Waddesdon Through The Ages

Ivor Gurney & Norman Carr

ISBN 0-9547310-1-8

Published in aid of Waddesdon Village Hall, a self-financing Charitable Trust since 1968.

Published by The Alice Trust, Waddesdon Manor
Produced by Mark Brandon, Waddesdon, Bucks. Tel: 07973 298094
Printed in Great Britain by Butler & Tanner, Frome, Somerset.

Photo on previous page "Beating the Bounds 2002".

CONTENTS

After a hundred years of service as the venue for every imaginable community activity, Waddesdon Village Hall was in serious need of improvement to meet modern requirements. The Management Committee approved a programme of works to include; a new heating system, remodelled toilets and kitchen, increased storage capacity, a gallery, a modern fire alarm system and an upgraded electrical installation, all to meet current legislation, and to be contained within the existing Grade II listed building. From start to finish the work was designed, scheduled, overseen and progressed by Mr Lesurf in a voluntary capacity.

Thanks largely to the perseverance of Mr Langton the Chairman, a grant for £60,000 was obtained from the National Lottery Charities Board. Also grants from Aylesbury Vale District Council and the Rothschild Foundation, together totalled almost £20,000, whilst royalties of £4,200 from "Waddesdon's Golden Years", and £4,700 from hall funds enabled completion of the project.

The photograph above was taken at a reception held on 20th November 1998, when the Hall was officially re-opened by Lord Rothschild. Entertainment at the event was provided by students from the Secondary School, and presentations on behalf of the Village Hall Management Committee, were made to Mr Lesurf and to Mr Langton, in recognition of their personal contributions to the project.

Left to right: Mr Alan Lesurf, Lord Rothschild, and Mr Andrew Langton.

FOREWORD

Compiling a comprehensive account of Waddesdon Through the Ages might appear to be a rather tall order, but to those familiar with Norman Carr and Ivor Gurney's earlier study, *Waddesdon's Golden Years 1874-1925* it will not come as a surprise that the authors have achieved another triumph. Based like its predecessor on a rich and eclectic mix of old and new photographs, press cuttings, letters, maps, archival material and personal recollections, this latest volume will be a source of delight, not only to those who know Waddesdon, but to anyone interested in history, archeology, genealogy, farming, the landscape or just the varied tapestry of village life.

It was the Rothschild family who in a sense put Waddesdon on the map in 1874, when Baron Ferdinand de Rothschild (persuaded by the commanding position of Lodge Hill), decided to build a Renaissance château there as his country retreat, but this book goes further, moving from traces of earliest habitation, through changing fortunes in the medieval period to when Waddesdon was part of the estates of the Dukes of Marlborough and on to the present day.

Three generations of the Rothschilds have indeed set their stamp on Waddesdon. Baron Ferdinand, the visionary, a collector of superb works of art, friend of the future Edward VII, politician and local philanthropist (founder of the Waddesdon Philharmonic Society which on one occasion he conducted from the balcony of the Five Arrows Hotel); Miss Alice, his sister and heir, redoubtable, passionate gardener and horsewoman, fiercely protective of her brother's legacy whether through her "Rules" for the preservation of his collection or her concern for the welfare of the Estate and village; James and Dorothy de Rothschild (the latter still affectionately known in the village as Mrs James) who saw Waddesdon through the war years and then had the generosity to hand the Manor to the National Trust; and my own involvement, a period which has seen the rebirth of the house and gardens after a major restoration project and visitor numbers rise to 250,000 in 2003.

During these years, the village and Manor have welcomed a huge variety of visitors, from Queen Victoria in 1890 and Edward, Prince of Wales (who came frequently), Lloyd George, King George and Queen Mary, Virginia Woolf and Winston Churchill to, more recently, Her Majesty the Queen and Prince Philip, Her Majesty Queen Elizabeth the Queen Mother, three prime ministers (Margaret Thatcher, John Major and Tony Blair), and Arnold Schwarzenegger, the Governor of California. Over this time, we have witnessed great changes. The neat, linear village which Baron Ferdinand knew has expanded to accommodate a thriving population. We are now under pressure as never before from the growth of Aylesbury, Milton Keynes and even the proximity of London in an age of commuters and teleworkers. As we move into the 21st century, there is much to celebrate and much to look forward to. Waddesdon Through the Ages is a vivid and timely reminder of how far we have come.

Rothschild

LORD ROTHSCHILD
May 2004

INTRODUCTION

When "Waddesdon's Golden Years 1874-1925" was published in 1996, we had not seriously considered further work of a similar nature. However the success of "Golden Years", the availability of large numbers of photographs, and not least the earnest persuasion of many Waddesdonians led us to undertake the compilation of this second book.

At the outset our thoughts were focused upon the remainder of the twentieth century; starting where our first book left off in 1925. However, we were anxious to present the new book in an historical perspective, and decided that episodes and interesting snippets from earlier days as well as the period 1874-1925 must be included. Some important neighbourhood developments, which affected Waddesdon, are also covered.

For those readers familiar with Rev. C Oscar Moreton's more scholarly book "The History of Waddesdon and Over Winchendon," and with our own "Waddesdon's Golden Years 1874-1925" some repetition is unavoidable, for this we apologise

Our view of "Waddesdon Through the Ages" is seen essentially through a comprehensive collection of photographs which records life in this locality since around 1870. An historical background is furnished by supplementary articles, documents and press cuttings interspersed at intervals throughout the book.

The opening section marshals a few significant items of interest concerning early settlement in this area, whilst subsequent sections deal with a progression of important events, characters, features and institutions related to Waddesdon in more recent times.

Limitations of space has precluded exhaustive coverage of some subjects, (we could have filled a book with photographs of cricketers and footballers!), whilst unfortunately a few entries which may have merited more space, are curtailed due to a shortage of suitable material. We realise also, there are sections where it may be perceived that some aspects, or individuals, deserve a mention, or perhaps more weight. We trust any shortcomings will be tolerated by our readers.

Finally we briefly comment on aspects of life in Waddesdon at the end of the second millennium, and include a group of contemporary views in colour, which record memorable images of our village for posterity.

Royalties from the sale of this book are to be donated in part to the two schools in the village, and the remainder to Waddesdon Village Hall. (A Charitable Trust, Registration No. 300343)

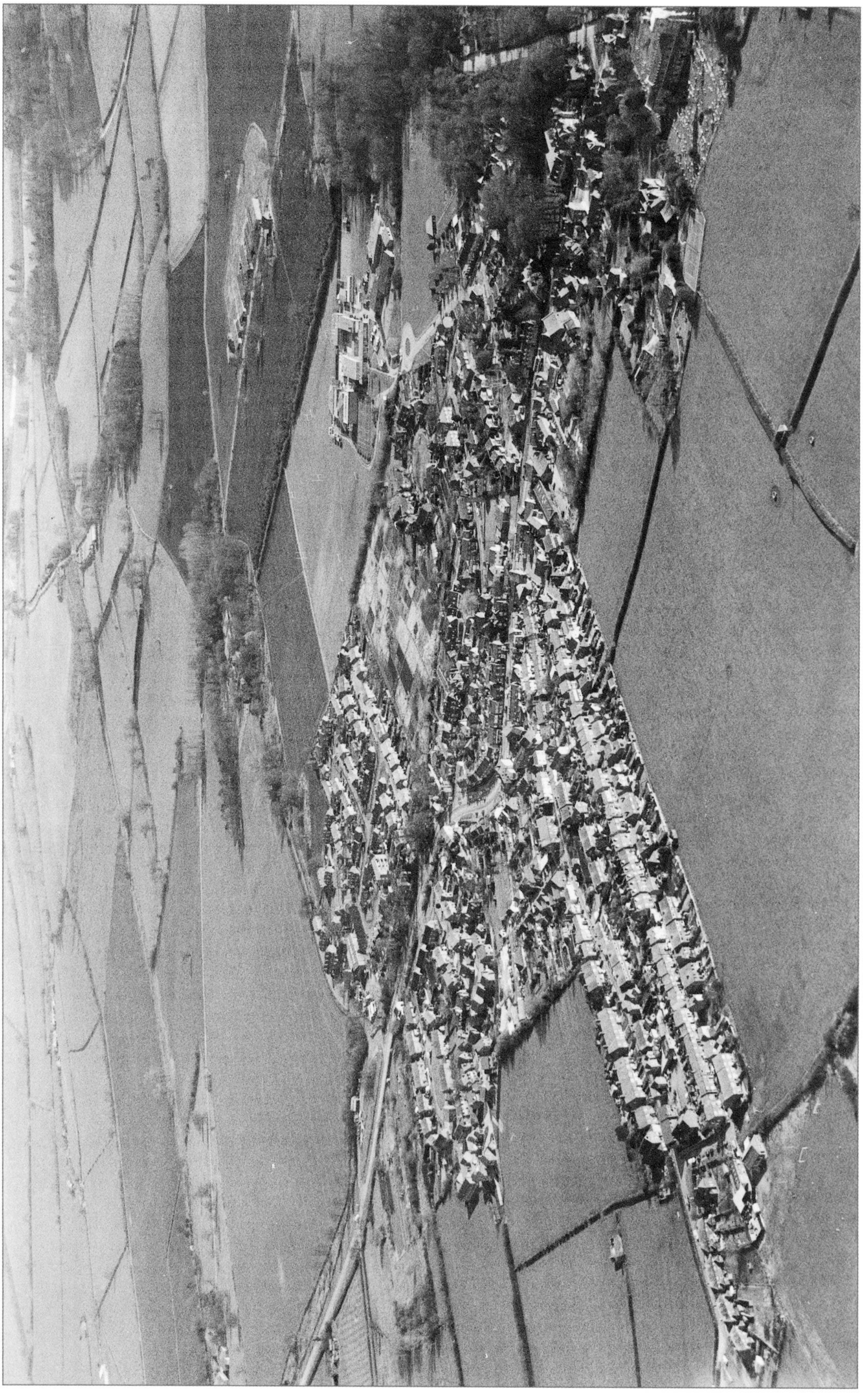

This aerial view of Waddesdon village was taken in 1994 by Ivor Gurney for inclusion in our first book "Waddesdon's Golden Years 1874-1925". The photograph shows the village from the west, and the parish Church is at the near right.

Section One

Origins and the Second Millenium

Ancient Origins

The land now occupied by the parish of Waddesdon and the countryside surrounding it, has supported human habitation for more than 8000 years. Flint tools from the Mesolithic period on Lodge Hill and the characteristic terracing (Linces) from the Neolithic period near Upper Winchendon clearly prove that Stone Age settlers were established here.

In 1855, five Bronze Age socketed celts were discovered on Lodge Hill and Saxon weaponry was uncovered at Philosophy Farm. More recently pottery sherds from the Bronze Age, Iron Age and Roman and Saxon periods signify a continuous human association with the area. On a much larger scale the Roman conquest left us with Akeman Street, which bisects the parish from east to west, linking St. Albans through Bicester and Cirencester with Bath. The Saxon name for Bath was Akemannes-ceaster (the city of invalids), and it was there that invalids hoped to cure their ills in the hot spring water.

In the 1960's, two school children Peter and Fiona Baron, unearthed several artefacts, which were identified as of Roman origin in the grounds of their home, Britain House. These included a bridle bit and part of a military helmet, there were also numerous items from later historical periods. Britain House was demolished to make way for the Little Britain development, which now maintains the proven use of this patch for human habitation, into the third millennium.

Until the late nineteenth century, the prime requisite for even the most primitive of permanent settlements was a naturally occurring source of water. In the Vale of Aylesbury, which lies on a thick bed of clay, water in summertime can be a very scarce commodity. However the flatness of the Vale is randomly relieved by hills and ridges where formations of Portland stone protrude through the clay, and on the slopes of these hills and ridges, water from subterranean aquifers finds its way to the surface in the form of springs. Where these springs were found to be continuous, human settlement could be a practical proposition. That is why the village of Waddesdon was originally located close to Spring Hill, part of Lodge Hill, and the early permanent dwellings were gathered close to the brook which collected the product of the springs.

Names which the settlement may have had in earlier times are lost, but historians have explained that "Waddesdon" is possibly derived from a combination of the Anglo-Saxon word for hill (don), and a chieftain by name of Wad or similar, who held the village, thus "Wotsdon". The brook which in Saxon times was called "Wottesbroke" and after the Norman Conquest was called "Wade," continued as an important source of clean water even after "Chiltern Hills" piped water was introduced in 1875.

The coming of the Anglo-Saxons brought conflict to the locality; records inform us that in AD 527 the Britons were defeated at Chearsley, and in 571 the Saxons took Aylesbury. At this time the forest of Bernwood covered much of this area and the native communities probably faced grim survival options when confronting the invaders. Inevitably the region was brought under the new order and to this day most place-names have Anglo-Saxon origins.

In 661 the district around Ashendon was plundered by Wulpher, King of Mercia, and in 871 a Danish army was defeated here by King Ethelred. The Danes returned in 921 and 941 plundering Aylesbury and Bernwood, and again in 1010 when they seized Aylesbury. This area had been near the fringe of the large portion of England ruled by the Danes, the Dane-law of the ninth century, but it obviously still held an attraction for them long after the division had ended.

During the Anglo-Saxon period local administration was organised through a system of "Hundreds". Buckinghamshire was divided into eighteen "Hundreds", each of which contained approximately 100 Hides of land, and may sometimes have been established according to land holdings instead of geographical practicality. In 1066 the Hundred of Waddesdon was largely composed of land held by Brictric a Saxon thane, and the area was nearly split into two parts, with Woodham, Westcott, Waddesdon, Fleet Marston, Quarrendon, Middle and East Claydon, Hogshaw and Granborough, but leaving Quainton and North Marston in the larger Ashendon Hundred. It is thought likely the meeting point was located near the boundary with Winchendon, which although about a mile from the village holds a commanding view of the surrounding countryside.

And so at the end of the first millennium we had a firmly established village that was based upon a very long period of human settlement. From there on record-keeping gradually improved and much of what is known results from scholastic study of written accounts over the centuries.

1.1 These fossils are from the Jurassic period, 150 to 140 million years' ago. The Waddesdon area at that time formed part of the sea-bed. The fossils and artefacts displayed in photographs 1.1 to 1.5 and their captions were provided by Mr Ken Machin. L to R from top: 1) Ammonite, Kosmoceras (like a shelled octopus), discovered in Oxford Clay at Woodham. 2) Belemnite (a squid-like animal), discovered in Kimmeridge Clay at Westcott. 3) Brachiopod, Torquirhynchia, has a bivalved shell but is unrelated to the Bivalves, discovered in Kimmeridge Clay at Waddesdon. 4) Gastropod, Pleurotomaria, discovered in Portland Limestone near Waddesdon. 5) Gastropod, Ampullospira discovered in Portland Limestone at Windmill Hill. 6) Bivalve, Protocardia, (an early cockle) discovered in Portland Limestone in the Waddesdon area.

1.2 Prehistoric artefacts discovered on Lodge Hill. L to R from top: 1) Flint Borer, Mesolithic, (Middle Stone Age). 2) Flint Core, Mesolithic, from this blades for tool making were struck. 3) Flint Scraper, Mesolithic, for scraping animal hides. 4) Pottery Rim sherd of clay, shell and grit, (Bronze Age). 5) Pottery Body sherd of clay, (Iron Age).

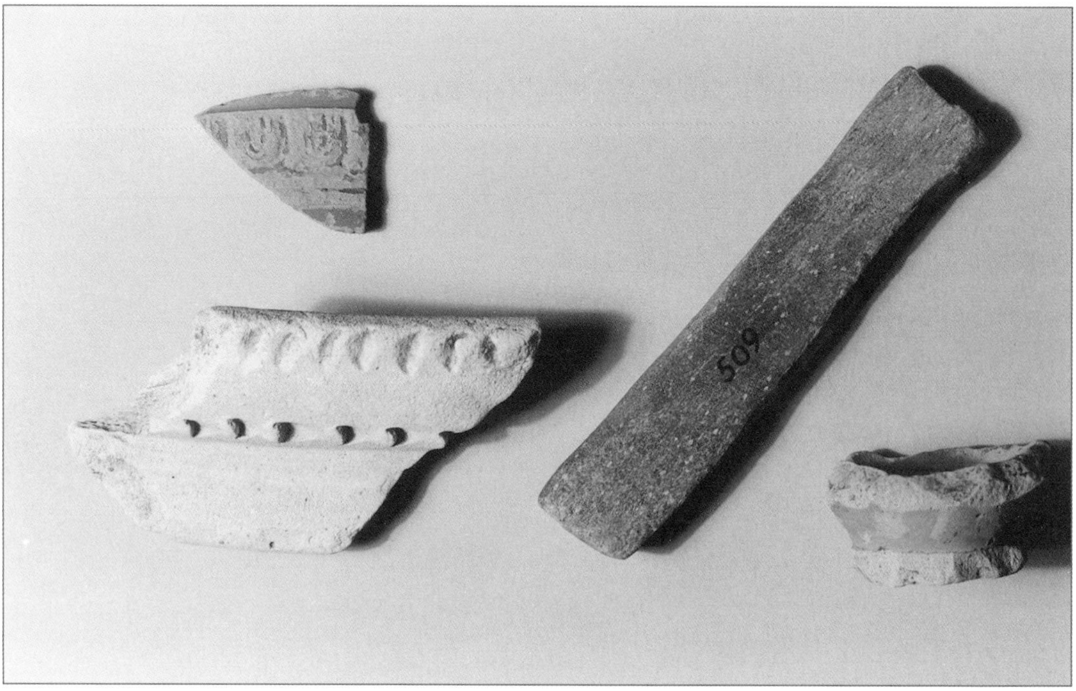

1.3 Roman and Anglo Norman artefacts discovered in Westcott. Top left: Body Rim sherd of decorated Red Samian Ware, Roman Found in Ayless Close.Bottom left: Mortaria Rim sherd (a gritted mixing bowl), Roman. Bottom right: Base of pot or vase, Roman. Found in Ayless Close. Top right: Hone of imported French stone, Anglo Norman. Found in Greatbury.

1.4 Artefacts of the Medieval Period Clay Spindle Whorl,12th to 13th century. Found in Greatbury Westcott. Iron 'D' Buckle, 13th to 14th century. Found in Greatbury. Iron Sickle Blade, Medieval type. Found in Ayless Close. Part of Jug Handle, Medieval. Note stylised 'Leaf' decoration. Found on site of a natural spring, Lodge Hill.

1.5 Post Medieval Artefacts discovered in Westcott. Two Georgian finger rings, probably worn by children. One shows traces of gilding. Found in Ayless Close. Centre: Flint Tinder Striker, 17th to 18th century. Found on a Farm at Westcott. Shoe Patten, worn on the sole of the shoes to raise them above mud. 17th to 18th century. Found at Lower Green. Georgian Book Clasps, G.R imprinted on Right Hand one. Found in Ayless Close.

1.6 In 1929 the Rev.Moreton explained the origins of unnatural ridges that occur on the slopes of local hills. Permanent settlements were first established in this swampy and heavily forested area as our Neolithic ancestors had acquired farming skills, which included the ability to construct hillside terraces for ease of ploughing and the cultivation of crops. Today, with modern farm machinery available, hillside fields have been put to the plough as never before and ancient contours have often been softened or erased. However this 1998 photograph has Mr Cyril Gurney standing on the second, of three discernable "steps" in the field "The Linces" near Upper Winchendon, the best local example of the characteristic Neolithic terracing. The name "Linces" is derived from the Anglo-Saxon for ridge, and it occurs again for a field on the northern slopes of Lodge Hill.

Waddesdon in the Second Millenium

The following text briefly provides some important historical aspects that are not covered in the illustrated sections of this book:

At the commencement of the second millennium the Kingdom of England was unified, well organized, wealthy and the envy of many of its neighbours. However when Edward the Confessor died in 1066 and Harold Godwin (Harold II), was elected to succeed him, there were two foreigners who coveted the throne and were to make his reign a very short one. Harald III of Norway invaded Northumbria in 1066, aided and abetted by Harold's brother Tostig Godwin. They were killed and their army was routed by Harold at Stamford Bridge on 25th September. Meanwhile William of Normandy invaded at Pevensey, Sussex, on 28th September; Harold hurried to repel him and was himself defeated and killed at the Battle of Hastings on 14th October 1066.

The Domesday Survey

The year 1066 witnessed the victorious William of Normandy established on the throne of England, and needless to say a large number of his supporters who had assisted in his campaign to defeat the English, had to be rewarded. One such was Miles Crispin, a Norman knight of considerable importance; he was awarded all the land owned by Brictric, an Anglo-Saxon supporter of the defeated King Harold. Brictric had owned most of the Waddesdon Hundred and numerous other holdings in the county of Buckinghamshire.

In 1086 King William instigated a nation-wide inventory of ownership and land values, (now known as the Domesday Survey), which provides us with concise information about the Manor of Waddesdon. It states: "Miles himself holds Waddesdon. In Waddesdon Hundred. It answers for 27 hides. Land for 12 ploughs: in Lordship 10 hides, 8 ploughs there. 50 villagers with 10 smallholders have 20 ploughs. 17 slaves. 1 mill at 12 shillings, meadow for 28 ploughs; woodland 150 pigs. Total value £30, when acquired £16, before 1066 £30. Brictric, Queen Edith's man held this manor."

Using the above information, historians have estimated the population of Waddesdon to have been around 500 persons in 1086, a large village for that period, and this was probably a reflection of its relative importance as the administrative centre for the Hundred. Unfortunately Waddesdon was never the seat of an important family, nor was it a site of strategic importance; therefore over hundreds of years, it rarely earned mentions in historical records. During the 14th century the Waddesdon Hundred was abolished, when it was absorbed into the Ashendon Hundred.

In these circumstances the written history of Waddesdon village until the late 18th century is extracted from Manorial and Church records, and details from those sources are included here and elsewhere in this book. However in the following paragraphs we also recount events that may have aroused extra-ordinary interest in this community.

Outlaws in the Middle Ages.

By the standards of the day, Norman England was an efficiently organized nation but it was quite sparsely populated and in the rural counties there was plenty of opportunity for skulduggery. In 1233 the vicinity of Brill was laid waste by Richard Sward and his gang of outlaws who terrorised this area. The Rev. Moreton informs us of a band of robbers, who in 1327 raided a settlement at Creslow. They stole horses, cattle, pigs and goods with apparent impunity, although they were known and named. Included in this bunch of outlaws was a certain William le Neuman of Wodesdon as well as two women! No further mention is made of the raiders, so we can only guess whether they were apprehended; however in 1346 after military service at the battle of Crecy, general pardons for past misdemeanours were earned by William Newman and Stephen Mareschal of Wodesdon, and William Frankeleyn of Westcote. A further twist was applied when William Newman returned home and was appointed keeper of the Aylesbury gaol.

Black Death. Pestilence and Epidemics

Waddesdon has no records of its fate during the Black Death in 1348. This outbreak of bubonic plague reduced the national population by a third in a few months and very few communities escaped without loss. We can assume this village suffered with all the others, especially as we have a clue. The field Blackpitte was formerly part of the Waddesdon common field, Staple-field, near the boundary with Quainton parish. From the name it is thought the Waddesdon victims of the Black Death were interred there, as far from the village as possible!

In 1665 the country experienced another epidemic of bubonic plague, historically well remembered because it preceded the Great Fire of London. The only mention in the records of Waddesdon is of one Richard Adams of Westcott, who was buried there because it was feared he had died of "ye sickness."

Smallpox is continuously mentioned in the Overseers' Accounts books of the eighteenth century because of payments made for nursing, airing of clothes, and provision of accommodation for families left without shelter as a result of the disease. There are also records of payments to medical practitioners for their services to the poor. In 1828 an Aylesbury surgeon, C M Terry agreed to "attend the poor" for one year at a cost to the parish of £45.

The nineteenth century also witnessed smallpox in the early years, and as the century progressed, the poor were caught in a downward spiral of living standards and were threatened by deadly illnesses arising from their own condition. In 1861 a typical budget for an "in work" labourer's family was listed: Bread- eleven shillings and nine pence, Flour- one shilling and six pence, Tea- four pence half penny, Firing- one shilling, Rent- one shilling, Other things- one shilling and a penny halfpenny, Total- sixteen shillings and nine pence (84p), no potatoes, milk, or meat, but probably some home-grown vegetables. Wages were usually around fourteen shillings (70p), but the women-folk earned a little, lace making or straw-plaiting. Hygiene in the primitive dwellings was impossible to maintain, and in dry weather water supplies were woefully short and often foul. These factors led to outbreaks of diphtheria, typhus fever, diarrhoeal diseases and scarlet fever, all highly infectious and particularly dangerous to the young, but in the "hungry forties" and beyond, no age-group amongst the malnourished was safe. Something had to be done.

Piped Water Supplies

At the suggestion of Thomas J E Brown, a surgeon resident in Waddesdon in 1861, steps were taken to "provide a pure and certain supply of water for the village". On Spring Hill the best and most reliable source was found after workmen had dug a shaft of 17 feet (5 metres).

The "pure element" was conducted in cast iron and glazed pipes to three cisterns with cast iron pumps placed on top, located at the entrance to Queen Street, the entrance to Silk Street, and the High Street opposite the Wood Street junction. The cost of this exercise was £130, which was raised by public subscription. However, although the improved water supply was an important basic measure for better health, records show that epidemics still regularly occurred, for instance an outbreak of scarlet fever in 1870 killed fourteen youngsters in three months.

Despite the interference with the principal spring, the Wottesbroke continued to flow. A small catchment basin with a stone step known as "the Sill", was constructed in the stream on the south side of Silk Street and water was collected from there by all and sundry. This convenient supply of water was still utilised early in the 20th century, especially when the piped supply was inadequate.

In 1866 the Chiltern Hills Spring Water Company supported by the neighbouring Rothschild families, commenced operations. Its pumping station was situated at Dancers End, near Tring, high enough to gravity-feed water in pipes to Aylesbury and beyond. A copious and reliable supply of water was essential for the building and running of Baron de Rothschild's country seat at Waddesdon. Consequently the Aylesbury pipeline was extended to Waddesdon via Stone and Eythrope, stand-pipes were installed at strategic points in the village and by the end of 1875 the villagers were able to enjoy this convenient supply of unpolluted water.

After 1875 there was a steady and discernable improvement in every aspect of life in the village, not least in the category of health. The many reasons for the improvement (a nineteenth century comparative judgment), included good water, education, medical care (accommodation for a resident doctor was provided by the Baron), regular employment, decent accommodation, diet and a consequent rise in morale. Epidemics became much rarer, and pestilence was consigned to the history books.

Mills and Milling

The Domesday Survey refers to a mill, apparently in the ownership of Miles Crispin, and subsequent manorial records suggest there may have been two in the 17th century. The Rev Moreton informs us that a Thomas East owned a water mill at Eythrope in 1640. Windmills were not yet in use in England, and these undershoot type water-mills were sited at Eythrope where they are commemorated in the field names Mill Close and Mill Ground, on either side of the road by the bridge. It must have been quite a relief to the locals when a windmill was conveniently built in the field known as Humphreys Ley, at Waddesdon in the 18th century. It was probably a post-mill, and again its locality is commemorated in the field names Mill Piece and Mill Field on the opposite (north) side of the Aylesbury road.

Although as a source of energy, the wind is not so predictable as water, windmills can harness the power of the wind almost anywhere, and as epitomized here the choice of site can invariably be selected closer to the need. In the early 20th century a new windmill was built in Humphreys Ley on the site of the old mill. It was not a practical proposition having been constructed for its aesthetic qualities for Miss Alice de Rothschild, and there is no doubt it was a fine looking mill. Unfortunately it was never operated commercially, (Mr. Taylor sometimes milled there at no charge, merely to demonstrate to Miss Alice and her guests that it could work), and on at least one occasion the Taylor boys turned the sails by hand when it was known Miss Alice was riding past on her return from France. The sails of the mill were badly made and after the Great War they began to disintegrate. Finally the windmill was demolished by dynamite a little more than thirty years after its construction.

Around 1855 Mr. George Taylor commenced operations at his new steam mill situated off Back Road next to the large pond, which stretched to Silk Street. The tall chimney was a local landmark until 1893, when George's son Joseph was persuaded by Baron Ferdinand de Rothschild to move to nearly identical premises down Quainton Road; there the chimney was not such a distraction for the Baron and his guests! The Quainton Road steam mill obtained its water from a specially dug 40 feet deep well, but in 1934 this became redundant when a diesel engine replaced the steam engine. The old pond in Back Road remained for many years as the trees matured about it, then it was reduced in the inter-war years and finally filled-in in the 1960's. Many of the older villagers will recall the steam-rollers and steam traction engines replenishing their tanks there, and the childhood hours of fun spent fishing for "tiddlers" in summer and sliding on the ice in those cold winters.

The steam mill in Quainton Road was in continuous demand after commissioning in 1893, mainly milling Persian and Russian barley for pig food, and also local wheat flour for farmers and villagers. A hundred years ago the price for milling a bushel of wheat was 6d, or quite often no money passed hands, the owner received the flour and Mr. Taylor retained the "offal", (bran and toppings). To allotment holders this was a very satisfactory arrangement.

Milling continued in Waddesdon in the hands of Mr. Alfred J Taylor, the son of Joseph, gradually reducing in volume until operations ceased in the 1960's, leaving the premises in use as a store for the distribution of animal feed. More recently the landmark chimney has been demolished and the mill building now accommodates a busy metal polishing firm.

The Akeman Street

During the passage of hundreds of years the old Roman road Akeman Street, which connected London and Bath via Aylesbury, Bicester and Cirencester, was abandoned in the vicinity of Waddesdon. Also for unknown reasons, travellers looped around the north of the village at the edge of the ancient common fields, leaving the Aylesbury road near Gullatts Furlong and rejoining the Bicester road at Home Ground, (see Field Map in Section 1). The title of "Black Waddesdon" was said to have been earned from the treatment of wayfarers; this by-pass may have been the result!

Maintenance of the road was minimal and in winter this track, once a road fit for Roman armies, disappeared under water for long stretches in the low-lying marshland. The unfortunate traveller, was therefore forced to follow that path which seemed the most promising.

On 10th November 1770 an Act was obtained for making a Turnpike road, to be known as the Aylesbury and Bicester Turnpike Road. Parliamentary approval was to take more than twenty years. Meanwhile in 1774 the Enclosures Act saw the end of Waddesdon Common and the old London Road ceased to bypass the village. No doubt this turn of affairs pleased all concerned, allowing more land to be enclosed, reducing the parish road maintenance responsibility and improving the prospects of shopkeepers and inn landlords.

Turnpike roads were privately owned ventures financed from the proceeds obtained at tollgates situated at the ends, and at intervals in between. The name "Turnpike" was derived from a shaft mounted horizontally above the top edge of the gate, able to revolve in trunnions, and with short pike-like spokes projecting around the shaft at intervals along its length. Thus providing a formidable obstacle to toll-dodgers. Usually, the only traffic not charged was pedestrian.

On 17th September 1793 the Bicester Coach left Aylesbury for the first time, and in 1795 the London to Bicester stagecoach service was inaugurated.

With the London Road now passing through Waddesdon the village assumed a new importance. The Marlborough Arms was a stopping point for the stagecoaches and in due course became the first Post Office. The maintenance of the road provided occasional work for the otherwise unemployed agricultural labourers. On the 2nd January 1831 it was recorded that "sixty men were lately employed on the road at Waddesdon, as no other employment could be found". Unfortunately the reputation of "Black Waddesdon" was not diminished by a legendary and unrecorded story of the murder of a Welsh horse-dealer at the Barley Mough Inn, later re-named The Chandos Arms, and situated in Silk Street. (See village map). Numerous assaults took place on tything-men and other officials, and a tendency was to return the friendly waves of coach travellers with a hail of stones and mud! Two Watchmen were appointed to patrol the streets at night, armed with pistols and fortified with rum and gin.

The rapid development of the railway system heralded the end of the turnpike road network. Locally the opening of the Aylesbury to Claydon line in 1868, brought rail travel at Quainton Road Station within walking distance for most parishioners, and erstwhile stagecoach travellers were attracted to the advantages of the train.

The Great War and the internal combustion engine caused main roads to regain their eminent position in the national infrastructure. Munitions lorries en-route from the midlands to docks in the southeast ploughed along the High Street, up to their axles in mud in winter and throwing up great clouds of dust in summer.

The last century has seen the Akeman Street prove to be a mixed blessing for Waddesdonians. In the year 2000 the convenience of public transport passing through the village has gone and due to the heavy incidence of commercial and private traffic, the main road is now regarded as a negative feature of the village.

The Civil War

Undoubtedly the most traumatic times of the olden days were during the mid-seventeenth century when the people of this country were divided, sometimes within families, in their support of King or Parliament. King Charles I, by his arbitrary actions had created a sense of outrage amongst many politicians, and his failure to heed the warning signs of rebellion in the House of Commons, led inevitably to Civil War in 1642.

Mid-Buckinghamshire predominantly favoured the Parliamentary cause and it is likely that Waddesdon and Over Winchendon people were even more biased in that direction as the Lord of the Manor, (Colonel) Arthur Goodwin, was a staunch friend and ally of John Hampden. Aylesbury was fortified as a major bastion of the parliamentary territory facing the Royalist forces at Oxford, and its garrison was constantly seeking to prevent incursions into the surrounding countryside by Royalist foraging parties.

The Rev. C. Oscar Moreton describes in "Waddesdon and Over Winchendon", numerous occasions when the parish experienced Civil War involvement, but thankfully it was never the scene of large-scale conflict. Military actions in the vicinity included; in November 1642, the Battle of Aylesbury when the town was successfully defended against an army which was reputedly led by Prince Rupert; in January 1643, Colonel Goodwin led a night attack at Piddington and captured three troops of enemy horse; in June 1643, a skirmish at Chalgrove Field when John Hampden was mortally wounded; in mid 1643 the Waddesdon minister was taken prisoner and conveyed to Oxford; in August 1643 a fierce skirmish at Bicester; in August 1644 the siege of Hillesden House a Royalist stronghold; again in August 1644, shortly after Hillesden House, a Captain Abercrombie who had taken part in the siege, though married to one of the ladies of that house, was involved in a skirmish at Eythrope and killed; in December 1644 a skirmish at Long Crendon, and finally in June 1646 the Royalist stronghold at Boarstall House fell to the Parliamentarians. The movement and quartering of armies in and around the area meant that locals suffered the demands which followed, including the plunder of Over Winchendon in 1645 by Parliamentary troops.

A bloodstained page in a Waddesdon church register, bears witness to the bravery in 1642 of a clerk (probably William Delafield). He was wounded in a struggle, but prevented the destruction of the records by a group of Parliamentary supporters who had just returned from the defence of Aylesbury. The overseer for improvements to the Aylesbury fortifications, was the same William Delafield, who also served as a "gunner" on the artillery battery stationed there.

Although the defeated King was arrested in 1646, he continued to scheme with the Scots for a Royalist revival. In 1648 he escaped and was recaptured, and in 1649 he was tried, condemned and executed. In 1651 the final battle of the Civil War ended in a crushing defeat for the Royalist forces at Worcester. Oliver Cromwell's route back to London passed through the parish of Waddesdon and his army camped between Quainton and Aylesbury. The Mayor and Corporation of the town rode out to welcome the legendary soldier, only to learn he was out hawking on Quainton Seche (Marsh)! Next day the army continued on its way with four to five thousand prisoners "driven in front like sheep".

There followed a period of social, religious and political constraint, which affected everyone, and was soon resented by most. However, a pleasant reminder of our links with the English Civil War lies in the existence of the Arthur Goodwin Alms Houses, built as instructed in the benefactor's will of 1645, "as soon as the distractions of these times would permit".

The Hamlets

When Baron Ferdinand de Rothschild purchased the Marlborough Estates in 1874, the parish of Waddesdon contained three hamlets; Wormstone, Wescot and Woodham.* They all originated from the Manor of Waddesdon established in Anglo-Saxon times, and their separate existence resulted from the fragmentation of the ancient Manor in the two centuries following the Norman Conquest. It was the custom for wealthy men to provide land as part of their daughters' dowries or occasionally to endow land to religious orders. As a result, a number of minor manors were created each with their retinue of servants and employees, and the accommodation necessary. Perhaps for reasons of communication the three hamlets developed at manors on, or near to the old Roman Road, whilst several other more remote minor manors including Eythrope, did not.

Westcott became a separate entity from the Manor of Waddesdon when land there formed part of the dowry of Egeline the daughter of Reginald de Courtney, who at that time was the Lord of the Manor. Other marriage settlements over the years increased the amount of land that was independent of the Waddesdon Estates, and no doubt this encouraged the establishment of a separate community. In 1885 Ordnance Survey recorded the Civil Parish of Westcott as totalling 1,410 acres.

Wormstone is thought to have been the original location of a farm belonging to a Saxon by the name of Waermod, hence "Waermod's Tun". In the thirteenth century mention of "Waermodesdon" indicates that by then it was an independent manor of some importance, but in 1540 with Westcott, it was again largely amalgamated into the Waddesdon and Winchendon estates, in the ownership of John Goodwin.

Wormstone was situated alongside the Wottesbroke, southeast of the parent village at a distance of about half a mile. It consisted of numerous cottages, smallholdings and Wormstone Farm, which had been the site of the Manor House. In addition there was the windmill that stood a short distance from the Aylesbury Road, a landmark for at least two hundred years until its demolition in the 1930's.

The Civil Parish of Wormstone is recorded on the Ordnance Survey map of 1884 as being 5,005 acres, the largest by far of the Waddesdon hamlets. However this settlement was by that date almost extinct, as the privately owned small buildings and dwellings were bought up for inclusion once more into the main estate.

The hamlet of Woodham stands near to the farthest western extent of the combined parish. It is positioned on the Akeman Street at the edge of the ancient Royal Forest of Bernwood, and in the neighbourhood the place-names include the name "wood". Kingswood, Wotton Underwood and Grendon Underwood are settlements which border the parish, whilst Queenwood and Mercers Wood are but two of the tree covered areas which are remaining from ancient times.

The Manor of Woodham has always been associated with that of Waddesdon, for despite a sizeable portion of the land being granted in trust in 1505 to the warden and community of the Mystery of Mercers as an endowment of St Paul's School, the Waddesdon Manor retained possession of the estate land.

The census of 1861 combined the population of Waddesdon and Westcott at a total of 1,786 persons. There seems to be no mention of Woodham, but it may be assumed that its population would also have been included in that total.

Unfortunately there is insufficient space to include separate historical accounts for the hamlets although much material is available, particularly for Westcott, which has grown quite independent of Waddesdon. However, ties are strongly maintained in the presence of descendants of the Adams and Goss families, stalwarts of the old parish for hundreds of years.

*Note: the spellings have changed over the years.

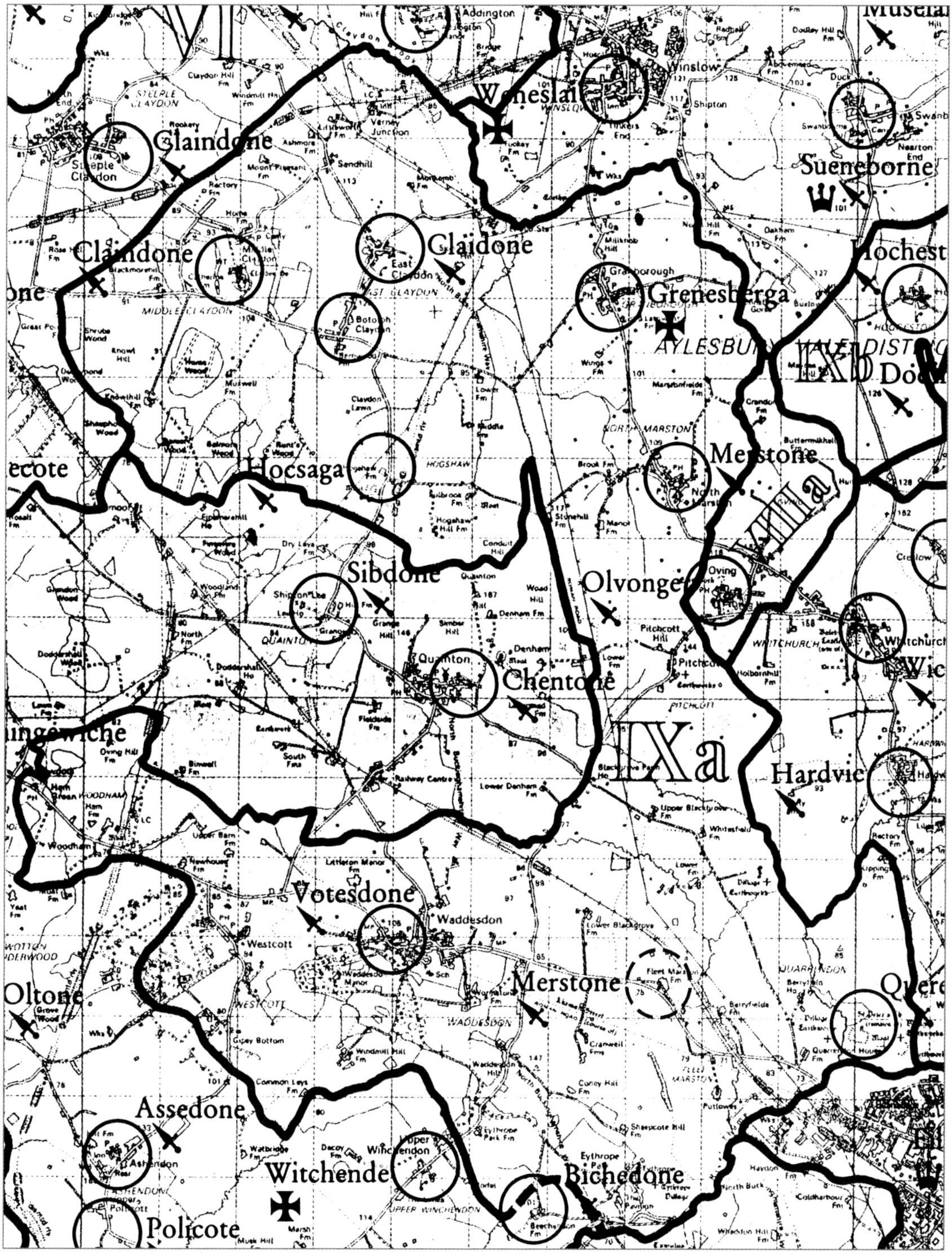

1.7 The boundary of the Hundred of Waddesdon shown here superimposed onto a modern map. Within the boundary lie Middle, East and Botolph Claydon, Granborough, Hogshaw, Fleet Marston, Quarrendon, North Marston, Eythrope, Ham Green, Woodham and Pitchcott. Altogether an area of 91 Hides (1 Hide approximated to 120 acres), somewhat short of the 100 Hides denoted by the title "Hundred".

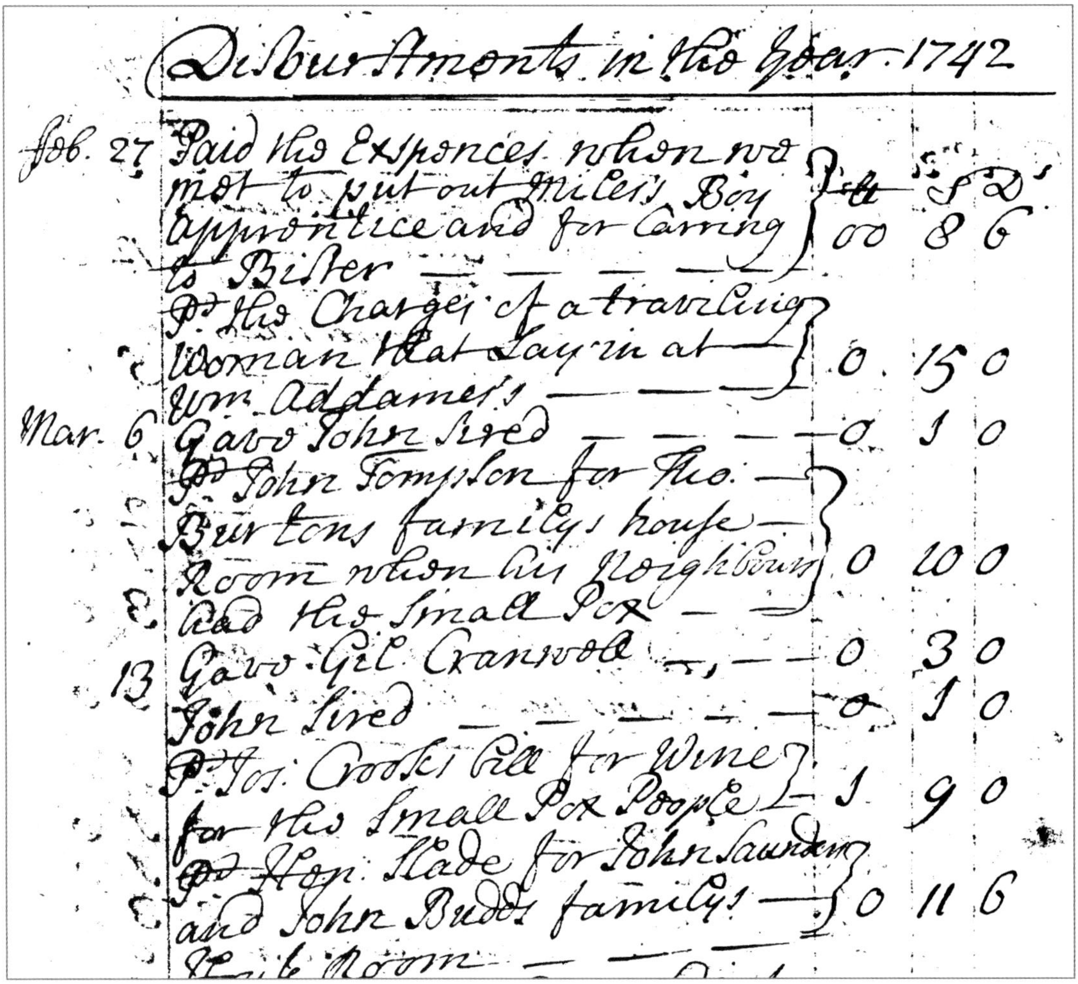

Disburstments in the Year 1742

		£	s	d
Feb. 27	Paid the Expences when we met to put out Miles's Boy Apprentice and for Carring to Bister	00	8	6
	Pd the Charges of a travling Woman that lay in at Wm Addames's	0	15	0
Mar. 6	Gave John Sired	0	1	0
	Pd John Tompson for Tho. Burtons familys house Room when his Neighbours had the Small Pox	0	10	0
13	Gave Gil Cranwele	0	3	0
	John Sired	0	1	0
	Pd Jos: Crooks Bill for Wine for the Small Pox People	1	9	0
	Pd Hon. Slade for John Saunders and John Budds familys House Room	0	11	6

1.8 Before the Poor Law of 1834 was enacted, it was one of the duties of the Overseers for the Poor to issue aid to the destitute of the parish. This copy from the Churchwardens Account Book for 1742 informs us how some of the Church Rates were expended in March of that year. (Clarified below).

Disbursments in the year 1742		
		£ s d
Feb 27	Paid the expences when we met to put out Miles's Boy Apprentice and for carrying to Bister	0 8 6
	Pd the Charges of a traveling Woman that lay in at Wm Addames's	0 15 0
Mar 6	Gave John Sired	0 1 0
	Pd John Tompson for Tho Burtons familys houseRoom when his neighbours had the Small Pox.	0 10 0
Mar 13	Gave Gil Cranwele	0 3 0
	John Sired	0 1 0
	Pd Jos Crooks bill for Wine for the Small Pox People	1 9 0

Further on there is mention of payment for "HouseRoom", "Necesareys" and "Beer" for the families with the smallpox. No doubt the wine and beer was considered medicinal although it may also have been in recognition of the hazards of drinking water. NOTE: Written and spelt as in original book.

1.9 Terraced Cottages in Silk Street 1875. Altogether a better than average class of construction and thatch in good order, rather more than can be said for the fence in the foreground. Unfortunately nothing is known of these buildings, not even the incongruous end house with tiled roof, suffice to say they went the way of all the Silk Street dwellings, demolished to make way for tree plantations.

WADDESDON WINTER GIFTS.

To the Editor of the Bucks Advertiser and Aylesbury News.

SIR,—It has been the fashion for many years, among some of our good friends in neighbouring parishes, to speak contemptuously of our place, as being always far behind in every good thing. Now, whether their over-fancied excellence justified them in so doing, I shall not waste words in discussing: all I can say is, that Waddesdon is looking up, and the Waddesdonians are going a-head, in a manner to show that if they ever were last in the race, they are determined not to remain so. I do not write, however, to trumpet forth our doings; but, in the hope that others may "go and do likewise," when they see what can be done in a parish like this, with a large labouring population, and no resident gentry. At the beginning of December, when the necessaries of life were daily becoming dearer, the Rev. W. W. Walton invited the ratepayers to meet him, to consider the condition of the labouring poor. The call was almost unanimously responded to, and the reverend gentleman having laid before the meeting the pressing nature of the call to assist our poorer brethren, at a time when there is a difficulty in large families in procuring a bare subsistence; he threw out a friendly challenge, to the effect that he would untertake to distribute in food any sum equal to that raised by the farmers and others, to be spent in fuel. The challenge was readily accepted, and it was determined to raise £25, and to cover a space of sixteen weeks in its distribution. Messrs. Adams, Payne, Goss, Cox (Lane-end), and Rose (Eythrope), were named, to form a committee to carry out the design, according to the plan proposed by Mr. Adams, the churchwarden, by which the price of the coal is lowered according to the size of the family. Our two clergymen, on their part, have put down £40, raised among their private friends. The result is that 54 families (being all containing more than two children) can buy every week 1 cwt. of coals, varying from 3d. to 7½d. Every week, 390 rations are distributed, each ration consisting of a pint and a half of good pea-soup, and 6 oz. of bread; of these, 230 are consumed before a good fire, in the rectory kitchen, by labouring men, after their work: the rest goes to the nursing mothers, the widows, the large families, and the aged. Miss Clarke has also kindly added five tons of coal, for those widows and old people who do not participate in the farmers' gift. In addition to the above, the Rev. H. J. Marshall and Mrs. Marshall have very kindly given away to many of the poor and needy a considerable quantity of good rice, milk and bread, which has proved an important help, just in the severe weather, and in these hard and trying times. Then there is the clothing club, which the Rev. W. W. Walton established soon after he came to reside among us: that also is doing a great amount of good to hundreds of the poor people. The following figures will show what has been done in the year ending Christmas last:—Free subscriptions, £22; deposits of the poor, £94 13s. 4d.; total number of depositors, 236; total number of tickets issued, 415; total sum spent in clothing, £114 19s. 7d. It is earnestly hoped that this timely benevolence will spread much comfort, stave off illness from many a working man, and excite a kindly feeling between the employers and the employed.

Your obedient servant,

Jan. 16, 1854. A WADDESDON MAN.

1.10 In 1854 the 21st January issue of the Bucks Advertiser and Aylesbury News contained this letter from "A Waddesdon Man". Despite the poor reproduction (in part) of the cutting, the reader is recommended to persevere to the end. The correspondent writes far more eloquently than we could, and encapsulated in the letter, are so many aspects of what life must have been like for many, in the winters of that period.

1.11 Traditional mid-Buckinghamshire houses in Silk Street 1875. Robustly built with thick walls, tiny windows and thatched roof, cool in summer and warm in winter (relatively speaking).

WADDESDON AND WESCOTT CLOTHING CLUB, 1870.

Receipts.

	£	s.	d.
Duke of Marlborough, K.G.	4	0	0
Duke of Buckingham and Chandos	4	0	0
F. Calvert, Esq.	3	0	0
Rev. T. J. Williams	1	0	0
Miss Adams............	0	2	6
Mrs. Belgrove	0	3	6
Mrs. Bliss	0	4	6
Mrs. Dodwell	0	5	0
Mrs. T. G. Goss	0	5	0
Mrs. James Goss........	0	3	6
Mrs. Mason, Fleet Marston	0	3	0
Mrs. Matthews	0	5	0
Misses Monck	0	10	0
Mrs. Payne	0	5	0
Mrs. Ridgway..........	0	5	0
Mrs. Rose, Cranwell	0	3	6
Mrs. H. Taylor	0	4	6
From Christmas Tree....	1	19	0
Interest at Bank........	0	8	2
144 Depositors	78	3	8
	£95	10	10

Payments.

	£	s.	d.
Deficit from 1869......	0	8	2$\frac{1}{2}$
Mr. Howe's Bill	21	3	2
" Longley's "	6	0	4
" Madder's "	9	12	10
" Stockwell's "	32	5	6
" Reid's "	5	8	6
" Copcutt's "	0	15	6
Mrs. Broad's "	3	6	4
" Figg's "	1	11	0
" Frank's "	3	11	4
" Saunder's "	1	2	4
Miss Tompkins' "	0	15	6
" Crook's "	3	4	6
Co-op. Stores "	6	17	4
	£96	2	4$\frac{1}{2}$

1.12 One of the numerous savings clubs initiated by the Rev. W. W. Walton. The members (Depositors) not only benefited from their own thrift, but also were encouraged by the donations from the supporters of the scheme, which enhanced the individual shares. This Statement of Accounts for 1870 displays the meticulous care with which 19th century finances were displayed for public perusal. No doubt these figures were studied with great keenness by those involved.

1.13 The Mason's Arms in Chapel Lane, near to Motons Farm, the Manor of the Second Portion of the Church Living. This ancient inn catered very much for the lower end of the market and was really a beer house, probably doing much of its business with the off-licensed trade. Note the earthenware jar carried by the workman.

The "Waddesdon Harmonic Society" has now been formed. The public meeting on Jan. 11th was well attended, and between 20 and 30 persons joined the Society. The Rev. T. J. Williams was elected President; Rev. E. C. Baldwin, Secretary; Mr. James Goss, Treasurer; Mr. O. King, Musical Director; and Messrs. P. Dodwell, W. Parker, Rev. T. Boniface, Bristow, and T. Ward, Members of the Committee. Terms of subscription:—Honorary Members, 5s.; Practising Members, 2s.; Boys and Girls under 14, 6d. per annum.

CHRISTMAS CHEER.

The following is a list of the Subscribers to the Beef and Tea distribution on Dec. 30th, 1870:—

	£	s.	d.
Balance in Hand	0	15	5
Rev. T. J. Williams	1	0	0

Messrs. Geo. Adams, John and Joseph Crook, James Goss, Mrs. Ridgway, W. and J. Rose, J. Seamons, W. Tompkins, and Wilcox, 10s. each.

Messrs. Geo. Anthony, Belgrove, Bliss, Rev. T. Boniface, Bulford, Cooper, Cox, C. Crook, Edwin Crook, L. Crook, Curtis, Dodwell, O. Duntling, Flowers, J. Garner, Howe, King, Napier, W. H. Rose, J. F. Saunders, 5s. each.

Mr. Thorne, 3s.

Rev. E. C. Baldwin, Messrs. Bridle, Cockerel, J. Crook, Ezra Crook, Gibbins, Mason, F. Mason, Paxton, Robbins, James Stevens, W. Stevens, Mrs. Simons, Terry, and Watson, 2s. 6d. each.

Messrs. Coughtrey, John Goss, J. Hook, and W. Ward, 2s. each.

Mr. Adams, 1s. 6d.

Messrs. Bradbury, M. Copcutt, a Friend, Moscrop, J. Saunders, Mrs. John Taylor, Miss Tubb, 1s. each.

As many as 92 houses partook of this acceptable gift. The Meat was supplied by

	£	s.	d.
Mr. Fisher, of Aylesbury, whose bill was	12	13	6
The Tea was supplied from the village shops	2	2	8
Total Expenditure	£14	16	2

1.14 A page from the Parish Magazine for February 1871 gives us a sign of hope for Waddesdon. The Waddesdon Harmonic Society article speaks for itself, some of the villagers were keen to make music together. Christmas Cheer on the other hand, has two aspects to illustrate. First there were 92 households at least in need of this Beef and Tea distribution, and second thankfully, there were a number of benevolent villagers willing to donate to make it possible.

1.15 The old Marlborough Arms in 1875 had always been part of the Manorial Estate and was soon to be renamed The Five Arrows Inn but to the villagers would always be known by its former name. Waddesdon's most important inn, it had been a coaching stop on the Aylesbury to Bicester Turnpike Road, and in 1847 was also registered as a Post Office with "letters received at quarter before 9 o'clock in the morn, and despatched half past 5 o'clock in the even". Mrs Sarah Eeles was the proprietor at that time. The old inn was demolished and the new Five Arrows Hotel was built in 1887. George Cockerill the landlord named above the doorway later became the licensee of the White Lion Hotel. The horse drawn vehicles shown, are from left to right; Gig or Trap a favourite with farmers, Brougham and Landau, both used by professional and well-to-do business classes.

1.16 Henry Turnham the new landlord of the Five Arrows Inn displays his Wagonette at The Square in the centre of old Waddesdon circa 1880. At the near right is the fork into Silk Street whilst farther back the Five Arrows sign can be discerned outside the former Marlborough Arms. It was in The Square and down the wide High Street that the annual Feast Fair was held each October, until one year the side-shows created an obstruction for the Duke of Buckingham and thereafter the fair was held on The Green, the enclosed field behind the row of elm trees in the rear of the picture. The only building in this photograph to survive the next thirty years is the three-storey house on the left, which was given the "Rothschild treatment" and stands to this day (2000).

1.17 A view from Lodge Hill showing the south and eastern side of old Waddesdon circa 1874. Clearly distinguishable on the right is the tall chimney of Mr Joseph Taylor's steam mill situated in Back Road (Baker Street), and nearer the camera at the right of picture are the cluster of dwellings, shops and small-holdings around the Square, (now the War Memorial). The spindly trees in the hedgerows have been lopped for firewood; they are mainly elms and in the years that followed would be surrounded by plantations within Waddesdon Manor Park.

1.18 Another view of Waddesdon from Lodge Hill circa 1874. This picture shows the houses and smallholdings stretching along Queen Street and the old Church tower clearly defined on the little rise at the right. At the left are two houses on the main road, down Bicester Hill and across the field can be seen the barn which still exists (just!), in the upper Parson's Close. (2000).

1.19 A typical nineteenth century rural village, this is the Waddesdon of "Olden Days". The wide High Street flanked by ancient cottages and business premises giving a careworn and somewhat neglected image. In the background at the left, the works are under way for Baron de Rothschild's mansion and the stand-pipe in front of the Alms Houses inform us the date is probably around 1878. For all the people in this photograph fundamental changes have already commenced.

1.20 Old and new in 1888. Between the new Reading Room on the left and Mr Edwin Garner's new Shoe Shop on the right we have another tantalising glimpse into the village of 1874. At the centre is the Co-operative which with the cottages on the left and behind on the right (in Queen Street) are remnants of the old Waddesdon which were soon to be replaced by woodland.

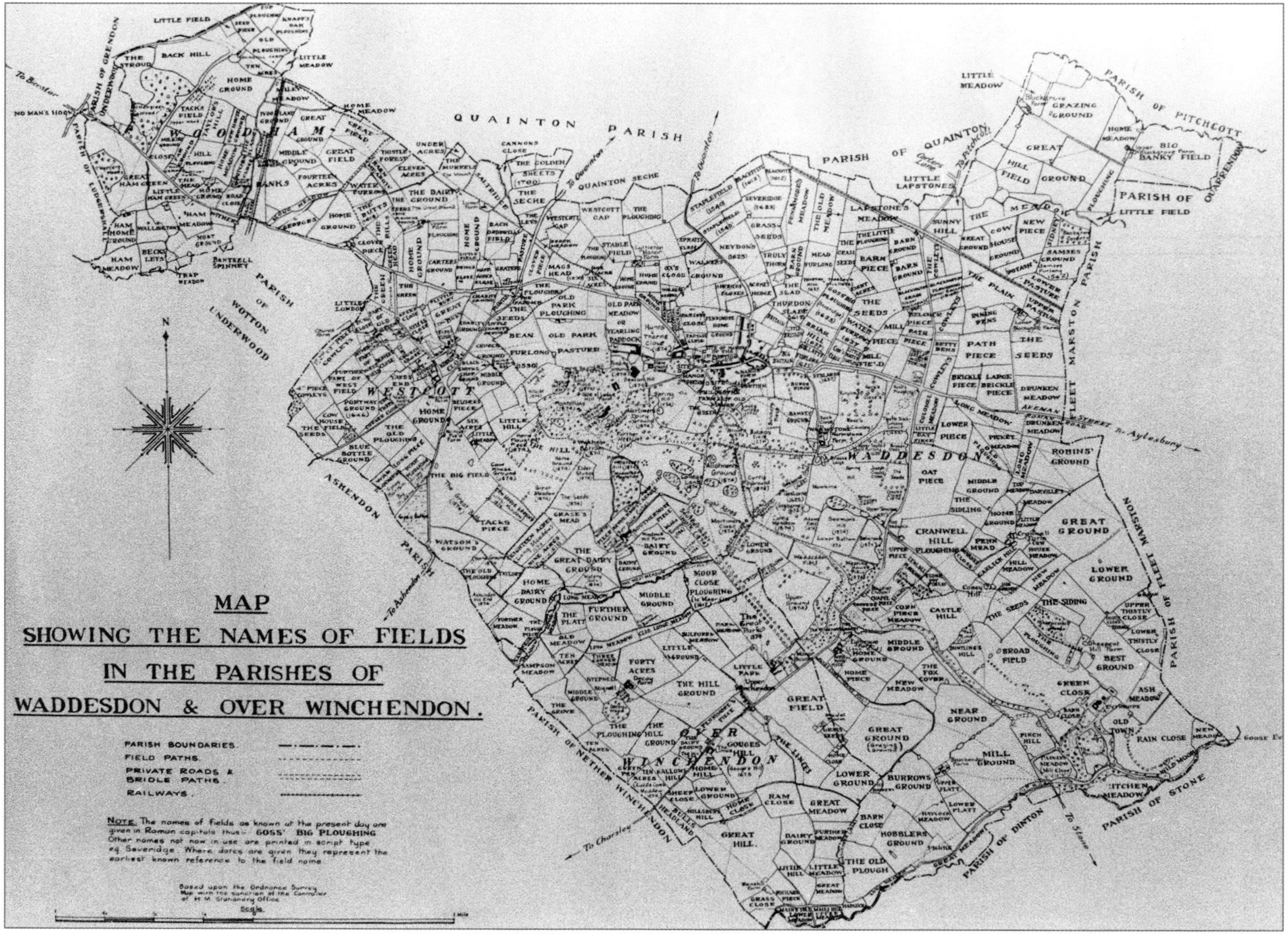

1.21 In his book "Waddesdon and Over Winchendon", published in 1929, the Rev. C. Oscar Moreton not only provided us with a fascinating account of local history but also meticulously recorded and mapped the field-names within the parishes. Because we feel it important to ensure future generations have ready access to this unique information we have copied the Field Map and reproduced it here at roughly a quarter the size of the original. The reader will observe the diversity of names ranging from owners, through to ancient titles of obscure origin in 1929, let alone the year 2000! One such is "Blackpitte" recorded in 1612, thought to have been so named as the burial place at the extremity of the parish, for Waddesdon's victims of the Bubonic Plague (Black Death) of the 14th century. (centre top).

Common, Close and Field

The archaic feudal system of medieval social order, left 18th century Waddesdon with substantial areas of unenclosed common land. On the northern side of the Akeman Street were two great tracts known as Staplefield and Brackfield whilst to the south were Wormstone field and Gosbourne. Divided into strips, these common fields had been essential features in the existence of our village, and although living conditions were harsh, a seemingly fair, familiar and closely integrated way of life had evolved. The villagers' use of common land had depended upon their individual social positions; some owned the right to graze and cultivate strips, whilst others just enjoyed the right to glean and forage, earning their living in employment on the larger farms.

Alongside the common fields were woods and enclosures belonging to the Lord of the Manor, the minor manor owners and the church, whilst nearer to the village itself were numerous small "closes" which were convenient and gave night-time security for animals. As long ago as 1540 King Henry VIII had granted to John Goodwin the Waddesdon and Over Winchendon estate, including an impressive list of fields including Court Closes, New Close, Staple Hill, Bush Leys, Blakedown, Siene Piece, Gibden Seche, Ship Slade, Lobbs Leys, Woddeston Park, Gilden Lease and Pulpit Acre.

By the early eighteenth century the ancient system of common land agriculture, though popular with its beneficiaries, was seen to be inefficient. An Agriculture Report for mid-Bucks in 1771 stated the land was poorly cultivated, badly drained, and also starved of improvement because the villagers removed any dried cow dung for use as fuel! Enclosing the common fields had long been seen as a step towards greater efficiency in English agriculture, and in the Vale of Aylesbury at that time the raising and fattening of cattle and sheep was the most profitable. To the church, a new Enclosures Act had a big attraction in the facility to resolve for ever the collection problems of many "small tithes". It is therefore not surprising the late eighteenth century witnessed a mass of Enclosure Bills, including the 1774 enactment, which saw off the remaining 1357 acres of common land in Waddesdon.

A separate and particular Parliamentary Bill was obtained for each parish, and the enactment of the Bill was carried out meticulously. Government Commissioners, experienced in dealing with the subject were appointed and they in turn engaged the staff necessary to fulfil the objects of the Bill. Surveyors to map and plan the enclosures, and contractors to plant the quickthorn hedges, erect protective fences, dig drainage ditches, and lay out access roads and footpaths.

The Commissioner at Waddesdon had to judge the values of various common fields and set to one-side, allotments to be awarded to each rector in lieu of "small tithes". This left a reduced area to be divided and allotted to the freeholders (or proprietors). The Commissioner awarded each proprietor a new field or fields equivalent to the combined value of their previously held strips. Appeals were settled, works completed and accounts finalised. The total of £1089-7s-0p was levied upon the owners of the new enclosures. Those who could afford it, paid up! Those who could not afford it had three choices; a mortgage, sell up, or try to avoid the levy - but beware, the commissioner's powers included the right to seize the goods and property of his debtors, sell them to settle the debt and return any surplus to the ex-proprietor! It appears from land ownership records that most chose to sell up. People were not happy; it was a "buyers market". A tale handed down by word of mouth tells of disgruntled villagers uprooting some of the newly planted hedges at Staplefield in the dead of night, but of course they were eventually defeated by the vicious quickthorn and the perseverance of the new landowners.

Waddesdon was left - a rarity in the locality - the only sizeable community without even a village green. (Westcott would have been in a similar plight but for the generosity of the Duke of Buckingham, who granted a small area for a green after the Enclosures there in 1766). Old maps show three locations in Waddesdon bearing the name "Green". One, off Silk Street and known variously as "Kings Green", "The Green", and "Walkers Green" and may once have been part of the common field "Gosbourne". Both King and Walker were land-owners. The second is the field next to "Atte Greene" (the Church Manor of the Third Portion), now containing the Police and Fire Stations and part of Chestnut Close. Although not at the centre of the old village this unenclosed land was known as "The Green", for in 1657 the Alms Houses were built "on a piece of land lately inclosed on Waddesdon Green". The third "Green" was the triangle of open land at the junction of Silk Street and High Street. According to old maps this was known as "The Square" as well as "The Green". Both above second and third greens were almost certainly village greens at different points in history, and both were appropriated by the church. The lack of a village playing field was rectified in 1939 when James de Rothschild presented to the village a substantial field, football pavilion and children's playground.

By the second half of the nineteenth century, ownership of the 6,010 acres in the combined parish of Waddesdon, Westcott and Woodham was divided between the Manor estate - mainly to the south of the main road, and an assortment of private owners including the church (Glebe Land) and Oxford University. The Manor was by far the largest area under single ownership at 2,762 acres, (including land in Upper Winchendon), but was divided into tenanted farmsteads and smallholdings.

The village and its hamlets were now entirely surrounded by a patchwork of fields whose shapes were irregular to say the least. Most fields were separated by hedges principally of quickthorn, but with older stretches of elm, blackthorn, maple, crab-apple and bullace, intertwined with blackberry bramble and dog rose. Huge elm trees, the occasional oak and ash provided shade at intervals, and somewhere in almost every field was a pond, often with willows growing next to it; the water for livestock and the willow for rick-pegs etc.

As the centuries passed, the fields were given names from many sources. Some of the names were ancient and the reasons for them are long forgotten, others were derived from owners' names, position or shape, type of ground, animals or plants. Scattered around Waddesdon are fields with names in all these categories including Coney Hill (animals; rabbit), Drunken Meadow (plants), Thistle Ditch Furlong (plant and size), Goss Big Ploughing (owner), Long Meadow (shape), Lower ground (Position), Redlands (colour of soil), and Golden Nob (probably earlier known as Gilden Lease). Drunken Meadow is believed to have been named after the Darnel grass which grew there, causing grazing cattle to become giddy. The three allotment fields in the village are Gullatts Furlong on the Aylesbury Road, Sheriffs Closes off the Quainton Road, and Golden Nob behind Baker Street.

There is little doubt that two of the oldest fields in the parish are those known as Parsons Closes. Situated to the north of the church, these two fields have always belonged to the first portion and have been enclosed since earliest times. The farthest of these formed the village-side boundary with the old London Road, which at that point followed the edge of Waddesdon Common.

The numerous other closes in the village were usually named after their present owners so that one small piece of land could have several names in succession over a period of many years. Thus William Gurney's Close which was formally a part of Lord's Waste could well have been renamed "Baron's Close" after its acquisition in the late 1870's.

After Baron Ferdinand de Rothschild purchased the Estate in 1874, he immediately commenced to buy out numerous smallholders on the fringes of his land. New woods were planted on ancient closes, open parkland appeared where once small farms had been, and some of the old tracks were straightened and upgraded. A hundred years' later in 1974, despite these changes it was still possible to discern many of the old enclosure lines because the Baron nearly always left the trees. Sadly, within ten years all those magnificent elms had been wiped out by Dutch Elm disease.

Since the end of the Second World War the face of the countryside around Waddesdon has drastically altered. There has been a trend to larger farms, larger machinery and intensive agriculture, therefore small farms, barns and inconvenient hedges had to go. After a few years of cultivation all traces of them had also gone. The number of farm workers has reduced to a fraction of that of the 1940's, specialist contractors carry out much of the work, and general conversation is no longer enriched with local dialect and farm husbandry terms. Field names mean nothing to most villagers, and soon may only be known to those who own or work them.

At the dawn of the third millennium the story of the local countryside is not all "gloom and doom", the removal of the hedges seems to be at an end. Most farmers have made efforts to redress the balance, by planting trees in those corners of fields that are difficult for large machinery to negotiate. There has been some official encouragement for tree planting and new plantations are being cultivated, particularly on the Manor estate. The loss of the ancient barns was inevitable, as was the loss of most of the dew-ponds; they were no longer needed and could not all have been retained for aesthetic purposes only. Thus we have a changing countryside producing crops and livestock as never before, and not as attractive as in yesteryear. But that, it seems, is the price of progress.

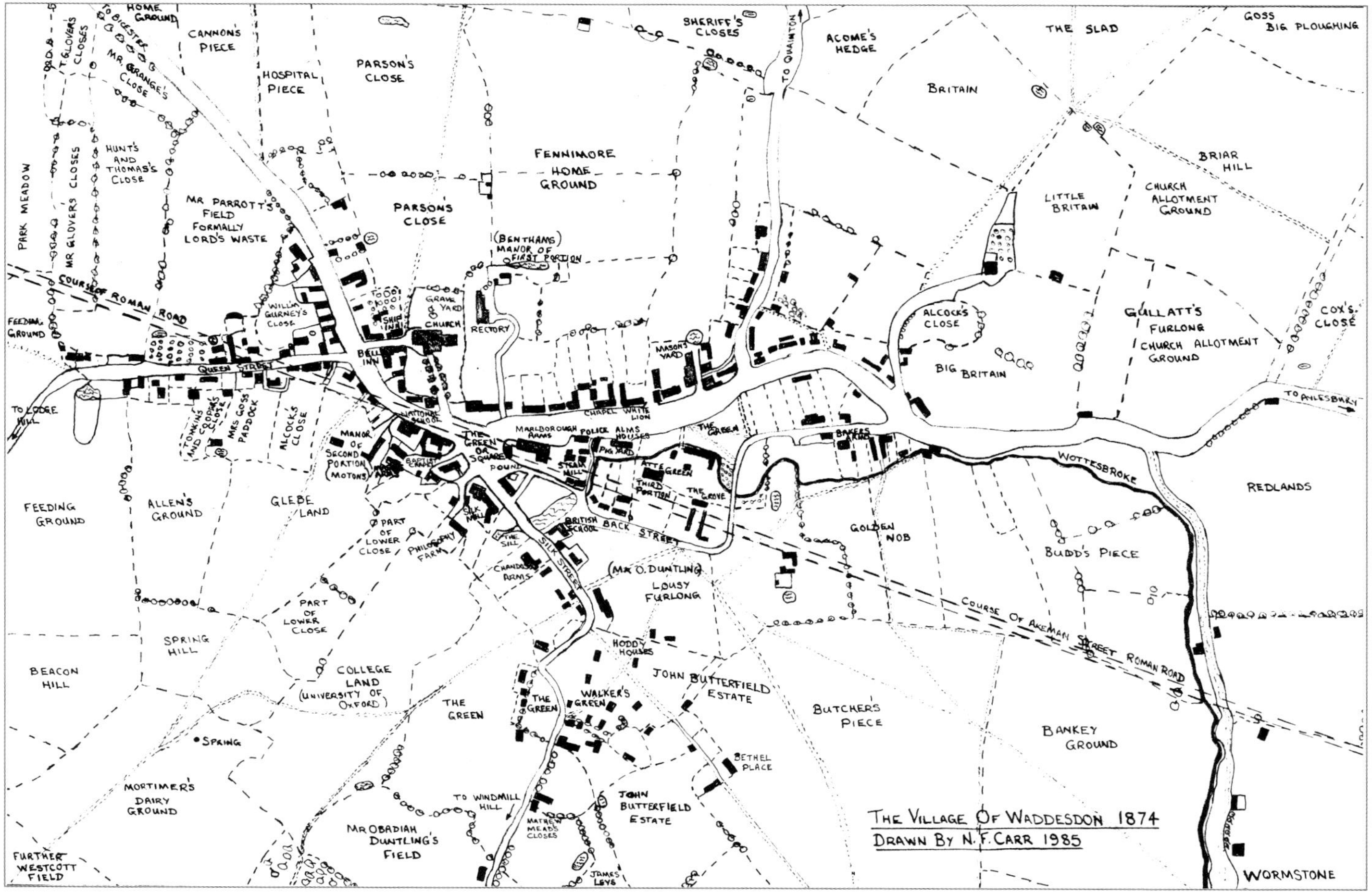

1.22 The first large scale Ordnance Survey map of Waddesdon was surveyed in 1886 and therefore records a village which had already, post 1874 undergone considerable physical changes. The map reproduced above was drawn by Norman Carr and was based upon the 1886 Ordnance Survey scale 1:2500x publication. Its purpose is to illustrate the old village layout in 1874 and was composed from numerous sources of information including photographs, ancient maps and most importantly from documents relating to the sale of the Manor of Waddesdon and Over Winchendon and other properties subsequent to August 1874. For the purpose of this book it was decided to superimpose the line of the Akeman Street (Roman Road), and once again an Ordnance Survey map was used as a guide. Although the original of this map was drawn in 1985, details were added as they became known.

Section Two

Lords and Ancient Manors

Although little detail is known of Waddesdon and its Manor prior to 1066, there is clear evidence it already had considerable local importance. When the Anglo Saxon system of Hundreds was devised, enabling government at local level, the Waddesdon Hundred was included in the original eighteen subdivisions for Buckinghamshire. Notwithstanding the need for good communications within a Hundred there was also due acknowledgement to allegiance, for although the Waddesdon Hundred was a very odd shape, much of it was owned by the Manor; held in 1066 by the Saxon thane Brictric.

Brictric had been an important member of the court of Edward the Confessor, on occasions representing England as an ambassador to the Royal Court in Flanders. It was there he incurred the animosity of Matilda, (future wife of William the Conqueror), when he spurned her amorous advances. Queen Matilda exacted her revenge upon Brictric after the Conquest by arranging his imprisonment and the confiscation of his estates.

The Norman successor to Brictric was Milo Crispin, a supporter of William the Conqueror of course; he also received substantial holdings of land at Quainton and Shabbington. The Domesday Survey of 1086 informs us that the Manor of Waddesdon had an area of 27 hides, (a hide was approximately 120 acres or 48 hectares, making the Manor of Waddesdon about 3,200 acres or 1,300 hectares).Records from this period do not indicate whether a manor house existed in Waddesdon.

The substantial Manor of Waddesdon, inevitably began to fragment and within a few generations saw the loss of numerous large farmsteads. As a result of bridal dowries, bequests, and gifts, minor manors were established in their own right, including Eythrope, Cranwell, Wormstone, Westcott, Blackgrove, Woodham, Collett and Beachendon.

In 1165 there commenced a period of nearly 400 years when the Manor of Waddesdon was held by the Courtenay family. Henry II granted the Manor to Reginald de Courtenay around 1165 and except for a few dramatic interruptions his descendants held it until 1539. The Courtenay family enjoyed very mixed fortunes during these sometimes turbulent years, for although the head of the family bore the important title "Earl of Devon", several of them managed to support the wrong side when it really mattered. In 1461, during the "War of the Roses", Thomas the 6th Earl supported the Lancastrians (Red Rose) and was beheaded after capture at the battle of Townton Field. His younger brother Henry was beheaded at Salisbury and John, the youngest brother was killed in 1470 in the battle of Tewkesbury. Consequently, Thomas, grandson of the 5th Earl was attainted and his estates forfeited to the crown (Edward IV). Not for the first time the Earldom of Devon was restored to the Courtenay family but in 1539 the earl was attainted and beheaded, and his property finally escheated to the Crown, (Henry VIII).

A manor house had been constructed during the time of the Courtenay ownership, though not as an Earl's residence! Evidence of a moated manor house, about 500 metres south of the Church, near the base of Lodge Hill has been described in the Rev Moreton's book "Waddesdon and Over Winchendon". A small remnant of the moat can today be found alongside the driveway near the Cricket Field.

In 1540 the Crown leased, for 21 years, much of the estate in the parish of Waddesdon to Edward Lambourne, "along with the capital manor house". Later that same year the King granted to John Goodwin "all the Manor of Waddesdon with its rights and advowsons" held together with Upper Winchendon. The combined Manors of Over Winchendon and Waddesdon became a single entity, and the manor house was already sited at "The Wilderness" near Upper Winchendon. John Goodwin lived, died (in 1558) and was buried at Winchendon.

In 1634 the Manor descended to Arthur Goodwin, upon the death of his father Sir Francis Goodwin. Arthur Goodwin had been Member of Parliament for Aylesbury in 1625 and later became the Lord Lieutenant of Buckinghamshire; he was a close friend and colleague of John Hampden and heavily involved with him in determining strategy in the turbulent days preceding the Civil War. As a colonel in the Parliamentary Army he was involved in various battles and skirmishes in the vicinity including the storming of Sir Robert Dormer's house at Ascott near Wing. John Hampden was mortally wounded during the Battle of Chalgrove Field in 1643, and Arthur Goodwin attended his dying friend at the house of Ezekial Brown in Thame. When after several days of suffering John Hampden passed away on 24th June 1643, it was Arthur Goodwin who supervised his removal to Great Hampden.

Arthur Goodwin died in 1645 leaving his estates to his daughter Jane. In a codicil to his will was an instruction to build six alms houses in Waddesdon. They stand to this day, his lasting memorial. (See photo no 4.16).

Jane Goodwin had become Lady Jane Wharton on marrying Philip, 4th Lord Wharton in 1637, and it was thus that Lord Wharton followed Arthur Goodwin as Lord of the Manors of Over Winchendon and Waddesdon and also Wooburn near Beaconsfield.

Philip, Lord Wharton was born in 1613, he was educated at Eton and Exeter College Oxford and succeeded to his title in 1625. The ancestral home was at Wharton Hall, Westmorland, but as a very young man he travelled extensively in Europe, spending a time in the service of the Prince of Orange. On his return to England he attended the court of Charles I, where he was popular and influential. At royal command he participated in several of the celebrated masques held in the 1630's, he was described as "the most accomplished gentleman, the greatest beau of his time with a particularly fine pair of legs which he delighted in showing when dancing".

The Whartons' main residence was at "The Wilderness", the manor house at Over Winchendon. They progressively extended and improved the building during the lifetime of Jane, but upon her death Lord Wharton moved to Wooburn. The House at Wooburn was graced with a 120 feet long gallery to accommodate Lord Wharton's extensive collection of portraits of the day, principally the works of Anthony van Dyck and Peter Lely.

During the Civil War, Philip 4th Lord Wharton supported the Parliamentary cause, fought at Edge Hill and other battles. He was much favoured by Oliver Cromwell but at heart was a monarchist, and he welcomed the restoration of the throne with Charles II in 1660. Throughout these troubled times he retained his influence and his fortune, and in later years he embraced the Puritan theology of Calvinism. In his will was a bequest for gifts of bibles to be awarded to deserving children of the parishes connected with his estates. The bequest has endured for three hundred years and Lord Wharton bibles have been treasured for generations in local families.

Thomas 5th Lord Wharton succeeded to the title upon the death of Philip, his father, in 1696. He was different to his father in many ways; described as a compound of the very best and the very worst, and attracted the type of unflattering comments which we still reserve for the more brilliant figures in our midst. The poet and satirist Alexander Pope was moved to target him thus:

"Wharton the scorn and wonder of our days,
Whose ruling passion was the lust of praise,
Born with what e'er could win it from the wise,
Women and fools must like him, or he dies".

The 5th Lord Wharton preferred to make his home at Winchendon (See photo no 2.2). He extended the old Goodwin mansion and added a large gallery for displaying the famous Wharton collection of portraits. Magnificent grounds were laid out in the Dutch style with parterres, gardens, an orangery, terrace walks, a bowling green, kitchen gardens and stables for his beloved racehorses and greyhounds, which were incidentally said to be the finest in England.

An ardent Whig and an extremely able politician, he was an eminent statesman, and Member of Parliament for Bucks. On the other hand he was a duellist and a rake who enjoyed his celebrated life to the full. His abilities and popularity both with royalty and society were recognised in 1706 when he was created Viscount Winchendon of Winchendon. In due course he was appointed Lord Lieutenant of Ireland, advanced to Marquis of Wharton and had earned further titles before his death in April 1715. (See photo and caption no 2.5).

Philip 6th Lord Wharton was the only surviving son of Thomas, and he inherited the title at the age of 16. Like his father he was well educated and highly accomplished but yet again quite different in his extravagances and his behaviour. When still under 21 he took his seat as Marquis of Catherlough in the Irish Parliament and was so successful that he was raised to the highest rank of peerage, Duke of Wharton. He took his seat in the House of Lords but his conduct was becoming increasingly unacceptable, his extravagance and lack of restraint in all things leading to "the utmost licentiousness". Eventually his expenditure proved his ruin and his estates by now suffering from neglect were vested in trustees.

In 1725 under a Decree of Chancery, the trustees sold the "Manors of Winchendon, Waddesdon and Westcote" comprising 2,700 acres, to the Trustees of the late First Duke of Marlborough, for Sarah, the Dowager Duchess. Meanwhile the famous collection of portraits was sold to Sir Robert Walpole for a reputed sum of £1500. These portraits are now scattered around the world, some in the U.S.A. and a number in the Hermitage museum in St Petersburg (Leningrad), having been purchased from the Walpoles by Catherine the Great.

Philip 6th Lord Wharton was given an allowance of £1,200 per year and he went abroad where he began a round of visits to countries, not all of which were friendly to Great Britain. He entered into the service of Bonnie Prince Charlie, the Young Pretender, and later served the Spanish King at the Siege of Gibraltar. He was indicted for High Treason as a consequence; refused to return to England and so was attainted and his property confiscated. On his death in a charitable convent at Tarragona in 1731, all his titles became extinct. The mansion at "The Wilderness" had long since succumbed to the ravages of neglect, and Charles, 2nd Duke of Marlborough had allowed the demolition of much of what had survived. In 1758 John Russell of Aylesbury purchased the salvaged materials including statues in the grounds, lead pipes lying from the Water House and sundry building materials for a price of £1,400. Sufficient of the grand house, stables and cow-houses remained for utilisation as a farm, and that is eventually what it became after initially serving as the residence of the Duke's Steward. The stables were demolished in 1860, they were described by Lipscomb "as a magnificent design, having carved pillars, cornices and stuccoed ceilings, partly gilt" ... etc.

For nearly 150 years the successive Dukes of Marlborough held the Manor of Waddesdon and Over Winchendon and during this period the inhabitants of Waddesdon gained little from that illustrious association. However, in Upper Winchendon several substantial cottages and a village school were constructed in the mid 19th century. The Manor house at Winchendon was reduced to the standing of a farm, and the ancient Manor house in Waddesdon though for a short time in the early 19th century accommodating a member of the Nugent family, (related to the Marquis of Buckingham), was allowed to degenerate until its remains were finally demolished in 1860.

As the Lord of the Manor of Waddesdon and Over Winchendon, the Dukes of Marlborough each held the advowson for the Church of England benefices within the manorial area. It is probable that in this way they exerted their most obvious influence (indirectly) upon the lives of the villagers.

In 1874 when Baron Ferdinand de Rothschild purchased the Manor of Waddesdon and Over Winchendon the advowson was retained by the House of Marlborough, and hence-forth the rectors have been appointed under the patronage of the Dukes of Marlborough. In 1900 the 9th Duke of Marlborough presented to the Church of St Michael, Waddesdon the ornate Italian pulpit, in thanksgiving for his safe return from the Boer War.

2.1 Philip, 4th Lord Wharton, who succeeded to the Manor of Over Winchendon and Waddesdon in 1645 through his wife Jane, the daughter and heir of Arthur Goodwin. This portrait by Anthony Van Dyck was included in the large collection held by the Whartons at Wooburn and Upper Winchendon. A lasting act of benevolence to parishioners adjacent to the Wharton estates was Phillip Lord Wharton's bequest to present Bibles and Prayer books to deserving youngsters, (See Charities, Section 5)

2.2 The Wilderness circa 1710. This magnificent Manor House at Upper Winchendon was the home of Thomas 5th Lord Wharton. The gardens as illustrated were set out in the Dutch style, whilst nearby was an orangery, kitchen gardens, stables for racehorses and kennels for greyhounds. It is hard to comprehend that within 15 years this view was to become a scene of neglect and terminal decay. This painting, now held at the County Museum is the only known illustration of The Wilderness in all its glory. (Copy of painting of Winchendon House reproduced from, Journal of Garden History, 1988, by Taylor and Francis Ltd, "The Anglo-Dutch Garden in the age of William and Mary". Copied and published by kind permission of Taylor and Francis Ltd, London, and Buckinghamshire County Museum Aylesbury (c)).

2.3 The Wilderness, circa 1910. This photograph by Albert Cherry of the residence of George Alfred Sims, land steward to Miss Alice de Rothschild, views the house from the north. Although this is still quite a large dwelling, when compared with the painting in 2.2 one can see it comprises only about a quarter of the 1710 mansion. Of particular interest in this photograph is the absence of any evidence of a cupola above the east facing gable end, and the curious spur of wall remaining at the end nearest the camera, presumably a remnant of the portrait gallery, which adjoined the building at this point. The seat by the tennis court is now on the site of the previous building.

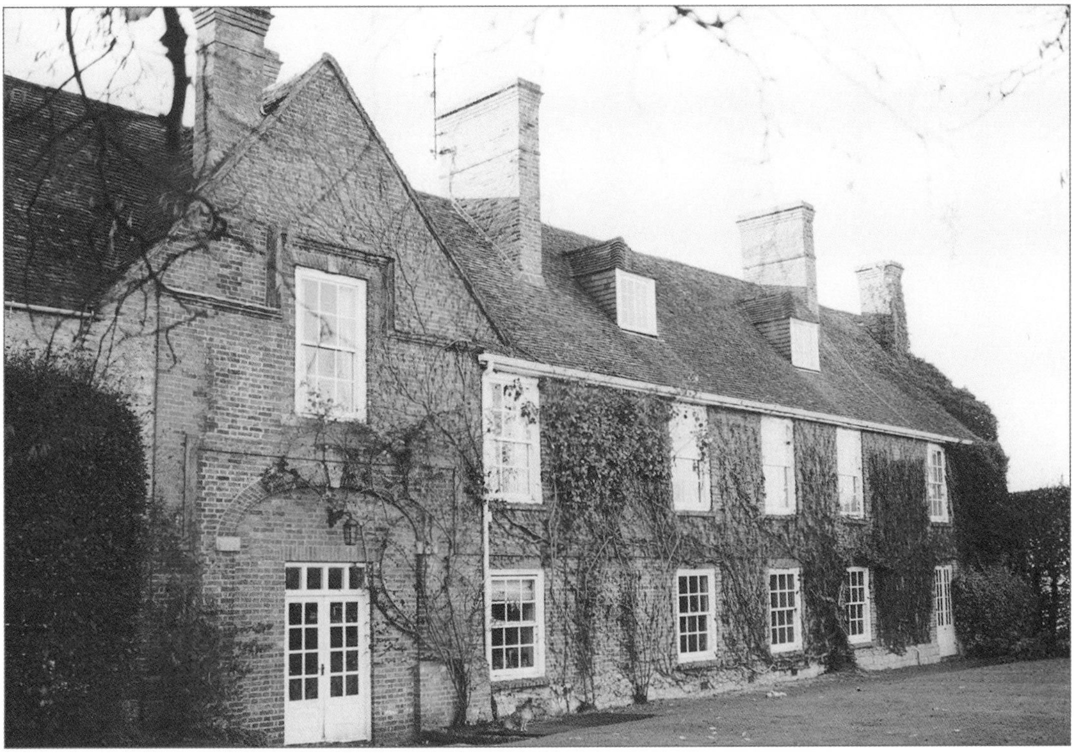

2.4 The Wilderness November 1999. This photograph by Ivor Gurney is taken at almost the same angle as the vantage point of the painter in 2.2 and is the best comparison obtainable due to the presence of trees and hedgerows. The photograph gives a good profile of the ornamental brickwork around the window on the east facing gable end which three hundred years earlier was faithfully copied by the artist. The brickwork spur mentioned in 2.3, at the far end has been removed during the past 100 years.

2.5 Keepers' Lodge. This photograph circa 1970 of the Lodge shortly before demolition records a sad end to a building with a mysterious and curious history. A hundred years earlier it was known as "The Folly" and for its final century in existence it was the home of a succession of estate gamekeepers. Standing on the gloomy western edge of "The Wilderness" wood, around 600 yards north-east of the old Manor house it was believed to have been built by Thomas 5th Lord Wharton for his "favourite" lady. This is especially credible as it appears to fit the contemporary description; however it is in the wrong place, as the "Lady's" abode was described as having a fine view from this spot overlooking a vast expanse of the county on the east. Strangely, Mrs Messenger the wife of the last gamekeeper to live there always claimed there was a tunnel linking the cellars of the Manor and Keepers Lodge; perhaps someone in the future will excavate and prove a point.

2.6 School Lane, Upper Winchendon circa 1870. This stark view of fairly substantial cottages off School Lane is reminiscent of nineteenth century frontier settlements in North America. With few windows the interiors must have been rather gloomy, but at least these homes would have been drier and warmer, judging by the wood-pile, than the cottages down in Waddesdon. All the houses in this photograph would be demolished in the following twenty or so years, being replaced by "Rothschild workers' homes", the land at the rear became allotments.

2.7 Upper Winchendon circa 1870. Another view in School Lane, but from nearer the main road. The houses at near left were built by the Duke of Marlborough, given the "Rothschild treatment" post 1874 and followed by two further rows. This completed a continuous line of dwellings down to the new school opposite, which had also been built by the Duke. In the 1920's the "Rothschild" house at left of photograph was occupied by the Tilly family. Mr Tilly worked on the Estate and Mrs Tilly would have jars of sweets on shelves in the porch for the children to spend their farthings* on, when leaving the school opposite. *(See notes at end of book).

2.8 Upper Winchendon circa 1895. The houses on the left, known as "Dukes Row" were built by the Duke of Marlborough circa 1870. They were a great improvement over the type of dwelling normally occupied by the workers in the district at that time, and illustrated an overdue involvement in the welfare of his employees by the absent lord of the manor. The lady leaning over the gate on the left is one of the Russell sisters. In the early 1900's the house at the far end of the row was also a small shop run by Mr and Mrs Hawkins. The Rothschild houses on the right are of post 1874 vintage and the house nearest the camera was, in the early part of the nineteen hundreds, a reading room for men only from the age of fourteen years, and occupied by Mr and Mrs Folly. After the Second World War the Reading Room was destined to become "The Club", and Mr James de Rothschild set the annual rent at one shilling, (5p). An ex army hut, remaining from the Second World War camp on the Eythrope Drive, was taken down piece by piece by Winchendon inhabitants in the 1950's and rebuilt next to "The Club" as the village hall.

13

LODGE HILL FARM,

With FARM HOUSE,

Containing One Attic, Four Bed Rooms and Lumber Room, Hall, Two Parlours, Living Room, Two Dairies, Granary over one, and Wash House,

AND THE FOLLOWING OUTBUILDINGS—

Cart Horse Stable for Seven Horses and Loft over, Fatting Shed for Eight Beasts, Coal Shed, Two Poultry Houses, Piggeries and Food House, Yard with Open Shed, Feeding House, Barn, another Feeding House, Cart Shed, Gig House, GARDEN and ORCHARD. Detached in the Fields are Sheds and Yards for Cattle, together with

THE FOLLOWING LANDS,—

No. on Plan.	Description.	Cultivation.	Quantity. A.	R.	P.	Parish.
173	Free Hill, Shed and Yard	Pasture	11	0	38	WADDESDON
174	Round Hill, Sheds and Yard	Ditto	20	2	35	Ditto
175	Lince's Piece, Sheds and Yard	Ditto	5	1	34	Ditto
176	Spinney		0	1	5	Ditto
177	Sand Piece	Pasture	3	3	1	Ditto
178	Wykham Bottom Ground	Arable	31	2	33	Ditto
179	House and Homestead		1	3	0	Ditto
180	Plantation	Wood	0	3	16	Ditto
181	Westcott Hill Field	Pasture	2	2	20	Ditto
182	Hill Side	Ditto	9	1	38	Ditto
183	Bean Furlong	Ditto	30	1	36	Ditto
184	Part of Old Park	Ditto	46	3	6	Ditto
185	Part of Old Park	Arable	27	0	0	Ditto
186	Park Meadow, Sheds and Yard	Pasture	24	2	37	Ditto
187	Feeding Ground	Ditto	29	0	30	Ditto
188	Beacon Hill	Arable	13	3	9	Ditto
		TOTAL ACRES	259	3	18	

In the occupation of JAMES BULFORD, as yearly Tenant, at a Rental of **£610.** per Annum.

THE MARLBOROUGH ARMS INN,

SITUATE IN THE CENTRE OF

THE VILLAGE OF WADDESDON,

Comprising Two Attics, Seven Bed Rooms, Two Parlours, Large Bar, Tap Room, Club Room, Kitchen, Wash-house, Dairy, Larder and Cellar,

AND THE FOLLOWING OUTBUILDINGS—

Coach-house, Stable for Four Horses, Three Loose Boxes and Loft over, Brew-house, Granary, Gig-house, Piggeries, Yard, Garden,

AND CLOSES OF RICH GRAZING LANDS, as follows,—

			A.	R.	P.	
189	Spring Hill	Pasture	8	3	13	WADDESDON
190	Allen's Ground	Ditto	6	2	10	Ditto
191	Close, Buildings and Yard	Ditto	0	3	25	Ditto
192	Part Lower Close	Ditto	2	0	0	Ditto
193	Part Lower Close, Sheds and Yard		2	1	3	Ditto
194	Marlborough Arms Inn, Outbuildings & Garden		0	1	14	Ditto
		TOTAL ACRES	20	3	25	

Let to WILLIAM TOMKINS and W. COOPER, as yearly Tenants, at **£94.** per Annum.

2.9 The unsuccessful Auction Sale of the Waddesdon, Winchendon and Westcott Manors on the 7th July 1874 had been preceded by the issue of an 18-page catalogue, which described the assets in some detail. Here we reproduce page 13, which deals with Lodge Hill Farm and The Marlborough Arms Inn. It may be of interest to note the "Buckinghamshire Giant", William Stevens, by 1874 had already left as tenant of Lodge Hill Farm and was residing at The Marlborough Arms. This sale marked the end of an era in more ways than one. It is also interesting to note the areas of the fields are given in Acres, Roods and Poles, measurements used until the late 20th century, and dating back many hundreds of years.

WADDESDON.

THE DUKE OF MARLBOROUGH'S ESTATES.—The announcement of the sale of the Duke of Marlborough's Buckinghamshire Estates caused considerable surprise in the neighbourhood, as the property is very extensive. The sale comprised a very important freehold manorial estate, principally tithe free and land-tax redeemed, situate in the parishes of Waddesdon, Upper Winchendon, and Cuddington, and hamlet of Westcott, about 5½ miles from Aylesbury, only one mile from the Quainton station of the Aylesbury and Buckingham Railway, and 12 from Buckingham; comprising the manor of Over Winchendon, the manor or lordship of Waddesdon, and also the manor of Westcott, with their rights, members, and appurtenances thereto belonging; Maynes-hill, Lince, Upper Winchendon, Decoy, Windmill-hill, Common Leys, Westcott-field, Lodge-hill, and Westcott Farms, with superior farm residences and very extensive and appropriate farm buildings the Crooked Billet publichouse, situate at Ham Green, and the Marlborough Arms, in the village of Waddesdon, about 50 cottages, part newly built, sundry enclosures of accommodation land, the whole within a ring fence, except as to a small part, in and near the villages of Waddesdon and Westcott, in one of the finest dairy districts in the county. The whole embraces an area approaching 3,000 acres, and produces, independent of the valuable woods in hand, a present inadequate rental of nearly £6,000 per annum. The property was offered at the Auction Mart, London, on Tuesday last, in one lot, but the biddings not coming up to the estimated value of the estate, no sale was effected, and the estate was bought in at £174,000. The principal biddings were made on behalf of N. G. Lambert, Esq., M.P.

2.10 A description of the Duke of Marlborough's Estate at Waddesdon and Over Winchendon and its failure to sell at the auction in July 1874, as it appeared in the Bucks Advertiser and Aylesbury News.

2.11 March 1998. Waddesdon Manor viewed from the driveway at the old Manor House, The Wilderness, Upper Winchendon.

Section Three

Waddesdon Manor & the Rothschilds

Baron Ferdinand de Rothschild

When in the summer of 1874 Baron Ferdinand de Rothschild purchased the Manorial Estate of Over Winchendon, Waddesdon and Westcott, he was a comparatively young man of thirty-four. A great-grandson of the founder of the Rothschild banking house, he was born and raised in Germany and Austria, although his mother was English. In the early 1860's the Baron settled in London, became a British subject, and married Evelina the daughter of Baron Lionel de Rothschild of the English branch of the family.

After only eighteen months of married life the Baron suffered the double loss of his wife Evelina in childbirth, and her unborn child. It is doubtful if he ever recovered from this bereavement, however with characteristic benevolence he endowed the Evelina Hospital in London as her memorial. Events would show that this act of munificence was not an isolated reaction arising only from grief, but was typical of the man throughout his lifetime.

In the early 1870's, almost eight years after the death of his wife, the Baron decided he would not find a suitable country house for sale, and so must construct one for himself. Already in or near the Vale of Aylesbury five members of the extensive Rothschild family had established their country homes and had happily assimilated into the local scene. Sir Anthony at Aston Clinton, Mayer at Mentmore, Leopold at Wing (Ascott), Alfred at Halton and Lord Nathanial Rothschild at Tring. At this time the Baron and his sister were residing at Leighton House, Leighton Buzzard. It was hardly surprising therefore that Baron Ferdinand should choose a nearby estate in which to build his country seat. In fact it was while hunting with the Duke of Buckingham at Wotton, that he first saw from a distance the commanding position held by Lodge Hill. This was in 1874 the year of his inheritance, and the Marlborough estate happened to be for sale.

After an unsuccessful auction on July 7th when the property was "bought in" at £174, 000, a private sale was swiftly concluded to the Baron at "around £200,000". As the following years would prove, Baron Ferdinand was a dynamic person who lacked neither the wherewithal, nor the determination to succeed with the creation of Waddesdon Manor. A French architect, Gabriel-Hippolyte Destailleur, and a French landscape gardener Elie Laine were soon appointed and briefed. In mid-September 1875 more than 100 workmen who were "engaged in preparing the approaches to the Mansion" were entertained to dinner, a hot meal and a pleasant and jovial evening. This little treat displayed the revolutionary approach to labour relations of the Baron, and while delighting the recipients, it may have caused a sense of unease amongst those who had been happy with the status quo! The tone of future relationships with village organisations, had already been shown when the Baron supplied prizes and "goodies" for the British School Treat, on 11th September.

Building and landscaping progressed apace. In October 1875 water was laid on to the site, and at Waddesdon, Eythrope and Westcott, standpipes were installed for use by villagers. Ever appreciative of innovative advances the Baron sanctioned the use of structural steel in the construction of the Manor (to the astonishment of engineers more than a century later!), and electric lights. On a different scale, in 1882 he commissioned the very first telephone installation in the area, one set in his study, one in his chief steward's room and one in the head groom's quarters.

Although Baron Ferdinand moved into the "Bachelors' wing" in 1880, the Manor was not considered complete until the housewarming in July 1883. However for visitors and locals alike, the creation of the Baron's country seat complete with park and woods, on this bare Buckinghamshire hill in so short a time was a marvel, and so it was often described.

From 1885 Baron Ferdinand was the Member of Parliament for Aylesbury until his death in 1898. At Waddesdon he frequently entertained the famous political and artistic personalities of the day, whilst the Prince of Wales (future King Edward VII) was a regular guest. Memorably in 1890, Queen Victoria bestowed the rare compliment of a "private visit" to the Manor.

The transformation on Lodge Hill was matched on a smaller scale in Waddesdon and Upper Winchendon. Inferior farms and houses on Estate land were demolished and sometimes replaced, a few of the better quality buildings that were suitable for retention, were given the "Rothschild treatment". In Waddesdon over a period of more than twenty years, the bulk of the Silk Street and Queen Street population moved into new houses in Frederick Street and Quainton Road. The village acquired a prosperous and successful outlook reflecting the improvements to every aspect of community life. Beneficial initiatives which may have faltered due to inadequate support were backed by the Baron, facilities were provided and improvement encouraged. A new British School was built in Baker Street, and the Church tower was completely remodelled, all by public subscription. A Reading Room and a Village Hall were provided. Annually, highly coveted School Prizes were awarded and a Philharmonic Society, two Brass Bands and numerous religious groups flourished. The Football and Cricket clubs played leading roles in the local sports-scene.

Away from Waddesdon the Baron also pursued his philanthropic habit, in many instances unknown to the general public until after his death. High on the list was his support for hospitals and improvement for the poor. In Aylesbury he donated £2000 of the £3000 costs for the construction of the Slipper Baths in Bourbon Street; to commemorate Queen Victoria's Diamond Jubilee he gave the Victoria Club for Working Men in Kingsbury Square, and the two magnificent cast bronze lions resting near the Law Courts in the Market Square, were a gift to the town which have become a familiar sight for everyone for over 100 years.

In 1898, after twenty-four years as Lord of the Manor, Baron Ferdinand de Rothschild passed away. During that period the lives of all the inhabitants in and around Waddesdon had been affected by his presence, almost always positively. Despite his consuming interests in fine art, epitomised in his collection retained at the Manor, his gift to the British Museum "the Waddesdon Bequest," and his political and social standing in the country, the Baron was and is still remembered by Waddesdonians, as the right man who came to the village at just the right time.

UPPER WINCHENDON.

SALE OF THE ESTATE

The estate known as the Winchendon Estate, and which was put up to auction last month by Messrs. Farebrother Clark, and Co., but bought in, has been disposed of, Messrs. Rothschild having added it to their already large possessions in this county. The extent of the estate reaches 2,763 acres, and the annual rent amounts to £5,723. We cannot give the precise sum at which the estate changed hands, but may surmise it to be somewhere about £180,000.

The property lies in the parishes of Waddesdon, Upper Winchendon, Cuddington, and in the hamlet of Westcott; it is principally titho-free and land-tax redeemed, and includes manorial rights in Winchendon, Waddesdon, and Westcott. The principal farms are Main's Hill, Linge, Upper Winchendon, Decoy, Windmill Hill, Common Leys, Westcott Field, Lodge Hill, and Westcott Farm, and the principal tenants are Mr. John Treadwell, Mr. Thomas Bliss, Mr. W. Cooper, Mr. J. Bulford, Mr. M. Mead, Mr. T. Matthews, &c.

There are also several plots of accommodation land, and the purchase includes the Marlborough Arms Inn, Waddesdon, the Crooked Billet, Ham Green, about 50 cottages and other properties. The farm tenants have mostly held under the late landlord for many years; they are of an enterprising and improving class, and some have taken prizes at the Royal Agricultural Show of England for their superior breed of sheep and oxen, and although the holdings are yearly, the tenants, as a whole, are such as no new occupier would feel disposed to disturb in their occupations. Great improvements have of late years been carried out on the property, under the immediate inspection of the agent to the late noble owner, by the erection of new homesteads on the most approved principles of modern farming; the remainder having been thoroughly repaired and kept in good order.

The late proprietor of the property was his Grace the Duke of Marlborough. The estate was purchased by the trustees of the will of John Duke of Marlborough, K.G., early in the year 1725, of the trustees of Philip Lord Wharton, under a Decree of Chancery, so that the Marlborough family have held it about 150 years. The property came to the Whartons in 1682, by the marriage of Philip 4th Lord Wharton, with Jane, only daughter and heiress of Arthur Goodwin, Esq., M.P. for Aylesbury, and granddaughter of Sir F. Goodwin of Wooburn and Upper Winchendon.

The mansion at Upper Winchendon was pulled down in 1758; it was the residence of both the Goodwins and the Whartons. It stood on the brow of an eminence, south-east of the church, and was enlarged, if not entirely rebuilt, by Thomas, Marquess of Wharton. The gardens and parterre were esteemed superior to any in the county, and this seat was celebrated for its fine collection of orange trees. No plan or description of the place exists to discover a specimen of the style of Dutch gardening, of which Lord Wharton was one of the most eminent patrons. The rectilinear terrace walks and division of the gardens may be traced, flanked by a grove now very appropriately termed the Wilderness. A good deal of brick-work in the shape of brick walls is still standing, and which are supposed to have formed the boundaries of the kitchen garden, and tradition points to the site of the bowling-green—the constant accompaniment of an old English country seat. Some of the outhouses, being the remains of large and magnificently designed stabling, with pillars, cornices, stuccoed ceilings, and gilt ornamentations, stood as late as the year 1860. In 1758, John Russell, of Aylesbury, purchased all the materials of the mansion, with the iron gates palisadoes, stone images, &c., in the gardens; the price was £1,400 agreed to be paid by instalments. The materials of the stabling and many items of fixtures were excepted from this bargain. It is probable that many of the ornamental items from the old mansion still grace some of the old houses in Aylesbury, but their identity cannot now be traced. The remains of the outbuildings were subsequently occupied by permission of the Duke of Marlborough by the family of Vassar, who was steward of the estate. In the Wilderness was a small turreted brick building, originally erected by Thomas, Marquess of Wharton, for the residence of a favourite lady. The spot, though solitary, commands a remarkably fine view, embracing the old race-course at Quainton, and neighbourhood. Some pictures and portraits from the old mansion were to be met with in the village a few years ago, but they probably by this time have all disappeared.

We hear that the purchaser of the estate contemplates rebuilding the mansion near the old site. It is a most charming spot for the erection of a gentleman's residence. Its elevated position affords views not to be excelled in any part of the Kingdom, and the immediate vicinity is already ornamentally and well timbered.

3.1 A report from the Bucks Advertiser and Aylesbury News of 22nd August 1874 informs us of the sale of the Marlborough Estate and gives an interesting review of its recent history.

3.2 Waddesdon village viewed from Beacon Hill, a field on Lodge Hill, photographed in 1874 as surveyors busily set out the works required for Baron Ferdinand de Rothschild's new mansion and grounds. No sign yet of the changes to come! The old church tower, the steam mill chimney and the cluster of dwellings in Queen Street and Silk Street can be discerned, whilst in the left foreground is the steep track leading to Lodge Hill Farm. This scene clearly shows Waddesdon as a typical mid-Buckinghamshire village and should be compared with photograph 3.8 which is of this view just a dozen years' later.

3.3 In an age when much of the work was done by hand, this photograph of workers near the redundant Lodge Hill Farm shows an ingenious if precarious runway to ease the labour of the barrow pushers, perhaps enabling transfer of the spoil onto a horse-drawn cart. At centre rear can be seen a plantation of young trees already in place, circa 1880.

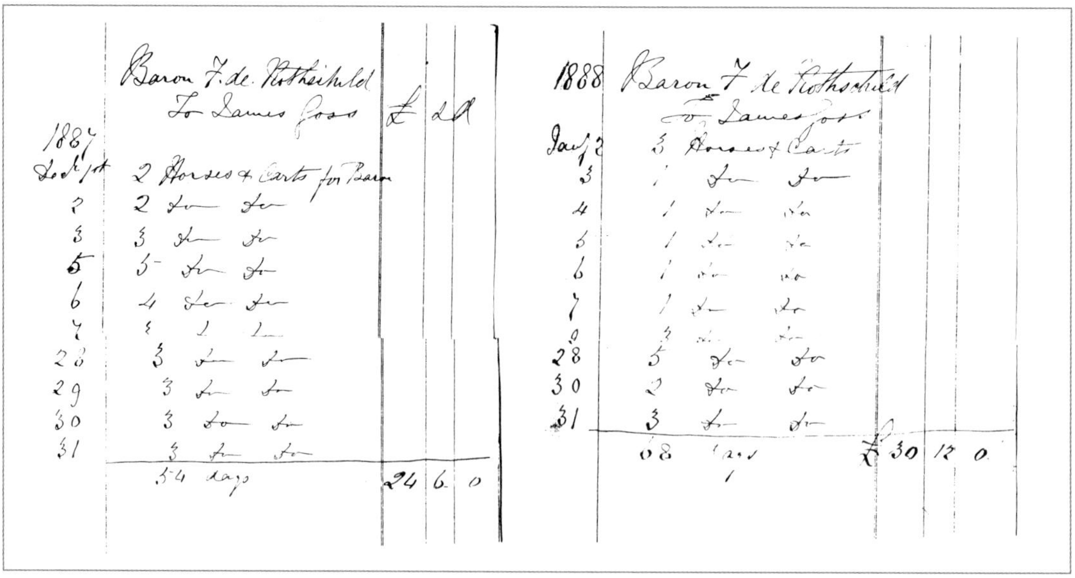

	Baron F. de Rothschild To James Goss	£	s	d
1887 Decr 1st	2 Horses & Carts for Baron			
2	2 do do			
3	3 do do			
5	5 do do			
6	4 do do			
7	[illegible]			
28	3 do do			
29	3 do do			
30	3 do do			
31	3 do do			
	54 days	24	6	0

1888	Baron F de Rothschild To James Goss	£	s	d
Jany 2	3 Horses & Carts			
3	1 do do			
4	1 do do			
5	1 do do			
6	1 do do			
7	1 do do			
9	3 do do			
28	5 do do			
30	2 do do			
31	3 do do			
	68 days	30	12	0

3.3a From the outset and for many subsequent years the Baron contracted local farmers etc to supply horses and carts with drivers on a continuous basis. We have reproduced a page from the ledger of Mr James Goss of the Glebe Farm on the Green, for December 1887 and January 1888. For the supply of the equivalent of 122 days' service in those two months the charge was £54 – 18s – 0d. (9 shillings (45p) per day!).

3.4 Work under way on the site of the new "mansion", as it was to be called by all and sundry. Circa 1875. Mr Judd, the works foreman in the top hat standing at centre of picture, married a Waddesdon girl and settled in the village. This photograph vividly depicts the labour intensive assortment of human tasks that were called for in this, the largest building project ever experienced in Waddesdon. The village had emerged from a century of hardship and hunger and now there was work for those who needed it, prospects for those who aspired and profits for those who had services or goods to sell. Every horse and cart not essential to the owner's requirements was continuously hired out for the mansion works.

3.5 Our Victorian ancestors were undaunted by the prospect of cutting a roadway through a hill, this was the age of the "navvy" and the work under-way in this photograph was "small beer" when compared with many railway and canal building enterprises. However, this cutting circa 1875, through the spur which connected Lodge Hill to Westcott Hill, enabled South Drive traffic to progress from Grand Lodge at the Waddesdon cross roads without undue effort for the horses. The curious pinnacle remaining at centre of picture indicates the volume of spoil so far removed, the glacial boulders scattered around give a clue to the origins of at least some of the rustic stonework later artfully sited in the grounds, whilst the rough contours of the sides of the cutting leave us with an impression of much work remaining to achieve the smooth profiles of the finished article.

3.6 Waddesdon Manor under construction in 1878. More than 100 years on this photograph appears the best of several which were taken to record how "modern" technology was assisting builders in their labours. A steam-powered hoist is operating from the ground whilst several scaffold-mounted cranes are working upon the building. The iron rails at right and left foreground are for wagons winched up the hill from a spur of the Wotton Tramway, and used to convey much of the heavy building materials for the project.

3.7 A landscaping gang circa 1878. Carefully posed so as not to spoil the lengthy exposure process, this rather well attired bunch of gardeners can already see the progress resulting from their earlier work, but can scarcely have imagined the woods and parkland which would give so much pleasure in the years to come. In order to speed the afforestation of Lodge Hill the Baron had employed the already established technique of transplanting nearly full-grown trees from the surrounding countryside, including the woods at Ham Green. Specially designed carts, drawn by Percheron horses imported from France became a common sight, making their slow progress along the roads with the trees anchored vertically and the roots swathed in hessian. Telegraph lines and other impediments were removed where necessary. In order to aid irrigation to the plantings in time of drought, an underground piping system was installed.

3.8 The Steep Path circa 1885 leading from the Manor to the Stables. Already the immediate farmland is taking on a park-like appearance, but Mr Taylor's steam mill chimney still rises in Silk Street, no sign yet of the new Five Arrows Hotel, and from this distance the old Church Tower looks good for a few hundred years!

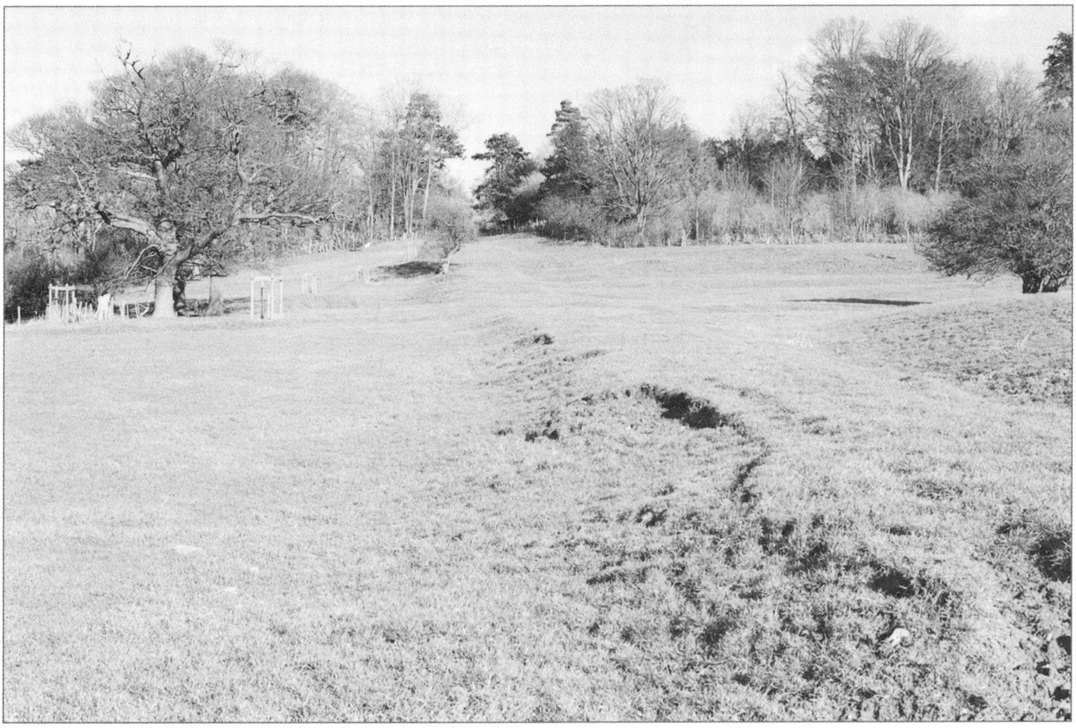

3.9 Spring 2000 and on the SW slopes of Lodge Hill the raised bed of the track on which the building materials for the Manor were winched is clearly still in evidence, whilst on the right of the picture one can discern two terraces (Linces) remaining from man's efforts at cultivation 7000 years' ago.

3.10 Waddesdon Manor circa 1885. The south front sparklingly new and without its mantle of trees must have seemed like a fairy-tale castle to the locals who well remembered the Lodge Hill of old.

3.11 The north front circa 1895. Although this picture illustrates the perfection of the Manor in all its glory, there is also an established air to the view, belying the relative immaturity of everything in sight. This is the first close-up view of the Manor the Baron's many visitors would have had, and no doubt they were suitably impressed.

3.12 Baron Ferdinand de Rothschild relaxing in his private sitting room at the Manor, as recorded in his "Red Book" November 1897.

3.13 Baron Ferdinand de Rothschild enjoyed the company of famous and influential guests at his house parties at Waddesdon Manor. A number of mature trees to be found near the Manor in the year 2000 were planted as young saplings by important visitors around 100 years' ago. In some cases the commemorative plaques remain. This photograph is of a Saturday-to-Monday party group in July 1897. It enabled such persons as the Grand Duke Michael of Russia, Countess Torby, the Russian Ambassador, the Brazilian Minister, Count Mensdorff, Princess Henry of Pless, the Earl and Countess of Warwick, and other military and political leaders to meet the Prince of Wales, shown here at the centre of this group. Invariably the party would travel from and return to London on the Metropolitan Railway via Waddesdon Manor Station. Non-scheduled stops if necessary, were made at the station for the convenience of the Baron.

3.14 On Wednesday May 14th 1890, Queen Victoria made a visit to Waddesdon Manor and although it was not an "Official Engagement" the local populace took the opportunity to welcome the Queen in grand style. This photograph shows the Queen's carriage with two postilions about to move away from the entrance to Aylesbury Railway Station, whilst the numerous on-lookers, officials and troopers of the Royal Buckinghamshire Hussars face their monarch as she commences her horse-drawn journey to Waddesdon. The route through Aylesbury was decorated with bunting, flags and loyal messages, and crowds of people lined the roads. At Fleet Marston a stand had been erected to enable locals to watch the royal party pass by, and a large crowd had gathered at the Grand Lodge at Waddesdon cross roads where the carriages entered the estate grounds. For her travel upon the gravel drives around the Manor, the Queen's pony and carriage with attendant (The brother of John Brown), had been sent in advance. Soon after the Royal visit the Queen arranged for her cook, head gardener, and furniture keeper to visit and learn from the Waddesdon methods.

Mr. Horwood's youngest daughter, Miss J. A. Horwood, a little girl some seven years of age, then presented a bouquet of Marechal Niel roses, lilies of the valley, and yellow heather to her Majesty, while two other of Mr. Horwood's children offered bouquets to the Princess Beatrice.

The school children in the stand sang a verse or two of the National Anthem, her Majesty listening with a pleased expression, and then the ceremony was over, the outriders got the signal to proceed, and amid ringing cheers the Queen was driven at a slow pace up the Market-square. The Baron and Lord Rothschild also received quite an ovation as they drove past. The streets and the windows were crowded with people, and nothing could exceed the heartiness with which they welcomed her Majesty. At the head of the procession rode Captain Drake, the Chief Constable of the County, while in immediate proximity to the Royal carriage were the Equerries-in-Waiting, General du Plat and Col. Carington. At the stand near the Infirmary about 350 school children from Aston Clinton, Mentmore, and Halton sang "God save the Queen," under the leadership of Mr. Pughe. The procession passed along the route indicated, and soon reached the open country.

THE VISIT TO WADDESDON.

Along the road to Waddesdon were numerous parties waiting for the Royal arrival, and here and there a waggon loaded to its utmost capacity stood by the roadside, while at many of the scattered cottages there was some slight attempt at bunting. It was not until Fleet Marston was reached that anything like an organised demonstration was seen. Skirting the road on the right by Mr. Sanders' pretty home, with its neat walks and closely-shaven lawn, was erected a comparatively small platform, while immediately opposite was one of larger dimensions, and both were crowded with eager sightseers, anxiously awaiting the arrival of her Majesty. A number of decorated Venetian masts, with flags, and strung with evergreen and parti-coloured flowers depending from mast to mast, had a very pretty effect. Mr. Sanders kindly lent his fields to the scholars attending Earl Temple's schools at Wotton Underwood, and also generously supplied them with refreshments. From this point to Waddesdon Cross Roads the scene became livelier, pedestrians and traps, carts, and waggons, filled with holiday folk, hurrying forward to the appointed rendezvous. The preparations for the reception of her Majesty at the Cross Roads were on a very extensive scale. A handsome arch had been thrown across the road with the words "Welcome to our Queen" running the length of the span, and on the reverse or Waddesdon side, "God bless our Queen." The arch was embellished with trophies and Royal flags, with the monogram "V.R.," and depending from the centre was a basket of flowers, with floral festoons, &c. A number of platforms were erected for the accommodation of the tenants and inhabitants of Upper and Lower Winchendon, Grendon, Marsh Gibbon, Quainton, Whitchurch, Oving, Pitchcott, Westcott, Ashendon, Waddesdon, and Long Crendon. These platforms were tastefully adorned with evergreens and various coloured artificial flowers depending from Venetian masts. The three arches over the entrance gate to the Park were neatly traced with festoons and evergreens, the centre one, in gold letters, on a crimson ground, bearing the words "God save the Queen." The venerable tree in front of the gates was transformed into an arbour, its drooping branches being encompassed by festooned uprights with depending tracery; and close at hand was the Royal Standard floating from a flagstaff. The patience of the large assembly was at last rewarded by the appearance of the mounted police, and shortly before two o'clock ringing cheers announced that her Majesty had arrived. The Royal carriage halted at the entrance to the Park, and Miss Sims and her sister, daughters of Mr. Sims, steward to and Lord Dalmeny and Hon. Neil Primrose from Mentmore.

NOTES FROM WADDESDON.

Our Waddesdon correspondent writes:—"There were splendid archways and other decorations at the Cross Roads (entrance to the Park); standing accommodation for 1,000 persons. Great enthusiasm was manifested when the Queen appeared. A beautiful bouquet was presented to her Majesty by the Misses Violet and Blanche Sims, daughters of Mr. G. A. Sims, the highly respected steward of the Baron, attended by daughters of the tenantry. Midway in the park about 600 school children were assembled under the direction of the Rector, Rev. T. J. Williams, Rev. E. P. Baverstock, Rev. J. S. Davis, Mr. J. Holland and the teachers: Miss Osborne, Miss Ridge, Mr. Lane, and Mr. Riddle. The children, with banners and flags flying, formed a very pretty picture. As the Queen came in sight the National Anthem was sung with great spirit. As the last note died away the royal carriage drew up in the midst of the scholars, and at a signal from the Rector, Katie Hemmings and Connie Day (dressed beautifully in white), representing the children of the different schools, presented a most exquisite bouquet to her Majesty. The Queen was evidently pleased, and thanked them very graciously. The Royal carriage then proceeded on its way to the mansion amidst great cheers. The children formed in procession, marched to the Cross Roads to see the decorations, and proceeded through the village to their respective schools, where a substantial tea had been provided by the Baron. After tea hearty cheers were given for the Queen and the Baron. A procession was again formed, and proceeded to the park to witness the return of her Majesty. As the Royal Party passed, cheer upon cheer was given. The children were highly pleased with the day's enjoyment. The Church bells rang in honour of the Queen's visit, but there was not much decoration in the village, because it was known that the Queen would not pass through."

AFTERNOON IN AYLESBURY AND THE QUEEN'S RETURN.

Whilst the Queen was away at Waddesdon, the visitors and holiday-makers at Aylesbury amused themselves in various ways, many taking great pleasure in viewing the decorations. "Creature comforts" were not forgotten, and the generosity of the Rothschilds provided for a large proportion of those on duty and even on pleasure bent. At the Crown Hotel Lord Rothschild's tenants dined at his Lordship's invitation. Mr. Stratton, C.C., presided and proposed "The Queen," while Mr. Dover (Risborough) proposed the health of his Lordship. Mr. A. de Rothschild's tenants were similarly entertained at the King's Head Hotel, Mr. Swanston representing the former and Mr. P. Hart the latter. In the Corn Exchange 600 Volunteers enjoyed a capital dinner supplied by Messrs. J. C. Garner and Co. at the order of the Baron, and a vote of thanks was accorded to their host by the guests. The Hon. Walter Rothschild entertained the Yeomanry at the George Hotel. In the Butcher's Market the out-of-town school children were supplied with a substantial tea by the same well-known firm of caterers, and on the motion of Mr. Pughe, hearty thanks were accorded to the Baron. About five o'clock the people began to line the stands and the streets in expectation of her Majesty's return, but it was not till much later that the procession made its re-appearance. When the Queen did arrive she was again enthusiastically cheered. She drove slowly, but without stopping, to the Station, and the train at once left for Windsor, which was reached at a quarter to eight o'clock, the arrival being about an hour later than had been arranged.

THE ILLUMINATIONS AND FIRE-

3.14a A visit by Queen Victoria, such as that made to Waddesdon Manor in 1890 was a very rare occurrence. For the Baron it was a compliment and honour of the highest order, and for those in the locality it was the opportunity to participate in an unprecedented pageant of patriotic zeal. Most survivors of the 20th century will find the excitement and sense of occasion of that time difficult to imagine, but something of the mood can be captured in these cuttings from the extensive report published in the Bucks Herald on Saturday May 17th 1890.

3.15 The Rock Garden was one of the attractions that the Baron developed in the parkland surrounding Waddesdon Manor. In the space of only a few years the bare slopes of Lodge Hill were cleverly concealed by trees and as this photograph illustrates, the use of water and ornamental rock-work combined with horticultural artistry produced an air of peace and tranquillity to delight the most stressed of the Baron's grand visitors. The Rock Garden and much other ornamental rock-work at Waddesdon was constructed by James Pulham who had pioneered a technique for manufacturing artificial rock. Its survival in good shape in the year 2000 bears testimony to his skills.

3.16 The Stables that were built in 1884 were designed by M.Gabriel Hippolyte Destailleur. The Baron had discussed requirements with his staff and the builders to ensure all the requirements were addressed.

3.17 The construction of Waddesdon Manor had barely been completed when the working men in the village were provided with this magnificent Reading Room and Club House in 1883. A library of 200 volumes, lecture and games rooms, a coffee bar and reading room gave the members facilities which matched the best in the county. The gate-house keeper who resided on the premises, had the additional unenviable job as club steward, a task requiring the firmness of a school master and the tolerance of a saint. Jack Uff the last steward prior to the Second World War was ideal for the job, and well remembered by all past members. After the Second World War the Reading Room was used for a Boys' Club, which was intended to be self-administered. The Chairman was always the Estate Agent but Committee members were elected from the boys. The premises and the Steward were provided by the Estate. The club evolved into a Youth Club but by the mid 1970's, due to the apathy of members and parents was closed down. Mrs de Rothschild donated the library of classical works to the Waddesdon Secondary School.

3.18 In constructing and maintaining the gardens and grounds around the Manor, the Baron employed a veritable army of men and boys who established a reputation for hard work, skill and precision. The grounds were described as "a wonderland" which must have seemed even more wonderful to those who knew this Buckinghamshire hill only 15 years' before. In this photograph of 1890, we have more than 50 staff at the recently constructed Rock Garden. Most of them were destined for a future of many years of secure employment and good domestic accommodation in Waddesdon, a village now brimming with confidence and initiative.

3.19 The Gasworks Lodge at Westcott. Circa 1900. This grand looking lodge contained two dwellings, the homes of staff employed in operating the Manor Gas Works. At the centre of this photograph, with the bicycle is Mr Albert Evans the works manager.

3.20 Waddesdon Manor Gasworks. Circa 1900. Situated at Westcott near Westcott Field Farm, the works enjoyed the convenience of railway access via a spur from the Wotton Tramway. The gasworks supplied coal gas to the Manor, stables and laundry on Lodge Hill from 1883 until 1916. Mr Albert Evans was trained at a similar works, at Mr Lionel de Rothschild's house at Ascott near Wing, and recruited by the Baron to take charge here. When during the First World War, coal was in short supply, the Manor requirements for gas were met from the Waddesdon village system, and this works at Westcott was closed down. The gasometer pit remained until the 1960's, but now the land shown forms part of the outer boundary of Westcott Cricket field.

3.21 On the 17th December 1898, his 59th birthday, and after a short illness, Baron Ferdinand de Rothschild passed away at Waddesdon Manor. This photograph records the sad crowd at The Reading Room Gates as the hearse bearing the body of the Baron passes on its way to the railway station for the journey to the Jewish Cemetery at West Ham. This is the only known photograph of this occasion and unfortunately it illustrates the limitations of contemporary cameras in recording moving objects.

THE LATE
BARON F. DE ROTHSCHILD, M.P.

Our readers will have received from other sources the information of the great loss we in Waddesdon have sustained in the death of Baron Ferdinand de Rothschild, M.P. It will, therefore, only be necessary in this place to record the mournful fact that after a very brief illness he passed away on the 17th inst,, which was also his 59th birthday. We have to deplore the loss of a kind and generous neighbour and friend, a liberal employer of labour, and a courteous gentleman, whose place will not easily be filled. A memorial service was held in the Parish Church on Thursday, December 22nd, at 4 p.m, when every seat was occupied. The address at the end of the service was delivered by the Rector.

3.21a The Waddesdon Deanery Magazine for January 1899 carried this notice informing readers of the death of the Baron and subsequent memorial service in December.

Miss Alice de Rothschild

Miss Alice de Rothschild inherited Waddesdon Manor and the estate when her brother Baron Ferdinand died in 1898. She was the youngest daughter of Baron Anselm de Rothschild of the Viennese branch of the family. Her mother died while Miss Alice was very young, and at the age of 13 she made an extended visit to the Aston Clinton home of Sir Antony and Lady de Rothschild. She shared a schoolroom with her cousins and established a lifetime friendship with them, for her stay at Aston Clinton was a happy time and Miss Alice learned to know and love this country and its customs. As an adult she was known for her brilliant intellect, her firm sense of duty and strong will power. In her early years she was a skilful and intrepid horsewoman and like her brother the Baron, she was very keen on hunting, even travelling to Ireland in that pursuit. Numerous commentators of the day have stated that Miss Alice was no beauty; one quotation attributed to her possibly sums up the reason for her not marrying: "No man will wed me for my looks, and I will make certain no man will wed me for my money!"

However, when her brother Ferdinand's young wife died in 1867, it was Miss Alice at the age of 20, who in the absence of their mother provided the close family support that he needed. For the following 30 years she was the widower Baron's companion, assisting in the realisation of his plans for the Manor, and assuming the role of hostess to his many guests. As the years passed her health became a major concern and she took to avoiding the British winters by moving to her villa in Grasse, in the south of France. Amongst her distinguished guests at the villa were numerous members of Europe's royal families, including in 1891, Queen Victoria, who was also residing in Grasse that winter.

Miss Alice's period as mistress of Waddesdon Manor can be described as legendary. For the local population she was generally perceived as having an extraordinary will power and sense of purpose. She was normally serious in all respects, and her manner forbade frivolity from others. She was an expert on the protection and preservation of the very large range of fine art at the Manor, and ensured her staff were trained accordingly. Her style of dress outdoors changed little, no matter the season, a grey suit and a Panama hat. Travelling in the neighbourhood, she was often to be seen driving herself in a phaeton drawn by two ponies. She did not employ a Land Agent, but like Baron Ferdinand oversaw the management of the property through stewards and head-foremen etc. Her staff were in no doubt as to the level of service required; the best at whatever cost in time or trouble. Most days she visited the gardens, the farm or walked the grounds, and ensured she was satisfied with every detail, often carrying a "spud" to remove offending weeds which had escaped the eye of a soon to be admonished foreman. It is no wonder the workers were advised to make themselves scarce when Miss Alice approached!

Down in the village there was hardly a family whose fortunes were not positively affected by the Manor and Estate, and whose members were well aware of how desperate things had been a mere generation ago. It is therefore not surprising that the custom of the womenfolk to curtsy as Miss Alice drove past was perpetuated from Victorian times. In later years this custom was often quoted as a criticism of Miss Alice, but maybe it was just a case of times changing quicker than customs.

Traditions which villagers were pleased to see carried on from the Baron's day were the annual Schools' Treat an event eagerly anticipated by everyone, the school prizes, and the regular hosting of the Bucks County Show. Miss Alice introduced some welcome customs of her own, including an annual Sports Day with generous cash prizes, the issue of gifts each year to the old folk, an unwritten instruction that no villager wanting work at Christmas-time was to be denied, and the delivery of nourishing food to families struck by illness. In 1910 Miss Alice provided a recreation ground off Baker Street near Golden Nob allotments, complete with playing area for football and cricket and with swings, see-saw and a large swinging boat, (and also an ex-policeman as warden!). Again in 1910 by a Deed of Exchange with the Church, Miss Alice secured the old National School and surrounding land previously part of the Church Manor of the Second Portion, and provided the new National School in Baker Street. The old school buildings were given the "Rothschild Treatment" and fitted out as a club known as "The Institute" for senior Estate officials and local professional men. By this last development Miss Alice completed the "model" estate village, it now had every conceivable amenity and by all accounts was just bursting with confidence and enterprise. What misfortune could possibly spoil all this?

During the Great War of 1914 - 1918 Miss Alice could no longer visit Grasse, and her health was deteriorating. Entertaining at the Manor ceased and was not resumed after the war, however the "Waddesdon Standard" was maintained. Although Miss Alice was now an invalid she resumed her visits to Grasse, and on the 3rd of May 1922 in Paris, on her return journey to Waddesdon, she died.

The funeral took place at Willesden Jewish Cemetery. Simultaneously a service of remembrance and sincere appreciation was attended by workers, tenants, schoolchildren and parishioners in the Parish Church in Waddesdon. It was the end of an era.

3.22 Miss Alice de Rothschild, sister of Baron Ferdinand and his heir, had divided her time between Eythrope and Waddesdon since the Baron first moved to the Manor in 1880. She maintained the development of the Waddesdon Estate and it is said, raised the standard even higher, such that the "Waddesdon Standard" became a by-word for excellence in all aspects of maintenance in grand houses and their grounds.

3.23 "The Pavilion" at Eythrope circa 1900. Built for Miss Alice de Rothschild in 1883 to the design of Mr George Devey, this house of somewhat unique appearance was constructed without a resident's bedroom. Miss Alice had been advised to avoid the risk from sleeping in damp low-lying locations, so she made sure the temptation was eliminated and travelled daily to and from Waddesdon Manor, whenever she was in residence. "The Pavilion" was a totally new construction, built a short distance from the site of the old manor house, which had been demolished in 1810; this new house therefore enjoyed much the same views of the river and the park as its ancient predecessor.

3.24 The name Silk Street had been given to this road after a Silk Factory was established nearby in 1843. During Miss Alice's time it became known as "The Carriage Drive" for obvious reasons, but also some knew it as Silver Street for reasons unknown. The two main gate columns served as plinths for the matching stone dogs which gazed down Silk Street ("waiting for the Church clock to strike at midnight when according to children's legend they leapt down and raced to the Church door," nobody knows why! Now in the year 2000, they still sit there and the story is still told"). Princes Lodge, the principal subject of the photograph, is attractively recorded here, partly hidden by the ivy and creeper, which Miss Alice liked to see on Estate property. The lodge was never the gate-keeper's abode, but has usually accommodated Estate managers, who have no doubt enjoyed this "perk" of the job.

3.25 The Grand Lodge at Waddesdon Cross Roads circa 1910. An imposing entrance to the grounds with its long and gently rising driveway up to Waddesdon Manor. This entrance was conveniently placed for guests arriving from the Aylesbury direction and was used for the visit of Queen Victoria in May1890. After the construction of the Manor Station in 1897 its positioning was even more convenient as the station was only a mile away.

3.26 The Buttery and Rose Garden at the Dairy circa 1904. Once again much evidence of the ivy and foliage, which Miss Alice so admired, and the roses in full bloom. On the left is a rather leafy pergola, which after the Second World War was removed to a position near the Aviary, but now is restored to its original site near the Dairy. (2000).

3.27 A hot summers' day and nothing to disturb the silence except maybe the distant ring of a blacksmith's hammer somewhere unseen. Queen Street and Home Farm in 1905. Taken from the Church Tower, this scene somehow captures the atmosphere that prevailed in a well-ordered Edwardian estate. The enclosed yard with its central dovecote was surrounded by workshops, stables, a smithy, cart sheds and all the premises necessary for farming operations at that time.

3.28 The decade following Baron Ferdinand's death witnessed a steady continuation of the Rothschild development in and around Waddesdon. This view from the Church tower records a newly completed "Cedars" standing on land formerly containing the pigstys, chicken coops and outdoor lavatories of cottages, and including The Ship Inn. (See photograph 3.27). The Cedars was built circa 1905 and was intended to become a maternity nursing home to be run by two friends of Miss Alice, the Misses Chinnery and Gilling-Lax. Garden staff and servants were seconded from the Manor.

3.29 Mr George Frederick Johnson, Miss Alice's Head Gardener, was appointed at the age of 26 after working at the Rothschild gardens in Vienna, and at Miss Alice's villa at Grasse. An exceptionally talented horticulturist who had learned both German and French in his travels, he set and maintained standards to reflect the exacting requirements of the Lady of the Manor. Mr Johnson is shown here in the straw boater surrounded by some of the 50 or so staff employed at the gardens in 1910, including Mr Wicks seated on the right, standing next in the jacket is Mr Alfie Saunders, and the boy on the far right is Ernie Dormer. The gardens were required to provide a continuous supply of flowers, fruit and vegetables for the house, and much ingenuity was employed in stretching the seasons to the utmost with a range of early to late varieties. To help achieve this, the vegetable seed list included 15 varieties of peas, 10 of beans, 8 of cabbage and 11 of broccoli. Mr Johnson, who never allowed the garden staff to whistle or be caught with hands in their pockets, remained Head Gardener at Waddesdon until his death in 1954, having served the Rothschild family for 62 years.

3.30 Something of the orderliness and symmetry of the gardens can be seen in this photograph of the rose beds viewed from the Dutch Gardens looking towards Top Glass circa 1905. Notwithstanding the importance of fruit and vegetables, flowers and their display consumed more time and energy, and established a proud reputation for Waddesdon and the gardeners. The raising of plants for the parterre at the Manor at this time was an enormous undertaking, when up to 50,000 were planted out each spring.

3.31 An unusual view of the Manor circa 1895. Taken from the field that now contains the cricket, tennis and bowls club, the relative immaturity of the trees on Lodge Hill is accentuated by the towering elms on the right of this photograph.

3.32 Weir Lodge at Eythrope in wintertime circa 1960. As with most country estates, distinctive lodges were built at practical locations to enable the maintenance of operations. This attractive house on the northern bank of the River Thame at Eythrope, usually housed senior Estate managers. In addition to their official duties they would ensure the weir gates were adjusted appropriately to maintain the required water level in the artificial arm of the river.

3.33 North Lodge c 1895. Situated at the end of Cat Lane, this lodge marked the junction of the driveway from Eythrope and the road leading to Sheepcot Hill Farm. Before the construction of the private estate road connecting Waddesdon Manor with Eythrope, the driveway shown at right foreground in this photograph, was the carriageway used by Miss Alice on her frequent excursions to The Pavilion. Subsequent to the building of the new drive, this ancient bridle road from Eythrope to North Lodge fell into disrepair. It was, and remains a public bridle road: for many years burial parties travelling from Eythrope to Upper Winchendon or Waddesdon, had to use this route to avoid the drive becoming a public right of way. Note: Cat Lane was so called because of The Cat public house that stood on the south side of the lane, and approximately 100 metres from the main road. Waddesdon, The Rothschild Collection (The National Trust) Sam Payne.

In Memoriam.

ALICE DE ROTHSCHILD, 1847-1922.

(BY A FRIEND AND RELATIVE.)

The name of Alice de Rothschild may not suggest any definite portrait to those who were not personally acquainted with its bearer, for, alas! she had been suffering from constant ill-health for many of the last years of her life, and had therefore partly if not entirely withdrawn from all social duties and pleasures. But in Buckinghamshire where, like so many members of her family she owned extensive property, her name was well known and justly respected; indeed, her generosity was as widely recognised as were her wisdom and strength of character. Her death will be deeply and sincerely regretted by many, but especially by the inhabitants of Waddesdon; by the many there whom she assisted in trouble and difficulties; by the young, in whose school life and recreative hours she gave proofs of practical interest; by the working men, for whose benefit she provided a comfortable club-room and a useful library; and last, but not least, by the many families for whom she built sanitary and attractive cottages.

Alice de Rothschild was the youngest daughter of Baron Anselm de Rothschild, head of the Vienna Banking House. She lost her mother whilst of tender age, and spent rather a lonely childhood, owing to the fact of her being the junior member of her family. Following a suggestion of her English cousins, during a visit of their's to Frankfort, she came to England in the late summer of 1860, with her French Governess, Mademoiselle Hofer, who became her lifelong friend, and proceeded on a visit to her aunt, Lady de Rothschild, at Aston Clinton. There, under the auspices of that beloved aunt, the mention of whose name would bring tears to her eyes, she first learnt what country life and its duties implied. It was a happy time for the young motherless girl, who shared a schoolroom existence with her cousins, soon to become her devoted friends. At that early age she already gave proof of very remarkable gifts, both mental and physical; indeed, her power of grasping the threads of an argument and of logical reasoning were unusual enough in one of her years to have aroused the admiration and astonishment of no less a personage than Matthew Arnold, who met her when staying at Aston Clinton as a guest of Lady de Rothschild.

3.34 The Bucks Herald recorded this obituary of Miss Alice de Rothschild in the issue of May 13th 1922.

James A de Rothschild

James A de Rothschild inherited the Waddesdon Estate and Manor from his cousin, Miss Alice de Rothschild. He was a member of the French branch of the family, but had completed his formal education at Cambridge and spent much of his early adult life in Britain and the Empire.

In 1913 James de Rothschild married Miss Dorothy Pinto, and at the outbreak of war in 1914 he enlisted in the ranks of the French army. He was seconded to the British army as an interpreter on the Western Front where he was seriously wounded. After recovering from his injuries he served under Field Marshall Allenby in Palestine, locally raising a battalion from the Jewish settlements.

As a young man Mr de Rothschild had for many years worn a monocle and was instantly recognised by this; however in 1919 he suffered the loss of his left eye in a golfing accident, and for that reason thereafter, was usually to be seen wearing a frosted monocle. It is perhaps not surprising that the visual image generally retained in the locality, is of a tall monocled gentleman who was seen briefly at village functions, usually as President of the organising body.

In 1919 he became a naturalised British subject, as had his uncle Baron Ferdinand more than fifty years earlier, and in 1922 James de Rothschild came to Waddesdon as the new owner.

Within a few years of his inheritance, James de Rothschild had introduced a more commercial approach to the workings of the Estate and Gardens. Whilst the Waddesdon Standard was proudly maintained in and around the Manor, elsewhere the same ethics were diverted to the cultivation of quality produce for the market-place.

Mr and Mrs de Rothschild were active in public life and often entertained at Waddesdon Manor. In 1926 King George V and Queen Mary made a private visit and the traditional ceremony of marking the occasion by planting a tree, is very much in evidence today in the form of a full-grown cedar. Their guests included many notable politicians of the day, among them Herbert Asquith and David Lloyd George both former Prime Ministers, and Winston Churchill a future Prime Minister.

Mr and Mrs de Rothschild supported the Liberal Party and sponsored large fetes on Spring Hill, throwing open the Manor Grounds in a similar fashion as the Baron a few decades earlier. The highlights of these events in pre-radio days were the addresses given by political personalities, including on a memorable occasion, Lloyd George himself. In 1929 James de Rothschild was elected Member of Parliament for the Isle of Ely and went on to represent that constituency until 1945.

The final expansion of the Estate had been completed during the early years of the century, and by 1922 it was an established entity. There were however always possibilities for development within the Estate boundaries. For example by 1930 James de Rothschild had indulged himself in two items, a three hole extension to the original nine hole golf course around Windmill Hill Plantation, and near the top of Waddesdon Hill an extensive stud farm to accommodate his string of brood mares.

As the 1930's wore on and the likelihood of war increased, it is not surprising that Mr de Rothschild, himself Jewish, became aware of the persecution of Jewish citizens in Germany. As a result early in 1939, he arranged safe passage for a group of pupils and staff from a school in Frankfurt-am-Main and housed them at "The Cedars" in Waddesdon. (See Section 6).

James de Rothschild spent the 1939-1945 war years as a Member of Parliament, ending up as Under Secretary to the Ministry of Supply in the Coalition Government of Winston Churchill. Back at Waddesdon he made anything and everything available to the "War Effort". The Manor was used throughout to accommodate 100 children with their nursery staff, the Estate parkland contained a massive petrol storage dump and associated army camp, "The Institute" was used as a Red Cross Sick Bay, the Village Hall was an Evacuation Reception Centre, and when necessary any building available was pressed into temporary use for evacuees, use by the Home Guard or any other organisation, whilst the Gardens and the Estate were devoted to food production.

In the General Election of 1945, Mr de Rothschild lost his parliamentary seat. His health was not good, his eyesight was failing and although he maintained his close support for the Liberal Party, his days as an active politician were over. For the remainder of his life his abiding interests were horse racing, and continuing his lifetime support for the emerging nation of Israel.

After the Second World War the Manor and Estate were both in need of repair and renovation, and several years were to pass before things could be deemed acceptable. This was the period when austerity was the watchword; every commodity was scarce and probably rationed in one way of another. By the mid-1950's work was under way to upgrade The Pavilion at Eythrope in preparation for Mr and Mrs de Rothschild to move there from the Manor. The reason for the proposed move was not common knowledge in the locality, and the work at Eythrope was still in progress at the time of Mr de Rothschild's death.

On 7th May 1957 James de Rothschild died. The villagers mourned the loss of a benevolent but distant Lord of the Manor, who had maintained the valued traditions established by his predecessors during a period of tremendous change.

In his will, Mr de Rothschild bequeathed to the National Trust the Manor with most of the art treasures contained within, and 165 acres of gardens and grounds surrounding the Manor. In addition a Trust Fund of £750,000 was endowed to finance maintenance for the future.

3.35 Probably the most enjoyable aspects of James de Rothschild's social life were derived from the ownership of racehorses and all that went with it. Long before he inherited Waddesdon Manor he had known considerable success through his racehorses. Here we show him at the age of 31 leading in "Bomba" the winner of the Ascot Gold Cup in 1909. His "Brigand" won the Cambridgshire in 1919, and in 1921 he triumphed again with "Milenko".

3.36 James and Mrs de Rothschild with members of the Isle of Ely Constituency Liberal Party 1929. Mr Rothschild represented this constituency from 1929 until 1945.

3.37 Before the First World War a nine-hole golf course had been laid out around Windmill Hill Plantation on the instructions of Miss Alice de Rothschild. The course was extended for James de Rothschild by the addition of three holes on the Westcott side of the wood. This photograph shows a group of golfers including Mr de Rothschild in the Rolls Royce and Mrs de Rothschild at left of picture having almost completed the course. The golfers were a welcome source of income to the young men of the village at weekends when they would wait at The Five Arrows Hotel in the hope of a caddying job at two shillings or Half a Crown (two shillings and six pence) if the player had a pleasing round. In the years just before the Second World War, Mr de Rothschild had to be hauled in an invalid chair between holes, with a car on hand where-ever possible. The golf course did not survive the war but the bunkers were discernible until the 1970's.

3.38 Around 1924 the Stud Farm was constructed on Waddesdon Hill, and yet another field of expertise was introduced to the local workers. This photograph by Ivor Gurney was taken on 17th November 1999 and has the Stud Groom, Malcolm Smith at the centre of the picture.

3.39 Mr P. Sidney Woolf was Mr James de Rothschild's land agent for over 25 years, from the early 1920's. Like his predecessor he lived at the Wilderness, and for many years travelled around the estate on horseback. He was a strict but fair manager; however all the employees knew he liked to see them busy, and those working in the Home Farm vicinity were always warned of his approach by a particular hammer rhythm devised by the blacksmith, Harry Gilson.

3.40 Chauffeur, George Fowler with Mr de Rothschild's Rolls Royce Phantom III in 1937. A Waddesdon man, George had graduated to chauffeur via a short spell at Cubitts Car Company, the Wilderness gardens, a learning period with Mr Jack Cox, Head Chauffeur and driving tuition at the Rolls Royce school at Cricklewood. The coachwork for this car was by Park Ward of London, and in the construction programme, allowances were incorporated to match George's height etc. In those pre-war days it was not unusual for Mr de Rothschild to fly to Paris for dinner and then return the same night whilst George waited at Croydon Airport, and sometimes to rush down to Newmarket for a particular race, then back to The Commons to vote. With a 7.34 litre V12 engine this car was capable of what was asked of it! George continued in this job, despite having to combine forestry and Covent Garden delivery work, for more than 50 years, finally leaving the service of Mrs de Rothschild around 1982.
Note: Most of the chrome on JdeR cars were painted black as the famous RR radiator grille shows in photo.

3.41 Sitting on the steps at the front of the Pavilion at Eythrope are Cyril Gurney, Sid Feasey, the head gardener and Mr Clark, Mrs Somerset Maugham's butler, in the summer of 1935. The rather functional wing at the centre of this photograph, was added in the 1920's to provide bedrooms and bathrooms. (See 3.23). In the programme of works carried out in the late 1950's this functional wing was rebuilt to more closely match the style of the original. Mrs Somerset Maugham lived at the Pavilion until 1939, and during the Second World War Vic Oliver the famous variety artiste resided at The Homestead at Eythrope.

3.42 In one of the glasshouses at Eythrope in the 1940's, where the emphasis was on production of high quality flowers for Waddesdon Manor and market, via Covent Garden. "Mossy" Dormer with son Bill.

3.43 The Bothy at Waddesdon Gardens here viewed from the south in the 1940's, comprised an old 19th century original and a "new" 20th century extension. Situated at the very end of Queen Street, opposite the Head Gardener's house, the Bothy first accommodated young men who had been recruited and trained to work in the gardens and grounds of the Manor. By the late 1940's, perhaps as a result of wartime employment of Land Army girls, the Bothy accommodated about 4 or 5 young men in the "New Bothy", and the same number of girls in the "Old Bothy". All were employed in "Top Glass", the Kitchen Gardens or in "Paradise" (the greenhouses nearer the office and yard). At this time Mr and Mrs Sartain also lived in the old Bothy, Mrs Sartain cooked the food and the cost was equally shared. Of course there were always plenty of vegetables from the gardens and milk from the Dairy. Mr Sartain worked with the yearling racehorses at the stables, which were also at "Paradise". There was no central heating so the rooms were cold in winter, but a duty gardener stoked the boiler to supply hot water for bathrooms and kitchen. The working day commenced at 7am, breakfast at 8am, lunch at 12, tea at 5pm, sometimes overtime followed. Everyone was expected to be in by 11pm, usually! The Bothy was demolished circa 1972.

3.44 This 19th century view of the magnificent array of greenhouses forming the core of Waddesdon Gardens is included at this point to provide an overall perspective for the photographs that follow. That part of the complex nearest the camera was known as "Top Glass", whilst to the rear were the greenhouses known as "Paradise". To the right of near centre the Vestibule can be discerned, and the tall domed house at left of centre contained the boiler and hot water tank for the convecting central heating system. Stretching from left to right at the back is the extensive fruit range. The glasshouses at Sandringham house were modelled on the Waddesdon pattern.

The Gardens

In the photographs which follow 3.44a we provide the reader with aspects of Waddesdon Gardens in winter and summer circa 1938. These photographs stand as an historical record and remind us of the many years of gardening excellence at Waddesdon.

Soon after his inheritance of Waddesdon Manor, Mr James de Rothschild began a process to commercialise the Gardens under the management of Mr Johnson. The emphasis was upon quality, and London hotels, restaurants and society homes provided the custom. Exotic fruit and flowers, surplus to the Manor's requirements were transported to Covent Garden market on a regular basis.

At the outbreak of the Second World War, Mr de Rothschild ordered the emphasis to be placed upon food production. Except for a sample stock retention, the large area under glass and in the beds was turned over to the growing of vegetables, and enormous quantities of tomatoes.

After the war years and during the austerity of the late 40's the Gardens gradually returned to their pre-war status, and once more became an attraction for visitors and guests at the Manor.

When Mr James de Rothschild passed away in 1957 work was already well advanced to make the Pavilion at Eythrope suitable as the family residence; subsequently Mrs de Rothschild lived there for more than 30 years. The smaller gardens and greenhouses at Eythrope were seen to be adequate for the needs of the house, and the greenhouses at Waddesdon Gardens were demolished over the next few years. There was much work of a melancholy nature for the surviving gardeners; cutting down and uprooting mature peach, nectarine, and fig trees, grape vines and many others.

Soon a large part of the area had reverted to a view not so different to that of more than 100 years previously, and large plastic clad, "Nissen Hut" shaped, greenhouses had been erected on the old kitchen gardens.

3.44a The vacant site of the "Top Glass" at Waddesdon Gardens in 1999. The wall at the edge of the woods on Lodge Hill is all that remains of the magnificent scene that met the eye in the vicinity of "Top Glass". This photograph was taken from a position where the man is standing at the main entrance in photograph 3.44, and looking towards the young trees on the bank at far left of "Top Glass".

3.45 The official main entrance to the greenhouse complex, known as the Vestibule. Over the years this was the access point for the many grand guests who would visit the gardens as a little gentle exercise perhaps, before lunch.

3.46 It is assumed this photograph was taken from the steps on the path leading to the Tulip Patch. It shows the Vestibule on the right, whilst on the left is the Dome. Most of the long houses stretching towards the camera would be filled with cyclamen and primula pot plants as Christmas-time approached.

3.47 The Dome photographed from the side of the Malmaison Carnation house (on right). Mrs de Rothschild particularly liked the sweetly scented pink malmaison carnations for table decorations, and they were cultivated as a speciality at Waddesdon. The door in view led into the Palm House which must have been more than 20 feet tall at the apex, whilst the top of the dome may have been double that.

3.48 On the left the Fruit Range taken from the Bothy end, and on the right the Fruit Border which ran the whole length of Paradise. Cliff Dan at the centre of the photograph worked at the gardens until the outbreak of war, when he returned to his native Norfolk.

3.49 Cliff Dan in the Peach House in the Fruit Range, having completed "tying in" the peach tree. As can be seen the Fruit Range comprised a south facing wall and a glass lean-to, perfect for its purpose.

3.50 Eric King, Jim Wicks and Harry Carter at the top of Paradise Frame Yard. At the rear on the left is the long Peach Case.

3.51 The Top Potting Shed and Reserve Garden with cherry trees "tied in " on the wall.

3.52 Potted and staked chrysanthemums on the ash patch, arum lilies resting in the foreground. The taller glasshouse at the rear was a show house, always full of carnations.

3.53 Eric King and Wally Stone at the rear of the Rock Garden.

3.54 The Manor Estate Fire Brigade circa 1935. The well-trained and skilful team was a credit to the Estate, here photographed in the Yard at the Home Farm. Rear L-R; Harry Atkins, Fred Whitlock, Arthur Hedges, L-R; ----, Bill Hedges, Willy Wheeler, Bert Jones, ----, John May, Mr Adcock, Harry Gilson, Dick Allen. All employees on the Estate.

WADDESDON'S CLAIMS

"Model of an Up-to-date Village"

OPENING OF A NEW PLAYING FIELD

Saturday was an important day in the history of Waddesdon. In the words of Mr. H. Rose, it became "the model of an up-to-date village." The great step which was taken on Saturday was the opening of a new playing field and recreation ground, which, with the pavilion that it contains, was given to the village by Mr. and Mrs. James de Rothschild.

Mr. James de Rothschild himself came along to perform the opening ceremony on Saturday, and was accorded a hearty welcome by the large crowd of villagers who had assembled. He was introduced by Mr. W. J. Hook, as Chairman of the Sub-Committee of the Parish Council which had considered the project.

Mr. James de Rothschild said it gave him very great pleasure to be there to perform the opening of the ground. Its history had originated in the many happy years which his wife and he had spent together. After being married for 25 years they had decided that they must do something to commemorate a happy and blessed time, and also they wanted to associate with their happiness the people of Waddesdon, among whom they had been living in friendship, affection and confidence for the last 17 years. (Applause).

"We thought," he continued, "that a good way of doing this would be to establish this ground where young people representing the Council School and the other the Church of England School.

A vote of thanks to the opener was then proposed by Mr. H. Rose, on behalf of the Parish Council, of which Mr. Rose stated he had been a member for about forty years. He expressed the thanks of the village to Mr. and Mrs. James de Rothschild for the great gift that they had bestowed. They could now call Waddesdon a model of an up-to-date village, for not only had they the cricket ground, bowling green and tennis courts, but on this new ground they had the football pitch, netball pitch, the equipment for children's games, and the pavilion with its dressing rooms and the necessary appliances. He was certain it must be the most up-to-date village in the county.

They had the project in mind for some time, but found that it would be a very costly affair, and then Mr. James de Rothschild came to their help, and offered them that field. So the Parish Council appointed a small sub-committee, and he thanked Mr. Hook, the Chairman, and Mr. Woolf for the work they had put in. They had also had help from the National Fitness Council and the Playing Fields' Association; and then Mr. Langley-Taylor came along, and the speaker did not know how they would have managed without him, for he had given them a great deal of helpful advice about the laying-out of the field. He had said it would prove a very suitable field, and he was right, though some of them had been rather doubtful; and he had also said it would cost very little to lay out, and again he had been right.

3.55 In 1938 Mr and Mrs James de Rothschild celebrated their Silver Wedding anniversary and in 1939 to mark the occasion presented the Playing Field, Recreation Area and Pavilion off Baker Street to the Village. Here we reproduce part of the Bucks Herald article that records the opening ceremony.

MRS DOROTHY DE ROTHSCHILD

On the death of James de Rothschild in 1957, the role of Lord of the Manor was passed to his widow Mrs Dorothy de Rothschild, a lady already well known and respected in the locality. She was a County Councillor and Justice of the Peace, Women's Voluntary Service Organiser, on the Management Board of the Royal Bucks Hospital and governor of Aylesbury College to list just a few of the public offices she held. Although by political persuasion a lifelong Liberal, Mrs de Rothschild always stood as an Independent in local government elections, and in the same way as her late husband, was committed to supporting the young state of Israel.

Waddesdon Manor, its contents and the surrounding parkland had been bequeathed by James de Rothschild to the National Trust, but meanwhile work was well advanced to make The Pavilion at Eythrope the country residence for Mrs de Rothschild, and it was here she made her home.

As chairman of the Management Committee for Waddesdon Manor, Mrs de Rothschild was always anxious to maintain its standing among the leading National Trust attractions. From the outset this required not only a focus upon presentation, but also a recognition of maintenance requirements and latterly as it became necessary, the restoration of the Manor. In her book "The Rothschilds at Waddesdon Manor", Mrs de Rothschild pays tribute to the team that assisted her through this period.

In the years following 1957 Mrs de Rothschild strengthened her bond with the local community. She maintained the Rothschild tradition in Waddesdon of unfussy support and interest in all that was good in village life, yet never-the-less encouraged a steady progress towards a higher level of independence. For example the announcement in 1968, to hand over the village hall with a £10,000 endowment in trust, was received with mixed feelings by many. In fact not surprisingly, more than a few would have preferred to leave things as they were! Subsequently, under the guiding hands of successive Estate Land Agent Chairmen, the Management Committee has fulfilled its purpose, and Waddesdon Village Hall remains an object of envy for most other villages.

From her earliest days at Waddesdon Mrs de Rothschild had enjoyed driving motorcars, and she was invariably at the wheel when travelling on the estate and in the locality. She became a familiar figure to everyone during those years when village fetes and events such as the annual horticultural show were still enormously popular. She would open fetes and present the prizes, and no one would have dreamt of, nor wanted anyone else. This was the public view. However there were many organisations in the village and around, which greatly benefited from the interest Mrs de Rothschild had in their welfare. Sometimes, as in the case of renovations to the Alms Houses, a degree of publicity was unavoidable, but publicity was never courted.

In December 1988 at the age of 93, Mrs de Rothschild died. The following comment is extracted from the January 1989 Waddesdon Newsletter. "The National newspapers carried extensive accounts of her importance as a member of the world-wide Rothschild family, and particularly of her dedication and benevolence to the State of Israel. For most of us these accounts were themselves revelations. The lady this community has known for more than sixty years, had simply and quietly endeared herself to us as a real friend."

3.56 We reproduce the photograph used in Mrs de Rothschild's 1955 election literature. She was re-elected as an independent member on the County Council.

3.57 In 1972 the Arthur Goodwin Alms Houses were extensively modified " with the help of Mrs de Rothschild". (See Photograph 4.16). This photograph, taken at the gate to the Alms Houses shows Mrs de Rothschild having just unveiled the plaque commemorating the history of the houses, together with the following notables: L to R; Mrs D. Campbell, Mr Boughton (Chairman Aylesbury District Council), Dr C.Campbell, Mr G.Baron, (Chairman Waddesdon Parish Council), Mr Creed (Builder), Mr Alec Harding (Parish Council), Rev H. Parker, Brigadier S.Cowan, (Estate Land Agent).

3.58 Mrs de Rothschild always showed a keen interest in village activities and gave support wherever it was needed. Here we see her bowling the first wood on the newly enlarged green at the Bowls Club, thus marking the opening of the extended facilities in 1965.

CENTENARY OF
THE WADDESDON
ESTATE

1874–1974

THE PAVILION
EYTHROPE

12 September 1974

3.59 Almost exactly one hundred years after Baron Ferdinand's purchase of the Manorial Estate, Mrs de Rothschild hosted a Centenary Dinner at Eythrope. The diners were entertained by the Orchestra of the Royal Artillery Mounted Band and later a spectacular firework display. Around 400 guests, including several members of the Rothschild family and numerous friends of Mrs de Rothschild dined with tenants, farmers, estate staff and village representatives and their partners. The guests were all listed alphabetically ("Lords alongside gardeners"), in the programme which contained photographs of the Baron, Miss Alice, Mr and Mrs James de Rothschild, and a short history of the Estate's past 100 years. We reproduce here the front cover of the programme.

Jacob Lord Rothschild

Nathanial Charles Jacob Rothschild was born at Cambridge in 1936. He was educated at Eton and then Christ Church College, Oxford, where he gained a 1st Class Honours degree in History. In 1961 he married Serena, daughter of Sir Phillip Dunn. He became head of the English branch of the Rothschild family, fourth Baron Rothschild, when he succeeded his father in 1990. Lord and Lady Rothschild have three daughters and one son, Nathanial.

On leaving University following National Service with the Lifeguards, he commenced his career at the family bank N.M Rothschild & Sons, and subsequently has been prominently involved with the world of finance. In the established tradition of the Rothschild family Lord Rothschild has an abiding and active interest in the Arts, and his work in the restoration of historic buildings and in the heritage conservation field is internationally acknowledged. In recognition of this work he became the first member in the history of his family to have been awarded the Order of Merit. He has been actively involved in numerous Arts organisations, serving as Chairman of the Trustees of the National Gallery, and Chairman of the National Heritage Memorial Fund. This latter office was an appointment by the Prime Minister, and included responsibility for distribution of National Lottery proceeds to the heritage sector. Lord Rothschild has continued the family support for the State of Israel and has undertaken important roles to further its interests.

In 1986 he undertook the duty of family member responsible for Waddesdon Manor, and upon the death of Mrs Dorothy de Rothschild in 1988, inherited the Manorial Estates at Waddesdon, Upper Winchendon, and Eythrope.

The years following have been eventful, both for the Manor and the Estate. Lord Rothschild has instigated and overseen a dramatic programme of restoration work for the National Trust at the Manor. The presentation and standard engendered has achieved national awards on a regular basis. Throughout the Estate there has been a continuous investment in improvements and renewal, and likewise in the village. High profile examples of the invigorating changes taking place are the restoration of the Dairy and adjacent Water Gardens, which has been transformed into an exquisite conference centre. The Five Arrows Hotel has also been extensively renovated and rejuvenated, to regain once again its prominent place amongst local hostelries.

In the year 2000 the Waddesdon Estate and the Manor are still the largest employers in the village, and the Lord of the Manor (a title never used in this day and age!), retains a benevolent interest in village welfare. The village continues to enjoy many of the benefits of a big house nearby, its grounds and the reflected fame, which places Waddesdon, very firmly "on the map".

3.60 To mark the completion of the first phase of the comprehensive repair programme to the fabric of the Manor, and the opening of the new gallery for the Sevres porcelain display, Her Majesty Queen Elizabeth and His Royal Highness Prince Phillip made a private visit to the Manor, as guests of Lord and Lady Rothschild. Local villagers were invited to greet the Royal party at the North Front at 11.00am on Friday 31st March 1995. Here we see Her Majesty receiving posies from a welcoming trio of small children. Meanwhile Prince Phillip beckons other children with posies from the crowd gathered nearby. (Photograph © Bucks Herald.)

3.61 The Pavilion at Eythrope 1995. The home of Lord and Lady Rothschild, this splendid house sits beside a substantial artificial lake fed by the fledgling River Thame which rises only a few miles away. Although the original was built in 1883, the house illustrated here in 1995 has been much enlarged, and bears little resemblance to the former bedroomless pavilion.

3.62 Waddesdon Manor circa 1990. This photograph records the external evidence of the first phase of the restoration of the Manor that commenced in 1990. The huge scaffolding tower and cover on the right protected the interior whilst the renovations were carried out. All aspects of the fabric and operational functions within the building were included in the restoration programme, from the roof to the curtains, from the plumbing to the fire and security installations. The stone and slate quarries in Wales and Bath which supplied the original materials were re-opened and ornate metalwork was commissioned from Italian foundries to ensure the replacements matched the surviving originals. The renovation programme has continued until the final phase is currently under way in the year 2000. The left-hand side of the Manor is under a similar scaffolding tower and the parking of cars on the pristine approach drive is now only permitted for special events. A tasteful but inadequate car park has been fashioned on the north-west shoulder of the hill and overflow parking is mustered on the access driveway to the Manor.

3.63 This photograph records the private visit of Queen Elizabeth the Queen Mother to Waddesdon Manor on 20th June 1994. She is shown here with Lord Rothschild, meeting some of the local school children that had been invited to welcome her on the driveway at the North Front. During her short stay, the Queen Mother helped to perpetuate the tradition for Royal visits to the Manor by planting a tree in the grounds.

3.64 Standing on the South Front of the Manor we have the Gardening staff employed there in August 2000. Standing L-R; Michael Walker, (Head Gardener), Paul Farnell, Tony Cooper, Ian Bolton, Richard Ernst, Peter Saunders, Frank Parge, Andrew Batten, Peter Thorp, David Hutchens. Front Row; Carolyn White, Radka Vaculova, Bronwen Thomas, Giulia Bohrer, Rachel Edwards.

3.66 The staff employed at Waddesdon Gardens and Garden Centre August 2000. Standing at the entrance in the wall where the former Fruit Range had been. L-R; Robin Mowatt, Derek Gardener, Mary Gardener, Karen Ayris, Jean O'Brian, Chris Tarbox, Deborah Mackay, Len Bellis (Head Gardener), Gary Marsh, Bill Fowler. Bill Fowler has worked at Waddesdon Gardens since the early 1950's.

SECTION FOUR

STREET MEMORIES

Within this section we have gathered some extremely interesting views which are historically unique; we believe they will prove pleasantly nostalgic for many readers, and remind us all of Waddesdon's recent past. Inevitably the older pictures are often considered the best, for not only were the photographers professionals, but the novelty of their art allowed them seriously to record everyday scenes which are now ignored. We no longer have a village photographer such as Albert Cherry, who produced so many excellent studies around 1900; regrettably, this section is therefore deficient of such photographs of the more recent developments on the streets of our village. However, aerial photographs included at 4.17, 4.18, 4.32 and 4.41, can be compared with the frontispiece on page 2, to see how and where Waddesdon village has expanded during the twentieth century. The main housing developments have been: Sherriff Cottages 1930's, Grove Way 1930's-1940's, Anstey Close 1950's, Goss Avenue and Sharps Close 1950's-1960's, Chestnut Close 1960's, Warmstone Close 1980's, Little Britain 1980's, and of course the Schools' complex which has continued since the 1960's. Meanwhile the population has grown from 1,610 in 1891, to 1,864 in 1991.

4.1 Church Row and the parish church circa 1900. At the far end of the row, nearest to the church is The Ship Inn, a popular and ancient public house, and venue each year for the annual Feast Day celebrations. Amongst other entertainment's, a prize was awarded to the man "pulling" the ugliest face through a horses collar. It was said that one man won this competition for many years without even trying! All the buildings on the left of this picture were demolished around 1908 and all that remains in 2000 is the rather stunted Horse Chestnut tree shown outside The Ship. On the right is The Bell Inn.

4.2 Occupying the land formerly containing The Ship Inn, Church Row and two houses at the top of Bicester Hill, The Cedars was built by Miss Alice de Rothschild to accommodate two friends, the Misses Gilling-Lax and Chinnery. It was rumoured that they were to operate a nursing home there, but in fact lived a kind of Grace and Favour existence with daily support provided by the Manor and Gardens. Several of the families from the cottages were re-housed in the aptly named New Street off Quainton Road. circa 1906.

4.3 Bicester Hill, the High Street looking towards Westcott. Circa 1925. On the left the ornamental gables of the Home Farm buildings and on the near right "The Homestead" so named since its procurement by Miss Alice de Rothschild around 1905 when all the property on this strip of land was added to the Estate. (See 9.6).

4.4 The Bell Inn circa 1935. A very popular roadside inn, The Bell attracted passing trade as well as loyal regulars from the village. The lawns and tea gardens allowed families to call there after a warm weekend walk, perhaps across the fields to Westcott. The larger thatched roof on the right was destroyed by fire in the 1950's, leaving only the smaller portion visible at the left of the building.

4.5 Circa 1888. At the centre of this picture is the new Reading Room provided by Baron Ferdinand de Rothschild for the use of the working men of the village (see 3.17). The building with the bell cupola was The National School and to the left we can see Mr Phillip Dodwell's shop. Beyond the Reading Room a cottage and a shop can be seen, the shop was the "Co-operative Store", better known as Moscrops (the name of the proprietor). Both Moscrops and Dodwells were general stores and bakeries, whilst in addition Dodwells was the village Post Office and Telegraph Office.
Note the sculpted dog on the gate pillar at the Manor entrance gateway.

4.6 Circa 1933. A similar viewpoint to 4.5 but a very different view. The shops and cottage had gone before 1900 and the school was converted to The Institute in 1910 (a club for local businessmen and Estate officials, provided by Miss Alice de Rothschild). The glass spherical light fittings on the gate pillars had replaced the sculpted dogs about 40 years earlier. A rare detail to be noted from a pre-Second World War photograph is the privet hedges in need of a trim. Had the Waddesdon Standard started to slip?

4.7 The Square circa 1910, captured on a summers day, a picture of near perfection, spoiled perhaps by the straggly poplar tree near the centre of the photograph. One is reminded of the maintenance effort demanded by the legendary "Waddesdon Standard" in the faint outline of the painters' trestles at the gates near Princes Lodge far away down Silk Street. The house at the centre of picture was until 1906 the residence of Dr Morrison who then moved across The Square to the Roses, a grander house provided by Miss Alice de Rothschild.

4.8 A similar view to 4.7 but around 22 years on. Sadly The War Memorial is now added to the scene. The poplar tree has gone but the ancient elms at the edge of "The Green" down the High Street were to stand for another 35 years.

4.9 The Five Arrows Hotel was built in 1887 on the site of the old coaching inn, "The Marlborough Arms," which itself had latterly been renamed "The Five Arrows Inn". (See 1.15). Designed by Bierton architects W. Taylor and Son, in the "Old English Domestic" style, it had a concert and audit room, a dinning room to seat one hundred persons, ten bedrooms, several bathrooms, and two smoking balconies. The stables and yard buildings were in the same style; the whole being contained in newly planted and spacious grounds. This photograph shows the completed hotel, clubroom and roadside garden, with its piper fountain and immature topiary. Ladies take tea on the near smokers' balcony, while the young chestnut trees at the rear, and the grass alongside the dusty unmetalled road, reveal the novelty of this scene.
Waddesdon, The Rothschild Collection (The National Trust). Sam Payne

4.10 "The Roses" circa 1910. A terrace of small cottages was demolished to make way for this grand house built by Miss Alice de Rothschild to accommodate the village doctor and his successors. Built in 1904, The Roses served its purpose until the early 1990's when the new Surgery opened in Goss Avenue. It is now rented out by the Estate.

4.11 These two houses in Bradfords Alley, adjacent to The Square, were built for the Estate by John Thomson and Son around 1882. They incorporate some of the internal structure of cottages previously on the site. This photograph was taken circa 1910, and illustrates the established air of the property and surrounding woods.

4.12 The High Street circa 1900. A busy scene on a summers day. Between the newly completed Village Hall and the Five Arrows Hotel is the old Police Station. The ivy -clad cottage next to the White Lion Hotel was the home of Kitty Allen who sold homemade sweets and rock.

4.13 Waddesdon Village Hall in 1996. The scaffolding was installed to enable redecorating and maintenance work on the weather vane in time for the centenary. In this day and age weathercocks are rarely used nor noticed, and it may be of interest to point out two other features, the chimney and the window in the roof which exist purely for aesthetic reasons, added it is said, when the baron was dissatisfied with the part-finished structure. To celebrate the centenary of the hall in 1997, drama students of Waddesdon Church of England Secondary School provided entertainment, including a re-enactment of Baron de Rothschild's address at the original opening ceremony, to an audience which included Lord and Lady Rothschild.

4.14 A reverse view to 4.12 circa 1973. On the left the petrol pumps previously owned by James (Jimmy) A. Jones and since the 1960's belonging to Clifford Goss. On the right of centre the Police Station and the new Fire Station.

4.15 The Frederick Street-High Street junction circa 1958. Baden Roads' barber's shop at left, Saunders' drapers and hardware at centre and down the road stands one of the large fleet of Midland Red coaches, which ran a number of regular daily services Birmingham-London-Birmingham, its passengers no doubt being refreshed at Gays' Cafe or across the road at The White House Cafe. The two tall poles by the roadside were vent ("stink") pipes for the sewerage system. The sign on the wall at far left was advertising Exide car batteries and was made of "cats eyes" type coloured glass, which reflected in vehicle headlights.

4.16 The Alms Houses circa 1972. The Arthur Goodwin Alms Houses were constructed by the executors of his will in 1657. They have been administered by the Lords of the Manor ever since, and their survival is due to successive rescue operations. In 1726 they were repaired by the Duke of Marlborough estate, in 1894 they were rebuilt by Baron Ferdinand de Rothschild and in 1972 they were extensively modified "with the help of Mrs James de Rothschild". On this occasion the six houses were reduced to four to allow the provision of a toilet, kitchen, living room, bedroom and bathroom in each. (See article on Charities).

4.17 An aerial view of Baker Street and the Green in 1932. At the centre of the picture is the farm of the Manor of the third portion of the Church Living, Atte Greene, and at the left is the old Manor House. "The Green", a totally enclosed field in the middle, reveals the worn turf caused by people taking a short cut from Baker Street. At near centre is the Church School and behind that is The Grove, with the small farm belonging to Ewart Newman whose fields include Butchers Piece and Lousy Furlong, the land at the right of picture (now Grove Way and the village Playing Field).

4.18 An aerial photograph taken around 1957. In the foreground is the new housing estate, Goss Avenue and Sharps Close. This ground had previously contained the Squatters' Camp, before that a Polish Army holding camp and during the Second World War, the living accommodation for troops of the Pioneer Corps and their support, employed in the Petrol Storage Dump on the estate. Golden Nob allotment ground to the left, not a spare plot in sight, Grove Way now completed and the new Fire and Police Stations, leaving precious little of The Green at the centre of the village.

4.19 The High Street from the Quainton Road junction in 1951. On the left is the thatched barn belonging to the farm at "The Green" and nearer the middle of this photograph is the ancient Manor House of the Third Portion. At this time and for previous generations this Glebe (Church) land was farmed by the Goss family. At right of centre the white field gate posts can be discerned, one of them has survived intact to this day, (2000) . The tall cast iron pipe at the roadside was one of a pair which were intended to vent sewer gases from the sewage pipes deep under the ground. The "Stink Pipes" were removed in the 1960's without detrimental effect, so far!

4.20 Shops and houses on the south side of the High Street viewed from the Quainton Road junction. circa 1921. On the right is the Saddlery of Mr T.Goss, then the Butchers Shop of Mr R. Price. Further on can be seen the petrol pump in front of Mr L.Thorne's Garage business, and to its left is the Greengrocers' shop of Mr T. Griffin.

4.21 The High Street circa 1930, from the junction with Wood Street. On the right is number 30 High Street, the house built in 1890 by and for Mr H.H.Sherwin, a contractor who "did well at the Manor". It was said and believed this house was constructed from surplus materials from Lodge Hill. The Baron arranged for the addition of the porch and conservatory to improve the appearance, (and succeeded in making it look like a mausoleum). The ex-Primitive Methodist Chapel next door has been converted into Mr Rhodes' Garage and remains an automobile workshop to this day (2000).

4.22 The opposite view to 4.21. The White House not yet white and the bungalow not yet built. Circa 1930.

4.23 The High Street looking east from Wood Street junction circa 1905. The main road is dry and dusty in this picture, but during winter in the Great War it was a sea of mud with ammunition lorries en-route from the midlands often "up to their axles".

4.24 The opposite view to 4.23 but this time the photographer in danger of being trampled by a flock of sheep! Circa 1891. The cottage adjoining Mr Sherwin's had the two yew trees clipped identically in the extraordinary shapes which drew more than a few nudges and giggles from naughty boys over many years.

4.25 A charming picture similar to 4.24 but circa 1898 and included because we like them both! Although unusually, Waddesdon had gas lighting, witness the lamp standard on the corner, for most households paraffin lamps were the normal source of artificial light, hence the American Lamp Oil horse drawn tanker.

4.26 The "Bottom Shop" circa 1900. The shop and adjacent housing were built for Aylesbury Brewery Company around 1895. This photograph shows Mr George Sharp the Wheelwright from Number 1 High Street at the doorway, the boy on the left is Percy Hicks, and the boy on the right is Bert Biswell. At the rear in Baker Street is Dodwell's bread cart. Langridge's shop sold "Ales and Stout in casks and bottles" and in addition offered cooked meats, bacon, ham and groceries, a typical corner shop of that period.

4.27 The "Bottom Shop" circa 1930. The Misses Figg and Moules not only provided a mouth-watering display of confectionery but also kept "Ye Olde Corner Café " though where the café customers were entertained is not clear. We know that in the summer the rear grounds were used as a tea-garden. The café was closed down before the Second World War, although the shop continued to thrive as always.

4.28 Unfortunately the "Bottom Shop" was closed when this photograph was taken in May 1997, giving us a rather uninspiring picture. Worse was to come however, within two years Roger Slade, the son of Jack (J.A.Slade), had ceased trading and soon converted the shop to living accommodation. This last general store in the village is now just a memory, and to all intents and purposes people are compelled to purchase their provisions from supermarkets in the local towns.

4.29 The old council school in 1997 some years after completion of its redevelopment. The property, painted white, includes the Head teacher's house on the left, new houses squeezed into the playground spaces, and of course the original school now converted into apartments. When the development was completed it was first called "Gibbs Mews", but this name was not officially adopted. A pity! (See article Section Twelve, 3rd paragraph). The school, which was funded by "public subscription" in 1895 and cost then £2000, was absorbed into the property portfolio of the County Education Authority. When the new County Combined School was nearing completion in the late 1970's, the Authority prepared to dispose of the old school, but not before they had completely stripped and replaced the roof tiles! The village received no financial gain from the sale of the property.

4.30 Baker Street circa 1905. This view is not so different after one hundred years, the biggest change being the state of the road and footpath.

4.31 Four little girls at play in the field near The Grove off Baker Street circa 1931. Sybil Jones, Margaret Wicks, Kathleen and Joan Clare sit where the entrance to Grove Way was to be built.

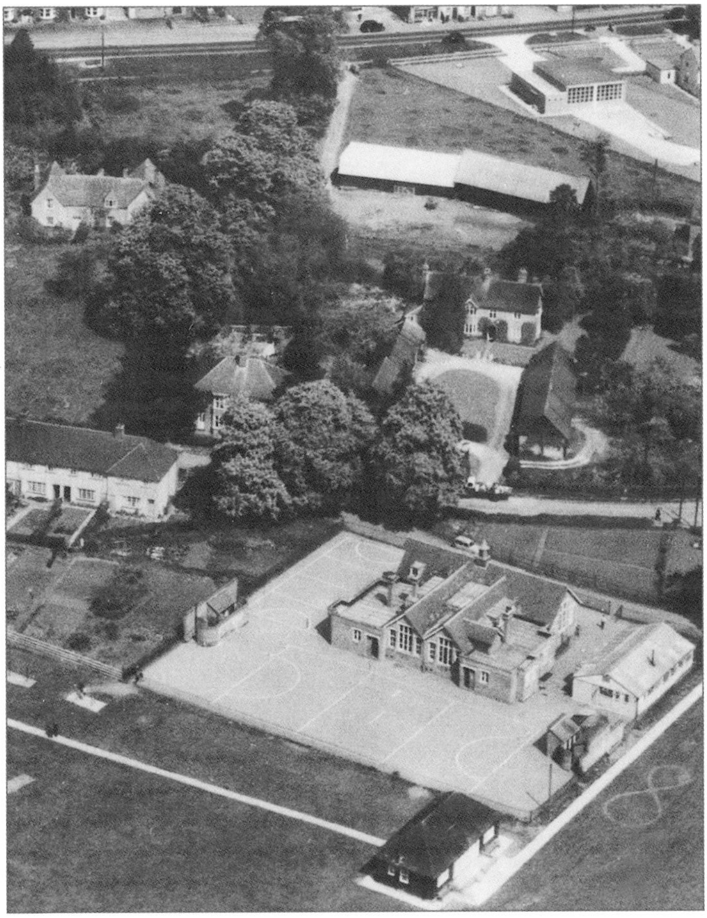

4.32 This circa 1955 aerial picture of the centre of Waddesdon provides us with excellent views of areas that have dramatically changed during the ensuing 45 years. At the near centre is the village playing field pavilion, built 1939, burned down in the 1990's. Next is the old Church School, built 1910, demolished for housing in the 1980's. Note the lavatory blocks, senior boys on the left, junior boys and girls on the right. The brick hut on the right was erected circa 1948 as extra classrooms. Right of centre is "The Grove", a smallholding of the past with redundant cow-sheds etc which were demolished in the 1970's for housing. Isolated left of centre is "Atte Greene", the Manor House of the Third Portion of the Church living, whilst nearby are the ancient barns forming part of the Green Farm and The Green, now reduced by the Fire and Police Station developments. Atte Greene was demolished and the whole area of Church land sold for housing, (Chestnut Close). Somehow it was decided not only to bury the manor house but also the unique name of the site!

4.33 In 1937 the Council House development, which was to be known as Grove Way was started, but progress was interrupted by the Second World War. Four pairs of semi-detached houses and a short entrance road had been completed. This photograph of 1946 shows German Prisoners of War working on the circular road, and Norman Carr reading a comic to Norman Atkins.

4.34 Quainton Road circa 1920 taken from the junction with New Street. On the left is the cart shed belonging to the house known as "Farthings" which was then a small-holding farm house. Gas street lights are visible and the Gas Works house and perimeter wall lie down the hill at the centre of the picture.

4.35 Harry Fowler's General Store at the junction of Quainton Road and Wood Street circa 1938. In the doorway is Ted Atkins, a typical young man of the village whose hobbies included music and (fatally) membership of the Territorial Army. See Section 6.

4.36 A very "Quaint" Christmas card. Quainton Road circa 1900. At the left is the sun- blind of Mrs Keedle's shop, a general store which stocked everything from sweets to paraffin, and Mrs Keedle would obtain rarer goods from Aylesbury on her weekly trips for that purpose. At the centre rear is a thatched cottage which was demolished to make way for the present No.1 Quainton Road and likewise the house behind the two ladies at the right of centre, demolished and now the site of a bungalow built for Mrs Kathy Cannon circa 1948.

4.37 Waddesdon Windmill circa 1932. Constructed in 1905 on the site of a much earlier mill. On the 12th November 1834 the first known Challenge Steeplechase took place from this site towards the steeple of St Mary's Church in Aylesbury. The finish line was at Ardenham Stile on Ardenham Hill. First prize was a silver cup and 50 guineas; entry 20 guineas, weight 12 stone 7 pounds, 21 entered. Weighing-in was at the White Hart Hotel and a crowd lined the course to witness the event. The winner was Captain Becher on Captain Lamb's famous horse "Vivian". "Vivian" was successful despite giving his rider a ducking in the river and falling over a gate during the race. The Marquis of Waterford and Count d'Orsay were among the riders. The windmill in the picture had been an impressive sight when new but its design was flawed and workmanship of the sails was poor. It was never a practical success although it was operated by Mr J.Taylor for a few years prior to the First World War, when conditions allowed. Miss Alice de Rothschild liked to see the sails turning and in truth they usually only turned when she was in residence. By the time of this photograph circa 1930 the mill was derelict and around 1935 was demolished by the use of an explosive charge. It was intended to re-use the bricks for building but they were found to be curved and therefore of little use.

4.38 Frederick Street circa 1902. On the left is the cart shed which in the 1920's was converted to become "The Frederick Street Room", a venue for numerous gatherings and meetings including a thrift club, Boy Scouts and Wolf Cubs, singing groups and musical practice sessions. Partly obscured in this picture, by the man in the bowler hat, is Herrings' bakery and grocery shop, the only purpose built shop in Frederick Street at this time. Prior to the Second World War the locals not only bought their daily bread from this shop, but often took advantage of the opportunity, at a few pence each, to use the residual heat of the bakery to cook their dinners! The boy in the cap is Harry Cripps.

4.39 Lower Frederick Street circa 1930. The elm trees have gone at the bottom of the road, but no sign yet of Waddesdon's first council houses, Sherriff Cottages, which will be named after the closes being used for allotments.

4.40 Frederick Street in May 1997. A sight familiar to villagers of the late 20th century, cars everywhere but the photographer did capture one gentleman on film. Quainton windmill in the distance partially restored during the past twenty-five years but soon to lose its sails once again and in need of repairs. At centre right of the picture are the premises of the shop formerly Herrings', Dodwells', Les Fowler's and latterly Tom Holdsworth's, but for nearly twenty years a private dwelling, the victim of modern shopping customs.

4.41 The eastern half of Waddesdon village from the air in 1932. We can see the compactness of the housing which then was scarcely 50 years old, but accommodated large families in a close-knit community. At the near left and upper centre are two large allotment fields, Sherriffs Closes and Golden Nob respectively. Down Quainton Road is the chimney of Mr Taylor's steam driven mill, and opposite the mill house is the Provincial Gas and Lighting Works Limited. In the works grounds can be seen the gasometer expanded almost to capacity. Scattered around the village can be seen many spaces where orchards and large kitchen gardens flourished, these of course are nearly all now gone, "in filled" with more houses. The sites of more twentieth century developments can be picked out, from left to right; Alcocks Close (Little Britain), Anstey or Big Britain (Anstey Close), Budds Piece (Goss Avenue), Butchers Piece (Grove Way), Atte Greene (Chestnut Close).

4.42 Mr Joseph Taylor's corn mill was built in 1893 by Waddesdon builder Joseph Holland, replacing the previous mill that had stood near Silk Street. In this photograph of May 1997 the mill house and mill buildings are largely intact, but the tall chimney a landmark for a century has gone, demolished for safety reasons. D.K.R. Metal Finishing Company occupy the premises now, putting a shine on innumerable ancient and modern metal artefacts.

4.43 Waddesdon Police Station and Houses in 1982. Until the 1950's the village Police Station had been accommodated in the end-of-terrace house, number 90 High Street, but then the combined Station and houses shown here were constructed on the field known as "The Green". Sergeant and Mrs Brown moved in to the far house, and one of the Police Constables stationed in the village moved in to the near one. In those days the office was manned most of the time, and in due course an Inspector was appointed and two more police houses built in Goss Avenue. Times have long since changed, like everyone else policemen and women want to own their own houses. In the year 2000, plans for a new Police Station were announced, and this building's days were numbered.

Section Five

Church, Chapel and Charities

Of Church and Clergy

From earliest times mankind seems to have embraced religion in one form or another as an essential element of communal life, and by the end of the first millennium England was an established Christian country. At that time there would have been a parish church at Waddesdon, probably on the site of the present church and possibly built of wood.

At nearly 160 feet (48 metres) in length and 50 feet (15 metres) wide the present larger than average parish church at Waddesdon gives an indication of the standing of the village in ancient times. The oldest parts of the building are of Norman origin, dating from around 1190, whilst additions and renovations over the centuries reflect the architectural styles that followed. During the eight hundred years since the Norman church was built, the building and clergy have played a key role in the life of the parish community, and it is no coincidence that resources have been afforded to maintain the church in a fitting manner.

During the 13th century the size of the parish and the value of the "living" had been judged sufficient to justify the appointment of three priests, each with their own "portion" of the living. Consequently for the next six hundred years Waddesdon sometimes had as many as three rectors and one or more curates. These clergy were appointed under the patronage of successive Lords of the Manor who held the advowson until 1874, since when it has been retained by the Dukes of Marlborough.

The "portions" were themselves small manors, having manor houses, land and tenant farmers. Each portionist was entitled to manorial rights from his tenants including one days labour at haymaking time, one day at harvest time, rent for the tenancy, and on the death of a tenant a Heriot, which is a payment in money or kind. The Heriot was often the best animal of the deceased, however anything of value might be acceptable, for instance on one occasion it was a feather bed!

The three manor houses were situated in the village, each within its enclosure of about two and a half acres known as priest's acre. The manor house of the first portion was located at the rectory near the church; it was known as "Benthams" and had 26 acres of open field, two closes and ten houses. The manor house of the second portion was located south-west of the church at a distance of 250 yards; it was called "Motons" (later known as "Muttons") but at one period in history was named "Raising". "Motons" portion included ten acres of open field and five houses. The manor house of the third portion was known as "Green End" or "At The Green". It was situated about 500 yards south-east of the church, adjacent to an area known as "The Green". This portion included 20 acres of open fields, five houses and a payment of £12 yearly from Pitchcott rectory. The third portion was obliged to provide straw and hay to litter the church.

When the enclosures of the last of Waddesdon's common land had been completed in 1774, the village found itself largely in the hands of three landowners; the Lord of the Manor and Oxford University holding the land to the south of Akeman Street, and the church holding much of the newly enclosed land on the north side. In 1881 the three portions of the living were amalgamated and the sole rector and curate resided at the new rectory near the site of Benthams, the manor of the first portion.

In ancient times the rectors were probably the only formally educated residents in Waddesdon, and one can imagine that life for some of them must have been intellectually quite lonely. However the energies and attributes of an educated man appointed as rector in one of the portions could always be of great value to the community, and numerous examples of charity and organisation are recorded.

Probably the most illustrious scholar who served as rector at Waddesdon was Gabriel Goodman. He was appointed to the first portion in 1569, and retained office until his death in 1601. Gabriel Goodman was one of the original subscribers to the Thirty Nine Articles of the Church of England and he assisted in the translation of the "Bishops Bible" (one of the fifteen portions bears his initials G. G.). On his death in 1601 he was buried in St. Benet's chapel at Westminster Abbey, where his monument was erected, a kneeling effigy in doctor's habit.

Of all the clergy associated with the Church of St. Michael, none can have carried out their duties with more dedication than the Rev W. W. Walton . He died in 1859 after nine years as senior curate to the three portions, but during that period when living conditions and poverty were as bad as at any time in history for ordinary villagers, the Rev Walton worked unceasingly to alleviate the suffering and improve the lot of the poor. In 1859, just prior to his untimely death, he was awarded the living of the third portion by His Grace the Duke of Marlborough. Shortly after his death a school-house was built by public subscription, in his memory.

The amalgamation of the three livings in 1881 coincided with a small reduction in the amount of Glebe land in Waddesdon. Motons was sold to Baron Ferdinand de Rothschild and about 80 years later, Green End was sold for housing development. Despite this, several hundred acres of farmland is still owned by the Church Commissioners, making them the second of the two main landowners in the village.

5.1 The parish church of St Michael and all Angels circa 1885. This is a view which greeted Waddesdon church-goers in the 18th and 19th century, but unfortunately when this photograph was taken, the tower had deteriorated and was in a dangerous state. The oldest parts of the church date from the 12th century, and the enduring importance of this building to the community is reflected in the evident additions and renovations over the centuries. Records from the past 150 years bear witness to a continuous struggle by the church-going community to maintain the fabric of this fine building. Lately it has become quite obvious that although fund-raising is targeted, the maintenance demands on such an ancient structure are never ending.

5.2 The parish church circa 1895. The tower had been completely rebuilt, the remainder of the exterior had been renovated and a pebble-dash finish applied. The total works cost around £3,000, and the contractor was Mr H. H. Sherwin a Waddesdon builder. At the base of the tower on the south side is a commemorative stone laid by the Bishop of Reading on the 20th October 1891. The chestnut trees on the right of the picture formed an avenue containing the path leading to the church porch from the village square. A lych gate was added at the churchyard entrance on the path in the early 20th century. The western doorway is in Ham Hill stone and the drip stone terminals are carvings of the head of the Bishop of Oxford on one side, and on the other Queen Victoria, by Mr S. Allen. Needless to say the new appearance as depicted here would have been unrecognisable to the Waddesdonians of old.

5.3 The interior of the parish church circa 1910. The rood screen was the gift of the Rector in 1902, Dr Henry Yule, in memory of his father. On the right are the three magnificent Norman arches dating from around 1190. Whilst just discernible beyond the arches is the Italian pulpit, the gift of the 9th Duke of Marlborough in thanksgiving for his safe return from the Boer War.

5.4 The view in the church from within the chancel circa 1910. The choir stalls were installed as a memorial to the Rev. T. J. Williams in 1901. The fine craftsmanship in these and the rood screen is well displayed in this photograph. On the upper right are the pipes of the organ, which was installed in 1902. This was soon deemed inadequate, and was replaced in 1912.

5.5 The Rev. W.W.Walton was an inspired worker for the good of the community, and during his nine years as Senior Curate of the three Portions, he continuously strove to improve the lot of the poor in and around Waddesdon. He received basic medical training, so was able to provide some treatment for the sick, whom he visited assiduously. However it was his efforts to engender a self-help culture, which were of the most practical and long-lasting help; a coal club, clothing club, soup and bread rations, and loans for purchase of seeds. He formed a library, kept an evening school, supplied stationary, promoted temperance and also revived the Bible Association, and established the Harvest Festival in aid of the Bucks General Infirmary. Perhaps inevitably he died from diphtheria, a disease contracted from visiting the sick in 1859.

5.6 This memorial tablet now rests in the parish church. Nearly a century ago it was replaced by a Five Arrows sign in the gable end of the house especially built in memory of the Rev. Walton, at the National School. The whole of the school premises and land had been transferred to Miss Alice de Rothschild in a rather favourable deed of exchange, and presumably the Church authorities decided not to object when the tablet was replaced. Why not retain both?

5.7 Completed in 1870, this is the Manor house of the First Portion (Benthams). Constructed to fulfil a multipurpose role as a manor house, rectory and farm house and including an adjoining house for a curate, Benthams was set in substantial gardens with stables and a cart shed, leading into the Parson's Closes. This photograph was taken circa 1970.

5.8 The Rev. T. J. Williams, Rector of the First Portion in 1867 and the first occupant of the new rectory at Benthams. In 1881 he presided over the amalgamation of the three portions of the living, whereupon he became the sole rector, supported by one, or occasionally two curates. A learned gentleman and a jovial character he became somewhat notorious in his battle for due payment with the Aylesbury and Buckingham Railway Company in the late 1860's. After 30 years' ministry at Waddesdon, and a bachelor for all that time, he prepared to retire and marry, and was teased in a good-natured way by his friends, including Baron Ferdinand de Rothschild (at the opening ceremony of the Waddesdon Hall).

5.9 The Rev. J.E.G. Farmer served as Rector in Waddesdon from 1905 to 1921. In those days the combined living at Waddesdon was extremely well-endowed, and the rectors had every incentive to remain here. The Rev and Mrs Farmer celebrated their Silver Wedding, circa 1910, by inviting all the elder villagers to a Garden Tea Party, and they and their family were considered very much part of the village. Sadly their son Henry Farmer was killed in action at Ypres in May 1915. A window in the Lady Chapel was dedicated to his memory by his parents, and a figure in stone of St George and the Dragon is mounted above the south doorway in the Porch, dedicated by his brother. Probably the last major ceremony at which the Rev Farmer officiated was the unveiling of the War Memorial on Easter Sunday, 27th March 1921.

5.10 The Rev. George Dixon, Rector in Waddesdon from 1921 to 1963. During his 42 years as Rector, the Reverend (later Canon) Dixon worked continuously at all the tasks traditionally associated with a country vicar. A bachelor all his life, he resided at the Rectory with his two sisters, and all joined in the many activities involving the church. Particular memories of parishioners include the Rev Dixon visiting outlying homes on horseback, his steadfast concern for those who were sick or bereaved, his interest in the welfare of the Church of England School, and latterly his ambition to construct a Church of England Secondary School. This last ambition was fulfilled just before his retirement, when in September 1963 the new C of E Secondary School was officially opened.

5.11 The old Manor House of the Third Portion, Atte Greene circa 1925. This old manor could be approached across a paddock from the south, Baker Street side, as in this photograph, or more conveniently from the north, High Street side, down a narrow path alongside the Alms houses. It stood where the junction of the roads in Chestnut Close now lies, and was sold along with the remainder of Atte Greene site, by the Church Commissioners in the mid 1960's. Standing at the gate in this picture is Mr Arthur (Pete) Goss, the last tenant of this house and the last person to farm at "The Green". Mr Goss was one of the final generation of this particular branch of the Goss Family. He was a stalwart Churchman, and a parish councillor for more than 50 years.

5.12 The Rev. Hugh Parker, Rector in Waddesdon 1963 to 1979. During the 16 years of his ministry at Waddesdon the Rev. Parker oversaw several significant changes in the living. First the selling of "The Green" for development, next the amalgamation of most of the church farmland into Glebe Farm, down Quainton Road. Then the sale of the rectory and land at "Benthams" and the building of a new rectory nearby. Whilst these rationalisation exercises appeared to realise substantial sums of money, it was the Church Commissioners' funds which benefited.

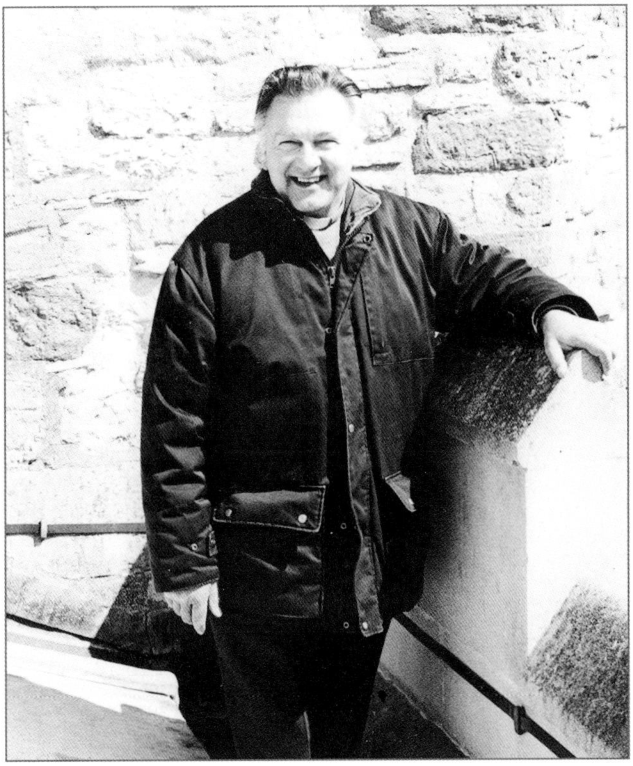

5.13 When the Rev. Colin M. Hutchings and his wife arrived at Waddesdon Rectory in 1982 they already had a family of three teenaged children, so were well aware of modern trends and issues. The Rector and Mrs Hutchings joined in village life, particularly the Royal British Legion branch and the Mothers Union, and it was during this period that various charities were revived.

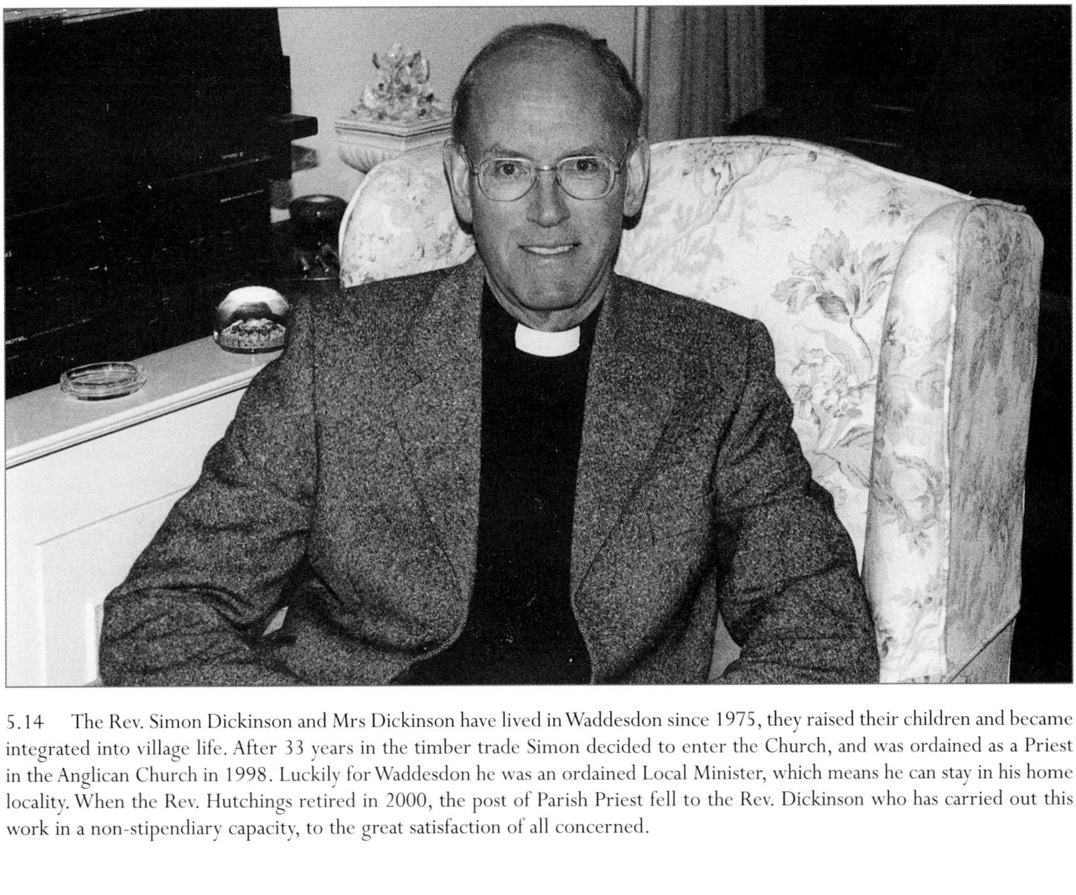

5.14 The Rev. Simon Dickinson and Mrs Dickinson have lived in Waddesdon since 1975, they raised their children and became integrated into village life. After 33 years in the timber trade Simon decided to enter the Church, and was ordained as a Priest in the Anglican Church in 1998. Luckily for Waddesdon he was an ordained Local Minister, which means he can stay in his home locality. When the Rev. Hutchings retired in 2000, the post of Parish Priest fell to the Rev. Dickinson who has carried out this work in a non-stipendiary capacity, to the great satisfaction of all concerned.

5.15 Waddesdon's Boys Brigade unit with its leader Mr A..Biswell and the Rev. Edward Norris (Curate). A splendid example of the participation in youth activities by the boys of the village, and the involvement of the Church in leading them. Photographed in 1895 at the front of the Rectory.

5.16 The Perseverance Bible Class 1896. The Rev. T..J. Williams had every good reason to look satisfied at the turnout for this class.

5.17 Three Curates pose here with a group of Church worthies, around 1898. Although the purpose of the gathering is not mentioned, it was probably the Church of England Men's Society, at least we have all the names of those present. The gentleman with the medals, Mr Walton, had served in the armed forces during the Crimean War 1854 to 1856.

5.18 The Church Garden Fete was a well established event by the commencement of the twentieth century, but during the Rev. G Dixon's ministry they became a much anticipated treat. For much of the period the annual Church Fete was held on Whit Monday and invariably included a Fancy Dress competition and entertainment by school children. Westcott School usually did Maypole Dancing, and the Waddesdon Church School performed traditional Country Dances. This photograph is of a Church Fete on the Rectory lawns in 1924.

5.19 A Church Fete in 1936. Judging the Fancy Dress competition. The "Alice in Wonderland" couple at the rear is Mr and Mrs Leybourne.

5.20 The annual Church Fete, Whit Monday 1963. Adults and children sit enthralled at the entertainment being presented at the popular garden fete. Nearest the camera are John Sturch, Karen Preston, Robert Barker, and Francis Norris. The children behind include Michael Holland, Roger Slade, Ivor Southam, Charles Jenkins, Roland Carter, Robert Carpenter, Margaret Norris, Vivienne Saunders and adults at the back include Mrs Taylor, Mrs Leybourne, Mrs Ashpoole, Mrs Goss, Mrs Kibble, Mrs Con Porter, Ted Porter, Ray Atkins and Dr Colin Campbell.

5.21 "Rev Crosby's Angels" circa 1944. During, and for some years after the Second World War, the curate, the Rev. Crosby had the additional task of Choirmaster. Here we have the choir with the Rector and curate, photographed at the church porch. Back: Bill Reynolds, Terry Hayes, Gerald Cyster, Vernon Mulcahy, Tom Lovell. Middle: John Cripps, Basil Reed, Derek Reynolds, Derek Lovell, Murray Saunders, Colin Hicks, John Carter, Ivor Cyster. Sitting: Tim Carter, Rev. Dixon (Rector), Rev. Crosby, George Hicks. The name "Crosby's Angels" was rather enviously given because it was reckoned the Rev Crosby refused to hear any criticism of the choirboys.

5.22 The new Rectory 1969 nearing completion. A move by the Church Commissioners to capitalise on some of the assets at Waddesdon, included the sale of the Manor houses of both the old First and Third Portions, Benthams and Atte Greene. At the same time it was necessary to construct a replacement rectory to accommodate the vicar, and this was situated in a small plot within the grounds of the old rectory. The remainder was sold off for development - Rectory Drive.

5.23 The bell-ringers in 2000. St Michael's has a peal of six cast steel bells, manufactured in 1862 by Taylor Vickers and Co of Sheffield. It is said steel bells are not as good as those cast in bell-metal, however our stalwart ringers provide a very welcome sound in the year 2000 exactly as their predecessors have done for many decades. Left to Right: Percy Richards, Ian McEwan, Joan Williams, Murial Wright, Tony Wright, Ivor Burnell (Tower Captain).

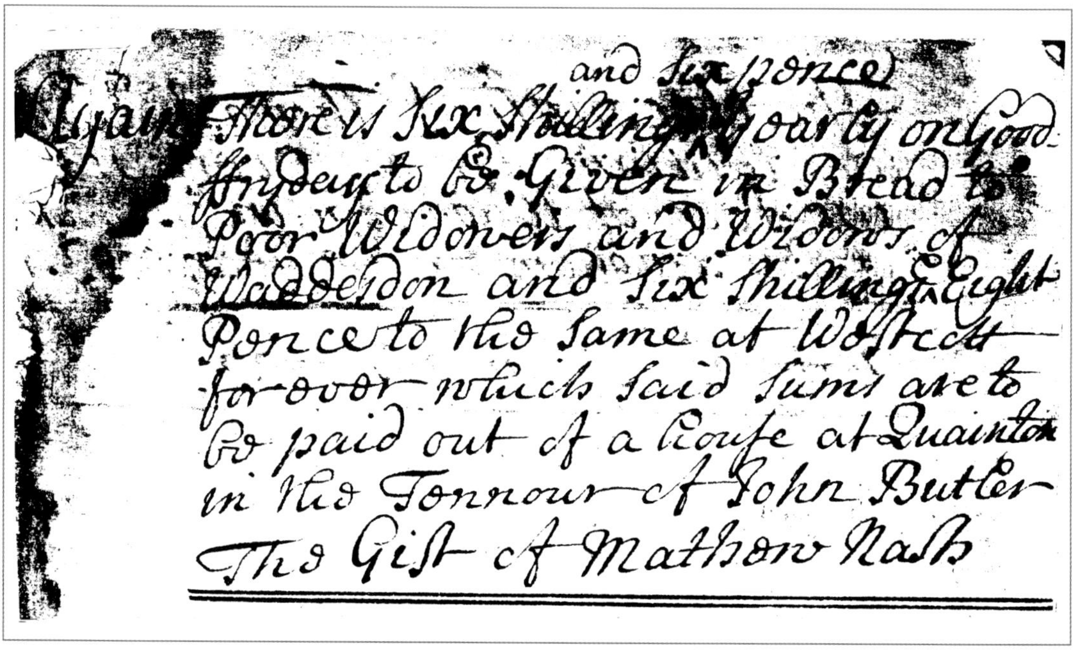

and Six ponce
Again There is Six Shilling yearly on Good
friday to be Given in Bread to
Poor Widowers and Widows of
Waddesdon and Six Shillings Eight
Ponce to the Same at Westcott
for ever which said Sums are to
be paid out of a House at Quainton
in the Tonnour of John Butler
The Gift of Mathew Nash

5.24 Reproduced from the Churchwardens' Account Book for 1742, this hand-written statement is as follows: "Again there is Six Shillings and six pence yearly on Good Friday to be Given in Bread to Poor Widowers and Widows of Waddesdon and Six Shillings and eight pence to the same at Westcott for ever which said Sums are to be paid out of a house at Quainton in the Tennour of John Butler. The Gift of Mathew Nash."

Waddesdon's Charities

Charity in thought, word and deed is a basic tenet of the Christian faith, which has under-pinned the evolving British way of life for many centuries. Our history in the second millennium has a profusion of acts of charity, usually in the form of bequests, and most old villages and towns have their particular charitable trusts; Waddesdon is no exception.

We describe below those Charities that have historical interest, some are now defunct while others continue to serve the community in the year 2000.

Please Note: In olden days the pound sign was denoted by a lower case letter L after the number. and is shown thus in quotations in this section. e.g £10 was written as 10.l

Philosophy Farm

In 1622 the old Waddesdon manor farm was purchased by the trustees of Sir William Sedley, who had bequeathed £2000 to endow a lectureship at Oxford University. The property yielded a rent of £120 per annum towards the Sedleian Professorship of Natural Philosophy. This rather remote act of charity probably had no direct benefit for Waddesdon, but Philosophy Farm (See map 1.22), carried out its function for 250 years. The acreage was increased to 339 in the 1774 enclosures, benefiting from an allotment in lieu of "four yardlands and four acres". The property was purchased by Baron Ferdinand de Rothschild circa 1875, when it yielded around £200 per annum; the buildings were demolished and the whole farm was absorbed into the Estate park. Presumably because of this association with the village, Oxford University contributed to the British School building fund in the late 19th century.

The Bread Charities and the Bunter Cow

In 1832 there were several long established "Bread Charities" in Waddesdon; they originated from the instructions of kindly persons who had endowed sums of money or property, the proceeds of which were to be used for the purchase of bread for the poor of the village. The endowments were not large, and the interest or proceeds from most would have been less than 10 shillings per year. Amongst these benefactors listed in 1832, but copied from a paper of 1733, were: Matthew Nash, "a sum of 6s. 6d. is expended yearly in the purchase of ...... quartern loaves which are distributed by the minister and churchwardens on Good Friday to about ten widows of this parish," (see 5.24)

Mrs Bethell's gift, "there is 10.l. which passeth from overseers to overseers, the interest to be given to the poor of Waddesdon and Westcott in bread on the feast-day of Saint John the Evangelist for ever,"

Mr Eggleton's gift, "there is 10.l. which passeth........ to the poor of Waddesdon in bread on May-day for ever,"

Mr. William Rice's gift, "again there is 20.l....... to the poor of Waddesdon, Westcott and Woodham, in bread on the feast-day of Saint John the Evangelist, for ever,"

By 1832 the endowments of Bethell, Eggleton and Rice, had been taken over by the parish, and annually around 27th December a baker was paid £3 to produce loaves costing less than one penny each, to be distributed to all the married poor of the parish having children under ten years of age, one loaf to each person. (More than 720 loaves for £3!).

Mr. Ross's gift, "there is 20.l. that passes from churchwardens to churchwardens... to be given in bread to such poor people as the churchwardens should think fit, six penny loaves every Lord's day, two Sundays to Waddesdon one to Westcott, to six poor people...". By 1832 this endowment had been taken over by the parish and £1.10s.4d. per year was spent on bread, and distributed to persons on parish relief.

In addition the tenant of Lodge Hill Farm was required to keep two cows for a regular milk distribution to the poor of the village. This, the "Bunter Alms Cow Charity" mentioned by the Rev. C Oscar Moreton, derived from an indenture of Sir Francis Goodwin dated 1631. The tenant of Lodge Hill Farm in 1825, complained the £10 rent allowance was inadequate and secured agreement to keep only one alms cow. In 1865 the solitary "Bunter cow" died, and the carcass was sold for £4, sadly that was the end of this Charity. (The origin of the name "Bunter" is unknown).

All these Charities were administered by the Churchwardens and Overseers for the Poor, who were also responsible for distributing the bread and milk according to the benefactors' instructions.

A Charities' Commissioners report of 1868 states the Eggleton and Ross charities had contributed £60 and £20 respectively on assisting emigration, this appeared to leave them with no capital and they were therefore defunct. In 1995 the sum of £29.48 consisting of £7 capital and £22.48 accumulated income held by the Church Wardens under the title of Matthew Nash Charity was transferred to the William Turner Charity in a "tidying-up exercise."

Arthur Goodwin's Alms Houses. (Charity Commission Registration No.203342)

The Manor of Waddesdon and Over Winchendon passed to Arthur Goodwin in 1634. He was heavily involved in the Civil War but in a codicil to his will, bearing the date 30th August 1645, Arthur Goodwin ensured the completion of six almshouses on land lately enclosed on Waddesdon Green. The terms of his Will "directed Lord Wharton, and Jane, (daughter of Arthur Goodwin and wife of Lord Wharton,) who were his executors, so soon as the distractions of these times would permit, to take in hand and speedily finish these houses, for which good stone and timber were already lying in the yard, ...". Meanwhile he allowed £5 yearly to be paid to six poor people until the houses were built, and then for a £30 a year rent charge out of the manor of Waddesdon for ever.

The six almshouses were completed in 1657, some ten years after the death of Arthur Goodwin. In 1832 it was recorded that six aged widows, four of Waddesdon and two of Upper Winchendon, appointed by the minister, were residing there, (the parish of Waddesdon included Westcott and Woodham). The alms people were paid two shillings per week for 50 weeks each year, and the houses "are repaired at the expense of the Duke of Marlborough, and they are now in tolerably good condition."

The almshouses were rebuilt in 1894 by Baron Ferdinand de Rothschild. In 1972 Mrs Dorothy de Rothschild paid for the complete modernisation of the terrace, consolidating the number to four comfortable self-contained homes.

The administrative and qualifying criteria have altered to take account of modern developments in care etc., and this charity is in a sound financial position to continue providing homes in the 21st century. Villagers, male or female, are publicly invited to apply for vacant homes and although the Alms Houses are no longer let free-of-charge, the modest rent of £25 per week includes heating, gardening, water and maintenance costs. The Trustees represent the Waddesdon Estate, the Parish Church, the local Doctors and the Parish Council. The Clerk to the Trustees is Mrs J Payne, c/o The Waddesdon Estate Office (2000).

John Beck's and Lewis Fetto's Charities (Charity Commission Registration No.203344)

John Beck (1598-1675) of Bicester left in his Will £6 to each of five executors, to use for the poor of Woodham, Westcott and Waddesdon, to apprentice out a boy, or to be used at the discretion of the trust. In due course a one acre field on the Pitchcott road was purchased and the rent in 1832 was £l - l5s - Od per year. In 1876 the rent of the field yielded £3 per annum, and it was resolved to accept the offer from Baron Ferdinand de Rothschild to purchase the land. The £167 proceeds were invested in 2.5 per cent Consolidated Stock. Unfortunately the value of this investment diminished over the years, realising only £49.40 in 1994, when the stock was sold. £50 was invested in 7.77 shares in the Charities Official Investment Fund, and now represents the capital value of John Beck's endowment.

Lewis Fetto of Wormstone, by his Will, dated 11th June 1724, left £140 to be invested in lands by his executors. From the clear rents and profits of such lands 40 shillings to be expended "........ for the Putting to school to learn to read and write or cast accounts, four poor children of the said town and liberty,.........", and the remainder of the clear rents and profits " ....for putting out apprentices such poor children.....". The first accounts book informs us this charity was established in 1727 when six trustees were appointed; a 13.4 acre field near Westcott was purchased and soon apprenticeships were being sponsored. For example a sum of £5 was paid to "Mrs Abbett for taking Henry Lee apprentice" in1734. Occasionally girls were apprenticed as in 1764, "4.l for apprenticing Ann Giner." The usual apprenticeship period was seven years. The field "Charity Ground" remains the property of the Trust, and represents the capital value of the Lewis Fetto element of the combined charity.

In 1814 the Beck and Fetto charities were combined under one set of Trustees, and the funds were joined and dispensed from a single account. This arrangement was formalized to the Charity Commissioners satisfaction in 1994!

In 1832 the Overseer for the Poor arranged the emigration to America of 39 poor villagers to help relieve the burden on the ratepayers. The "Beck and Fetto" Trustees awarded a grant of £50 towards the costs of the journey. Also in 1832 it was reported that "Eighteen boys are taught free at a school in Waddesdon, at 10s. a head. The 9.l paid for these boys is made up of 3.l contributed voluntarily by the three rectors of Woodham, Westcott and Waddesdon, and 6.l from the charities Fetto and Beck. The remainder of the two charities, 7.l. 15s. has been laid out from time to time until 1832 in apprenticing boys."

In 1904 a £2 annual endowment, payable from income was established as Fetto's Educational Foundation, and this was reconfirmed when a revised scheme for administering the combined charities was promulgated in 1948.

Since their inception the John Beck's and Lewis Fetto's Charities have aided innumerable local youngsters in education and work training. Today the six Trustees comprising the Rector and representatives of the three parishes, dispense grants to applicants who are under 21, resident in Woodham, Westcott or Waddesdon, and embarked upon academic or formal training leading to a career. Fetto's Educational Foundation, now £40, is awarded to the village Primary School for equipment or materials to foster literacy. The Clerk to the Trustees is Norman Carr (2000).

William Turner's Charity. (Charity Commission Registration No 203343)

In the early 18th century when William Turner was a young boy, he arrived in Waddesdon with his mother. Although they were penniless vagrants, they were fed by the rector and given shelter in the rectory barn, but it soon became apparent that William was suffering from smallpox. In those days this highly infectious disease was often fatal, and vagrants with smallpox could expect to be driven from any community. However the mother and child were lucky for they were given care, and miraculously William recovered, although it is said that some of the villagers who contracted the disease at that time did not. William always remembered his debt to Waddesdon.

William Turner went on to become a successful trader in butter and cheese and at his death in 1784 was a man of considerable means. In his will he bequeathed all his residuary personal estate for the benefit of the poor of the parish of Waddesdon. This estate was represented by two sums of stock, "2,265. l. 11s 6d. and 1,000. l. three per cent. Consols," the dividends of the latter sum to be enjoyed by his executrix during her life. The executrix Hester Draper, alias Turner (William's daughter?), died in 1806, and the stock was transferred to the Trustees of the charity bringing the total value to £3,265 – 11s – 6d.

It was recorded in 1832 that "the dividends, amounting to 97. l. 19s. 4d. are most injudiciously distributed, ... by the curate, churchwardens and overseers, amongst all the married poor of the parish having children under 10 years old age, amounting with their families to about 800 individuals, in shares varying from 1s. to about 10s. according to the size of the families". The parish comprised Westcott and Woodham as well as Waddesdon. Despite the distribution being deemed injudicious, it must be remembered that for a labourer earning perhaps 1s.3d. per day when in work, a gift of a few shillings would have made a big difference.

The charity has survived to the present day, for much of the past relying on the original investment in three per cent Consols, which was reduced to two and a half per cent, and distributing the inflation-eroded dividends according to the criteria noted in 1832. The capital value of the charity's stock dropped and in 1974 half the stock was sold, realising £338. 54, which was invested in the Charities Official Investment Fund. In 1979 the remaining stock was sold for £320.10 and the proceeds invested likewise. At around the same time the Trustees devised a different criterion for distribution of dividends, to help alleviate financial problems associated with sudden change of circumstance.

The Trustees include the Rector and representatives from organisations in the parishes. The Clerk to the Trustees is Mr David George (2000).

Lord Wharton's Bible Charity (Charity Commission Registration No. 200298)

Phillip Lord Wharton, by a deed of 1692, gave to trustees the clear yearly rent out of certain lands in York, for the purpose of distributing annually 1,050 Bibles, with the Singing Psalms and 1,050 Catechisms. The said Bibles and Catechisms to be bound, the former in calves' leather, and the latter in sheep's leather. The covers to be inscribed as instructed.

The areas of benefit for this charity were originally communities closely associated with the Wharton estates at Waddesdon, Wooburn and at Wharton Hall in Westmorland, Cumberland and Yorkshire. The recipients of the bibles and catechisms were to be poor children able to read, who could recite from memory Psalms 1,15,25,37,101,113, and 145. The restrictions upon areas of benefit were relaxed, and by the early 20th century the numbers of Bibles distributed had increased from the original 1,050 to several thousands.

Lord Wharton Bibles were awarded to local children over many years. They were treasured and handed down by the village families, and in many cases survive to this day. Unfortunately this ancient tradition seems to have foundered in Waddesdon around the 1960's, but nationally the Charity has survived and evolved. The bibles are now distributed to applicants (clergy, church officers or head teachers) across the country, for presentation to scholars under 18 years who have an acceptable comprehension of the scriptures.

Seven Trustees, four Anglican and three Nonconformists, are responsible for the Charity, and the day to day administration is carried out by the Clerk Mrs R.J.H. Edwards, 30 Prentis Road, Streatham, SW16 1QD (2000).

THE FAITH BEAUMONT CHARITY. (CHARITY COMMISSION REGISTRATION NO 1068452)

Major Michael Beaumont of Wotton House, Conservative M.P. for Aylesbury in the 1930's, wished to create a lasting memory of his wife Faith who had died in this period. He made a gift of a twelve acre field opposite the Crooked Billet public house in Kingswood, on which to erect a Church of England Secondary School. The Second World War intervened, and in 1947 a formal conveyance of the field was made to appointed Trustees. However the preferred site for the new school had by then become Waddesdon, and eventually the Trustees obtained Charity Commission approval for a Scheme setting up the Charity. The income of this Charity "to become available to individuals and organisations for the promotion of education, including education in accordance with the doctrines of the Church of England."

The area of benefit is the parishes of Waddesdon, Westcott, Woodham, Grendon Underwood and the neighbourhood thereof. The trustees include the incumbents of Waddesdon and Grendon Underwood and nominees of the Parish Councils of Waddesdon, Westcott and Grendon Underwood. The Clerk to the Trustees is Mr Ron Copcutt (2000).

WADDESDON VILLAGE HALL (CHARITY COMMISSION REGISTRATION NO 300343)

The Waddesdon Hall was built by Baron Ferdinand de Rothschild in 1897 to serve as a venue for enlightening functions for the villagers. The Hall was totally maintained by the Waddesdon Estate, and booked and used according to conditions set by the Baron. Dances and consumption of alcoholic drink were not allowed! Over the years the rules were relaxed, dances became commonplace but the sale of drink on the premises was forbidden until after 1968.

In 1968 Mrs Dorothy de Rothschild conveyed to Trustees under the condition of a Trust Deed, the land, the Hall and a £10,000 endowment, "for the use of the inhabitants of Waddesdon and the neighbourhood ...."etc. This gift (The Foundation) was vested in the Official Custodian for Charities, with the endowment invested in the Charities Official Investment Fund.

The Waddesdon Village Hall has a Committee of Management, which is responsible to the Trustees for the management of the Foundation. The Committee comprises a Trustee and representatives drawn from the Parish Council and village organisations. Co-opted members are also included.

5.25 The Roman Catholic Church of St Jude in Frederick Street. This building started life in the 1920's as the Butchers shop of Mr Ernest Saunders. Then after the Second World War it was the Co-op Butchers shop, before eventually being converted to its present use in the 1960's. The Waddesdon members of the Roman Catholic Church were never very numerous, but displayed a willingness to work and raise funds in the 1960's and 1970's, sufficient to build and run their own church that still operates, albeit in a reduced role. Since its establishment St Jude's has provided the village with a meeting place for smaller gatherings.

5.26 The Wesleyan Chapel shortly after its construction in 1877. This was a tremendous achievement by the members of the chapel. To raise the money to embark on such a development, to complete the task and pay off the final bill at £1280, at a time when most men earned less than £1 per week is little short of a miracle. Note; the grass verge and pathway leading to the "main road".

Methodism in Waddesdon

In the year 1774 the village witnessed two important occurrences. The first was the enclosure of the remaining common land, and of course this was an immediate, memorable and shattering event which affected everyone. The second probably had little immediate impact on the village as a whole, but was of incalculable importance to some because it marked the beginning of the Wesleyan church in Waddesdon. This was not however the first connection with the Wesleys in this locality, for on Sunday 3rd October 1725, the freshly ordained John Wesley preached at both Fleet Marston and Over Winchendon.

William Goodson, was an agricultural labourer of Waddesdon, living in rented accommodation with his wife, five children, his widowed sister and her small daughter, and he had joined the Methodist Society at Weedon on its formation in 1772. From their home in Waddesdon, he and his wife walked to hear "Wesleys Preachers" whenever they could. The distances were always considerable, sometimes as far as Wendover, illustrating perhaps the particular attraction that those nonconformist preachers had for many in the area. At the Midsummer Sessions in 1774 William Goodson's house was licensed as a place of worship, bringing the Methodist preachers to Waddesdon for the first time.

The first Methodist service in Waddesdon was attended by Joseph Bradford a travelling preacher, and the regular services which followed soon attracted an impressive membership. With the existence in the village of a non-conformist congregation there was a polarisation of opinion and undoubtedly these early Weslyans were considered as fair game by some of different persuasion. At the outset it was not unusual for services to be interrupted by "Quickers", the itinerant workers who were employed from parish to parish in planting quick-thorn hedges around the enclosures. These men were used to being unpopular by the nature of their work, and needed little encouragement to disrupt the services of religious radicals. None-the-less the new church flourished in adversity, and William Goodson's house served its special Sundays' purpose for 12 years.

Fresh premises were licensed in 1786, and in 1805 the first purpose-built chapel was opened. The following years saw strong growth in membership such that a larger, modern chapel was necessary, and in 1869 it was resolved to raise necessary funds. At a cost of £1280 the new chapel was built and was opened in 1887. The adjacent old chapel became the Sunday school.

The old chapel stands to this day, having been used continuously as a Sunday school and a venue for numerous other activities. These range from, Methodist Guild and Woman's Hour meetings, to wartime canteen for local armed services' personnel. In the days when Waddesdon had two bands, the Temperance Prize Silver Band practised and stored musical instruments there, and by providing music for the Annual Sunday School Treat, paid the rent in kind.

Despite the hard times of the 19th century most villagers could discern a gradual improvement in their lot; education was playing its part and so more people were able to articulate their thoughts. Church or chapel going was the normal thing, and practically every family attended either the Church of England or one of the Non-conformist Chapels in the village. In the late 19th century the sense of religious emancipation was displayed still further when a Primitive Methodist Chapel was built and for a few decades thrived, before closing in the 1920's (now a vehicle repair workshop).

The Methodists in Waddesdon have always considered Sunday school to be an important function of the church, and have provided the village with a valuable and enjoyable service without a break, ever since the early beginnings. For successive generations of scholars there were additional highlights in the year, which added to their happy memories of the chapel. In February or March was the Sunday School Annual Prize-giving when, depending on attendance and diligence, every pupil received a book suitably inscribed by the Sunday School Superintendent. Those who had achieved maximum points were duly presented with a medal, and in subsequent years bars to pin on the ribbon, it was not unusual to see medals with more than four bars proudly displayed at the prize-giving. On the second Sunday in July was the Anniversary of the opening of the chapel, and on the following Tuesday the Annual Sunday School Treat. Depending on which field had been recently mown the treat was held in either Anstey, Redland, or Britain field. The excited children met at the Sunday school in the early afternoon and marched to the field preceded by the banner and the Temperance Band. Games were played and races held while the band provided music. Teas were laid out on trestle tables beneath the elm trees, and later everyone marched back to the Sunday school where each child was given a bun from Franklins bakery.

In later years the venue for the Treat was normally the Cricket Field, but some time after the Second World War the Treat became an outing by coach, often to Wicksteed Park. The Temperance Band disbanded more than 60 years ago, and other village traditions and events have ceased, but for the Sunday school members The Treat is fondly remembered from the days when little things meant a lot.

There has been a steady decline in religious activities in the village during the last fifty years, and membership of the Methodist Church has reduced in common with other denominations. However, Methodism still exists in Waddesdon, and even after more than two hundred years the movement nurtured by William Goodman and his contemporaries has influence on everyday life in the village.

In place of the Sunday school classes there is now a thriving "Shell Club" providing the scholars with the same teaching and values, but in a modern style. The Women's Hour still meets at regular intervals. Periodically the Methodist and Church of England congregations join in combined services at either church.

In the latter part of the twentieth century much maintenance and improvement work has been carried out to the Chapel and old Sunday school. Internally the Chapel is now easier to heat and maintain and has toilets, whilst the old Sunday School has a new kitchen and floor. Both buildings are a credit to the members who have worked hard physically and otherwise to achieve their aims.

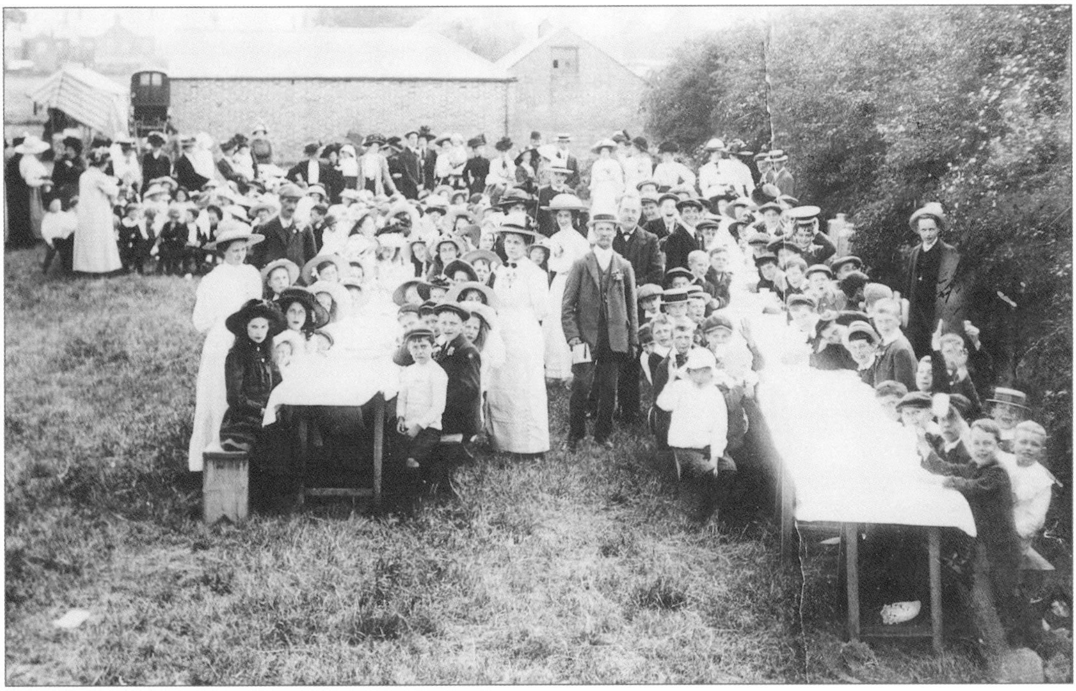

5.27 The Wesleyan Sunday School Treat circa 1910. On this occasion the treat is being held in Mr Joseph Taylor's field (Britain Field), and it is clear that a good time is being had by one and all. This is one of the few photographs from this period showing the young boys especially, " playing up" just like they do 90 years on. A rough head count indicates around 150 children in the photograph.

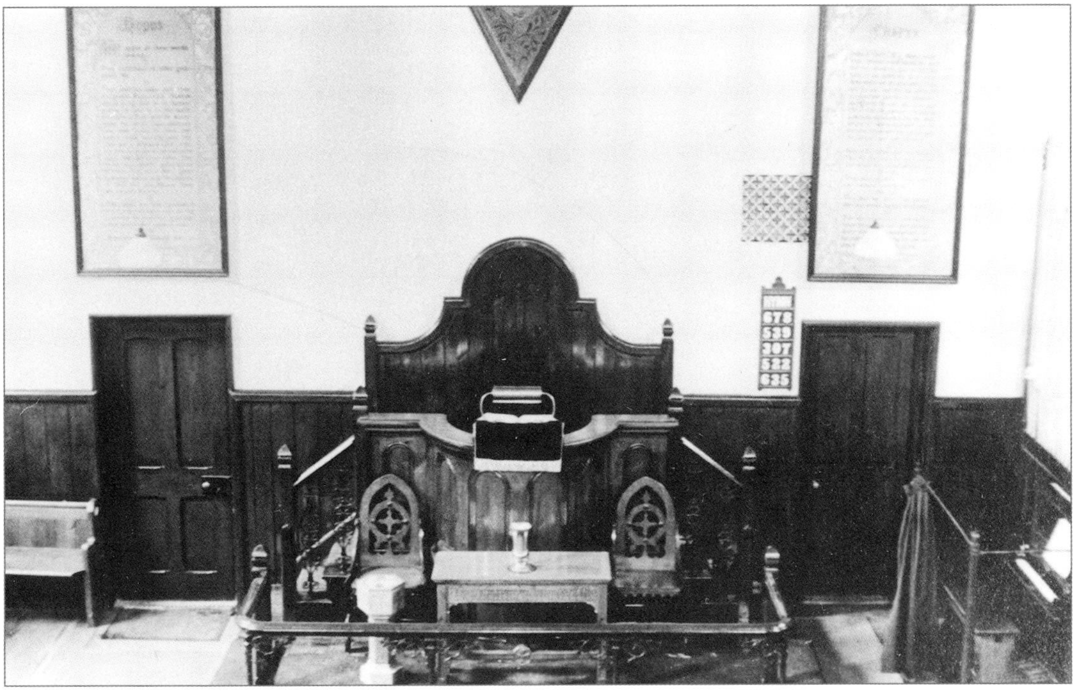

5.28 Inside the Wesleyan Chapel, a familiar scene to chapelgoers for nearly one hundred years, the simple but impressive pulpit with the Ten Commandments displayed on the rectangular frames, and the Lord's Prayer on the central diamond frame. Photographed from the gallery.

5.29 At the Sunday School Treat of 1927 in the Cricket Field, these little tots were given their tea on their own little picnic area. Standing with refreshments: Jack Atkins, Ruby Jones, Kitty Speed, Audrey Holland. Children at back L-R starting with the girl in white hat - Elsie Walker, Mary Cheshire, Ruby Saunders, Phyllis Martin, ----, Amy Evans, Harry Carter, Sid Carter, Ron Cripps, Ron Carr, Betty Harding, Hilda Cannon, Freda Richmond. Front row L-R starting with girl without hat - Rosie Biswell, Barbara Read, Elsie Sharp, Freda Atkins, Len Wood, Andy Speed, Alec Cripps, ---, Doris Scott, Outside the fence: On the fence twins Iris and Ivy Carr, Joy Carr (in pram) Mrs Annie Carr, Mrs Louisa Cripps, Mrs Harding.

5.30 The Methodist Chapel Sunday School Treat circa 1930, photographed at the Cricket Pavilion with the banner displayed behind. "United we stand divided we fall" is the motto on the banner. Back Row L-R; Arthur Cheshire,-----, Len Copcutt. Second Row; Gladys Saunders, Evelyn Scott, Josie Fowler, Joan Harding, Hilda Cannon. Third Row; Len Wood, Rose Evans, Bernard Holland, Mary Cheshire, Harry Carr, Elsie Sharp, Cyril Biswell, Ted Ewers, Doris Scott, Doris Rolfe. Forth Row; Nancy Carter, Amy Evans, Harry Carter, Ron Carr, Alec Cripps, Ron Cripps, Ron Cupcutt, Ken Rolfe, Norman Warren, Sid Carter, Betty Harding, Ruby Saunders. Front Row; Rex Cripps, -----, Joan Rolfe, Freda Atkins, Nellie Atkins, Lil Carter, Phylis Martin, Iris Carr, Ivy Carr, Renie Martin, Betty Biswell.

5.31 The Methodist Shell Group, the modern-day Sunday school continues to thrive in Waddesdon. This photograph records a gathering of members of the Waddesdon Group together with friends from Whitchurch (Wh), Princes Risborough (P.R) and Stone (S) circa 1998. At the back L-R ; Stuart Milton (S), Amy Milton (S), Back Row; Rebecca Booroff, Rebecca Inwood, Laura Bradford, -----, -----, Elaine Chambers, Kimberley Saunders, Livvy Meek, Rebecca Swatton, Rosie Short, Laura Bull, Laura Ashton, -----. Second Row; Tammy Addison, -----, Lucy Bradford, -----,-----, -----, -----, Rachel Adams. Third Row; Mark Goss (Wh), Lana Jay, Ashley Hollings, -----, -----, Nathaniel Redding (P.R), Lewis Ashton, Jacob Redding (P.R), Abbie Garrad. Front Row; Kimberley Hollings, Brian Brown (S), Megan Thorne, Lucy Inwood, Lynn Marlow, Gina White, Abby Meek, Lucy Coates.

5.32 Members of the Primitive Methodist Chapel about to leave on an outing circa 1905. On the right is the chapel, which was built in 1876 in the traditional style, including gallery. Despite the obvious dedication of the original members, it was not to last and the chapel closed down in the early 1920's. The building was sold to Mr Rhodes, who carried on a garage/engineering/radio sales business. It is now a vehicle repair and sales workshop (2000).

Baptists in Waddesdon

Local records prove that the parish had associations with the Baptist Church as long ago as 1679, for on the 30th of January that year, Thomas Monk's 50 Articles of Faith were signed by fifty-four residents of the Aylesbury area. Amongst that group of signatories was John Mountegue junior, Yeoman of Waddesdon, who was known to preach at his father's house, and that of William Alley's. John Mountegue was constable of Waddesdon in 1714, and chief constable of Ashendon in 1715. On the 12th July 1722 the dwelling of Edmund Dorrell in Wormstone was registered as a Baptist Meeting House.

After the enclosures of 1774 when the last of Waddesdon's common land was taken, there was a steady decline in living standards for many of the villagers. This was not unique, and it was not only the poor who were affected and were questioning the order of things. In Waddesdon and elsewhere there was an upsurge in popularity for non-conformists; in France, in somewhat different circumstances there was a revolution.

What became of John Mountegue, and his co-signatories and their descendants, or of Edmund Dorrell is not mentioned in records of Waddesdon. However more than 100 years on, the village was again formally associated with the Baptist Church when Mr W. Hitchcock, a farmer of Wormstone, applied to have his home "licensed for preaching". The first meeting of the "Particular Baptists" as they were known in this vicinity, was held there in February 1791. Exactly where the house stood is not known, but in those days the hamlet of Wormstone consisted of a number of dwellings and farms.

The following year (1792) The Waddesdon Hill Meeting House, as it was first known, was opened on the 8th August. Built by Mr Francis Cox, a farmer of Cranwell (his name is etched above the doorway), miles from the nearest community, this little chapel never had a local congregation in the normal sense. It was the first Baptists' chapel in the area, and drew its members from a radius of about 10 miles. They travelled, on foot mostly (although a horse mounting block still exits at the road verge), from Waddesdon, Aylesbury, Bierton, Long Crendon, Westcott and numerous hamlets in between.

In May 1795 Mr Henry Paice was ordained pastor of the Meeting House, and on the 19th July seven persons were baptised by him, the first baptisms at Waddesdon Hill. Membership numbers rose as people were attracted to the Baptist cause, and fell correspondingly as groups such as the Aylesbury members (in 1799) decided to build their own chapels. However a strong nucleus remained so that in 1809 the membership was 136.

Mr Francis Cox died in 1803, and in his will left the Meeting House and a legacy of £1000 to the Baptist cause. He also left £100, the interest of which to be distributed to the poor of the Baptist Church. These legacies were secured on mortgage of a farm at Owlswick.

In 1811, Mr H. Cox of Cranwell, "fitted up a room at Waddesdon for preaching", with the meetings allowed on Wednesday evenings. Soon afterwards the Waddesdon Baptists were allowed to hold "Lord's Day evening services" on two Sundays in each month at Wormstone, and the remaining Sundays at Waddesdon.

The Waddesdon Meeting Room was situated in an area, which is now wooded to the east of the exit to the Manor grounds. Many older villagers have heard of Chapel Lane, this started in the vicinity of the Square (War Memorial), ran behind the cottages in Bradfords Alley, roughly parallel to the main road, and led to the Baptist Meeting Room (Chapel), The Masons Arms public house, and several small cottages.

On the 16th of May 1826 Mr Henry Cox died, leaving the Waddesdon meeting room and two adjoining houses "for the benefit of the cause at Waddesdon Hill."

The Waddesdon chapel as it became known was extensively renovated in 1867, at a cost of over £100, and re-opened on the first Sabbath in August of that year. In 1870 the burial ground of the Waddesdon Hill Chapel was enclosed by a brick wall, which stands today, and in 1887 the chapel was renovated at a cost of £161-8s-0d, (£161.40)

On the 8th January 1888 Baron Ferdinand de Rothschild purchased part of Home Close off Frederick Street, and erected a chapel and outbuildings on the land. This new Baptist Chapel was opened on the 7th June 1888. The original chapel and two cottages in Chapel Lane at the rear of the National School were sold to the Baron in 1889 for £300. This sum was placed on the mortgage of two houses in Watford, the income to be used towards the new chapel expenses.

Over the following 60 years there was a dwindling of local Baptist membership and as a result of this the Frederick Street Chapel became redundant. On the 25th April 1951 it was auctioned and sold at the Bulls Head Hotel in Aylesbury. It was altered to become a dwelling place, and still retains many features from its original construction.

The Waddesdon Hill Chapel stands to this day. It is no longer used but preserved by the "Friends of Friendless Churches", who acquired the property "through the generosity of descendants of the original donor, and Buckinghamshire Historic Buildings Ltd" in 1986. Public access is possible through instructions on the exterior information board.

5.33 Waddesdon Hill Baptist Chapel photographed 1999. Built in 1792 by Francis Cox whose name is etched above the doorway. Local members of the Particular Baptists used it for almost 200 years. By 1986 it was no longer required for its original purpose, and was acquired by the "Friends of Friendless Churches". A notice at the entrance gives relevant information.

5.34 Waddesdon Baptist Chapel in Frederick Street photographed 2000. Mrs Jean Warr at the entrance to her home in the old chapel which was converted to living accommodation by Mrs C. Percival in the 1970's. The chapel was opened in 1888, having been constructed for Baron de Rothschild and transferred to the Baptists, in part exchange for the previous chapel which stood where woods now grow, not far from the War Memorial.

Section Six

Waddesdon and the Wars of the Twentieth Century

In this section we have endeavoured to record something of life in twentieth century Waddesdon during wartime, together with some details of villagers' experiences in the armed forces. Although this was the era of the photographer, in wartime, security was paramount, and as a result there are no photographs of the army camp, and fuel storage dump which transformed parts of Waddesdon Estate during the Second World War. However, we have described how the village responded to the demands of the conflicts, from the Boer War to the First and Second World Wars, and we show how those who lost their lives are remembered. We also wish to acknowledge the service of the post-1945 Nation Servicemen from the village, some of whom saw active service in colonial emergencies.

The Boer War, 1899-1902

At the start of the twentieth century Britain was at war with the Dutch South African settlers, known as Boers. Things had not gone as expected, the British Army with world-wide commitments was short of manpower, and consequently volunteer units of militia were used to bolster the forces in action.

The Royal Buckinghamshire Hussar Yeomanry Cavalry, more often known as "The Bucks Yeomanry", sent two companies to South Africa in 1900, under the command of Lord Chesham (statue in Aylesbury Market Square). They included three men from Waddesdon, Cyril Sims, Frederick Grace and Walter Roads, and were known as the "Hunting men of Bucks". These volunteers gained much respect for their horsemanship and endurance, as they trekked thousands of miles to bring the elusive Boers to battle. After serving for a year they were relieved by a fresh contingent, and arrived home in June 1901.

Waddesdon's contribution to the armed conflict also included the service of its regular soldiers, Pte. G. Biswell, Oxford and Bucks Light Infantry, and two who are listed on the Coombe Hill monument (Wendover): Ashby and Charlott.

The Boers were finally defeated in 1902 after a campaign which gained for Britain the control of South Africa's immense mineral wealth, but raised many questions regarding military tactical leadership and propriety in the treatment of a hostile civilian population.

6.1 This "Welcome Home" arch across Waddesdon High Street was constructed for June 17th 1901 to greet the Waddesdon group of militia-men who returned home after a tour of duty in South Africa. The Royal Buckinghamshire Hussars Yeomanry cavalry spent over a year in action against the Boers during the Second South African War (later known as the Boer War). The arch was rebuilt to welcome home Private George Biswell, a regular soldier in the Oxford and Bucks Light Infantry, who returned from South Africa in August 1901.

horses were taken out, and the brake conveying the three Yeomen drawn with ropes to a platform close to the Waddesdon Hall, when the following address was read by the Rector, who was Chairman of the Committee.

"To Lieutenant Cyril J. Sims, Sergeant Frederick Grace, and Trooper Walter Roads, of the 38th Company of the Imperial Yeomanry.

"We, the inhabitants of Waddesdon, here assembled, desire to offer you our most hearty congratulations on your happy return from the South African War.

"It is an intense satisfaction to us to know that by God's goodness you have been restored to your homes safe and sound after the dangers and toils of a campaign which has called forth more conspicuously than ever the highest qualities of the British soldier—discipline, courage, and endurance. The distance of the seat of war, the slender knowledge possessed of the recources of the enemy, and the character of the country itself, together with the existence of the fatal enteric fever, all these things might well make the South African War a very serious undertaking even for the professional soldier, whose business it is to uphold the honour of his Sovereign and his country in any quarter of the globe whither he may be sent. But, when it was found that the ranks of the professional soldier required reinforcement by the voluntary service of those who were engaged in more peaceful pursuits, we can never forget the instantaneous and enthusiastic response the invitation to fight for Queen and Country met with throughout the Empire. And this was the case not only here but also in our Colonies, who have in this war so nobly comented, with their blood and treasure, the bond which unites them to the Mother Country.

"It is therefore with justifiable pride that we in this place recall the fact that those I am addressing relinquished their own private interests, and postponed their family ties to the call of duty, and went forth fearlessly under the protection of

6.2 We reproduce here part of the article from the Waddesdon Deanery News for July 1901, describing the reception for Lieutenant Cyril J. Sims, Sergeant Frederick Grace and Trooper Walter Roads.

6.3 Army manoeuvres involving the regular forces and the Territorial Force comprised of all the old volunteer reserve militias, were held annually. For several years they were welcome to camp and exercise on the Waddesdon Estate. Here we see an officer studying a map near Grace's shop circa 1910, whilst a light field gun trundles past into Quainton Road.

6.4 Again mounted troops making their way past the Bell Inn, perhaps en-route to Westcott where units were regularly encamped in Great Butts (Westcott Big Field) circa 1910. Note the tea-garden of the Bell Inn alongside the footpath.

6.5 A column of field artillery travelling past the old Square (or Green), back towards Aylesbury, perhaps having completed their two weeks of manoeuvres. The locals could once again return to their normal life, secure in the knowledge that the army would deal with any foreseeable adversary. They could not know of the horrors awaiting these soldiers and many of the men-folk of the village, in the Great War only a few months away.

6.6 One of the "Old Contemptibles". Richard Wood was a regular soldier at the outbreak of war, serving in the Royal Field Artillery. He had met his wife Florence Annie Speed, a Waddesdon girl working "in service" at Boxmoor, and after the war they settled back here. Kaiser Wilhelm II of Germany had famously described the British Expeditionary Force as a "contemptible little army" and expected to easily and swiftly obliterate it under the weight of his immense forces at the outbreak of the war. Despite facing overwhelming odds and incurring high casualties, the B.E.F. immediately established a very high reputation in helping to stem the German advance, and its members proudly adopted the name "Old Contemptibles" for their post-war association, of which Dick was a leading local organiser. Here we have a portrait of Dick Wood in a sentimental setting, popular in this period, with an image of his wife superimposed, "in his thoughts", circa 1916. He served throughout the war despite being badly injured through gassing, which left him with bronchial problems for the rest of his life.

The First World War 1914-1918

For more than ten years prior to 1914, informed opinion had pointed at the growing military ambitions of the German Kaiser and his court, and warned that war in Europe seemed inevitable. On the 28th June 1914 the heir to the Austrian throne was assassinated in the Serbian capital of Sarajevo. There followed a complicated sequence of events that culminated in the German invasion of neutral Belgium, and as a result on the 4th August, a British Declaration of War on Germany.

During the following four and a quarter years as the conflict spread around the world, all the eligible manpower of the opposing nations was drawn into the fray. In Britain the whole population became employed in work supporting the war effort. For the first time women did "men's work" thus releasing men for the armed services. A few wartime photographs of women working in Waddesdon fields have survived, and one is included in this section.

Waddesdon was represented in all services and in most theatres of operations, but it was on the Western Front that most Waddesdonians served, and where the majority of those listed on the War Memorial fell.

The British Army of the First World War relied heavily upon units that were raised and recruited from specific areas. Typical of this tradition, especially in the early years of the war, were the Bucks Battalions of the Oxford and Buckinghamshire Light Infantry. The recruits included groups who had grown up together as neighbours, attended school, played, enlisted and trained together. They then went off to war, and too often died together. The horrendous numbers of casualties suffered by "Pals' Battalions", drawn from highly populated industrial areas, accentuated the folly of this recruiting ploy, and before the end of the war recruits were more likely to be dispersed to other regiments.

There is reticence on the part of most ex-servicemen to talk about the serious side of their war-time experience, and if one considers the appalling casualties of the Great War it must have been of supreme importance to the survivors, that the loss of so many mates should not in any way be trivialised. For this and probably other humane reasons, nothing, (citations apart) regarding Waddesdon servicemen has been recorded. The writer recalls three short stories from long-past chats with veterans: George (Nicky) Ewers was in the 2nd Bucks Battalion in France, and survived going "over the top" three times, including during the 3rd Battle of Ypres on 22nd August 1917, when six Waddesdon men were amongst the 120 killed. Forty years later he still could not believe how he survived, when so many of his mates all around him, had been mown down. Cecil Atkins joined the Northants Regiment at the age of 18 in 1917, and the following year on 21st March took part in a desperate action to stem the German advance near Amiens. When they withdrew after the action, the fit survivors of his battalion were able to crowd into one lorry. Fred Marriott was in the 1st Bucks Battalion hurriedly transferred from the Western Front in November 1917, to support our Italian allies, who were in danger of defeat by the Austrians. There on the mountainous slopes of northern Italy the battle-hardened British Army covered itself in glory, but inevitably yet more men fell. Amongst them was Fred's pal Robert Cripps of Waddesdon, who was fatally wounded when they were exposed to concentrated fire while advancing up a rocky mountain-side in May 1918.

As the war ground on into its fifth year, the end was undoubtedly in sight, for despite the Russian withdrawal from the conflict, the allies, now including fresh troops from the United States were advancing everywhere, and German society was in chaos. And so it was at 11.o'clock on the eleventh day of the eleventh month in 1918 that an Armistice came into force, the German armed forces were defeated in all but name, and the war-weary people could look back in sorrow at this "War to end all Wars".

Waddesdon's War Memorial records the names of sixty-two men of the village who were killed while serving in the armed services of this country. Their sacrifice was the price our community paid for the honour of our nation, and the freedom of untold millions across the world. Every family in the village was affected by this loss; most having close relatives amongst the fallen. They found comfort in the knowledge that this conflict, "The war to end all wars", would never be repeated. No country would again embark upon an aggressive course of action which could lead to World War!

6.7 Early in the war the sight of an aeroplane was still a rare occurrence, and in this photograph Albert Cherry chose to record the scene in Waddesdon High Street, as everyone strained to catch a glimpse of the aircraft. Circa 1914.

6.8 Ben Thorne enlisted in the R.A.S.C. (Royal Army Service Corp) shortly after the war started and served in France for nearly four years. Although he had worked as a baker for Mr P. Dodwell, he was soon involved in mechanical transport and never happier than when at the controls of a motor vehicle, in this case a Douglas combination.

6.9 As the war progressed and more and more men enlisted or were conscripted, many jobs had to be undertaken by womenfolk. In this view taken in the Old Park Meadow off Bicester Road, a group of ladies are removing kale or brussels' stems before the cultivation process commences once more in the spring. The conventions of the time dictated the work-wear of those concerned, they must have envied the men whose trousers and shirt sleeves were much more practical. Circa 1917.

6.10 Once again women doing work normally in the male province. On this occasion it is the Rectory glasshouse circa 1916, the girl on the step-ladder is Zilpha Fowler. Note the cast iron stove.

6.11 Gunner William Jones of the Royal Field Artillery. Killed in action on the 25th September 1917. See illustration 6.12.

Another Waddesdon young man, in the person of Gunner William Jones, R.F.A., son of Mr. and Mrs. James Jones, of Quainton Road, has made the supreme sacrifice, official intimation having this week been received by his parents that he was killed on the 25th September. Gunner Jones, who was 23 years of age, was formerly employed by Miss Alice de Rothschild on the Waddesdon Manor Estate, and joined up in March, 1915. He was drafted to France in June of the same year, and after being there for about eighteen months he was invalided home with trench fever. He was taken to a Glasgow Hospital in December, 1916, and remained there for about four months. After a short home leave he returned to the Front last May. The deceased soldier's Commanding Officer, writing to Mr. Jones, states:—"Your boy was hit in the temple by a bullet while going to assist some of his mates, who were in trouble, and killed outright. His Brigade has only recently come under my care, so I did not know him, but I hear on all hands that he was a most promising gunner, and his loss will be deeply felt by the Battery. Your loss will, of course, be a heavy one, but you will have the consolation of knowing that he died at his post while engaged on a dangerous piece of work for the assistance of some of his comrades. May God lighten the burden to you with this thought." Sergt. J. Robinson, in the course of a letter tendering the sincere sympathy of the other N.C.O's and men of the Battery, states: "A better lad I never wish to have. He was

6.12 The local newspaper cutting of November 3rd 1917, recording the death of Gunner William Jones. It is thought provoking to contemplate the task of Commanding Officers, who at the end of the day (probably), had to write words of condolence and comfort to the next-of-kin of so many young men. This article gives a particularly good example.

6.13 The Dolls Fair at the War Charities' Sale in the Waddesdon Hall. This is described in 6.14.

6.14 A cutting from the "Bucks Advertiser" of Saturday 3rd November 1917, describing some of the work by those on the "Home Front" to raise money for alleviation of the effects of the war. Interestingly it mentions the "rag-dollery" illustrated in photograph 6.13.

WADDESDON WAR CHARITIES SALE.

OPENING CEREMONY BY MISS ALICE DE ROTHSCHILD.

The picturesque village of Waddesdon was the scene of an interesting and successful patriotic function on Thursday, when the second annual sale of live stock, etc., in aid of war charities was gracefully opened by the lady bountiful of the district, Miss Alice de Rothschild. For many weeks past the local Committee, of which Mr. G. A. Sims is the Chairman, Miss Elsie Turnham and the Rev. L. O. Mott the Hon. Secretaries, and Mr. James Reid the Hon. Treasurer, had been working with rare energy to ensure the success of the effort, and their endeavours were splendidly backed up by every resident of the district. Those who could not help with money or with gifts of goods for the sale willingly gave of their labour, and the interior of Waddesdon Hall, where one part of the sale was held, was stacked with a bewildering variety of useful and fancy goods, as well as with provisions and produce from the Waddesdon allotments which had been generously given for the laudable objects in view. A most interesting feature was a stall devoted to dolls, the girls of the village having discovered in rag-dollery what may develop into a not unimportant local industry. The dolls had been fashioned under the supervision of Miss Elsie Turnham, dressed by lady friends, and their faces beautifully painted by Mr. T. Tindall Wildridge, who also rendered assistance in a variety of other ways. The fancy stall contained many articles which had been made by the ladies of the neighbourhood, and the vegetable stall was laden with a

TO THE EDITOR OF THE "BUCKS ADVERTISER."

DEAR SIR,—We have always looked upon horse chestnuts as of no commercial value and they have been the perquisite of the boys for the noble game of "Konkerers." This war has taught us many things, and amongst them that it is possible to extract a spirit from these chestnuts, which is of use in the production of high explosives. A ton of chestnuts saves ten hundredweight of barley, so that it is easy to see how valuable they are to the country.

Every chestnut is wanted, and it is hoped to secure at least 250,000 tons this year. I have been entrusted by the Bucks County War Agricultural Committee with the duty or organising their collection, and I want to enlist the help of the schoolboys in our County Schools, but I now appeal to all landowners, householders, and farmers who have chestnut trees to be good enough to have the chestnuts all picked up as they fall and reserve them. If they will kindly send me a postcard saying about what weight they have on hand, I will send them word what to do with them. I hope to have a local Receiving Agent in every village and district who will take in small quantities, but in the case of those who can collect a ton or more, I should then notify the Ministry of Munitions, who will send a motor lorry for them as soon as possible.

I hope that Bucks will do all it can to help provide "Surprise packets" for Fritz.

Yours truly,

COLIN TAYLOR.

Riverside,
Rickmansworth.
August 21st, 1917.

6.15 Raw materials not normally considered of economic consequence were harvested assiduously during the Great War, and one such in Waddesdon was horse-chestnuts. This newspaper cutting of September 1917 urges readers to collect "conkers" to help in the manufacture of explosives. No doubt Waddesdon was able to donate an impressive amount to be included in the National target of 250,000 tons!

THE GREAT WAR.

THE ROLL OF HONOUR.

KILLED IN ACTION.

LANCE-CORPORAL F. A. CUFF.

Mr. and Mrs. H. G. Cuff, of Quainton Road, Waddesdon, have received the following letter from Capt. Bowen informing them of the death of their son, Lance-Corporal Fred A. Cuff, Bucks Battalion, Oxford and Bucks Light Infantry, who was killed in action while in command of his Lewis Gun Section, during an attack by the Battalion on the enemy's positions:—"He was in my Company for a considerable time, and it is impossible to say how much I feel his loss. He was always cheery and intelligent, and by the splendid interest he took in his work encouraged his men in no small manner." The deceased soldier was 21 years of age, and previous to joining the Colours in June, 1915, he was employed as a baker by Messrs. Garner and Son, Aylesbury, and for several years by Franklin Bros., Waddesdon. He had been in France 16 months.

PRIVATES J. and A. EVANS.

Mr. and Mrs. E. Evans, of Quainton Road, Waddesdon, have had official information that their sons, Private John Evans, of the Machine Gun Corps, and Private Alfred Evans, of the Royal Warwick Regiment, who had previously been reported missing, are now believed to have been killed on the dates they were reported missing. Mr. and Mrs. Evans, with whom much sympathy is felt, have now had three sons killed in the war, and they have four others serving with the Colours.

6.16 Two entries in the Bucks Herald of 1st September 1917, recording the deaths of three Waddesdon men, two of them brothers and particularly poignant is the fact that previously a third brother had been killed. For reasons not apparent to the writer, the name of Fred A. Cuff does not feature on the Waddesdon War Memorial. Possibly his family moved from Waddesdon before the memorial was constructed.

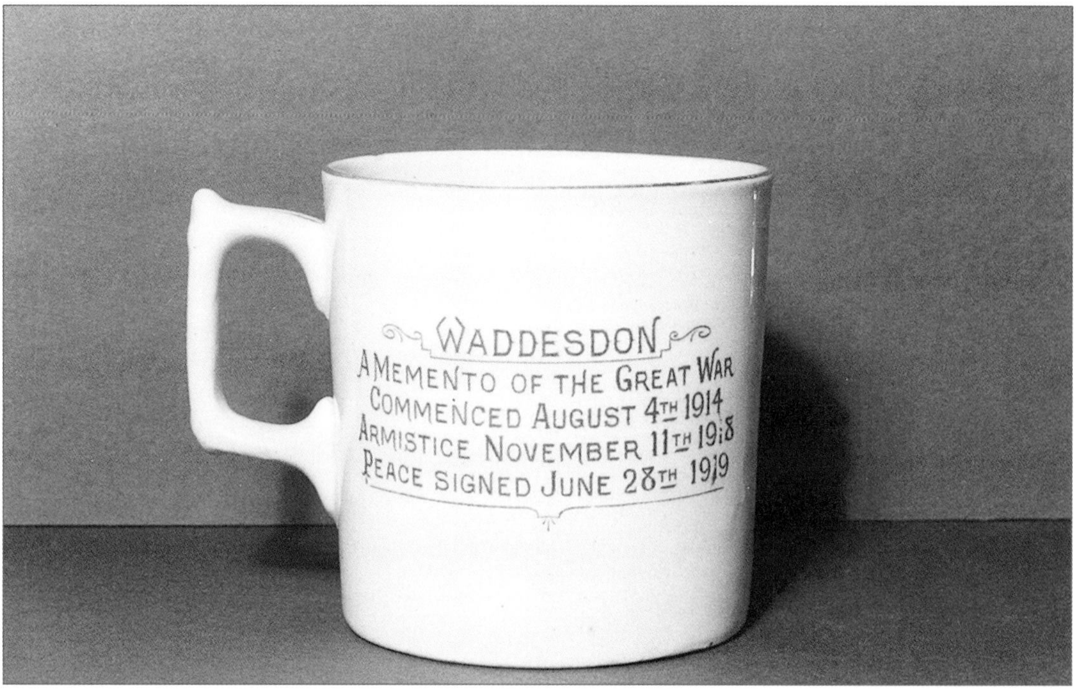

6.17 The end of hostilities was enacted "at the eleventh hour on the eleventh day, of the eleventh month" in the year 1918 under the terms of an armistice. The peace agreement was signed on June 28th 1919, and that is why numerous Great War memorials record the war period as 1914 -1919. Celebrations were held to mark the new "Peace", and in Waddesdon all the school children were presented with a suitably inscribed mug. A surviving mug from that occasion was photographed for this book in 2000.

6.18 A fund-raising scheme was organised in Waddesdon and the parish, for the purpose of constructing a suitable memorial to the 62 local men who had lost their lives in the Great War. The Memorial Cross was dedicated on Easter Sunday, 27th March 1921. This photograph shows the long ranks of ex-servicemen, part of the large crowd, the sadly depleted band (comprising the remnants of the Old Prize Band and the Silver Temperence Band), and the Memorial Cross swathed in the Union Flag, before the unveiling ceremony.

6.19 The newly dedicated Memorial Cross, 27th March 1921. Manufactured and erected by Hemms and Sons of Exeter this Cornish granite cross was later embellished by the addition of granite posts and iron chains around the base.

6.20 Prior to 1939, Services of Remembrance were held each year at 11a.m. on the 11th November. This photograph of the early 1930's show the village school children and a mainly female congregation attending the service, administered by the Rev. George Dixon in the Surplice, and assisted by his curate the Rev. Smith (in cloak).

6.21 & 6.21a On the east and west facing sides of the base of Waddesdon's War Memorial are inscribed a total of 62 names, the fallen of the village in the First World War. We have included these photographs and (6.60) the south facing side (Second World War), so that readers may scan them and maintain the promise of our predecessors "We Will Remember Them".

6.22 Joe Cripps in the dress uniform of the Oxford and Bucks Light Infantry, Territorial Army, Buckinghamshire Battalion. Circa 1938.

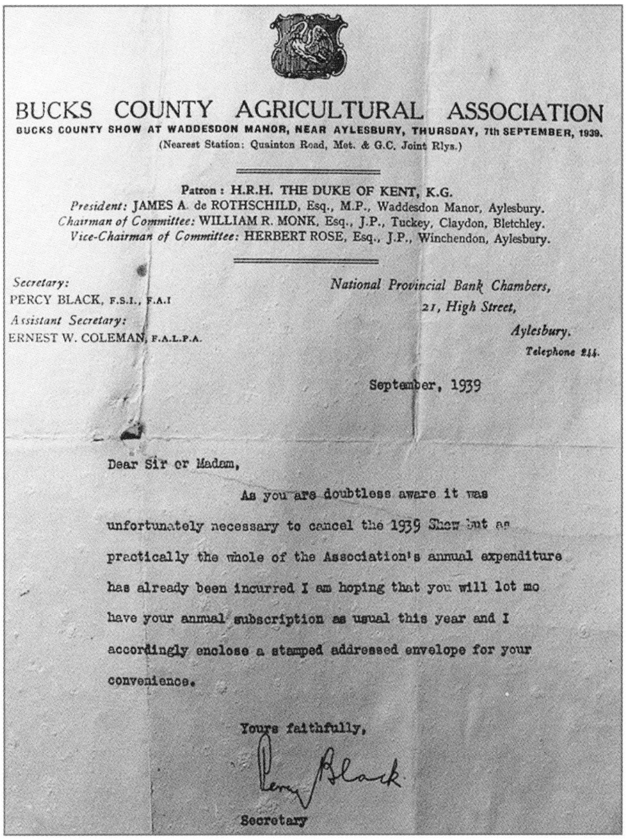

BUCKS COUNTY AGRICULTURAL ASSOCIATION

BUCKS COUNTY SHOW AT WADDESDON MANOR, NEAR AYLESBURY, THURSDAY, 7th SEPTEMBER, 1939.

(Nearest Station: Quainton Road, Met. & G.C. Joint Rlys.)

Patron: H.R.H. THE DUKE OF KENT, K.G.

President: JAMES A. de ROTHSCHILD, Esq., M.P., Waddesdon Manor, Aylesbury.

Chairman of Committee: WILLIAM R. MONK, Esq., J.P., Tuckey, Claydon, Bletchley.

Vice-Chairman of Committee: HERBERT ROSE, Esq., J.P., Winchendon, Aylesbury.

Secretary:
PERCY BLACK, F.S.I., F.A.I
Assistant Secretary:
ERNEST W. COLEMAN, F.A.L.P.A.

National Provincial Bank Chambers,
21, High Street,
Aylesbury.
Telephone 244.

September, 1939

Dear Sir or Madam,

As you are doubtless aware it was unfortunately necessary to cancel the 1939 Show but as practically the whole of the Association's annual expenditure has already been incurred I am hoping that you will lot mo have your annual subscription as usual this year and I accordingly enclose a stamped addressed envelope for your convenience.

Yours faithfully,

Percy Black

Secretary

6.23 In 1939 the Bucks County Show was arranged to be held at Waddesdon Manor on Thursday 7th September. With the Declaration of War on 3rd September the Show had to be cancelled, but as this letter illustrates, bills still had to be paid.

The Second World War, 1939-1945

When Nazi Germany invaded Poland on the 1st September 1939, Great Britain and France were treaty-bound to go to her aid, and by the evening of 3rd September both had declared war on Germany. This honourable, if desperate act was of negligible value to the doomed Polish nation, but it was an unavoidable first step which eventually led to the defeat of the Axis alliance. With the luxury of hindsight, we can see so clearly how utterly evil the Axis regimes were, and we are entitled to feel proud of the parts our communities played in the Second World War. The "diary" which follows lists the more noteworthy occurrences in the locality during the war.

1939

Spring: Households requested to state how many evacuees they could accommodate.
Easter: The Cedars' Boys arrived with Dr. and Mrs Steinhardt.
June: Waddesdon allocated 175 evacuees if and when Evacuation ordered.
Summer: Waddesdon Cricket Pavilion, the Water House at Upper Winchendon and the Bothy at the Gardens were requisitioned under the Government Evacuation Scheme.
August: Members of the Territorial Army (T.A) mobilised. (Those with allotments had already harvested their crops as far as was possible!)
War Declared 3rd September 1939
September: Evacuees from London arrive and were placed with local families.
100 small children and nursing staff settled-in at Waddesdon Manor.
Five Arrows Hotel Clubroom accommodated a class from a Roman Catholic girl's school and their teachers. They also used the Cricket Pavilion.
The Bothy was opened as a Maternity Home. The Bothy Boys were housed at the Manor where during air raid alerts; they helped carry the children to the cellars.
The Institute converted for free use by Aylesbury Rural District Council as a sick bay.
Selected privately owned commercial vehicles requisitioned for use by the Bucks Battalion.

1940

March: Many of the evacuees had returned home as "The Phoney War" had led to no attacks on London.
April: Letters from "Terriers" in France mentioned thanks for parcels from Waddesdon: Old Comrades Association, and "Jimmy" (de Rothschild). No action so far!
Girls of the Womens Land Army were employed locally to release male farm-workers for military service.
The racehorses at the Stud Farm were sent to Ireland for the duration of the war.
The Hospital Contributory Scheme received a total of £256-12s-11d from Waddesdon, Wescott and Upper Winchendon.
May/June: Bad news from France followed by Dunkirk evacuation and confusion as to the fate of Bucks Battalion.

The village learns of its first service-man killed in action.
Local Defence Volunteers' (later renamed Home Guard) contingent formed at Waddesdon.
July: Village Hall requisitioned as an Emergency Rest Centre.
A second Evacuation Programme brought a new wave of children to the village.
From now on men and women could be directed to employment in evacuated companies arriving in Aylesbury etc., including E.K.Cole (ECHO), International Alloys and Negretti and Zambra.
Prisoners of War, Italians and later Germans, held in camps at Quainton, Bicester and Hartwell were employed on local farms.
November: Incendiary bombs from German aircraft fell across Waddesdon, causing little damage.
The Waddesdon, Westcott and Over Winchendon Clothing Club had 119 member families; their combined savings amounted to £130-4s-5d. 111 members qualified for a bonus donated by Mr J. de Rothschild.

1941

The main drives and parkland of the Waddesdon Estate was requisitioned and prepared with all the constructions necessary for an Army open air fuel storage dump. Much of the work was done by Italian P.O.W's.
Airfields and other military installations were being built every few miles, receiving their complement of staff as soon as they were tenable
A land mine was dropped in The Slad by enemy aircraft, and a bomb in Humphrey's Ley. Big holes in the Waddesdon clay but fortunately no one was hurt.

1942

Westcott airfield completed, commissioned and commenced work as No.11 Operational Training Unit (O.T.U.). Some of the permanent staff had lodgings in the village.
Windmill Hill wood was completely felled to reduce dangers for low flying aircraft using the airfield. The tree trunks were removed for timber production, but the branches provided many villagers with valuable fuel to supplement their precious coal ration.
Soldiers and airmen from the local camps were now a familiar sight, using the local pubs and the canteen in the Sunday School-room of the Methodist Chapel.
Home Guard and Fire and Rescue drills held every Wednesday evening and Sunday morning at the Estate Yard.
Air Raid Protection (A.R.P.) training held at the Frederick Street Room.

1943/1944

Huge quantities of petrol and oil in cans and drums ferried from Quainton Station into the Dump by a stream of lorries, and there stacked ready for rapid use.
The Village Hall no longer required for evacuees, became available for "normal use", and

functions such as dances, concerts and fund raising sales held regularly.
Crashes of aircraft from nearby training and operational airfields were occurring with dreadful frequency. One crashed into trees on Lodge Hill, and as a result obstruction lights were installed on and around the Manor for use when appropriate.
Servicemen (G.I.s) of the United States armed forces, many of them black, became a common sight as they poured through the village in endless convoys of massive lorries. Any G.I to be seen on the streets were soon tailed by youngsters asking "Any Gum Chum?" Usually their cheek was good-naturedly rewarded with a stick of American chewing gum, a real treat for children starved of such luxuries.
Military manoeuvres seemed to be continuous with armoured vehicles and aircraft providing plenty of noisy distractions. Over-night, fields became parking areas for tanks and other military vehicles. Troops made camp, slept, ate and drank, and then just as suddenly they were gone!
The Five Arrows Hotel Club Room and part of the Ladies' toilet room was requisitioned for War Department ("W.D.") use in April 1944.
"D Day", 6th June 1944
The Dump busy as the stocks of petrol and oil are transported away to fuel the innumerable engines of war.
Village life was quieter now but everyone perhaps more anxious about the Allies' progress across the world. The end may have been in sight, but would all our loved ones survive?

1945

Despite some setbacks and a sustained aerial attack on southern England by V.1 and V.2's it was obvious the war in Europe was nearing its end. Newspapers were scanned avidly.
Soon the Allies were on German soil, and before long horrific stories of Concentration Camps were published. Troops including local men, hardened by years of warfare were horrified by what they found, and those of us back home were suddenly faced with examples of human debasement of which we had no inkling, (although it transpired the "Authorities" had been aware of the "Final Solution" for several years).
The Sick Bay at the Institute, which had been unused for some months, was closed down.
Meanwhile in the Far East, where the Japanese were also being pushed back, stories of their inhuman treatment of Prisoners of War and "liberated" natives, confirmed in people's minds the righteousness of the Allied cause, and the need to bring the war to a swift end.
R.A.F Westcott became a focus of interest as fleets of aircraft returned with thousands of British servicemen who had been liberated from Prisoner of War camps in Germany.
Cessation of Hostilities in Europe, 8th May 1945
Troops of the Free Polish Army move in to the "Camp" at Wormstone.
The "Five Arrows" Clubroom etc handed back for normal use.
Victory over Japan (agreed 15th August and surrender officially signed 2nd September 1945)

6.24 Edward (Ted) Atkins aged 29, a member of the Bucks Battalion, Oxford and Bucks Light Infantry photographed here with his wife Margaret and sons Barry aged two and Lionel, less than one year old in late 1939. Ted had been one of the pre-war Waddesdon contingent of "Terriers" mobilised in the Bucks Battalion in August 1939, and subsequently within the B.E.F. in France. The battle to protect the Dunkirk evacuation at Hazebrouck cost Ted his life, he was killed on 27th May 1940, the first fatal casualty of the war, from Waddesdon. It is difficult to imagine the task facing the young recently widowed Margaret Atkins, and the fact we find it difficult is perhaps some measure of the debt we owe to those who sacrificed so much.

6.25 Members of the Bucks Battalion Band after mobilisation in 1939. At the centre, with the Tenor Horn is Harry Carr, a peacetime member of the Waddesdon Old Prize Band. As part of the B.E.F. on the Franco-Belgian border at the village of Wahagnies, the Bucks were ordered to move swiftly into Belgium on May 10th 1940. Un-essential equipment had to be left behind, and the band instruments were buried near a farm for safe keeping. Within a few days the Allies were in retreat, and the B.E.F. was heading for evacuation at Dunkirk to avoid annihilation. Band and instruments were far from everyone's mind for the time being. Due to his badly blistered feet Harry Carr was put on a lorry that delivered him outside Dunkirk, and so he missed the rearguard action at Hazebrouck, and was one of the 337,000 Allied troops evacuated. Four and a half years later Wahagnies had been liberated, and a squad of Bucks men under Sergeant Stan Fowler returned there, retrieved the instruments, and shortly afterwards had them back in working order!

"St Omer"

The Bucks battalion was mainly drawn from the area of the county north of High Wycombe. The Battalion Band included members of Waddesdon Old Prize Band, Joe Cripps, Stan Fowler and Harry Carr.

General Mobilisation was ordered in late August 1939, and before war was declared on September 3rd, local communities had witnessed the departure of their "Terriers", who were soon undergoing intensive military training at Newbury racecourse. On the 17th January 1940 the battalion embarked for France, on to the Franco-Belgian border, for yet more training, and preparations for defence.

Germany invaded neutral Belgium and Holland on May 10th, and the Allies were suddenly exposed to threats from unexpected quarters. The prepared positions were vacated and the "Bucks" sent into Belgium to try to stem the German advance. As with most of the British Expeditionary Force, (B.E.F.) the Bucks then spent the next two weeks with practically no sleep, little food, lots of digging defensive positions, a series of withdrawals and very little contact with the enemy. On the 24th May the battalion was loaded onto lorries for transporting to "rest billets in Calais". Orders were suddenly changed and the eventual destination was Hazebrouck. In the confusion some of the vehicles did not arrive.

A massive evacuation was being planned and the "Bucks" were given the task of guarding part of the flank and rear of the B.E.F. as it fell back towards Dunkirk. Bolstered by a few artillery units and a miscellaneous bunch of soldiers who had arrived in Hazebrouck by chance, the weary "Bucks" prepared to face the might of the German Army. They had little ammunition, little food, no tanks, no mines and no barbed wire, whilst the front to be held was too long for the number of defenders. However throughout the next day tremendous efforts were made to prepare company positions, as news came through that the mass evacuation was under way. During the 27th May a full scale assault was launched by enemy air and ground forces and all the attacks were repulsed, but losses were heavy. Companies were cut off and survivors gathered at the Headquarters building, a convent, where the wounded were placed in the cellars.

The fighting continued around the convent throughout the 28th May, enemy tanks and machine guns were firing at point-blank range, while mortar bombs rained down on the remaining defenders. As ammunition ran short, it was decided to continue the fight until nightfall then let the fit men try to escape. Joe Cripps, a member of H.Q. Company was with a squad of men who prepared to break out by removing some bricks, then waited for dusk when they might slip out unseen. Unfortunately they had been observed, and when Joe led out the men a burst of machine gun fire cut across his legs almost severing one just below the knee. His nephew Frank Knight dragged him back; miraculously the German stopped firing and Joe was carried down into the cellar.

The main building was on fire and collapsed, and although the fit men rallied in the garden before making off, a large number were captured. Joe Cripps was lucky, for some wounded in the cellar were killed by falling debris, but he was dug out and taken to the Convent of St.Omer where a French doctor amputated his leg. The nuns nursed him back to health, and consequently he endured more than three years of P.O.W. confinement, before repatriation at the end of 1943.

His lasting gratitude to the nuns is displayed by the name over the doorway to the bungalow he built in Baker Street - "St Omer".

Over 200 Bucks' officers and men eventually made it back to Great Britain, forming the nucleus of a restored Battalion which continued to the end of the war.

6.26 Betty Harding joined the Woman's Land Army in 1940 and worked at the Waddesdon Gardens throughout the war - a home posting! Recruits were issued with a uniform including shoes, wellington boots, breeches, shirts, sweaters and a hat, and no forfeiture of clothing coupons!

6.27 Arthur (Happy) Gurney shown here at centre of photograph in Antwerp during the hard winter of 1944/45. A driver with the Royal Army Service Corp he landed at Mulberry Harbour, Arromanches on "D" Day + 17 (23rd June 1944), and was continuously engaged in ferrying supplies, mainly at night, to forward positions until the war ended. Arthur's wife had tragically died in childbirth in early 1944, leaving him with the task of raising his family whilst still away in the army. Fortunately, relatives in Waddesdon and Upper Winchendon rallied around, and the children were given good homes until Arthur was demobbed. Meanwhile in the Netherlands immediately after the war the R.A.S.C were involved in distributing food to the starving civilian population. Happily it was there that Arthur met the Dutch girl, who eventually came to Waddesdon to become his wife.

6.28 Len Wood shown here in the uniform of the Cameronians, had originally "joined up" in the Royal Artillery, and been employed on a Searchlight unit in 1941. He was transferred to the infantry, and was a member of the 15th Scottish Division fighting in Holland during 1944. A machine-gun bullet through his mouth was followed by extensive surgery to repair the damage, leaving an indelible reminder of the less than glamorous side of the war. In the years following the war Len combined his family life with an active involvement in village organisations and particularly rose growing to the highest standards.

6.29 Len Thorne "joined up" in the (R.A.F.V.R.) Royal Air Force Volunteer Reserve in September 1939, and commenced training in April 1940. He gained his "wings" in 1941 and was initially posted to 602 City of Glasgow Squadron stationed at Drem, and later at Kenley. Len progressed from Flight Sergeant to Flight Lieutenant during the war, and was twice "Mentioned in Dispatches". A fascinating aspect of his service at Duxford was on evaluation trials of captured enemy aircraft. In this photograph he is leaning against an authentic Messerchmitt Bf 109, which had been captured after a forced landing on Malta. Now in R.A.F colours the aeroplane was damaged after Len made a crash landing at R.A.F Wittering. Photographed late 1944.

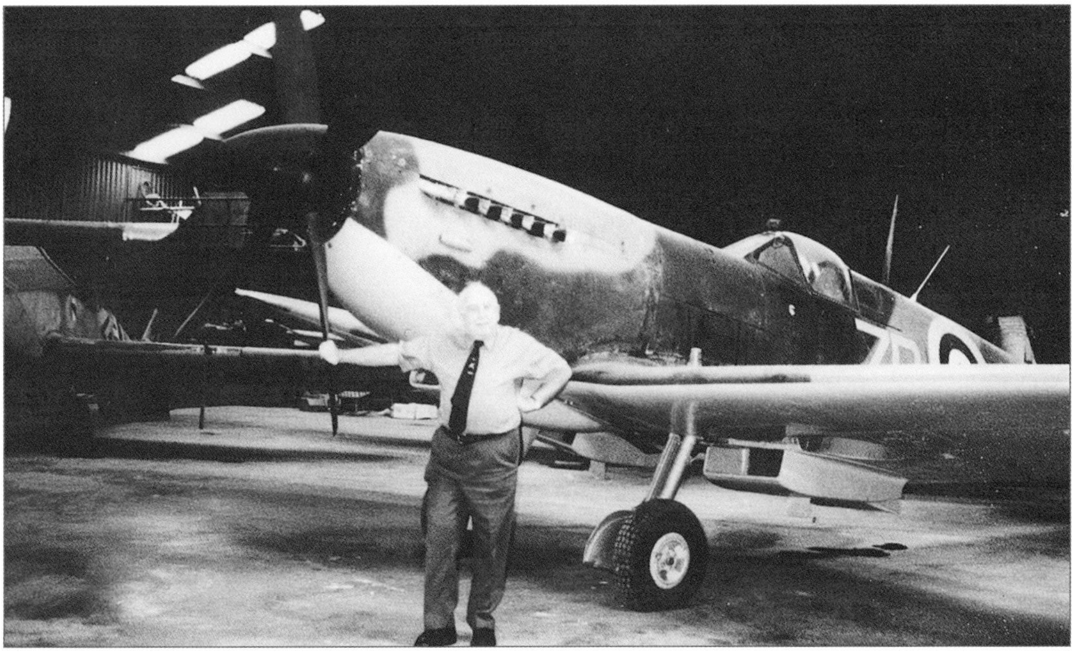

6.30 In 1944 Len Thorne piloted Spitfire Mk 9, MH 415 in a series of trials to evaluate the aircraft in Ground Attack role. For this purpose two wing-borne 250lb bombs and one fuselage-supported 500lb bomb were carried. Len met up with the Spitfire once more in the late 1990's when he made a trip to America, and was photographed with it at a private collection there. At the age of 80 Len still holds his pilot's licence and sometimes flies over Waddesdon from his home in Worcestershire. He maintains his interest in his home village in his regular visits to relations still residing here.

Year 1941 Month	Date	Aircraft Type	Aircraft No.	Pilot, or 1st Pilot	2nd Pilot, Pupil or Passenger	DUTY (Including Results and Remarks)
-	-	—	-	—	—	— Totals Brought Forward
AUG	2nd	SPITFIRE	P-8791	SELF	—	AIR TEST, CANNON TEST. 34,500'
"	2nd	SPITFIRE	P-8791	SELF	—	CANNON TEST
"	2	SPITFIRE	W-3638	SELF	—	AIR TEST, CANNON TEST. 35,100'
"	5	SPITFIRE	P-8423	SELF	—	BOMBER ESCORT.
"	7	SPITFIRE	P-8791	SELF	—	OPERATIONAL SWEEP.
"	7	SPITFIRE	P-8799	SELF	—	GUN & AIR TEST.
"	7	SPITFIRE	P-8799	SELF	—	GUN TEST

Single-Engine Aircraft Day Dual (1)	Single-Engine Aircraft Day Pilot (2)	Single-Engine Aircraft Night Dual (3)	Single-Engine Aircraft Night Pilot (4)	Multi-Engine Aircraft Day Dual (5)	Multi-Engine Aircraft Day 1st Pilot (6)	Multi-Engine Aircraft Day 2nd Pilot (7)	Multi-Engine Aircraft Night Dual (8)	Multi-Engine Aircraft Night 1st Pilot (9)	Multi-Engine Aircraft Night 2nd Pilot (10)	Passenger (11)	Instr/Cloud Flying [Incl. in cols. (1) to (10)] Dual (12)	Instr/Cloud Flying [Incl. in cols. (1) to (10)] Pilot (13)
55-25	162-25	3-30	7-40							3-30	9-35	7-40
	1-10											
	-40											
	1-05											
	1-25											
	1-35	FLEW AS RED 4. BOMBER ESCORT COVER TO STARBOARD OF 6 BLENHEIMS. WHEN 10 MILES WEST OF ST. OMER RED SECTION DIVED ON BY 4 109 E's. W/C. KENT ATTACKED 1st EA. & FOLLOWED IT DOWN. I ATTACKED 2nd EA. FIRING SHORT BURST FROM ASTERN & BELOW. E.A. TURNED ONTO BACK & WENT DOWN VERTICALLY, LEAVING TRAIL OF WHITE SMOKE. PROBABLY DESTROYED. SGT. GARDEN ATTACKED 3rd. EA. FIRING SHORT BURST. EA. DAMAGED. P/O THORNTON MISSING. 1. E.A. CONFIRMED AS DESTROYED										
	-35											
	-40											

6.31 Extracted from Len Thorne's Log Book, this cutting records the first of Len's five "kills" (Two confirmed, three probables). The date was 7th August 1941, when Len was a member of 602 Squadron at Dram in Scotland, and he was piloting Spitfire P- 8791 in an "operational sweep".

6.32 Oliver Franklin, shown here kneeling on the left with a group of American soldiers at Chartres in France, September 1944, was a member of G.H.Q. Liaison Regiment. For the duration of the war, and beyond, this unpublicised organisation performed a critical intelligence gathering and distribution role under its radio code-name of "Phantom". Although only 350 strong, it took part in every major campaign after 1939 and had units attached to the American armies in Europe. Oliver was attached to the American army in North Africa in 1943, and in France in 1944/5. Oliver recommenced his interest in playing cricket for Waddesdon after the war, and with his brother John, became well known and respected in the game throughout the locality.

6.33 George Blake was called up in February 1941, and drafted to the Duke of Cornwall's Light Infantry. In this photograph George is shown third from left, at a rest area just outside Rome, during the Italian campaign in January 1945. He was demobbed in 1946, and became well known in the village as a small-holder, jobbing agricultural contractor, and church-man.

6.34 Peggy Lines, daughter of the Waddesdon Policeman, like many other young women during the war had the choice of "joining up" or being directed to factory work. She chose to join the Auxiliary Territorial Service (A.T.S.), thereby taking on work which previously had been carried out by male soldiers. She joined the A.T.S. in 1943 and was trained on the operation of searchlight batteries. After a few weeks she was posted to South Mimms as a plotter on a search light site, carrying out all the operational duties necessary, including night-guard. Towards the end of the war Peggy, her crew and mobile search-light battery was moved to Herne Hill, South London to not only search and plot the course of aircraft, V.1s (Doodlebugs), and the new flying bombs (V.2) but to illuminate the site where they impacted and caused such massive destruction - an eye -opener to the horrors of this type of weapon. Peggy was demobbed in 1945.

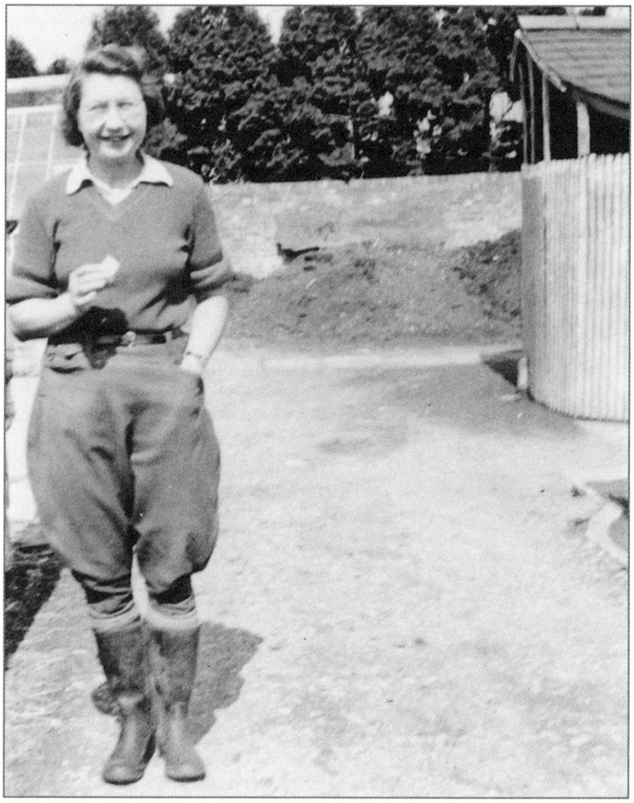

6.35 Joyce Clark spent most of the war in the office of a factory manufacturing uniforms in Nottingham, but then joined the Land Army, and after a spell at Taplow came to Waddesdon Gardens, and lived in the Bothy. It was here she met her future husband Jim Wicks.

6.36 Ken Rolfe was "called up" at the age of 18 in 1943, joined the Royal Navy Fleet Air Arm, and was trained as an Air Mechanic (Ordnance). He served with the Eastern Fleet on H.M.S. Unicorn, an aircraft repair ship, and was at the Battle of Okinawa in 1945. Upon "demob" Ken returned to the building trade as a bricklayer, and resumed his hobby as a Waddesdon footballer, mirroring the sporting exploits of his father and other members of the Rolfe family. In the year 2000 he still maintains contact with his old shipmates of H.M.S. Unicorn.

6.37 V.E.Day (Victory in Europe), May 3rd 1945. Harry Carr pictured here offering a toast and sporting an Orange (the national colour of the Netherlands) handkerchief in the Dutch town of Delft. The handkerchief was presented to him by a lady in Delft. With the surrender of Germany on this day, the allies had allocated units, ('T' Force), to secure sensitive installations, and to prevent revenge attacks on enemy troops. The Bucks Battalion were part of 'T' Force, and on May 3rd a contingent was en-route to Den Helder submarine base and passing through Delft. The Mayor and Corporation, and citizens were awaiting their official Liberation by the Canadian army, and mistook the Bucks Battalion for the vanguard of the parade. To the bewilderment of the soldiers, they were feted and given an official welcome. After a while they hurriedly drank up, made their excuses and left, as in the distance could be heard the approaching tanks and vehicles of the official Liberators. 50 Years on, Harry and his wife Joyce enjoyed the hospitality of the City of Delft, and he was able to enlighten them on the picture taken by the local photographer just before the official Liberation Ceremony. The handkerchief has been retained to this day.

6.38 Percy (Tucker) George photographed with his fiancée Ivy (Chalkie) in 1943. Tucker was "called up" in 1941 and after "square bashing" at Blackpool, was posted for training in Air / Sea Rescue. In 1943 he was stationed at Gorleston on the east coast, carrying out rescue operations in the North Sea, but by the end of that year was posted to the far east, India. There he was employed at various coastal stations until the war ended, and subsequently was involved in ferrying P.O.W.s as the infamous camps were liberated. Chalkie was posted to R.A.F. Westcott in 1942 as a member of the Women's Auxiliary Air Force (W.A.A.F.). She was employed in packing safety equipment for air-crews, parachutes, dinghies, etc. Chalkie recalls how the service-men and women at Westcott would walk to Waddesdon for dances in the Village hall, to visit pubs or the canteen at the Methodist Sunday School building. At Hall Farm, Mrs Cox sold teas to passers-by, and in Waddesdon those with bicycles could park them at Jimmy Jones's Garage, before catching the bus to Aylesbury, (last bus back was at 8.30pm!).

6.39 "Chalkie" and "Tucker" were married on Tucker's return from the Far East in 1946. Here they are shown after the ceremony in the garden of the family home down Bicester Hill.

Royal Air Force Westcott

No 11 Operational Training Unit transferred from Bassingbourne, to the newly constructed Royal Air Force station at Westcott, and its satellite airfield at Oakley in September 1942, and remained there until it disbanded in August 1945. No 11 O.T.U. had the distinction of training almost all the New Zealand air crews who joined Bomber Command, and the connection with that country is perpetuated in the design of the Unit badge which contains two Maori spears. Individuals came to Westcott for training, and eventual grouping into Air Crews of Pilots, Navigators, Bomb Aimers, Wireless Operators, Air Gunners and Flight Engineers.

The course lasted for approximately 10 weeks, at the end of which the crews moved on to Heavy Conversion Units, leaving the twin engined Wellington bombers at Westcott, for crew conversion to four engined Stirlings or Lancasters. Contrary to local legend, the station was never used operationally for bombing raids, but did take part in "Nickel" operations (leaflet dropping on enemy occupied cities). More frequently the airfield was used in emergency, by operational aircraft diverted from their home airfield, sometimes these "Cuckoos" (birds from another nest) landed whilst still "bombed up", and on some occasions this resulted in fatal accidents. One such is commemorated in a memorial window in Westcott Church - Flight Lieutenant E.C.Bulmer.

Near the end of the war R.A.F. Westcott received liberated British Prisoners of War. Around 53,000 P.O.W's, some of whom were seen to kiss British soil, were flown into Westcott and Oakley by every conceivable aircraft, from Mosquitoes to Lancasters. On 10th May 228 aircraft landed with their 5,418 happy passengers. On June 3rd Liberator aircraft landed bringing the final P.O.W,s from Italy. This was a time of exceptional effort by all concerned, including local members of the Women's Voluntary Service, (now W.R.V.S). They were organised to serve teas and form sewing parties to alter new uniforms and sew on the stripes, medal ribbons, regimental flashes, and other insignia as appropriate. The ex-P.O.W's were de-loused and kitted out in new uniforms, to ensure they were smartly turned out for their homecoming.

A steady flow of lorries passed along the Akeman Street, en-route for Aylesbury and thence to Beaconsfield, for P.O.W de-briefing etc. As they passed through Waddesdon they were cheered by the children and greeted with the cry of "Souvenirs!", and the response was invariably a few foreign coins or recently issued sweets. The coins were avidly collected and in some cases hoarded to the present day, the sweets were quickly consumed!.

No 11 O.T.U. disbanded on 3rd August 1945. It had produced 1,157 trained bomber crews from 121 courses, of which 62 were held at Westcott. The satellite station at Oakley was returned to mainly agricultural use, whilst the Westcott main base was put on a "Care and Maintenance" basis. The approximately 2,000 service-men and women who had staffed the Unit were demobbed or transferred. In Westcott churchyard lie the bodies of just nine of the dozens of young men who died in flying accidents in and around Westcott and Oakley in the three years of the existence of R.A.F. Westcott.

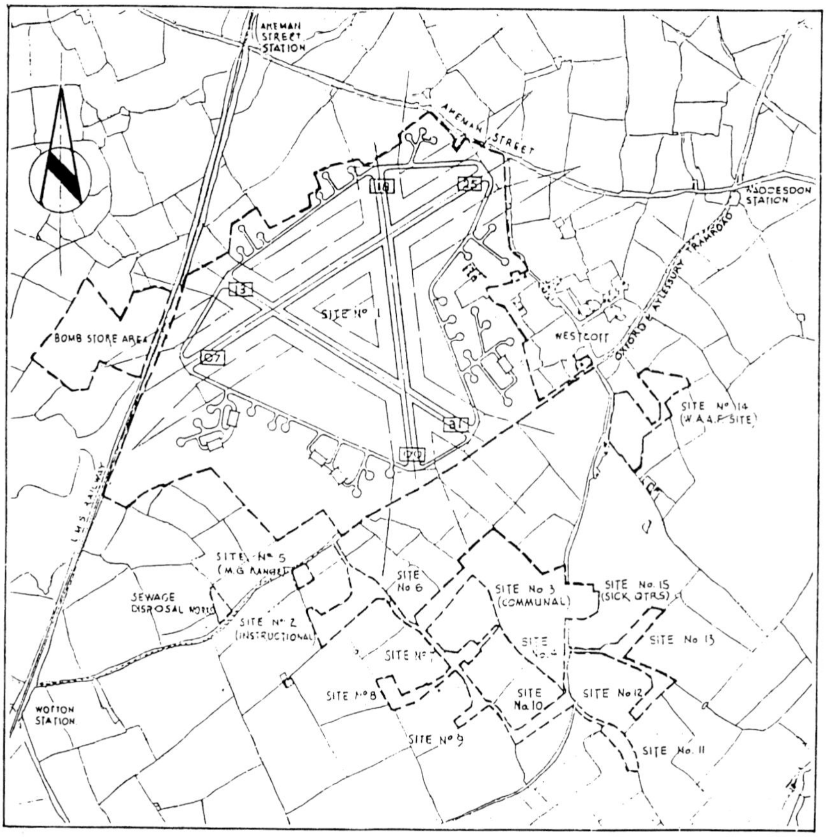

Site plan of RAF Westcott

6.40 This plan is included to show the extent of the R.A.F. Westcott site, and to give just a small glimpse of the tremendous effort made by this nation in the early 1940's when the "chips were really down". This amount of civil engineering was by no means rare at the multitude of military installations across war-time Britain.

6.41 Harold Goss and his three brothers all served in the armed forces during the war. Joe was in the R.A.F., Steve was in the Army whilst Harold and Eric were in the R.N. Harold joined up in 1941 and was posted to the Royal Naval Patrol Service (RNPS) at Lowestoft. This arm of the Royal Navy was essentially formed from requisitioned fishing vessels and crewed by fishermen reservists. Known affectionately as "Harry Tate's Navy" this organisation was highly respected for their bravery and seamanship. They went out in all weathers to sweep enemy mines from allied sea routes, and were also used to combat U-Boat attacks on convoys. Although RNPS craft were active across the world, Harold's service was confined to the coastal waters of Great Britain.

Note; Harry Tate was a comedian of the pre-war years whose act included an old motor-car which progressively fell apart during the performance.

6.42 Eric Goss joined the Fleet Air Arm in 1942 and was trained as an Air Mechanic on Beaufighters and Defiants, (neither carrier-borne aircraft). Consequently all his service was spent at Naval Air Stations, first in Egypt and later in South Africa. This photograph shows Eric (left) and a crew-mate on the wing of a Martlet aircraft in South Africa in 1945.

6.43 Robert (Bob) Snelling, the son of Waddesdon's pre-war police sergeant, took part in the airborne assault to capture the bridge at Arnhem in Holland. One of the most famous actions of the war, and thanks partly to the success of the film "A Bridge too Far", is still well known by modern generations. It is also known for the large numbers of casualties inflicted on the British and Polish Airborne troops during the nine days from September 17th to 26th 1944. Sadly Bob Snelling was one of these, he died of his wounds on September 21st 1944. His grave is in the military cemetery at Oosterbeek, Arnhem, which along with others in the Netherlands and many other countries, is lovingly maintained by the Commonwealth War Graves Commission. (See photograph 6.61).

6.44 Waddesdon Home Guard unit-comprising men from Westcott, Upper Winchendon and Waddesdon. circa 1944. Standing L to R. Ralph (Chunnel) Saunders, ------- ,Sid Brown, Len Gurney, Harry Turner, Bill Caterer Jnr, Percy Hicks, Harold Radwell, George Fowler, Tom Goss,------, Eddie Barnett,------, G.Atkins, Tom Mortimore, Pat Radwell, Ralph Saunders, Dick Schneider, Bert Pittam, Aubrey Hicks, Bill Holloway, Will Franks, Wally Mason,------, Graham Whitlock, George Reid, Will Cowley, Jim Wicks,-------, Jock Millar, Cecil Burgess, S.Watkin, Arthur Cowley,-------.Seated. R.Tissot, William Seckington, ------, Arthur Hicks, Bill Caterer Snr, Frank Cripps, Jack Rolfe, W. Jerrams, Bill Reynolds, Cecil Atkins, Cyril Gurney, Jack Cox, Sid Walker, Frank Saunders, T. Clark.

WADDESDON HOME GUARD

The Home guard or Local Defence Volunteers, as it was initially called, was formed in May 1940 and at the outset consisted of male volunteers aged between 17 and 65 years. They were either too old or too young for conscription, unfit for the services, or in reserved occupations. After January 1942 any man aged 18 to 51 could be directed into the Home Guard, and be subject to fines and imprisonment for not attending training drills.

In time all personnel were issued with uniforms, rifles and ammunition and with the threat of invasion, full military exercises were carried out despite the men carrying on their full time employment. Key observation posts were also constructed and manned every night as look-outs for the possible landing of German paratroops, and in the case of the Upper Winchendon section a small hut was constructed in the orchard of Mr Harvey's Model Farm, from where a good view was to be had of the Chiltern Hills. The hut was constructed from the wooden boards that were used to protect the statues at Waddesdon Manor during the winter months. It had a bed inside and was manned by three men every night, on a rota of two men off and one on. (After the war it was used as a Chicken House). Waddesdon's look-out was on top of the Manor, and the H.Q. was in the estate yard in Queen Street, as were the parade areas and armoury. Parades were held mainly on Sundays and Wednesdays but the men were on call at all times, day and night.

The rifle range of some 300 yards (277 metres) was in "The Linces" at Upper Winchendon, and we believe that some of the new members were initially not too good with their newly acquired rifles, as bullets were often found in and beyond the garden of Mr Harry Dormer and his son, who lived in an old cottage just over the brow of the hill. Harry Dormer would often complain to the Officer or N.C.O in charge that he was afraid to work in his vegetable garden during rifle practice for fear of being shot. Another precaution taken against the threat of invasion at Upper Winchendon was for three fir trees to be cut down, and in the event of invasion they were to be chained between posts on either side of the road. One at the edge of a wood about midway between the "Drive" Lodge and Waddesdon Hill Chapel, another between the Church Drive and the village, and the third south of the village at the end of "The Limes" farm wall on Gallows Hill.

One exercise at Waddesdon was for the Upper Winchendon section to "capture" Waddesdon Village Hall from members of Waddesdon Home Guard who were guarding the approach roads. The Winchendon section set out across fields near Quainton Station at night and approached Waddesdon, which was in complete darkness due to the "blackout" (no street lights or lights from any properties.) They found the rear of the Post Office, knocked on the door, and Mr Collyer the village postmaster, let them in the back door and out of the front, from where they ran across the main road, missing the patrols, and "captured" the village hall.

Perhaps from the outset, the Home Guard was treated as an object of amusement, and no doubt many of the comical events which occurred fostered this image. However it should not be forgotten that many of these part time soldiers were veterans of the terrible conditions during the Great War, and they had no illusions about what they would be facing if Germany invaded. The Home Guard in Buckinghamshire reached a peak strength of 19,816 in May 1943, and number 3 Company at Waddesdon consisted of around 80 men at this time. There is no doubt that membership of this and other civilian defence organisations heightened the overall sense of involvement in the total war situation. And although in Waddesdon thankfully, there was no emergency to fully test the people concerned, we have no reason to suppose the reaction would have been less than expected. The Home Guard was stood down on 3rd December 1944.

Thank goodness they were not called upon to fire their rifles in anger.

6.45 The stretcher-bearers and medics of Waddesdon Home Guard. Standing L to R: Harry Turner, Ron "Jackie" Church, -------, ---------, ---------. Seated L to R: Jack Rhodes, -------, Marley Walker, Dr Norman Black, Tom Copcutt, Ralph Saunders, Jack Cox.

6.46 The Air Raid Protection (A.R.P.) Rescue Wardens Standing L to R. Tom Evans, Teddy Sharp, Will Atkins, Vic Radwell. Sitting L to R. Charles Smith, Mr Saunders, Dick Carter, Tom Mole, Charlie Marriott. The A.R.P. (Air Raid Protection) organisation was formed for civil defence prior to the outbreak of war, and was initially staffed by volunteers. The Wardens are famously best remembered for their zealous checking of the blackout, "Put out that light!" was their watchword, and woe betide any householder displaying a chink of light after dark! Their duties included all aspects of civil defence, primarily concerned with air bombing attacks but the A.R.P. Wardens could deal with all manner of catastrophies. Fortunately again in Waddesdon, there were no serious incidents to test the mettle of the A.R.P.

6.47 L to R George Fowler, Jock Millar, Tom Mortimore and Pat Radwell at the ready with a machine gun circa 1944.

6.48 In November 1940 an enemy bomber jettisoned a load of incendiary bombs across Waddesdon, probably whilst returning from the destruction of Coventry. This tail-fin was salvaged by Tucker George from the middle yard at the Estate Home Farm, where the front incendiary portion had burned itself out. The bombers' loads consisted of a mixture of high explosive bombs and incendiaries, fortunately none of the former were dropped on Waddesdon on this occasion. Other incendiaries fell in Baker Street, High Street and Frederick Street, causing no serious damage and were dealt with by A.R.P. wardens or members of the public. A single incendiary bomb caused a fire at Watbridge Farm, which was attended by Waddesdon and Quainton Fire Service.

6.49 On the 17th September 1941, "the Park" at Waddesdon Manor was requisitioned for use by the Army, and work was soon under way to install Nissen Huts and all the paraphernalia associated with a military fuel storage depot. Apart from the living quarters ("the Camp"), with its main gate and sentry box just off the Warmstone Road in Budd's Piece, now Sharps Close / Goss Avenue, there stretched alongside the Estate driveways, from the Cross Roads Lodge almost to the Manor, and right down to Eythrope, a complex of large concrete standings, spaced to reduce fire-spread risk, on which were stacked thousands of filled petrol and oil cans of all sizes. There was a Fire Station, administration accommodation, guard huts at the numerous entrances, huge Nissen huts for equipment, workshops, and vehicle storage, large water tanks for fire-fighting, and of course miles of barbed wire perimeter fence. The cans of petrol and oil arrived by rail at Quainton Road Station, they were loaded onto lorries and ferried to "the dump" in a constant stream. After "D Day" the stocks were steadily reduced. Hidden from air observation by the trees it was said this was the largest petrol dump in the country. Much of the initial construction work was carried out by Italian P.O.W.s from Sedrup camp, near Aylesbury. The several hundred troops stationed at Waddesdon Camp, mainly Royal Pioneer Corps were drawn from every background imaginable, so it was no surprise they were able to organise social activities for all tastes. Here we have a photograph of the Pioneer Orchestra in the Camp theatre (Nissen hut!), with "guest player" Ron Carr with saxophone on the right. At the end of the war the Camp was closed down, and then re-staffed with a unit of the Free Polish Army. They left around 1946 and civilians ("squatters") moved in. The site was adopted by Aylesbury Rural District Council, and eventually developed into Goss Avenue, Sharps Close and Warmstone Close.

Waddesdon and the Evacuees

In 1937 government experts predicted that if air attacks on civilian targets continued for 60 days the casualties could be 60,000 killed and 1,200,000 wounded. (These figures were based upon civilian casualty numbers from First World War air attacks, at 50 casualties per ton of explosives. Thankfully, in the event the numbers were around 15 to 20 per ton of explosives). In view of the worrying deteriorating state of relations with Germany, it was imperative that plans for wartime evacuation of certain categories of city dwellers be put in hand.

The evacuation plans were necessarily extremely complex but their aim was simple enough. To remove from likely target cities those persons whose presence was not essential for the operation of that city, and whose presence would place unnecessary burdens upon the remainder. Several categories of evacuees were listed in order of priority by the Ministry of Health: 1 Schoolchildren, 2 Younger children with mothers, 3 Expectant mothers, 4 Blind adults and invalids.

Only 40 miles from the city, yet with a widely dispersed population in villages and small towns, the Aylesbury Vale was considered an ideal reception area for evacuees from London. And so Waddesdon and dozens of similar communities prepared for an aspect of modern warfare that was to be a new experience for everyone. (See also article "The Cedars Boys").

In the spring of 1939 households were canvassed to determine how many evacuees they would be prepared to take, and whether they could accept unaccompanied children. The weekly remuneration ranged from 10/6 (52 pence) per single child and 8/6 (42pence) each if more than one child, to lodgings only for teachers at 5/- (25 pence). These figures were increased later. Waddesdon whose population in 1931 had been 1,294, returned an offer to accept 457 persons! It is worth noting that at first evacuation was not planned to be compulsory, also the government would stand all costs except where evacuees were able to contribute towards their keep.

Voluntary organisations were enrolled to help in every way, and branches of the Women's Voluntary Service sprang up in every sizeable community. Waddesdon was no exception, especially as Mrs de Rothschild was a District Organiser! On 11th June the plans were announced; Waddesdon was to receive 175 evacuees who were to be debussed at the Village Hall. War however might yet be avoided.

Germany invaded Poland on 1st September 1939, and as a result of treaty obligations Great Britain declared war on Germany on 3rd September. Evacuation plans were immediately put into effect, and 1,500,000 evacuees travelled out of London in the official arrangement. A further 2,000,000 left in an unplanned exodus giving the authorities a foretaste of future problems. Evacuation services were swamped.

Meanwhile with a minimum of fuss, one hundred children, all less than five years of age, arrived at the Manor from Croydon with their nurses, furniture and ancillary staff. The children were drawn from four nursery homes, and included fifteen patients who were from Chicken Pox and Whooping Cough isolation wards! A strict routine was followed from 6 a.m to 7 p.m, including a morning and an afternoon walk, playtime and bath-time. Although the total staff numbered around 30 persons they were each allowed only two hours off duty daily, and one half day per week. The novelty of living in a mansion deep in the countryside soon paled for many of the young nurses etc! Because of the numbers involved, the task of evacuating the youngest children to the Manor cellars at night, whenever an air raid alarm sounded, was shared with the "Bothy Boys", who had to sleep at the Manor. The Manor was to remain a very grand nursery home for young children throughout the war-time years.

Where possible London school children were evacuated under the control of their teachers. Waddesdon received children from Ealing Grange School who shared the Council School, and the girls from St. Annes Convent, Ealing, who had classrooms at the Five Arrows Hotel and the Cricket Pavilion. The teachers who accompanied the convent girls were the first nuns many of the younger villagers had ever seen!

With such a large influx of youngsters, the village schools experienced a host of problems which included overcrowding, unruliness and not least, culture differences. At Christmas time in 1939, the schools were opened to provide additional recreational space under supervision. This led to a somewhat tetchy report of a spate of minor damage, including the consequences of a snowball fight in the C of E school assembly hall!

It is clear that villagers were prepared to tolerate a great deal of inconvenience, and make extra allowances for the poor unfortunates who had been removed from their nearest and dearest. There was generally a feeling of "doing to others as one would be done by", and "to do your bit", but there must have been quite a few sighs of relief amongst the host families, when the evacuees began to drift back home. In many cases this had not been a happy experience for hosts or evacuees. A large proportion of children came from desperately poor homes, they suffered from complaints associated with their background, skin diseases, poor resistance to illness and some had lice; whilst for others bed wetting was perhaps a not surprising result of the domestic trauma to which they had been subjected.

The dreaded devastation of British cities had not occurred during the early months of the war, and this period later known as "the phoney war", was used by the authorities to improve rapidly the evacuation organisation and infrastructure. Meanwhile a majority of evacuees had returned to their homes.

In the spring of 1940 the German armies succeeded in defeating all the allied forces on the continent of Europe. The majority of the British Expeditionary Force was evacuated from Dunkirk, and the remainder of the allied forces in France were nullified after the French and German governments signed an armistice in June. The English Channel separated the military might of the Axis powers from the remnants of the allied forces, and all of Great Britain was therefore within range of German bombers.

The Battle of Britain commenced in July with devastating attacks on airfields in southern England, but early in the autumn the main targets of the Luftwaffe were British cities. This phase of the war became known as the "Blitz", and it precipitated the second mass evacuation for British city dwellers. This time however, everyone was better prepared.

In Waddesdon the Village Hall was requisitioned as an Emergency Rest Centre, and was to remain thus until July 1943, at a cost of two guineas (£2.10) per week. The Institute was provided free of charge as the District Sick Bay, and the Bothy became a short term home for expectant mothers. On the 1st November the Council School received a teacher and 38 pupils from Croydon.

Some evacuees stayed only a short period at Emergency Rest Centres, others until the Blitz appeared to have ended in May 1941, others re-evacuated when a second Blitz occurred as the V1 (Doodlebugs) and V2 rockets were deployed against southern England in 1944. A minority settled with their "second families" for the duration of the war, and amongst these were some who were staying with relatives or family friends. By the end of the war a few evacuees had integrated so well with their host families that they stayed on.

Last and probably the least significant strand of the local evacuation story is also the least known. A few better-off families in the locality were able to take advantage of a scheme whereby children were sent to Canada for the duration, thankfully an unnecessary precaution as things turned out.

As with many of the involuntary situations, which had to be tackled during the war, the evacuation scheme brought out the best in ordinary people, and in addition caused a huge shift in official opinion of the need to improve the social services. As a result school children received free milk, expectant mothers and young children received cheap milk, cod liver oil, vitamin tablets, orange juice and dried milk, and the welfare of babies and mothers was regularly monitored.

In Waddesdon the Evacuation Scheme was a wartime experience which presented little personal risk, but demanded enormous goodwill and effort from all those involved. It is to their credit that they saw things through to the end.

The Cedars' Boys

By the late 1930's Germany was committed to a policy of persecution for any of its citizens of "non-Aryan" origin. The main focus of this policy was directed at the Jews, who had been deprived of their rights and were subjected to violence and humiliation with increasing regularity. Escape from this situation was difficult, as permission to leave Germany was refused for most people, even if a country of refuge could be arranged.

Some boys who had been forbidden to attend local schools because of their Jewish faith were sent, by their anxious parents to the Flerscheim-Sichel Siftung, from where they attended the Philanthropin, a Jewish school in Frankfurt-am-Main. In charge of the Home was Dr. Hugo Steinhardt, and with him was his wife Lilly, and their two teen-aged daughters, Lore and Helga.

The violence of "Kristallnacht" in early November 1938, and Dr.Steinhardt's arrest and removal to Buchenwald Concentration Camp, moved Lore and Helga to write to anyone who might be able to help. Fortunately a copy of the letter found its way via Lord Rothschild, to Mr and Mrs James de Rothschild.

The Cedars was made available, Mr de Rothschild arranged release of the group from

Germany, and undertook sponsorship in Britain for as long as necessary. On the 16th March 1939 they arrived in Waddesdon; 26 boys aged 7-15 years along with Dr. and Mrs Steinhardt, Lore and Helga. They were joined shortly after by 8 more boys and Miss Butzbach, who was to resume her duties as their cook.

After little more than a year Dr. Steinhardt died, never having properly recovered from the ill-treatment he had received in Buchenwald. Mrs Steinhardt took on the task of running the Cedars until all the boys had grown up, through the wartime years and beyond.

Things were not easy for the boys, and at first to speed up their acclimatisation, they were forbidden to speak German, they attended the village schools in equal numbers, and initially some were boarded out in the village. It is no wonder therefore, they quickly learned English, and were assimilated into the local community. Locals can recall how the boys took on the village Salvage Collection duties, pulling hand-carts around the streets, and calling at households for waste materials to be recycled for the war effort.

Some of the boys excelled academically, some on the sports field and at their careers. As they reached enlistment age they joined the British armed forces.

When the war ended a few of the Cedars Boys was reunited with members of their relatives, who had somehow survived the horrors of the "Holocaust", but the remainder learned that they were now orphans.

It is almost certain the action of Mr and Mrs James de Rothschild in 1939 saved the lives of this group, and even now they look back on their time at Waddesdon with a sense of gratitude, and affection for all those involved.

In the Waddesdon Estate park, near the Cricket Field, a Cedar tree has been planted with a plaque commemorating "The Cedars Boys", and at the Manor the "Boys" have installed an engraved memorial plaque to the memory of Mr and Mrs de Rothschild.

We are indebted to Uri Sella (who as Ulrich Stobiecha was one of the Cedars Boys), for providing the information, for this article.

6.50 In the summer of 1939 Waddesdon was already getting accustomed to the presence of nearly 30 Jewish refugees from Germany. In this photograph are three sisters; Emmie, Nancy and Nellie Atkins making friends with one of the refugee boys who was always known as "big Henry", to differentiate from a smaller "little Henry". The picture was taken in the top of Parson's Close near to "The Cedars", home for this refugee contingent until well after the war.

6.51 A group of "Cedars Boys" with Mrs Steinhardt circa 1945.L to R. Gert Heumann (now Gerry Hartman), Peter Gortatowki (now Peter Gort), Ulrich Stobiecka (now Uri Sella), Bernd Katz, Otto Decker, Harry Rothschild (not related to THE Rothschilds), Mrs Steinhardt, Hans Bodenheimer, Rolf Decker, Hans Greenberg, Irvin Freilich, (youngest Cedars boy). Gert became a lecturer at Harvard. Ulrich joined the Israel Foreign Office and was twice posted to the London Embassy. Otto Played football for Wycombe Wanderers, emigrated to the U.S.A. and played for America against England. Rolf emigrated to the U.S.A, served in the forces and played for America against England. The others became engineers, gardeners, a stockbroker, teachers etc, mostly ending up in the U.S.A.

R.G. 24

FOOD CONTROL (NATIONAL RATIONING).

NOTIFICATION TO RETAILERS OF CANCELLED REGISTRATION.

From the Aylesbury Rural local Food Office,
To (Name of Retailer) Stewart Adams.
(Address of Retailer) High St.
Waddesdon.

This is to notify you that the undermentioned person(s)
Elsie Hillier RDC Sick Bay —
The Institute Waddesdon.

who was* ~~were*~~ registered with you for Meat* ~~Bacon and Ham* Butter and Margarine* Cooking Fats* Sugar*~~ ~~have*~~ has* ceased to be registered with you for the following reason :—
Removed out of District.

The counterfoils which were deposited by you with this office in respect of this customer* ~~these customers*~~ have been cancelled.

At the end of the next four-weekly period for the food or foods in question your requirements will be reviewed and your permit will be adjusted if necessary.

Signed on behalf of the Aylesbury Rural Food Committee
[signature] Executive Officer.

Date 12/8/40

* Strike out words which do not apply.

Wt. 48745/4883. 1500m. 3/40. R. & C. Gy. 51-6439.

6.52 As this illustration shows, although the war had started less than a year earlier, by 1940 rationing was an established detail of everyday life and Elsie Hillier, who had perhaps been a patient at the Sick Bay at the Institute, was no longer there. Stewart Adams, family butcher, was therefore no longer provisioned to supply her meat ration.

Letters should be addressed— "The Secretary."
Telephone: ~~Whitehall 7681~~ MORECAMBE 1387.

TEMPORARY ADDRESS: The Elms, Morecambe, Lancs.

Enclosure

CHARITY COMMISSION,
Ryder Street,
St. James's,
London, S.W.1.
25th November 1940.

At the head of your reply please write— C 5818

County - Buckingham.
Place - Waddesdon.
Charities - Lewis Fettoe and John Beck.

Sir,

With reference to your letter of the 13th instant I am to say that the Request that the dividends on the sum of £10.15s.11d. 3½% War Stock belonging to Fettoe's Charity should be remitted to an account entitled "Waddesdon Parish Council Allotments Account" at the Aylesbury Branch of the National Provincial Bank is not understood. The Parish Council are not the Trustees of the Charity and it is not clear what Allotments are referred to. Moreover, as you are no doubt aware, the Official Trustees of Charitable Funds have long held a sum of £167 2½% Consols representing the endowment of Beck's Charity which has for many years at any rate been administered with Fettoe's Charity. The dividends on this sum of Consols is remitted by the Official Trustees of Charitable Funds to an account at the Aylesbury Branch of

T.G. Goss, Esq.,
Rectory Farm,
Waddesdon.

6.53 In November 1940, defeat was staring Britain in the face yet the comparative minutiae of the affairs of a small charity in Waddesdon, was given the consideration, which would help it flourish for another few centuries. Here we show that despite its temporary exile from London to Morecambe, the Charity Commission was still reassuringly protecting the interests of John Beck's and Lewis Fetto's Charity.

6.54 During the war, grass grew and children danced at Waddesdon Manor where pristine flower beds had once been. In this picture are some of the children who were evacuated to the Manor from two Croydon nurseries in 1939. Although all the art treasures had been removed for safe storage, inevitably the six years of use as a nursery created the need for a large restoration programme to the curtains, walls and other damageable furnishings by the end of the war.

6.55 There is little doubt that Baron Ferdinand and Miss Alice de Rothschild would have approved the scene we have here, in the circumstances of the Second World War, but anyone would have to admit to the incongruity of the setting. These tiny evacuees on their spartan camp beds amid the splendour of the Dining Room at Waddesdon Manor had a relatively peaceful and very different war to their contemporaries in Croydon their hometown. At least one little evacuee was plucked from the relative austerity of the nursery school at the Manor, and given a loving family home in the locality. Mr and Mrs Shirley of Upper Winchendon gained their daughter Violet by adoption, when she was only two years' old. She grew up here, and still lives in the area.

6.56 This photograph shows a mixture of evacuees and local children in Waddesdon Village Hall circa 1940, after the Women's Voluntary Service (W.V.S.) inaugurated a scheme to provide lunchtime meals on weekdays. At the back is Jack Uff, then the W.V.S. ladies L to R: -------, Mrs Loader, Mrs Harding, Mrs Long, Mrs M.Saunders, Mrs Newman, Mrs Robinson, Mrs Wheeler, and Mrs Reynolds (seated). Children - second row from front: -------, Rose Washington, Audrey Taylor, -------, ------, -----, ------, Bill Reynolds, Ken Wheeler.

6.57 Tom and Derek Lovell were evacuated from Willesdon in North London at the start of the Blitz in 1940. They were collected from Aylesbury station by Mr Willy Wheeler in the Estate van, and delivered to the Village Hall for allocation to "billets". Naturally they didn't want to be separated, (Derek says he cried for two days), and they were initially taken in by Nurse Edwards. Then they went to Mr and Mrs Win Walton at 74 Quainton Road, but were "too lively"! Not having experienced livestock before, they were caught throwing conkers at the backyard chickens in their coop, and were soon on their way. The third billet was a great success; Mr Levi Evans and his wife Annie proved to be admirably suited to the two brothers, and this arrangement continued until Tom had returned to London after the war, and Derek married and settled in the village to bring up his family. In this photograph we have Phyllis Martin a neighbour in Quainton Road, with Tom at the back and seven year old Derek, looking none too happy and probably looking forward to the next visit of his mother, with whom he has maintained close ties to the present day.

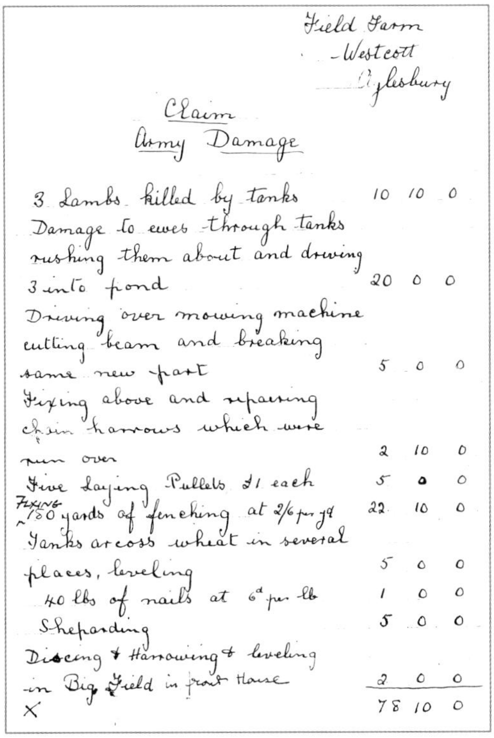

Field Farm
Westcott
Aylesbury

Claim
Army Damage

3 Lambs killed by tanks	10	10	0
Damage to ewes through tanks rushing them about and driving 3 into pond	20	0	0
Driving over mowing machine cutting beam and breaking same new part	5	0	0
Fixing above and repairing chain harrows which were run over	2	10	0
Five laying Pullets £1 each	5	0	0
Fixing 180 yards of fencing at 2/6 per yd	22	10	0
Tanks across wheat in several places, leveling	5	0	0
40 lbs of nails at 6d per lb	1	0	0
Shepharding	5	0	0
Discing & Harrowing & leveling in Big Field in front House	2	0	0
X	78	10	0

6.58 "War Damages", a fund to compensate owners of civilian property, for damage caused by enemy action and allied troop manoeuvres etc, was raised by a levy on property, according to Rateable Value. In the case of this illustration, army exercises had inflicted damage leading to a claim for £78 - 10s -0d, including the need for 40 lbs (18.2 kgs) of nails! This example reveals the extraordinary contrasts, which had to be tolerated in wartime to enable normal essential activities to proceed, in this case farming. A mile away from Field Farm, young men were being trained for extremely perilous aspects of modern warfare. Everyone knew the odds were stacked against their survival to the end of the war. There could be no adequate compensation for their War Damages.

6.59 All the people in this photograph lived at the top end of Quainton Road and it is thought the venue is the Five Arrows Hotel Clubroom. The occasion is the marriage of Albert Spaghagna to Phyllis Martin, coinciding with the end of the war in Europe, 1945. Back L to R: Violet Cannon, Linda Cheshire, Will Cannon, the child in front of Will Cannon is Christine Cheshire being held by her grandmother Elsie Cheshire, Bill Holloway, Phyl Cheshire with Roy Cheshire in arms. Middle: Evelyn Cheshire, --------, baby and mother Amy (nee Evans), Mary Cheshire, Henry Kelly, Irene Martin, (peeping) Derek Lovell, Mrs Tearle, --------, Kath Harrison with baby in arms, Terry Fowler, Mrs Evans, Peter Atkins in arms of Margaret Atkins, Sarah Turner, Levi Evans. Front: Harry Turner, Lionel Atkins, Alice Holloway with dog, John Fowler, Albert Spaghagna, Phyllis Spaghagna, Mrs Martin, Lorna Fowler, Nina Marriott, "Buttercup" Carter, Margaret Evans, Barry Atkins, Annie Evans, Anne Cheshire. Little boy at right of table is Alan Tearle.

6.60 "Lest we Forget". As with the First World War the names of the fallen of the Second World War were added to Waddesdon's War Memorial.

6.61 The gravestone marking the last resting place of Robert Snelling in the Oosterbeek military cemetery near Arnhem, Netherlands. See 6.43. For an unknown reason Bob had given his family instructions that in the event of his death, his name was not to be placed on the village War Memorial. We have however received permission from his family to display this photograph.

WADDESDON WELCOME HOME FUND

Jan. 1946

Dear Mr Carr

I enclose £11-10-0 as a small expression of the gratitude of your fellow parishioners, and to convey to you our WELCOME HOME.

We send it with thanks for the services you rendered your country in its *"hour of need,"* and with best wishes for your future.

Yours sincerely,

George Dixon.

Chairman,
Waddesdon Welcome Home Fund.

6.62 As in the Great War, there was a local Welcome Home Fund, which issued sums of money to the returning servicemen and women (presumably!) on their demobilisation. The Committee Chairman was the Rev. G. Dixon, and altogether the scheme made it possible for those who were not "called up", to show their approval of those who were. The recipient of this award served from before the first day, until some months after the last day, of the war.

6.63 In 1946 German P.O.W.'s were employed in building the circular road for Grove Way, a development that had been postponed by the war. Despite the recent past the local children quickly made friends with our erstwhile enemies who were found to be much like ourselves! Sitting at the front L to R: Anna Fowler, Mavis Carr, Phyllis Saunders, Norman Atkins, and Norman Carr. The P.O.W.'s travelled by lorry each day from the camp at Sedrup. They were held for about two years after the war ended, working mainly on civil engineering projects. Several of them collected willow and dog-wood "whips", which they fashioned into baskets in their spare time and others made wooden toys, which they sold for additional pocket money. Some P.O.W.'s working on farms, met local girls, courted and eventually married them, subsequently raising families fully integrated within the community.

6.64 A Fancy-Dress competition as part of a war-ending celebration in 1945 in Waddesdon Village Hall. Back Row L to R: Olive Hicks, Averil Cheshire, ----------, Valerie Haigh, Janet Atkins, Elsie Saunders, Edna Griffin, Betty Foley, Nina Marriott, Derek Lovell, Terry Fowler. Middle :- ? Ball, ? Ball, Glenda Pennington, Jill Rhodes, Bernard Linnell, Barry Atkins, Lionel Atkins (cat), Margaret Evans, Ann Cheshire, Lorna Fowler. Front:- ? Ball, John Fowler, -------, Alan Tearle, Linda Cheshire, Harold Pennington, -----.

6.65 For more than one hundred years events of great national importance, war and death etc had been commemorated on the stage in the form of tableaux. This vogue for abstract patriotic scenes was especially popular at functions relating to the Great War, and as this photograph shows four of the great battles of the Western Front are depicted in the tableau organised by Mrs Violet Cannon. Taken at the Church School around 1950, this was a rehearsal for an Old Contemptibles function in Aylesbury's Alfred Rose Park. L to R :- Stan Fowler (cornet- Last-Post), Cathy Charters (Wales), Daisy Cherry, Averil Cheshire,----------, ---------, Anna Fowler (nurse), Jacqueline Gurney (Angel of Mons), Ann Cheshire (wounded soldier) --------, --------, Wendy Saunders, Barbara Wheeler, Shirley Rolfe (England). Jacqueline recalls the tableau was mounted on the platform of a coal lorry, leading a parade around Aylesbury. She was stood on a chair relying upon the massive sword impaled into the floor to steady her from toppling as they lumbered around the streets.

6.66 Les Carter joined the Oxfordshire and Buckinghamshire Light Infantry as a National Serviceman in April 1956, and arrived in Cyprus to carry out the so-called "Internal Security" duties hitherto performed by the Parachute Regiment. This released the "Paras" for the ill-fated Suez operation. Cyprus at this time was far from being the idyllic holiday centre of today. A political group "EOKA" led by ex-wartime allies of Britain, were employing terrorist tactics to separate from the Empire, and achieve union with Greece. A sad and bitter time leading to disappointment from all viewpoints. Les returned home at the end of his two-year period, one of the few Waddesdon National Servicemen to spend nearly all of his stint in an emergency zone.

6.67 11 a.m Remembrance Sunday 1965. Viewed from a bedroom window of The Roses, this picture is more or less replicated every year. And now in the new millennium, there seems to be a greater awareness than ever, of the need to acknowledge society's debt to our 20th century servicemen and women, and in particular to those who never returned to enjoy the freedom for which they fought.

Section Seven

By Road and Rail

Waddesdon and the Railways

In 1839 a railway branch-line was inaugurated, connecting Aylesbury to Cheddington and thus providing access to the services of the London to Birmingham Railway. This was the first of the local railways offering direct access to London and the north, allowing travellers from Waddesdon for example, to arrive in the capital less than five hours after leaving their homes.

Following the opening of the Aylesbury arm of the Grand Junction canal in 1814 and the existing 18th century network of Turnpike roads, the railway was the latest manifestation of Great Britain's accelerating industrial revolution. In rural Buckinghamshire, as in other agricultural areas, the benefits of nearly one hundred years of industrialisation would have been hard to list; whereas hardships associated with that period of change would take a lifetime to dissipate. The last enclosures, shortages of food and work, introduction of labour-saving machinery (The Machine riots), and the civil unrest of the early 19th century were still recent memories. In the Waddesdon of 1840 there would certainly have been no spare funds for joy rides up to London. But the era of mechanised travel had arrived, even though another 30 years were to elapse before Waddesdon would hear the distant whistle and clank of steam engines.

On the 23rd of September 1868, after nearly ten years of planning and construction, the Aylesbury and Buckingham Railway Company commenced services. This fledgling company under the directorship of the Duke of Buckingham and Chandos (Wotton House), and Sir Harry Verney (Claydon House), had expended more than £100,000 to build a railway connecting Aylesbury to Verney Junction.

Thanks to the influence of the Duke of Buckingham the line did not follow the most practical and shorter route through the Pitchcott Gap, but looped to the west so as to close with the Duke's estate lands. As a result Quainton Road Station was established, and glebe land, (church land) at the northern edge of Waddesdon's parish was bisected by the track.

During the construction period several disputes provided some diversion for the locals, but perhaps none more than that involving the Rev T.J. Williams, rector of Waddesdon, who was adamant that work should not proceed before payment for the land was settled and paid. In public he resorted to the law, but it is reputed that in private he may have known something about the men who at the dead of night stripped freshly laid track and fencing from the disputed land!

At the outset the A. and B.R. relied upon the Great Western Railway Company to provide the rolling stock and locomotives, and to operate the trains, whilst employing its own staff to provide all other services. Initially there were three passenger trains each way daily, and it was clear the advantages offered by rail travel were quickly grasped by both commerce and the general public.

On the 8th September 1870 the Duke of Buckingham's workers commenced construction of a tramway, and the reasoning behind the strange diversion of the A. and B.R. became clear. The tramway was to provide access to Quainton Road station for the Wotton estate, and would cover a distance of nearly four miles, almost entirely over the Duke's land. This venture was totally private and therefore, unlike public railway company developments, did not require a Parliamentary Bill. However existing Board of Trade regulations had to be observed, including a speed limit of 12 m.p.h. As the intention was to use horse-drawn trams, this aspect was not perceived to pose an operating problem.

Work progressed rapidly, the labouring element being carried out by Wotton estate staff, and the skilled laying of track by contractors. The rails were laid upon longitudinal sleepers to facilitate equine propulsion, and at the standard gauge of 4 feet $8^1/_2$ inches (1.435m).

Where the tramway crossed public roads, at the cross-roads near Quainton Station, the Bicester road junction near Hall Farm, and the Ashendon Road in Westcott, level crossings were employed. Intermediary stations were built at Hall Farm (Waddesdon) and Westcott, each eventually having rudimentary passenger facilities and sidings for goods wagons.

Thanks to the flat nature of the land no major embankments or cuttings were necessary, and the Wotton Tramway was officially opened for business by the Duke of Buckingham on 1st April 1871. Long before that date he had already decided to extend the line to Brill, and the workers were retained to that end, completing the job in March 1872.

Although originally intended for goods traffic, popular demand resulted in the introduction of a passenger service within the first year, and in the same period it was found necessary to purchase two Aveling & Porter steam locomotives, to take on the additional work. The early passenger service comprised two return journeys from Brill each day, starting at 7.00 am and 3.05pm. Calling at the intermediary stations, the trains arrived at Quainton Road around 1hour 15 mins later. Adult fares to Quainton were: from Brill 1shilling, from Wotton 6d, Westcott 3d, Waddesdon 2d.*

The goods conveyed on the Tramway comprised a very wide range of commodities, farm produce especially milk and stock, bricks from numerous brickworks in the vicinity, coal, chalk, general merchandise and by far the greatest volume, horse manure from the London stables. 3,200 tons in 1872 off-loaded at trackside fields by arrangement, at the cost of 1d per mile per ton.

At this time Quainton Road Station was situated on the north side of the village road level crossing, with a turn-table arrangement to connect the Tramway to the main line on the Aylesbury and Buckingham Railway. The bridge and the removal of the station buildings to the Aylesbury side of the bridge came later in 1899.

Over the years the Tramway was developed to meet requirements. A branch line to Kingswood was constructed and another spur facilitated delivery of Bath stone and local bricks for the building works at Waddesdon Manor. The final haulage up the slopes of Lodge Hill being powered by steam winch. Later this spur was reduced to facilitate the delivery and removal of feedstock and by-products from the Manor gas-works in Westcott.

A plan to extend the Tramway to Oxford was approved by Act of Parliament in 1883, but partly due to the death of the Duke of Buckingham, this project progressed no further.

The Tramway changed hands on several occasions and benefited from the provision of better rolling stock and track. In 1890 the Metropolitan Railway Company acquired the A. and B.R., and in 1901 the Brill tramway became the farthest outpost of "The Met".

In 1897, Waddesdon at last got its own main line railway station. Thanks to Baron Ferdinand de Rothschild, who had commercial interests in the Metropolitan Railway Company, a new station, "Waddesdon Manor" (later called "Waddesdon"),was opened. Located just off the Pitchcott road, approximately two miles from the village, this station offered the most convenient point of access to the outside world for the Baron and villagers alike. For almost forty years the locals would commute via "Shanks' Pony" across the fields, or bike, pony trap or carriage on the roads, to and from the "Manor Station". The Baron and his guests enjoyed the added luxury of an arrangement whereby "through trains" could be halted at his request.

The railway network in this part of the country was almost complete, but the parish was to see one more incursion. An amalgamation of the interests of the Grand Central Railway and Great Western Railway, dictated the need to provide a link between their joint line to Birmingham and the G.C.R. line north. This link bisecting the parish via the Akeman Street station near Woodham, and including a new station at Wotton was completed in 1905. Offering direct main line access, this service soon attracted commerce away from the tramway.

Each strand of the local network swiftly became established as an accepted element of community life. Travel to far-off places was still a novelty, but by no means unusual. However for most villagers it was not passenger travel that exemplified the benefits, but rather a host of indirect factors. The railway employed numbers of locals on track maintenance, running the stations, level crossings and on the trains themselves; meanwhile there were jobs in coal deliveries, parcels and other goods, and the improved trade for farm products, especially milk and stock.

In 1922 "Waddesdon Manor" station on the main line was renamed "Waddesdon", and the Tramway station at Hall Farm became "Waddesdon Road". Neither of these stations were to survive much longer, as road transport was already beginning to demonstrate its advantages to the people of Waddesdon.

The Tramway, which by now was known as the Brill Branch, was operated for its final years by London Transport, and was the remotest outpost of the transport system of the metropolis.

Despite having earned a deep affection from all who used it, (many who came out of London for a day in the country), the last scheduled service train ran on 30th November 1935, and the old tramway was soon closed down.

Meanwhile the remaining rail services in the locality were suffering from the competition of road haulage and bus operators.

On the 4th July 1936 Waddesdon Station was closed, and notwithstanding an understandable upsurge of utilisation during the Second World War, the steady decline in railway use continued. The 1948 nationalisation of the railways had no beneficial long term effect on the process, and the well-known "Beeching axe" in 1962 largely completed the destruction of most of the local railway services. The old Great Western and Grand Central link from Ashendon Junction to Grendon was closed in the 1960's.

A single track now remains in operation from Aylesbury to Claydon, primarily for the passage of London rubbish trains en-route to the ex-brickwork clay-pits.

Little remains to remind us of the old railways, but at Quainton Road Station the Buckinghamshire Railway Centre provides a very popular link with the age of steam, still using the rail-bed first put down in the 1860's. Meanwhile Aylesbury Vale District Council has established "The Tramway Walk", following the course of the old Tramway.

The Wotton Tramway and the other main line railways in the vicinity of Waddesdon feature in numerous books on the history of rail travel, all of them with relevant photographs.

Following the recent privatisation of British Rail and the opening of the Channel Tunnel, there have been strong indications of expansion of the railways once more. Locally, plans have also been considered for railways to be incorporated in propositions for large housing developments. Time will tell!

*1 Shilling which was 12d = 5p in the currency of the year 2000.

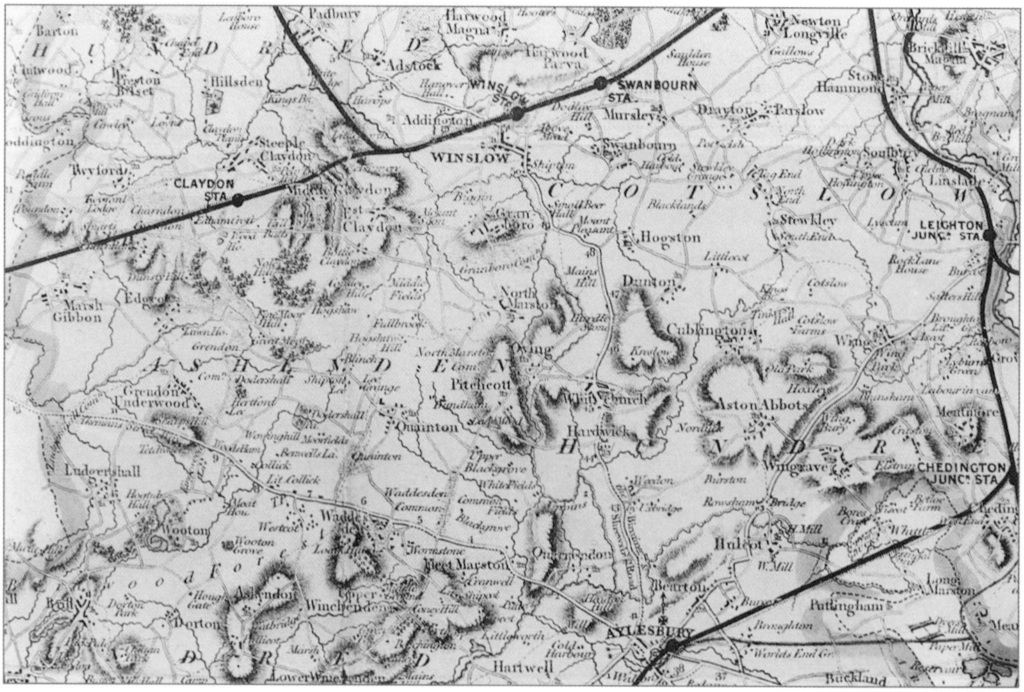

7.1 The first railway line in this area, showing the Aylesbury (1840) link via Cheddington to the London to Birmingham Railway. To the north is the London North Western Railway connecting Oxford to Cambridge. The illustration is taken from "Cruchley's Railway and Telegraphic County Map of Buckingham" and it was composed by superimposing the railway details upon an 18th century map of pre-enclosure vintage. The main London Road by-passes the village to the north and the common land is clearly shown.

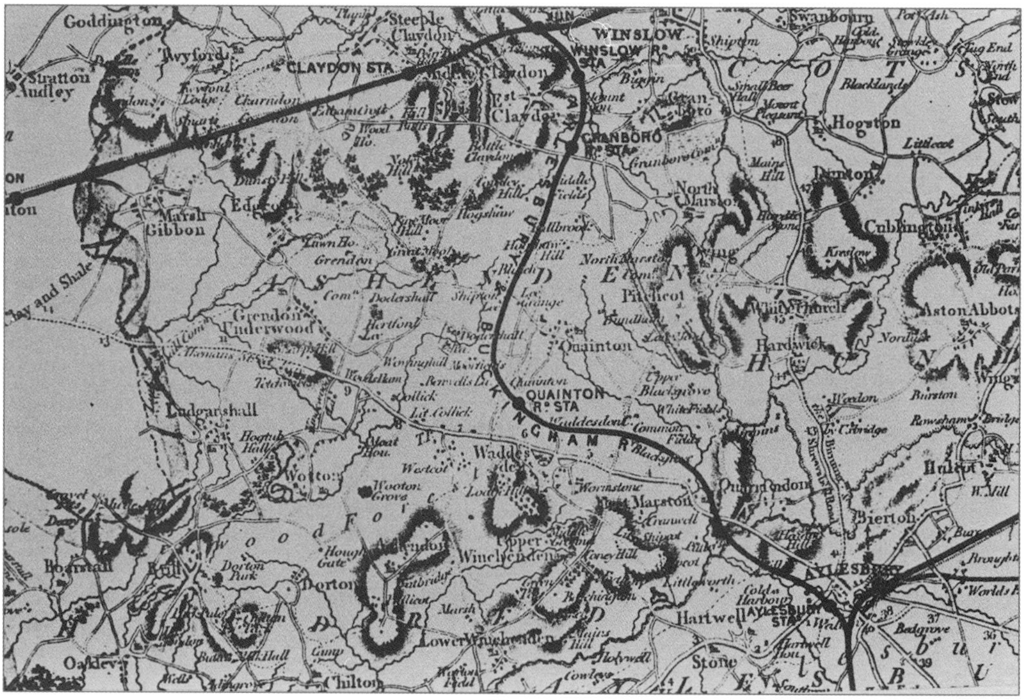

7.2 The local railway network in 1870, once again the same map was used as a backcloth with additions inscribed. This illustration shows the convoluted route taken by the Aylesbury and Buckingham Railway in 1869, but strangely also retains two scribed lines through the Pitchcott Gap where the original route was planned.

CHOIR TREAT.

The long contemplated excursion to London came off on Monday, August 24th, when twenty members of the choir, accompanied by the Rev. E. M. Evans and the Rev. F. Baldwin, started from the village at 5.30 a.m., en route for the great metropolis of England. Aylesbury was reached about a quarter to 7; and Chalk Farm Station in the North West of London at 9.15. This place was chosen for the party to alight from the train because of its proximity to the Gardens of the Royal Zoological Society of London. A thorough inspection of the gardens was made—two hours being profitably spent amongst the many curious and noble specimens of the animal creation. An adjournment was then made for the purpose of dinner, which was well served at a neighbouring coffee house; after which a pleasant ride in an omnibus brought the party to Trafalgar Square, and Westminster Abbey. Here the Service of Consecration of the Bishop of S. Davids and Central Africa was hardly concluded, so our Choir had the privilege of seeing the Archbishop of Canterbury and Assistant Bishops of London, Rochester, and S. Asaph; and of hearing the concluding voluntary upon the fine old organ. The brief visit to the noble fane being ended, the party made their way to Westminster Bridge; and after a glance at the exterior of the Parliament Houses, and S. Thomas' Hospital, all were soon safely on board one of the Metropolitan Steamers. The trip on the river was as far as London Bridge. All seemed thoroughly to enjoy the fine view of the Thames Embankment; and the varied scenes of busy life amongst the numerous ware-houses on both sides of the river. After the safe disembarkation at London Bridge, a wish was expressed by some to ascend the Monument. This was accomplished by those who were so desirous, and a fine view was obtained. At 4 o'clock the whole party entered S. Paul's Cathedral, and remained to the Service, which was of course chorally and effectively rendered, the Anthem being suitable to the Festival of S. Bartholomew, "How lovely are the Messengers" Mendelssohn. After leaving the grand old Cathedral, the party turned their steps towards the Holborn Viaduct, and at Messrs. Spiers and Pond's Refreshment Buffet enjoyed a good cup of tea. Euston Square Station was reached about a quarter to 7; and at 7 o'clock the party were on their road to Aylesbury, which was made about 8.40 p.m. All arrived safely at Waddesdon about 10 o'clock. Thanks are due to those who so kindly assisted in providing the treat, notably to Mr. Belgrove and Mr. Levi Crook, for so generously providing a horse and cart to carry the party to Aylesbury and back. We are glad to say that a very happy day was spent, and that no mishap occurred to mar its enjoyments.

7.3 The Choir Treat 1874. Since the introduction of the railway service to Aylesbury, the occasional trip to London was possible for some Waddesdonians. However the Choir Treat was probably the biggest event of the year for the working class members, and in this case would provide a subject of conversation for many years to come.

7.4 This Aveling & Porter 6 H.P. engine was first used on the Tramway in January 1872. It was based upon the company's successful road traction engine and cost £400. The engine motive power derived from a single cylinder of 7.75 inches diameter by 10 inches stroke (197mm by 254mm) and was transmitted to the wheels by means of a continuous chain around sprockets on the drive shaft and each wheel axle. Total engine weight was less than 10 tons and the running speed ranged between 4 and 8 m.p.h. A second engine was acquired in June 1872, and after various injuries to the drivers and firemen they were eventually both fitted with drivers' cabs, running boards and funnel spark arrestors. One of these engines ended its working life in the 1940's at a brickyard at Nether Heyford. It was restored and now rests on display in the London Transport Museum at Syon Park, Brentford.

7.5 This photograph of circa 1900 shows the Tramway train with the old original coach, a more recent bogey-coach, and a milk truck, patiently awaiting the Baker Street connection at Quainton Road station, at 4.13 on this summers afternoon. The locomotive is "Huddersfield" a Manning Wardle 0-6-0 Class K weighing some 17 tons, built in 1876 and bought for the Tramway in 1894 for £450. More sophisticated than its predecessors, but with a weight of 18 tons, this and other considerations had precipitated a reinstatement programme to gain Board of Trade approval, at a cost of £10,728, and was completed in 1894. The Metropolitan Railway Company took over the lease of the Tramway in 1901, paying £320 for Huddersfield in the "job-lot" deal. The other locomotives in the K class were named Wotton, and Earl Temple, named after Earl Temple, (Mr Gore Langton), who inherited the principal interests in the Tramway on the death of his uncle the Duke of Buckingham in March 1889. (Note: the engine Earl Temple was re-named Brill No 1 circa 1899.)

7.6 Waddesdon Road Station on the Brill Tramway circa 1930. From the outset permission for the level crossings over public roads was conditional upon the gates normally being closed across the tramway as shown here. The A41 road to Waddesdon is at the right side of the picture and Rag Hall, the road to Quainton is forking left. From 1872, when the Tramway was inaugurated heavy materials especially coal, timber etc were delivered here for Waddesdon dealers.

7.7 Waddesdon Road Station circa 1930 viewed from Rag Hall road. Hall Farm lies behind the station across the A41 main road, whilst to the left rises Lodge Hill with its mantle of trees. The siding, which branches left behind the station building, was for the loading and unloading of goods wagons. The main users of this facility in the early decades were Messrs Turnham of the Five Arrows, and Alcock whose premises were opposite the Alms Houses. Both of these were coal merchants in addition to their other business activities.

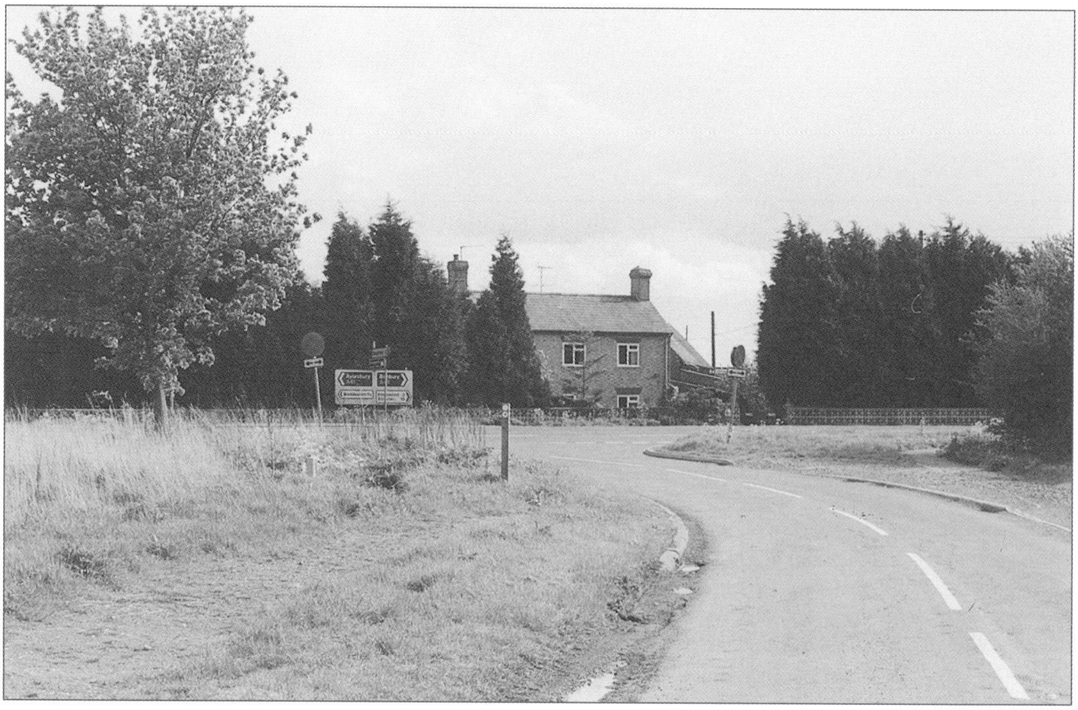

7.8 Rag Hall and Hall Farm 1997. Only the wide flat verge betrays the possible existence of the old Waddesdon Road station of 70 years' ago.

7.9 Metropolitan engine number 41, a class A Beyer-Peacock 4-4-0 T, at the level crossing on the Waddesdon / Quainton / Westcott / Claydons cross-roads. The Tramway was now (1934) the farthest outpost of London Transport.

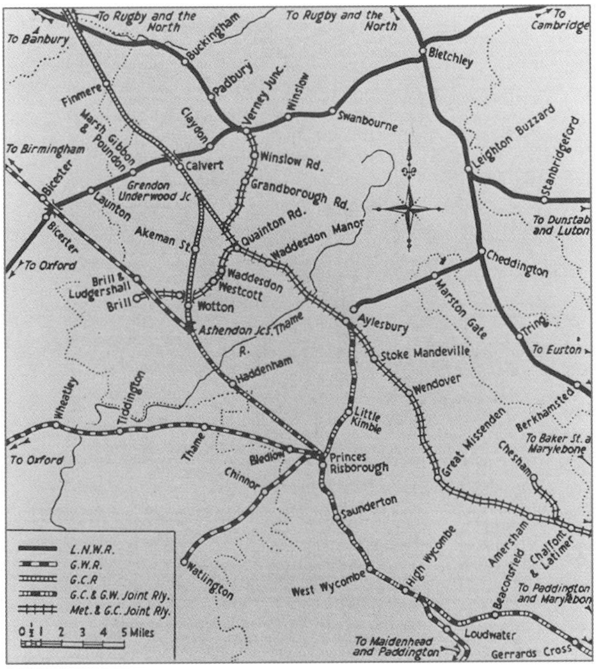

7.10 This network diagram shows the extent reached by railway development in this area, at its peak in circa 1920. From here on the railways, which had provided an economical and relatively convenient service for passengers and freight, would commence a downward spiral not to be halted for 50 years. Arguments for re-opening lines are now aired regularly as a possible means of reducing road congestion.

7.11 Waddesdon Manor Station on the Aylesbury and Buckingham line. circa 1910. The engine is a Grand Central Robinson Atlantic travelling south. This station differed from all others on this line in that the buildings were on the "down side" of the track whilst the others had their buildings on the "up side".

7.12 In 1922, "Manor" was dropped from the title of Waddesdon's main line station, and on the Tramway "Waddesdon Road" was substituted for "Waddesdon" at Hall Farm. This photograph shows the "up" platform and pedestrian bridge, with the Verney Junction to Aylesbury motor train heading south. In 1936 this station was closed and all except the platforms demolished.

7.13 The site of the old Waddesdon Manor Station in 1998. The "up" platform has long gone, but just discernable on the near right is the brickwork of the "down" platform. The road-bridge is still used by traffic on the Pitchcott road. The remaining single track is now mainly used by the rubbish trains that operate nightly from London, transporting waste to the redundant clay pits at Calvert. Occasionally the line is used by the Buckinghamshire Railway Centre at Quainton when they ferry visitors to and from Aylesbury.

Road Transport in Waddesdon

Road transport has been a key factor in the evolution of our society over many hundreds of years. The photographs that follow in this section give only a brief résumé of the differing modes of transport used in the village, and the characters involved, during the past century.

7.14 William Alcock, animal feed and coal merchant had these premises opposite the Arthur Goodwin Alms Houses, and made use of the railway sidings at Waddesdon Road Station on the Brill Tramway, for deliveries of coal etc. This photograph of circa 1880 has Mr Alcock's coal delivery cart's on the left and his trap for light deliveries on the right. The space in front of the last house in the terrace later provided the site for Humphrey's shop, now The Estate Agent. William Alcock's stables and close for his horses was in a small field now developed as Little Britain.

7.15 An Aylesbury delivery wagon at the White Lion Hotel in 1897. The cottage at centre of picture was the home and shop premises of Kitty Allen who made sweets and rock. The house was demolished and replaced by "Southview" in 1922, Humphrey's shop is at the left of picture.

7.16 The very smart delivery van used by Mr Dodwell's baker's roundsman around 1905. At this time Waddesdon had five bakeries, Dodwell, Grace, Herring, Franklin and Humphrey, all of them had their "rounds" and no doubt competed by smart turnouts, to attract non-committed customers.

7.17 This photograph shows Ben Thorne on the right, outside the workshop of his first business enterprise. The boy holding the smaller bicycle is Ben's son Leslie and the year is around 1913. Ben not only maintained and repaired motor-bikes and motor cars but also sold and hired bicycles. Note: the carbide lamp on the small bicycle.

7.18 Bob Price, the son of Waddesdon butcher Joseph Price, is shown here as a very young man with his James motor-cycle. It must have been one of the very first in the village as this photograph was taken around 1907.

7.19 Outside the White Lion Hotel we have landlord, Fred Paxton in the sidecar and in the saddle is Hubert St. John Wildridge, a colourful character and local artist who was employed in the administration of the Estate.

7.20 The very first motor-bus service for the village was inaugurated by the enterprising Ben Thorne from his business premises on the High Street, opposite the Primitive Methodist Chapel in 1920. Named the "Waddesdon Queen" and based upon a Model "T" Ford, the bus provided a service on market days - Wednesdays and Saturdays. The driver in the picture is Mr Percy Goss, and the boy is Leslie Thorne, and Ben Thorne stands at the front of the vehicle. The bus was used for hire as well as regular service, and was fondly remembered by the village football team, which hitherto had used a wagonette for away fixtures. After only around two years the "Waddesdon Queen" caught fire returning from Aylesbury and was destroyed. This picture shows the service provided by Mr Thorne from his small premises, and as the sign on the wall indicates, he also sold petrol. This was dispensed in four gallon cans which for safety reasons were stored in a special pit in the back garden.

7.21 The successor to the first "Waddesdon Queen" this very similar vehicle which offered considerably more protection to the driver, was also based upon a Model "T" Ford. In 1924 Ben Thorne became landlord of the Five Arrows Hotel, gave up the motor business, and eventually also the bus service. The bus was from then on used for hotel services, but including private hire as before. This photograph was taken circa 1926 in the yard of the Five Arrows Hotel. Tragically Mr Thorne died in 1927, but for the following four years his widow succeeded him as landlady at the hotel.

7.22 Charlie Cherry took on the regular bus service to Aylesbury using this omnibus which was affectionately known as the "Cherry Blossom". In this photograph of circa 1930 the bus had made the journey to the seaside (apparently), which if the driver, Stan Fowler, complied with the plated maximum speed of 30 m.p.h, would have taken a large part of the daylight hours for the journey. But time was not so important then! The "Cherry Blossom" service was sold to the Red Rover Bus Company in the mid 1930's, and Charlie Cherry went into semi-retirement, farming the smallholding adjacent to Britain House.

7.23 In the inter-war years roads, transport, and safety never really became co-ordinated. This photograph of circa 1930 shows the result of a collision between a United Dairies bulk-liquid tanker and a brick lorry on the hill leading out of Waddesdon towards Aylesbury. Apparently the brakes failed on the tanker causing it to run out of control and "jack-knife" in the path of the brick lorry. Note the solid tyres on the tanker tractor, also the seven (at least) policemen available to attend the accident.

7.24 This fleet of buses parked across Waddesdon High Street early in the 1930's demonstrates the low level of main road traffic in those days. For a number of years it was quite common for football supporters from the Midlands to take a refreshment halt in Waddesdon, whilst on their way to the F.A. Cup Final. The six identical buses were built by the Birmingham & Midland Motor Omnibus Co on an S.O.S "M" type chassis, with bodies built by a company called Brush. They hailed from Peterborough, and were delivered new to the Peterborough Electric Traction Company in 1929. The girl on the right is Myrtle Collyer whose father had the Tailor's business, which is now the Post Office. The policeman is Sergeant Snelling. We have no idea of the occasion, nor where the passengers had gone!

7.25 Percy Goss started his haulage business in the inter-war years using a horse and cart, but he soon progressed to a lorry and commenced to develop the business, Goss Transport. His son Sid Goss learned the business and in due course took charge. In this photograph we record the farewell to one of the Goss Transport lorries in 1939. It had been requisitioned for the Bucks Battalion and went with the B.E.F to France in 1940. When the remnants of the army were evacuated, all heavy equipment and vehicles were left, including the entire Bucks' transport. On the left is Pamela and next is Lena Goss, the daughters of Sid Goss, and with them is Charlie Cross who worked for Goss Transport. Note: The blackout /convoy light shield, fitted to the far side headlight of this Bedford lorry, not only restricted, but also deflected the small amount of light onto the road just in front of the vehicle, and with the near side headlight disconnected, no light would be visible to enemy aircraft.

7.26 Sam Evans' Garage at the Baker Street / High Street junction now the site of Waddesdon Tyres (2001). Sam is shown here dispensing petrol for Mr Dancer's Austin Seven in the 1950's. Around this time Mr Dancer at 93 years of age, was reckoned to be the oldest driver in the country. Evans' Garage was opened by Sam's father David around 1900, and he gained a reputation for ingenuity and engineering enthusiasm which has passed down the family line to the present day.

7.27 Ben Marlow leaning against Mr Alf Taylor's Austin lorry outside the Mill, down Quainton Road. The photograph dates from the 1960's, by which time milling at Waddesdon had halted, and the buildings were used for storage of cattle feed and corn.

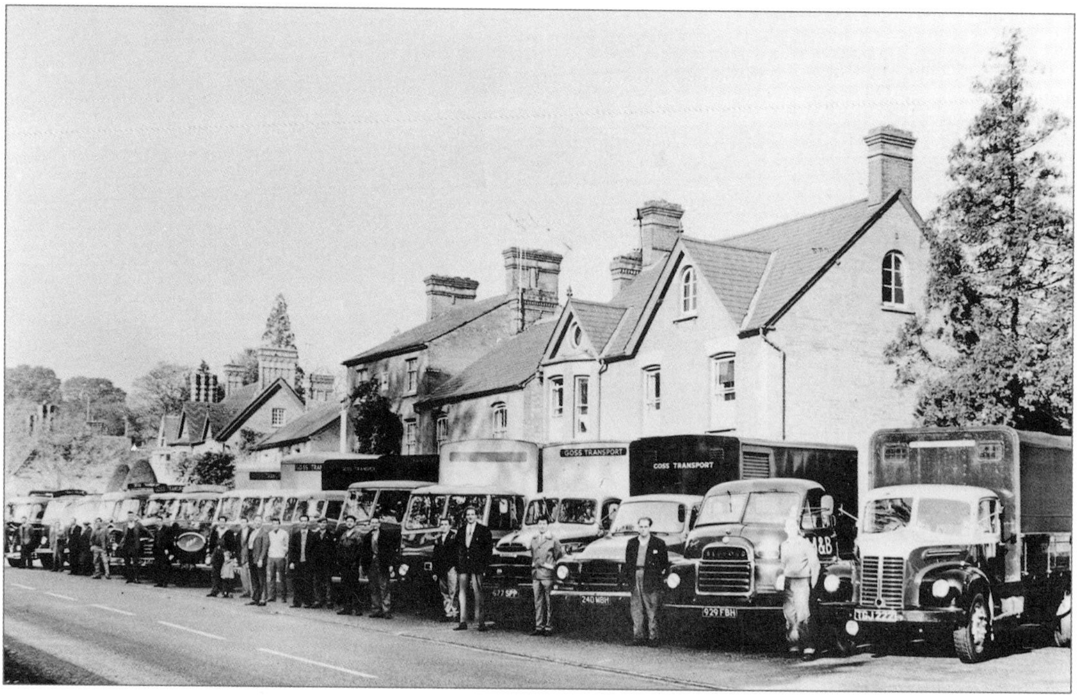

7.28 The business premises of Goss Transport were in the yard and outbuildings of the old gasworks down Quainton Road, but by 1962 when Sid Goss sold out to Amey's Transport,the number of lorries could not be fitted in the yard. This photograph shows Goss Transport formed up in the High Street in 1962, just before it was transferred to Amey's Transport. Amongst this interesting line of British commercial vehicles are names that, during the latter part of the twentieth century, had either disappeared, or been "swallowed up" by other national or international vehicle manufacturers. Some of the discernable names in this picture are, Dodge, Bedford, Austin, E.R.F, Foden, A.E.C, and Leyland.

7.29 Predominantly a village firm, here we have the drivers and other staff of Goss Transport 1962. Standing L - R: - Charlie Cross, Sid Goss, Clifford Goss, Percy Goss, Malcolm Cross, Jack Cartwright, Geoff Burgess, Ron Willis, George Clements, Fred Cook, Gordon White, Jim Zealey, Ben Marlow, David Marlow, Jesse Jones. Front Row: - Ken Butler, Frank Davis, Don Marlow, Eric Barnes, Don Stone, Cyril Gassor.

7.30 Alan Evans on the left of photograph is the grandson of Fred Evans the founder of the business in 1900. During the past century this village coal merchant has progressed from horse and cart and local deliveries, and has extended its area of operation. At the outset the coal arrived at Quainton Road Station and was stored there, but over the years, with the axing of many rail services, the storage depot is currently at Wheatley! This photograph was taken in January 2000. L - R: - Alan Evans, David Marlow, Stewart Evans (son of Alan).

7.31 Waddesdon Transport is very literally "the son of Goss Transport", for the founder is Clifford Goss who is the son of Sid Goss. See 7.29. Based in the High Street, at premises which includes the ex-Garage of Jimmy Jones, Waddesdon Transport operates a large fleet of heavy goods vehicles countrywide. Their distinctive paintwork in dark and light green and their immaculate appearance make them instantly recognisable wherever they are encountered. In this photograph are L-R: Nicholas Goss, Brian Sear, Paul Goss, John Johnson and Clifford Goss.

Section Eight

Clubs, Groups and Organisations

Ancient Churchwardens' accounts remind us that bellringing has been a spare time activity in Waddesdon for many generations, however the pursuit of organised non-secular recreation is not apparent until much more recent times.

By the last quarter of the nineteenth century, aspects of life for many ordinary people in rural Buckinghamshire were beginning to improve, and this engendered an upsurge in spare-time activities. Nowhere was this more evident than in Waddesdon.

Baron Ferdinand de Rothschild's arrival in 1874 and all that followed, sustained a memorable period for recreational pursuits, for in those days of little travel, the village accommodated numerous Estate officials as well as the Rector, Curates, Doctors, and School Teachers, most of whom were only too willing to support community activities. Crucially, the Baron himself never failed to give every possible assistance, to ventures and initiatives that would improve the lives of his neighbours.

The church and the chapels already had their long established groups, (see section 5), and intertwined with these were important non-denominational elements which aided community life. These included Night School classes held at the National and British schools, the Allotment Seed, Coal and Clothing Clubs founded in the "hungry forties", and the Penny Readings and Musical Concerts usually held at the National School. Distinct from, but similar to some of these, were the three Benefit Clubs, working men's sick clubs, which in return for a weekly subscription, paid a nominal sum to members unable to work through sickness or injury. A fledgling Cricket Club already existed and a Football Club was soon established, although facilities were spartan!

Over the years a multitude of recreational groups was formed in the village, ranging from sports clubs through to branches of national organisations. From the date of their inception these groups were properly constituted, many having the Baron or his successors as President. They invariably enjoyed success for many years, and in some cases it was inconceivable they would ever fail. However by the outbreak of the Second World War the signs were already clear; the Philharmonic Society and Temperence Band were gone and the struggling Old Band was "temporarily" closed down when several of its younger members were called-up; it never restarted.

A resurgence in community activities followed the war, principally energised by the men and women who had served in the forces etc. It is a matter of fact the succeeding generations have produced fewer community minded persons, and even fewer wanting to spend their spare time in community activities. Despite this there are still some successes, and we have endeavoured to include them in this section of village organisations over the years.

Waddesdon Football Club

Village football in the area took its first step towards competitive organisation when representatives of local villages, including Waddesdon, met at Oving in 1889 to launch the "Oving and District Villages Association". Rules were agreed and players' eligibility was treated with due seriousness. The competition was a knock-out tournament for a cup, the most coveted village prize in the district, known to this day as the "Oving Village Cup". For many years Waddesdon held the record for most often winning this competition.

The Aylesbury and District League was founded in 1891 and Waddesdon became one of the most successful members, regularly winning league and cup competitions.

Involvement in football, whether for recreation, as a club player, or supporter has raised much passion, and been the most popular male sport in the village since those early days. As a result the Football Club saw periods of great success over the years. The two World Wars interrupted the Club's progress and of course some footballers were among those who were killed or wounded. Despite this, the village fielded formidable teams in the Aylesbury and District League (A.D.L) during the inter-war years and after the Second World War, as the photographs show.

Perhaps the most successful period of the Club's history was in the mid-1960's when it dominated the A.D.L with a squad predominantly of village players. A move up to the Hellenic League followed, involving much more travelling and the necessity to recruit more players from outside the village. However, the teams performed very creditably for several seasons, entertaining crowds of several hundreds at home games. New rules demanding improved facilities and ground ownership spelt the end of Hellenic League football in Waddesdon, and several seasons in the South Midland League followed before the club returned to the A.D.L. in the 1990's.

It can be seen that the foray into the Hellenic League accelerated a trend which damages the concept of village football. Some village players went elsewhere for their football or packed up altogether, their families no longer supported the club, the fund-raisers gradually lost interest, and the players (from outside) having no ties with the community simply moved on. The pattern of more than seventy years was broken.

Thankfully the club survives, playing on the Juniors' ground off Frederick Street, and still encourages local boys and men to participate in organised football. However the fortunes of the football club no longer command the attention of the majority of Waddesdonians, and sadly the partisan pride, passion, loyalty and support of bygone generations have long departed.

8.1 Waddesdon Football Club was at the forefront of local competition for most of the 25 years before the First World War. This victorious team is pictured at the newly varnished Cricket Pavilion circa 1905. Back Row L-R: Tommy Franklin, Harry Gilson, -----. Middle Row L-R: Eustace Sims, Walter Raven, Charlie Cox, Fred Atkins, Jack Hilsden, George Richards, Charlie Cherry, Harry Olliffe, -----. Front Row: Billy Brown, Fred Charlton, Joe Saunders, Charlie Scott, Cyril Rolfe.

8.2 Unfortunately we do not know exactly which season this photograph celebrates but the most likely is 1924/25. At this time the village side was unbeaten in the Aylesbury and District League, Senior Section, and winners for the ninth time of the Oving Village Cup. The only side in the A.D.L. which could match Waddesdon, was R.A.F. Halton. After two "deciders" both drawn after extra time, Waddesdon and R.A.F. Halton had to share the Senior Section Cup as the third decider was cancelled due to the official termination of the season. Back Row: L-R ; T.Mole, J.Gilson, W. Whitney. Middle: R. Wood, E.Southam, G. Ewers, G.Finch, ?. Cripps, F. Eldridge, F. Winchcomb, A. Hicks, J. Uff. Front:---------, G. Rolfe, J. Rolfe, W. Eldridge, E. Atkins.

8.3 Waddesdon Minors May 1939. Anstey Minor Cup Final. On this occasion the Waddesdon team were runners-up in the second replay to Wycombe Old Technicians. Back Row: Ron Southam, Frank Wheeler, George Dyer, Harry Carter, Fred Caterer, Eric Hicks, Jim Ryder, Fred Cook, Charlie Cherry, Sid Carter. Front Row: Len Copcutt, Fred Woodbridge, Ray Young, Arthur Dormer, Percy (Tucker) George, Ken Rolfe.

8.4 Waddesdon Minors 1946 /47. Shown here after winning the Division 'A' inter-divisional championship on 24th May 1947. Back Row: Bill Haddow, Tom Mortimore, Garth Beckett, Ivor Hicks, Fred Cripps, Gerald Thompson, Reg Cyster, Ken Wheeler, Ron Southam. Front Row: Roy Southam, Vernon Atkins, Stewart Mulcahy, Den Schneider, Tim Carter.

8.5 Waddesdon First Team 1948. L –R: Ralph Saunders, Jack Callingham, Jim Neary, Harry Carter, Ken Rolfe, Brian Green, Rolf Decker, Den Eldridge, Bern Holland, Jim Kempster, Frank Horner. A talented and fit team, most of whom had recently left the forces. Frank Horner was the new Head Teacher at the Council School. Rolf Decker was to gain international honours playing football for the United States of America.

8.6 The winners of the Oving Village Cup 1956/57. To date the last time Waddesdon won the cup! At this time the original rules still applied, so the teams could comprise only players who were born in the parish or had resided there for more than six months. The cup-final was played, as always on Easter Monday, and Waddesdon who had lost in the Field Shield final on Good Friday, were the under-dogs. The opposing finalists, Bierton, had been invincible of late, having won the Village Cup for the past four years. Six of the team were less than 21 years of age, but on the day everything went well and Club Chairman Charlie Cherry realised his big ambition for one last time. Waddesdon won the Cup! Result Waddesdon 5 Bierton 2. Standing L-R: Ken Rolfe, Norman Carr, Tony Cherry, Eric Hicks, John Saunders, John Carter, Charlie Cherry. Kneeling: Fred Carter (Trainer), Meldwyn Price, Roy Southam, Derek Lovell, Don Marlow, Douglas Rolfe.

12—Bucks Advertiser & Aylesbury News, Friday, June 12, 1953

Truth Is Much Stranger Than Fiction!

ROLF DECKER

WITH our pen still dripping with excitement, we hasten to tell the most fantastic footballing fairy tale that has ever been our lot to relate.

It concerns an international, a much-decried affair, in which England were all set to scrub out a 1—0 World Championship defeat by the United States in 1950.

And they did, 6—3, under the floodlights of the Yankee Baseball Stadium in New York on Monday night.

But here are we rooting more than somewhat for the Yankees.

Local Lads

For in that American national team were two local lads, who just a few seasons ago were gracing the fertile football fields of Aylesbury and the Vale villages.

Recall the Decker brothers, Rolf and Otto, strong, strapping lads from Waddesdon, fearless footballers?

Some say that Otto came into the Aylesbury United half-back line too young. Anyway he hiked off to High Wycombe and was going great guns with the Wanderers when he eventually got the call of the U.S.A.

Big brother Rolf, who preceded him, stayed longer in the United rearguard. Then he returned to Waddesdon and was willing to stop his village rivals from scoring or have a go at getting the goals himself. Incidentally he picked up a Berks and Bucks junior cap — junior we said, mark you!

Then Rolf returned to Aylesbury and was still holding the fort at full-back when he got the call of the U.S.A.

They gave him a farewell gift, plenty of pats on the back, and off he went to return to his footballing friends later as a citizen of the U.S. Army.

Against England

Since then G.I. Rolf's twitching feet have been getting him places in the world of American football.

And only a few weeks ago he was in the American All-Stars team which lost 4-1 to First Division Liverpool. And he got that American goal from a penalty.

But imagine the consternation that there was in football circles of the Vale when the news came through that Rolf Decker was picked for America against the might of England at the Yankee Stadium. At centre-half, too, marking the great Nat Lofthouse of Bolton Wanderers.

The match, we know, was rained off once, so our anxieties were postponed for another day.

Two For Otto

And we awoke on Tuesday morning not with the question how did England fare—the odds on them winning were as tall as the Woolworth building — but how did Rolf Decker get on?

Well it seems he did pretty well in the first half because England did not register until two minutes before half-time. Lofthouse got two in the second half, but this news was dimmed locally by the fact that Rolf's younger brother Otto was brought in as a substitute at outside-right after half-an-hour and netted two of the American goals in the space of eight minutes.

In fact, according to all that we have read about England's 6-3 win, Otto was one of the stars of the "Stars and Stripes" side.

So it is "Vive la Waddesdon, Aylesbury United and Wycombe Wanderers" as we write finis to the Decker fairy story.

And now we must be off to take a census of all the local football artists who are thinking of packing their boots and hiking off to America and fame!

SPECTATOR

8.7 The Waddesdon (Cedars Boys) Football Internationals! An interesting aspect of this report is the failure to mention how Rolf and Otto came to be in Waddesdon, illustrating the situation which saw Britain sheltering untold thousands of refugees in the aftermath of the Second World War. Local football was one area where many excellent foreign players were welcomed and swiftly integrated.

8.8 Under the leadership of Eric (Roddy) Rhodes, (Quainton born but then a Waddesdon resident), this was the young Waddesdon team of 1961 which began to make its mark in the A.D.L. Roddy who had played for Aylesbury United and Wycombe Wanderers, and had performed at county level, drew the best out of the young talent in the village. Players in the back row L-R; Bryan Goss, Eric Rhodes, John Speck, Michael Sharp, Roy Porter, Tony Cherry. Referee "Budge" Horne. Kneeling L-R: Arthur Richards, Meldwyn Price, David Butt, Peter Williams, Douglas Rolfe. Club officials and supporters at the back: Paddy Williams, Ken Rolfe, Dick Carter (trainer), Malcolm Wheeler, Jim Fowler.

8.9 Waddesdon First Team 1963/64. This team had won the Aylesbury District League, Premier Division, and the Buckingham Charity Cup and were about to set Waddesdon on a trail of success covering the next ten years. Standing L-R: Fred Carter (Trainer), Tony Graham, Eric Rhodes, -----, Roy Pearce, Mick Sharp, Jim Fowler. Kneeling: Pete Atkins, Arthur Richards, Lito d'Giralomo, Dave Butt, Les Mills, small boy Graeme Fowler. All of this team either lived in the village or as in the case of Les Mills and Lito d'Giralomo had attended Waddesdon school..

8.10 Waddesdon's First Team circa 1967. By this time a force to be reckoned with, in Division 1 of the Hellenic League, but nearly half this team were from outside the village. Back Row L-R: -----, Stuart Shillingford, C.Makepeace, Eric Rhodes, Steve Hawkins, Rex Goodin, -----. Front: R. Oliver, David Butt, J.Stranks, Peter Atkins, Brian Hayers.

8.11 Waddesdon first team 1985. Competing in the South Midlands League. Back Row L-R: A.Young (Sandy), -----, Gary Crabtree, Neil Mack, Mark Giles, -----, Dennis Hill, Mick Brooks. Front Row: David Wilkinson, Darren Nichols, Anthony McKenna, Tim Brown, Mick May, Dave Cook, Roy Robinson.

8.12 Waddesdon Reserves circa 1992. Standing L-R: David Wilkinson, Anf Tearle, Peter Coyne, Andrew Carr, Neil Mack, Tim Brown, Martin Powell, Mick Brooks (Manager). Front: Tim Cowles, Simon Rawlings, Daren Willis, Ian Price, Stewart Green.

8.13 During the celebrations for the Queen's coronation in 1953 a football match between "Married" and "Singles" men was inaugurated. From time-to-time the idea is resurrected. This photograph records such an event organised by the Football Club and shows mostly villagers who played or had connections with the club. Circa 1994. Back Row L-R: Nick Slade, Steven Jones, Eddie Clark, Barry Hough, Chris Hough, Peter Coyne, Neil Hurlbatt, Martin Powell, Stewart Green, Rob Green, Nigel Cox, Stephen Green, Peter Webster, Darren Willis, Ian Brown, Marcus Powell. Front Row L-R: Nigel Saunders, Ben Richardson, Arry Coyne, Paul Coyne, Tom Lennard, Kenny King, Lee Richards, Stewart Powell, Anf Tearle, Bryn Wilks.

Waddesdon Football Club (Juniors)

Formed during the 1970's in view of the near disappearance of schools football, the Juniors set out to give village boys the opportunity to play competitive football. It was hoped village boys would progress eventually to the senior teams, but within a few years these aims were dashed when more and more "outside" players were recruited to produce a league winning team, with only two Waddesdon boys. Meanwhile the hard-working committee converted old allotment land into a Football Field in Frederick Street and constructed the Pavilion there. The Juniors was a founder member of the Westcott Friendly League and the club was able to revert to its original aims; there was never a shortage of players at this level. Unfortunately since the late 1980's the club has suffered from time to time, from chronic shortages of adult help, (a typical sign of modern times). A brief revival occurred in the late 1990's when three teams were in regular competition, but now (2002) there are no Junior teams in the village.

8.14 Waddesdon Football Club (Juniors). The successful Six-a-Side team shown here at Quainton circa 1988. L-R: Jack Rees, Jamie Ewers, Andrew Partington, Daniel Wright, Greg Masters, -----.

8.15 Waddesdon F.C.(Juniors) Under Elevens Team 1989/90. Standing L-R: Jamie Underhill, Andrew George, Dean Homewood, Sam Milin, Paul Bonner, David Janovic, David Davis. Front: Jason McEwan, Tommy Price, Louis Soulsby, Andrew Cunningham, Philip Masters, Lee Homewood.

Waddesdon Bowls Club

The origins of the Bowls Club lie in the formation of a Bowls Section within the Waddesdon and District Sports Club in 1923. The section played its first match, a friendly against Aylesbury, on Dr Black's green in the garden of "The Roses" in 1925, and used this green as the "home" venue until 1935.

The Bowls Section had special reason to celebrate King George V's Silver Jubilee when on that day in 1935 Mr James de Rothschild officially opened a three rink green at the Cricket Field.

The Sports Club was wound up in 1961, and the very popular Bowls Club, by now included women members. Mrs Dorothy de Rothschild had succeeded her late husband as president and had approved the Five Arrows crest for the club badge. The Club was affiliated to the Bucks County Bowling Association, additional rinks and a new pavilion were added, and in 1974 the facility expanded to include a licensed bar. In 1989 Lord Rothschild succeeded the late Mrs de Rothschild as president.

Over the years numerous successes have marked the progress of the club, including The Bucks County Benevolent Triples competition in 1976, (Tony Graham, Arthur King, Roy Southam), 1988 the men's team won the Gargini Cup, 1990 the men's team were quarter-finalists of the Bucks Cup, 1991 the men's team reached the semi- finals of the Bucks Cup, and again in 1995 when they also came second in the mid-Bucks League. In 1993 the woman's team reached the semi-final of the Trundell Trophy, and in 1997 women members were (at last!) granted full membership rights.

Waddesdonians of the 21st century have a reason to be grateful to the hard working Bowls Club members of the past. The facilities are very good, the setting is excellent and membership is open to all. Long may the club prosper!

8.16 The President of Waddesdon Bowls Club, Mrs Dorothy de Rothschild bowls the first wood when she inaugurated the extended and improved bowling green and Club-house in 1965. Watching closely are from the left:- Harold Sharp, Roy Southam, Arthur Brown, Ernie Southam (in cap), Francis Carter, and at right is George Knibb.

8.17 Waddesdon Bowls Club played host to a Bucks County Side and both visitors and home members are shown in this photograph circa 1972. At this time women players did not enjoy full membership status. For many years the club has included members who live outside the village, some who are exiles, some who have family connections with the village, and others whose only connection is through the Bowls Club. They have combined to establish a club, which can serve as an inspiration to others. The names of the visiting players are not known and are denoted below as "Visitor" Back Row L to R : Visitor, Visitor, Visitor, Arthur Brown, Visitor, Derek Stevens, Eddie Dymock, Francis Carter, Bob Barker, Roy Wheeler, Jock Kettyle, Joe Jordon, Roy Southam, Jock Cochrane, Jock Millar, Visitor. Middle Row: All Visitors. Front Row: Bill Mays, Reg Cant, Harry Cotterill, Jack George, Visitor, Tony Graham, Peter Brown, Ernie Southam, Arthur King, Harold Reid, Bill Crotty, Charlie Carter, Phil Conway, Harry Wheeler-Cherry, Visitor.

8.18 Four Bowls Club stalwarts showing off their trophies, circa 1975. L-R: George Knibb, Bill Haddow, Jim Ewers and Joe Jordan.

8.19 A timeless scene at the Cricket Field. A few clues betray the 1910 vintage of this photograph and inform the 21st century viewer that time has indeed marched on. The towering elm trees at the left, marking an old original hedge line from pre-Rothschild days, were lost in the Dutch Elm disease epidemic of the 1970's. The thatched roof of the Tea Room, built by Miss Alice in 1907, has been replaced by a tiled roof. The balcony rail on the Pavilion, built by the Baron, was removed for safety reasons in the 1960's. However this scene will be instantly recognisable to Waddesdonians and visitors alike, it shows the magnificent cricket facilities and the setting in all its splendour.

WADDESDON

SPORTS CLUB

FIXTURES

1955

for

BOWLS

CRICKET

TENNIS

S. G. Cross, Printer, Waddesdon, Aylesbury, Bucks.

SPORTS CLUB OFFICIALS

President :
JAMES de ROTHSCHILD Esq.

Vice-Presidents :

M. B. BROWN, Esq. K. A. SAUNDERS, Esq.

D. M. STORMONT MOWAT, Esq.

S. W. CROOK, Esq. Major WYMAN,

A. J. TAYLOR, Esq. R. J. BATCHELOR, Esq.

I. C. MACLAREN, Esq.

Chairman :
J. H. SMITH

Hon. Secretary :
Mr W. H. EVANS

Hon. Treasurer :
Mr H. COTTERILL

BOWLS SECTION

Chairman :	J H. SMITH
Hon. Secretary :	F. A. GOWLETT
Hon. Treasurer :	C. E. BUCKWELL
Captain :	F. A. GOWLETT

FIXTURES

Date		Opponents	Venue
May	12	Wendover	Away
	14	Bletchley	Away
	21		
	28	Stone	Home
June	4	Long Crendon	Home
	9	Wendover	Home
	11	Cholesbury	Away
	15	Calvert	Away
	18	Bletchley	Home
	25	Aston Clinton	Away
July	2	Buckingham	Away
	9	Long Crendon	Away
	14	Chilton	Home
	16	Wingrave	Home
	20	Aston Clinton	Home
	23	Wingrave	Away
	30	Prestwood	Home
Aug.	3	Calvert	Home
	6	Holidays	
	13	"	
	20	"	
	27	Prestwood	Away
Sept.	1	Chilton	Away
	3	Stone	Away
	10		
	17		
	24	Cholesbury	Home

CRICKET SECTION

Chairman :	J. H. SMITH
Hon. Secretary :	O. FRANKLIN
Hon. Treasurer :	C. BURGESS
Captain :	O. FRANKLIN
Vice-Captain :	R. SAUNDERS

FIXTURES

Date		Opponents	Venue
April	30	Westcott	Home
May	7	Swanbourne	Home
	14	Monks Risborough	Away
	21	N.A.L.G.O.	Home
	28	Bicester II	Away
	30	(W.M.) Beanacre Melksham	Home
June	4	Whitchurch	Home
	11	Princes Risborough	Away
	18	N.A.L.G.O.	Away
	25	Aylesbury Gas Co.	Away
July	2	Kimble	Away
	9	Whitchurch	Away
	16	Bicester II	Home
	23	Princes Risborough	Home
	30	Bledlow	Away
Aug.	6	Monks Risborough	Home
	13	V. 100	Home
	20	Kimble	Home
	27	Swanbourne	Away
Sept.	3	Aylesbury Gas Co.	Home
	10	Bledlow	Home
	17	Aylesbury II	Home

8.20 Dating from the 1920's the combined Sports Club for Bowls, Tennis and Cricket survived until the 1960's. Here we show the fixture card for 1955, listing also the President, Vice President and Club Officials. After 1961 each of the sports groups formed a separate club.

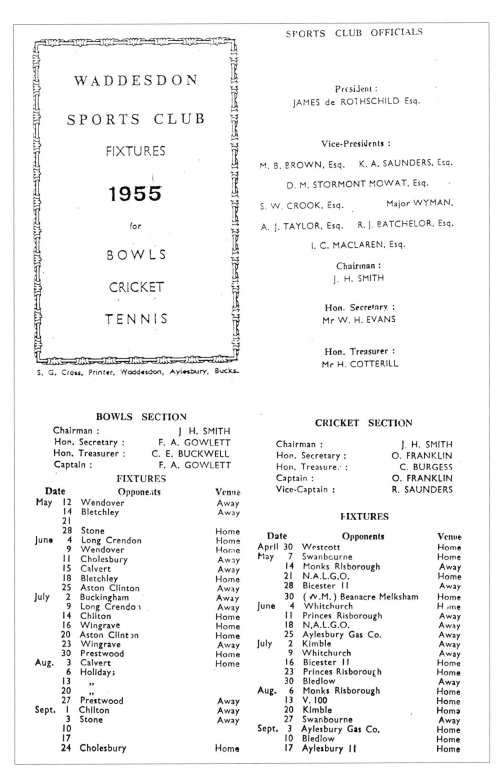

Waddesdon Cricket Club

Waddesdon Cricket Club was involved in regular competition in 1878, but at that time probably had no home ground suitable for matches, because all games reported in the Bucks Herald were played "away". However in 1879 a home ground was used, for a report states – "5th July 1879 Waddesdon 24, Weedon 30 – 0. The above teams played a friendly match at Waddesdon on Tuesday but the unfavourable state of the weather prevented any high scoring, stumps were not pitched until 4pm so that the match had to be decided in one innings each. Weedon won the toss and sent Waddesdon in, and were again victorious and the first two batsmen running up a score of 30 without losing a wicket. An excellent supper was provided by host Cockerill of the Five Arrows Inn."

Waddesdon's team :- J. Price, J.Lane, W.Chappell, G.Ward, J. Franklin, R.G. Marks, D. Nedwell, E. Grace, W.Bushnell, J.Saunders, H.Thorne.

In 1879 other names mentioned included :- J.Sims, G.Cannon, W & J Griffin, J.Uff, J. Dimmock, S.Wheeler, H.Judd, A.Holland, and R.Dodwell, all family surnames which are still familiar to older villagers.

The Cricket Club prospered apace as did the village itself, benefitting from the patronage of the Baron and later Miss Alice de Rothschild. Excellent facilities were provided and a certain rivalry grew between the other Rothschild model villages in the locality. A full-time groundsman was employed during the season, and talented cricketers were attracted by jobs on the Estate. Invitation matches were played against sides brought to Waddesdon by London based friends of the Rothschild family, and the far from ordinary village side frequently held its own against town teams.

These extracts are from reports in the Bucks Herald in 1908:

"Thursday May 21 st. Aylesbury v Waddesdon. Played on the County Ground resulting in a win for Waddesdon. Aylesbury 75, Waddesdon 79.

Waddesdon :- J.Hillsdon, J.Adams, J.T.Grace, A.Price, T.Gilson, A.T.Morrison, E.Pinnock, W.Biswell, W.J.Parry, T.Franklin, E.Creed".

"August 22nd. Waddesdon v Paddington. At two o'clock the players adjourned for lunch to the dinning room adjoining the pavilion, an excellent repast being provided by Mr Lander of the White Lion Hotel.

Miss Alice de Rothschild visited and invited the visitors to see her gardens and greenhouses".

The Great War saw Waddesdon's well tended cricket field revert back to agricultural use, hay was harvested where previously the crop was measured in "runs", "ducks", and "hat tricks", one of the insignificant sacrifices of that terrible war.

Between 1918 and 1939 the Cricket Club regained and sustained much of its earlier standing and importance in the community. The club still enjoyed the excellent facilities at the Cricket Field, and some of the contacts with London teams were re-established. Then came the Second World War.

Village cricket all but stopped, but the ground at Waddesdon was maintained to a good standard, because it was used for athletics as well as cricket, by the local Royal Air Force and Army servicemen.

The Cricket Club returned to normal in 1946, the field by now accommodating tennis courts and bowling green, to make an enviable summer sports' complex for the village. During the ensuing 45 years the fortunes of the Cricket Club have generally been good, although in common with all community activities there has been a steady fall in dedicated membership.

Then in the 1990's the club made determined efforts to recruit and involve the younger generation both in youth cricket, and in running the club. The trend has been reversed, more people are playing cricket and the teams are enjoying success. Long may it continue.

8.21 A Waddesdon XI and umpires in 1912. Photographed at the Cricket Pavilion, naturally! Standing L-R: ----------, Fred Crook, Ewart Newman, ----------, Arthur Goss, Thomas Franklin, Henry Turnham (Umpire) Sitting: Harry Dodwell, Edward Humphrey, Harry Gilson, John Grace, John Adams. Prior to the Great War cricket matches were often played on week-days. It may be noticed that all the above players were business men of the village, therefore the game on this occasion was probably a mid-week fixture.

8.22 Two stalwarts of the Waddesdon Cricket team of the late 1930's, Oliver Franklin (left) and Bill Heritage. Waddesdon's openers on Whit Monday 1938 they shared an opening partnership of more than 100 against Belmont, a London club.

8.23 The post Second World War team circa 1947. A tough side with a reputation for hard hitting. Standing L-R: Aubrey Hicks, Joe Cooper, Den Eldridge, Garth Beckett, Frank Eldridge, John Franklin, Rolf Decker. Sitting: Oliver Franklin, Dick Curtis, Harry Clark, Ralph Saunders, Dick Creed.

8.24 Waddesdon XI 1974. Standing L-R: Dick Schneider, Oliver Franklin, Tony Cherry, Eddie Barnett, Andy Tomlinson, Mike Clark, Fred Watts. Front: Brian Stone, Pete Atkins, Mark Edwards, Steve Hawkins, Barry Kent.

8.25 Waddesdon XI 1983. Standing L-R : Alan Bentley, Steve Hawkins, David Pegg, Andy Carr, Pete Atkins, Will Wright, Oliver Franklin. Sitting: Tony Cherry, David George, Mike Clark, Barry Kent, Ken Cherry.

8.26 The Waddesdon squad photographed before their first game in the Kookaburra Mid-Bucks League 1995. Back Row L-R: Richard Skym (Umpire), Tony Cherry, Richard Croker, Rhym Skym, Gerallt Skym, Paul Irwin, Kyle Biswell, Luke Thomas, Ian McEwan, (Scorer). Front Row: Graeme Foster, Adam Fowler, Alan Bentley, Julian Rolfe (Captain), Liam Biswell, Lee Homewood.

8.27 Waddesdon Tennis Club like the Bowls Club was originally formed as a section of Waddesdon and District Sports Club before the Second World War. The tennis courts were created within the cricket field and the members shared the facilities originally provided for the cricketers (this is still the case). Although the club has provided innumerable hours of pleasure for tennis players of the locality and has regularly entered in league and cup competitions, there appears to be very few photographs in existence. Here we have a team at Calvert circa 1953. Back Row L-R : Derek Lovell, Brian Beckett, Bill Read, ----------, Ron Copcutt. Front: Daisy Cherry, Sheila Southam, Molly Read, Dorothy Fowler, Alma Church.

8.28 Parish Councils were set up at the end of the 19th century. They undertook the administration of local government at the "grass roots", and gave parishioners the opportunity to stand as a candidate and / or elect their councillors at regular intervals. Democracy at local level. Despite the office of Parish Councillor being unpaid and largely unthanked, for many decades elections were necessary in Waddesdon as the number of candidates exceeded the vacancies on the council. Unfortunately in recent years this has not been the case, and the Parish Council sometimes has to function with a short-fall in its membership of councillors. This honourable and worthy community service has suffered often unfair criticism, apathy and poor support from the village at large; a sad reflection of contemporary parish life. This photograph shows the Parish Councillors who attended the Annual Parish Meeting in April 2002. This is an annual public meeting but the number of parishioners who attend rarely exceeds twenty persons. L-R: Robert Saunders, Hedy Richards, Roy Whitney, Margaret Morgan-Owen (also the Aylesbury Vale District Councillor), Catherine Ward, (Vice Chairman), Melanie Armstrong (Chairman), Fiona Russ (Clerk), Yvonne Barham, Alasdair McKenzie. The full complement of the Parish Council is nine persons and the Clerk.

8.29 Dr Colin Campbell is shown here officially opening the Adventure Playground in the Playing Field in February 1998. Also in the photograph are members of the Parish Council (P.C) and the Waddesdon Playground Action Group (A.G). L-R: Ann Gower – Clerk to the P.C., Sue Williams, Sandy Dean, Jane Olliffe – Joint Secretary A.G., Dr Campbell, Anne Kettleborough – P.C and Chairman A.G., Sarah Hamilton – Joint Secretary A.G., Sharon Ashton, Yvonne Barham P.C., Tracy Bradford, Debbie Short. The Playground Action Group was formed in 1996 with the aim of renewing the children's playground in the village playing field. In around 18 months they raised the funds, obtained grants and reached the stage shown in the background of this photograph. A second stage followed shortly after. A remarkable achievement in these times of relative insularity. Unfortunately, it has to be reported that vandalism commenced almost immediately work was complete, and a continuous repair programme seems to be necessary.

8.30 Waddesdon Old Prize Band circa 1895. This brass band was formed around 1850 and is often mentioned in reports of village fetes and similar functions of the nineteenth century. It was customary to include "Prize" in the title of bands after they had won first prize in a band contest. On the left standing with trombone is Eli Cripps who subsequently became Bandmaster. It was during his "reign" that the Old Band was a founder member of the Oxford Association of Brass Bands. The band regularly competed in Band Contests held by the Association as well as playing at local fetes, feast days and concerts etc.

8.31 The Waddesdon Temperance Silver Band "carolling" at Christmas time circa 1900. The making of music was popular and well supported by the villagers; they all knew plenty of tunes, thanks to hymn singing from early childhood, and readily progressed on to Souza marches, Gilbert and Sullivan operettas and the popular classics of the day. The Temperance Band used the old Wesleyan Chapel rent-free as their practice room, and in return led the parade and played without charge at the Chapel Sunday School Treat each year.

8.32 Bert Jones with the drums of the Temperance Silver Band circa 1912. Other photographs show Bert with a Baritone Horn, so it is safe to assume that like many versatile brass bandsmen he progressed from one instrument to another as needs arose. Bert worked as the agricultural engineer for the Estate farm, a well-liked and respected villager who in later years also ran the Sunday newspaper business for Waddesdon and the surrounding villages.

8.33 Members of Waddesdon Old Prize Band at Stanton St John Club Fete circa 1938. (Near Oxford) A regular engagement. Prior to the Second World War just about every village celebrated its Feast Day with a procession to the church, a service of thanksgiving, a dinner (lunch time) and usually a fun-fair. The celebration took place on the date or on a certain day of the week following it. The Waddesdon band was often hired by neighbouring villages to perform on their feast days, usually "half a band and drummer" to reduce costs. The hire fee was shared between the players to recompense them for loss of wages. On this and other occasions the band was transported by bus, no doubt driven by Stan Fowler, cornet player. Band members L-R: Charlie Thorp, Joe Cripps, Harry Carr, Teddy Fowler, George Rolfe of Wotton Underwood, George Fowler, Stan Fowler, George H.Biswell, Alfie Seymour, Herbert Owen, Fred (Knocker) Evett, The Conductor (with baton) is Bert Hopkins, ex R.A.F Staff Band and conductor of Aylesbury British Legion Band. The last remaining village locally, to retain this tradition, is Marsh Gibbon where the Greyhound Club still thrives.

8.34 On Thursday 9th July 1908 a fete entitled "Old English Revels" was held in the Rectory grounds to raise money for the newly completed renovations to the "side screens, panelling and pavements" in the church. The Morris dancers were "under London tuition", but the majority of the entertainment included the fairer sex, (such as in the dance illustrated). School-children performed singing games and choruses, in a programme which continued into the evening, when the Old Band played for dancing on the lawn. The sheets draped upon framing were to help evoke a bygone farming scene with thatched cottages and ricks of hay and corn. A large number of people took part and the venture was described as "fairly successful", despite a few showers that fell during the day.

8.35 In March 1905 Waddesdon Philharmonic Society gave three performances of "Les Cloches de Corneville" and the star of the production was undoubtedly William Uff. The following is reproduced from the report in the parish magazine: "Mr William Uff, an old favourite, gave an excellent rendering of Gaspard, the miser, his acting in Act 2, as the ghost which scared the village, being capital". This photograph taken at the rear of the village hall (where the Committee room now is) shows Mr Uff dressed for the part. The performances by the Philharmonic Society were always enhanced by the scenery and costumes, which were hired from London.

8.36 "The Mikado" by Gilbert and Sullivan transformed these six ladies for the photographer's lens circa 1906. L-R: Edie Garner, Milly Herring, Alice Crook, Annie Cripps, Molly Morgan, Kitty Ward. The headmaster at the National School, Mr S.C.Camp A.R.C.O. was paid an additional "retainer" by the Baron and Later Miss Alice de Rothschild to direct the String Band and the Philharmonic performances. It is little wonder that musical and acting talent was developed to the full.

8.37 This photograph of the cast for a play is thought to date from 1916 and includes a high proportion of the local farming community. L-R: Standing at back on platform ; Mrs Thompson, Gracie Thompson, Daisy Adams. Standing L-R: Nell Butler, Elsie Todd, Harry Payne, Winnie Denchfield, Gladys Saunders, Nancy Antonini, Arthur Tompkins, Gwen Terry, Poppy Terry, Molly Adams, Jack Newman, Dutchie Gurney, Nancy Monk, Phylis Manning, Lilian Curtis, Miss ? Turnham. Sitting L-R: Nell Figg, Aubrey Cooper, Miss Rushton, Dolly Wildridge, Poppy Simons, Mrs Eustace, Roy Curtis, Edith Adams.

8.38 Homespun entertainment at village fetes was the normal thing in the early 20th century, and in Waddesdon the standard was often very high, with lots of effort expended in the "props" as well as costumes and rehearsal. This "gypsy group" provided a colourful interlude between the serious business of money-raising at a Church Fete circa 1930. Back row L-R: Arthur Crook, Frank Howe, Dolly Wildridge, Nell Hedges, Rev. Deighton, Mary Read, Nora Pearson, Madge Walker. Front row: Dorothy Hinton, Mary Dennis, Mrs W. Evans, Dorrie Franks, Jack Sullivan, Win Dennis, Will Dennis, Irene Read, Nora Cherry.

8.39 By 1935 when this photograph of the cast for Gilbert and Sullivan's "Mikado" was taken, the Waddesdon Philharmonic Society had long since given way to the Choral Society. For some years up to 1939 this was a very successful group with a good core of lead singers and a reputation for entertaining performances. Back row L-R: ------, George Figg, Frank Howe, Dorrie Franks, Will Cannon, Reg Harding, Mary Rose. Standing: Randall Styles, Norah Pearson, Will Evans, Mrs Edwards, Malcolm Tooley, Miss Taylor, Will Franks, Mary Crook, Nell Hedges, Jack Uff, Will Dennis. Sitting: Mrs J.Uff, Win Jones, Miss Tooley, Mrs M. Tooley. Kneeling: Nancy Collyer, Audrey Holland, Nancy Franks, Una Taylor, Mary Dennis, Win Dennis.

8.40 A most remarkable ensemble which could only have existed between the wars, "The Blue Bell Symphony Orchestra" consisting of side drum, rattle and bazookas. The conductor the Rev. Smith was known as a very genial gentleman with a penchant for the theatrical! From the back L-R: Leslie Crook, Eunice Goss, Norah Pearson, Rev. Smith, Joan Bishop, Nancy Franks, Mary Crook. This group was undoubtedly a light hearted act, probably performing at church fetes and other fund-raising events. Circa 1935.

8.41 These boys are dressed appropriately for the sailors' horn-pipe they are about to perform, circa 1930. L-R: Peter Franks, Jim Colyer, Bob Snelling, Ron Whitney, Bert Cannon, Reg Baker.

8.42 Once again entertainment for the church Whit Monday Fete. Costermongers L-R : Joan May, Josie Fowler, Rita Crook, Dorothy Fowler, Sybil Jones. Circa 1937.

8.43 The Waddesdon Girl Guides circa 1937. Not a "high profile" group; this is the only photograph we have of them. Back row L-R: Josie Fowler, Sybil Jones, Iris Carr, Joan May, Rita Crook. Middle row L-R: Margaret Wicks, Emmie Atkins, Peggy Roads, Sheila Rolfe, Nellie Atkins. Front row: Joy Carr, Barbara Harris, Ruby Read.

8.44 After the Second World War the Brownies, Cubs, Guides and Scouts were re-formed, thanks largely to the initiative of Mr and Mrs Frank Horner. Mr Horner was the Headmaster of the Council School. In this photograph of 1952 we have the 1st Waddesdon Brownies with Brown Owl Faith Fowler and Tawny Owl Elsie Biswell. Middle Row L-R: Doreen Saunders, Freda Fowler, Anita Knibb, Gwenda Carr, Carol Shillingford, Susan Saunders, Rosemary Ewers, Barbara Sharp, Pat Davis, Pat Green, Veronica Sharp, Rowena Evans, Josie Biswell, Jessie Emerton, Joyce Franks. Front Row : Paula Rhodes, Lyn McKenna, Valerie Radwell, Joan Gilson, Geraldine Ashfield, Roseanne McKenna, Marie Fowler.

8.45 After the Second World War the Reading Room and its excellent facilities was used as a Boys' Club whilst every Monday evening Mrs Laybourne ran the Girls Club in the Village Hall. There were no special facilities in the hall but the girls were taught dancing and took part in amateur dramatic productions. Each year the Club produced a pantomime which played to packed audiences in Waddesdon Hall and then toured the local villages including Stone, Quainton and even Kingswood. This photograph shows the cast of "Babes in the Wood" circa 1949. Back row L-R: Brenda Hicks, Daphne Carr, Olive Hicks, Dorothy Clarke, Doreen Church, Averil Cheshire. Middle row: Wendy Saunders, Pearl Marriott, Patricia Hayes, Mavis Carr, Jill Roads, Doris Drydale, Barbara Wheeler, Anna Fowler, Gwen Rolfe, Ann Cheshire, Daisy Cherry, Jacqueline Gurney. Front row: Doreen Saunders, Vera Cripps, Gwenda Carr, Doris Cripps, Phylis Saunders.

8.46 Here we see Mrs Leybourne surrounded by some of the senior girls circa 1952. Back row: Margaret Evans, Betty Foley, Shirley Rolfe, Jacqueline Gurney, Valerie Haigh, Jill Roads, Phyllis Cooper. Remainder: Cathy Charters, Gwen Rolfe, Daisy Cherry, Pam Goss, Peggy Wheeler, Wendy Saunders, Phyl Green, Averil Cheshire, Barbara Saunders, Nina Marriott (behind), Mavis Sharp, Rosemary Howes, Mrs Speed, and Mrs Leybourne sitting at table.

8.47 The Girls Club presentation of "Snow White and the Seven Dwarfs" circa 1947 was like all their productions, an outstanding success. Cast members included a number of young boys who portrayed the seven dwarfs, and simultaneously caused the ever-tolerant Mrs Leybourne with more than a few "headaches". Standing L-R : Shirley Rolfe, Brenda Thompson, Jill Rhodes, Doreen Church, Barbara Wheeler, Olive Hicks, Averil Cheshire, Daphne Carr, Alma Church, Brenda Hicks, Murray Saunders, Jacqueline Gurney, Wendy Saunders. Front L-R : -----, Patricia Hayes, Norman Carr, Phyllis Saunders, Anna Fowler, Doreen Saunders, John Cripps, Gwenda Carr, Pearl Marriott, Mavis Carr, Doris Cripps, Rosemary Saunders, Gordon Whitney, Doris Drydale, Robert Drydale, Kneal Marriott, Colin Marriott, Ivor Gurney.

The Royal British Legion

The Waddesdon Branch of the Royal British Legion was wound-up at the end of the twentieth century after seventy-five years of exemplary service in the community. This organisation which had been the leading village branch in the area, suffered from the inevitable dwindling of its membership as the years took their toll. Its final days were extended only by the efforts of a dedicated few.

This account is drawn from some of the old Minute Books and personal memories.

The Waddesdon Branch of the British Legion, was formed in 1922; it included Upper Winchendon, Fleet Marston, Westcott, Quainton, Kingswood, and Grendon Underwood, and from the outset enjoyed universal support. Membership was open to all ex-service personnel and auxiliaries, and honorary membership could be granted where appropriate. The Branch President was Mr James de Rothschild, and the Chairman was Mr P. Woolf (Agent for the Waddesdon Estate). They and the remainder of the membership were veterans of the Great War; they shared a special bond.

The Charter of the British Legion placed emphasis upon the values of comradeship, service and helpfulness, and the objects of the organisation were to perpetuate the memory of the fallen, assist ex-servicemen and women in their transition to civilian life, and promote the welfare of dependants of those who had laid down their lives in the war. All these principles appealed to the nation, and nowhere more-so than in Waddesdon, where every family had been touched by the tragedies of war.

Branch operations focussed upon the main objects, involving fund raising for both National and Branch finances. There were regular meetings, an annual outing, an annual Armistice Dinner, visiting sick ex-service personnel, delivering financial and welfare aid to the needy members and dependants of the fallen, and last but not least to organise Poppy Day activities and the annual Armistice Day service. The maintenance and care of the Waddesdon War Memorial and the provision of a regular Christmas-tide Party for local children was also undertaken.

Fetes and Gymkhanas, combined with Waddesdon Gardens "open for inspection", were huge fund-raising successes, whilst Whist Drives, Dances and a travelling Cinemategraph apparatus provided more regular income. As with all voluntary organisations, the essential boring majority of the work, fell upon a relatively small group out of the more than 200 members, and the Branch was lucky in having a significant proportion in this group who were employed by the Estate. Members regularly accepting office in addition to the President and Chairman, during the first 25 years included: Rev G. Dixon, Dr N. Black, Messrs Herbert, Harvey, May, Mole, Leybourne, Wildridge, Adcock, Gurney, Wootton, Walton, Court, Cox, Cannon, Skinner, Copcutt, Harding, Wood, Cripps and Saunders.

The A.G.M. held in the Bell Inn on the 29th September 1939, shortly after the outbreak of war, noted an increase in membership of 40, and the annual dinner was planned "subject to wartime conditions". Later that year Mr Tommy Mole reported on his monthly visit to Stone Mental Hospital where four Waddesdon patients (among 132 ex-servicemen) had received parcels from the branch. The children's Christmas Party went ahead as usual, Mrs de Rothschild sponsoring the entertainment and gifts. In the new year the branch loaned recreational equipment for the crew of a Search-light Battery stationed in Cat Lane, (early days!).

War-time expediencies put a strain on spare-time activities, yet to their credit the officials maintained the normal function of the Branch throughout, and in 1943 the importance of women in the service was recognised in the decision to form a Woman's Section (actioned in 1950!). In 1945 as the war entered its final phase, the Branch lobbied the Rural District Council to give housing priority to returning servicemen. A "Welcome Home Fund" was inaugurated and fund raising dances etc were held. The 23rd A.G.M. on 26th November 1945, held in the Five Arrows Hotel Clubroom was attended by 46 members and was noted "the best ever" by Mr Jack Cox, the secretary. In 1948 the Quainton Branch was formed and 75 members transferred en-bloc.

Rejuvenated by an influx of new younger members, the post-Second World War Waddesdon Branch, resumed its vigorous pursuits of the Objects of the British Legion. Fundraising and social events reflected the energy of the Branch, officially helped now by the Women's Section which was also separately raising funds, e.g. they inaugurated an annual outing for the children. For some years efforts were made to obtain a club-house, even resolving in 1947, to "squat" in the Warmstone ex-Army camp, however by 1958 the building fund had stagnated and the club-house project was cancelled. The branch remained an important and influential organisation in the village, and its long-term future was in little doubt. This is exemplified by the fact that in 1968 when the Village Hall Charitable Trust was established, the stated management committee was to include representatives from the Waddesdon Branch of the British Legion.

During the 1960's and 1970's the Waddesdon branch hosted an annual Festival of Remembrance in the style of the national event at the Royal Albert Hall. These were extremely popular engagements for all concerned, with Marsh Gibbon Band and other appropriate entertainment, the parade of Standards from dozens of Branches in the Region, and finally the familiar religious ceremony and Act of Remembrance. These Festivals were initially held in the Village Hall, but as the numbers grew it became necessary to transfer the venue to the Secondary School where parking and other facilities were more suitable.

The big fundraising fetes were superseded by more reliable and less demanding "Bingo" sessions, and for many years these were a major source of income; the branch even laying on coaches to collect players from surrounding villages. Meanwhile the work of the Services Committee, which carried out the welfare tasks at Branch level, was assuming greater importance as the average age of members increased. Worryingly despite regular attempts to recruit new members and associate members, insufficient numbers were attracted to the organisation to guarantee its future. By the early 1990's the active membership was reduced to a handful of worthy men and women who soldiered on, given the occasional fillip as a new member arrived, but facing the inevitable end of the branch before the end of the millennium.

Listed here are a number of members who served as Waddesdon Branch officials for many years post Second World War: Major Costeloe, Dr Bellamy, Dr Campbell, Messrs E.Standen, P.Ashfield, F. Howe, J.Hayes A.Shillingford, L.Woods, W.Jones, P.Ades, W.Caterer, A.Bowler, F.Trimm, R.&D. Saunders, T.Read, J.Edwards, D.Skinner, S.Davis, Mesdames G.Tucker, D.Snell, J. Dormer, E.Washington, B.Davis. This list is by no means exhaustive and does not include the intrepid Poppy Day organisers, the Standard Bearers, nor many of the officials of the Women's Section; the records available do not have this information.

The remaining members were transferred to local branches still in existence, and the annual Service of Remembrance at the War Memorial is now organised by the Parish Council.

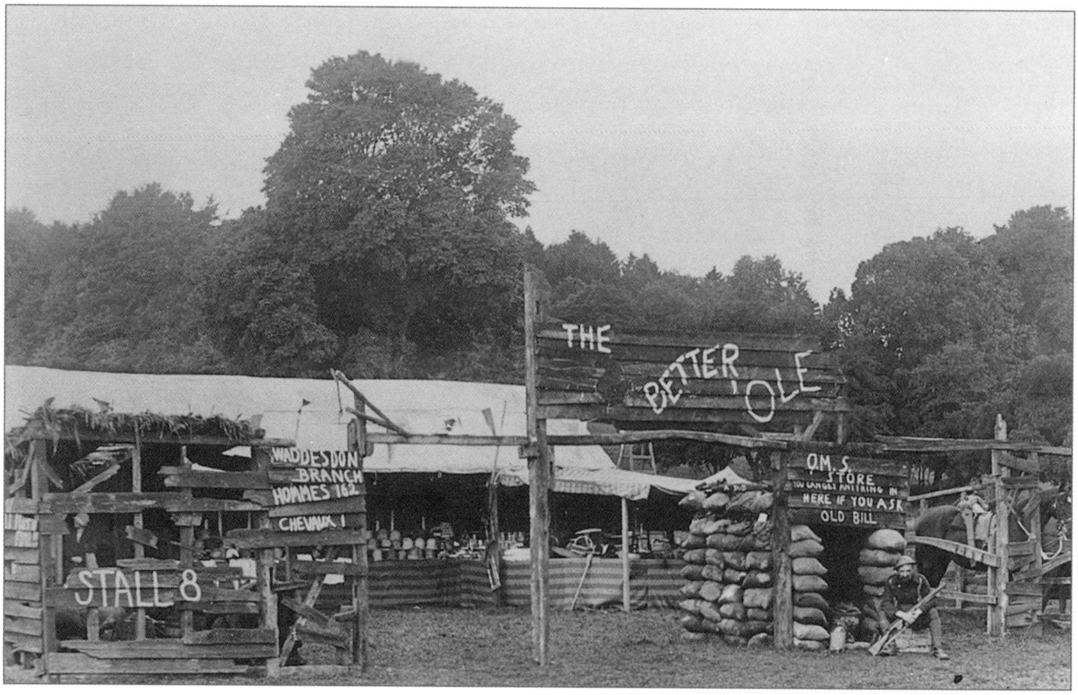

8.48 On Saturday 23rd June 1927 the Buckinghamshire County Committee of the British Legion held a fete in the grounds of Waddesdon Manor. The attractions included a " Mounted Gymkhana", a Display by 300 R.A.F. Halton Apprentices, Cabaret Concerts, a Push-ball Tournament, the Central Band of the Royal Air Force, Dancing in the Evening and finally a Grand Firework Display. This photograph records the stall which was Waddesdon's contribution, one of 28 such enterprises run by Branches from all over the county. "Old Bill", the Great War cartoon character who famously stated "If you know of a better 'ole, go to it!" is depicted here by Sam Court, sitting at the entrance to his bunker.

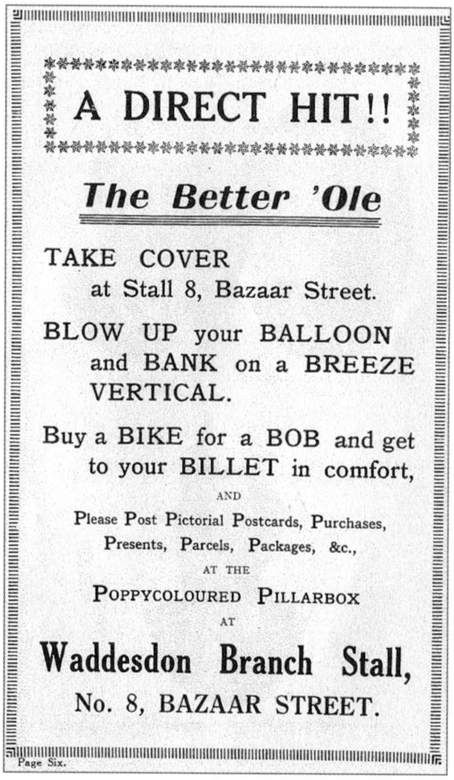

8.49 The advertisement for the stall of the Waddesdon British Legion Branch, "The better ole", at the Grand Fete held in June 1927.

8.50 The value of comradeship, which had been such an important factor for the servicemen of the Great War, is exemplified in this 1930's photograph of British Legion veterans on their annual outing. The outings always set out from the Branch Headquarters, which at this time was the clubroom of the Five Arrows Hotel. The cost of the outing was subsidised from Branch funds. On this occasion the charabancs were from the Aylesbury Omnibus Company. Although most of these in the photograph are unknown there are a few well-known faces still recognisable; at the front, third from left Fred Harding, then further to the right Charlie Scott, Dick Wood and Alfie Saunders (with boater).

8.51 The most emotive object of the British Legion has always been the very firm commitment to honour the dead of the Great War (originally), but then to include the fallen in the Second World War and subsequent wars involving British Armed Forces. All British Legion meetings commence with a period of silence for this purpose, but to the public the annual Service of Remembrance on the Sunday nearest to the 11th November is an opportunity to join in that commitment. This photograph shows the Remembrance Sunday Parade in 1952, led by the British Legion Standard Party. The Standard Bearer is Tom Read with Percy Ashfield on his left. Following the Standard are members of the Waddesdon Branch with the Chairman, Major Costeloe and visible in the party following are George Gurney (Upper Winchendon), Jack Slade, Ernie Hill, Ernie Southam, Sid Kibble, and Dr Bellamy. The Woman's Section's Standard Bearer was Mrs Brenda Davis with Mrs Adamson. Then come the Girl Guides led by Mrs V.Sharp, the Brownies, the Scouts and Clubs out of shot and as always the rear brought up by the Fire Brigade. On this and many subsequent Remembrance Sunday parades the numbers marching would have been in excess of 100; this number swelled by a large crowd of people at the War Memorial, many of them to hear once more the name of a long-lost relative in the list of those who "shall not grow old, as we that are left grow old".

8.52 The Five Arrows Lodge of "The Royal and Ancient Order of Buffaloes", an organisation whose main functions were for mutual benefit and charitable fund raising in an unobtrusive style. As with nearly all similar organisations, the younger generations have not been attracted to it, and after years of dwindling membership the Five Arrows Lodge closed down in the 1970's. In this photograph of circa 1925 we can name only a few. Rear; Extreme left Jim Carter, extreme right Ben Thorne, Middle; ------,-------,-------, Lou George, Bill Holloway, Bert Jones, Sam Court, Les Thorne.

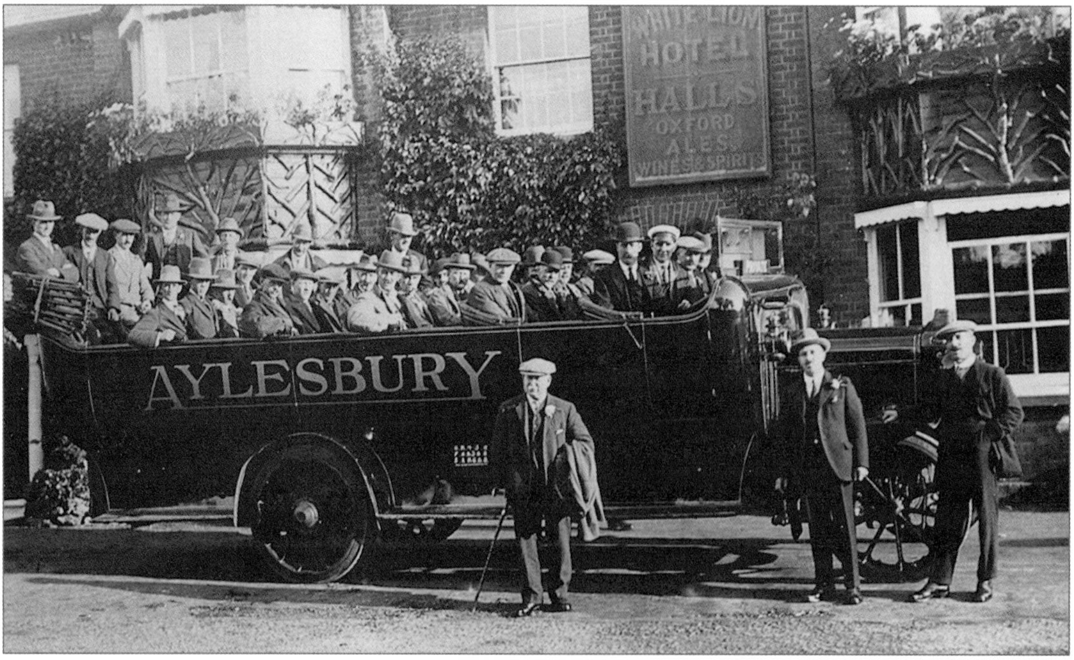

8.53 In the nineteenth century the White Lion Club was a "Sick Club", one of three in the village. As the years passed the emphasis changed from welfare to a social function, although for many years the club continued to pay sick members a small sum, so long as they obeyed the rules! This photograph of a charabanc about to leave the White Lion for an outing, circa 1928, shows the members packed tightly into every possible seat. Included from L-R: Teddy Sharp, Tom Evans, Horace Holland, and standing, centre, is Fred Paxton (landlord) and at extreme right Chris Hicks. Note; Solid tyres on the bus.

8.54 Waddesdon's "Cherry Blossom" with its passengers at the seaside? Circa 1932. L-R: -----, Jim Saunders, Glad Saunders, Mrs J Saunders, Charlie Cherry, (owner of Cherry Blossom), Stan Fowler (driver), back Jack Buckle, front Connie Owen, Rene Fowler, Ruby Buckle, Mrs Buckle, Bern Holland, Horace Holland, Charlie Thorp, Mrs Thorp.

8.55 In the early 1950's, day-trips to the seaside were very popular "mini-holidays" for many rural villagers. The White Lion Club ran at least one trip every year. In this photograph are a group of White Lion regulars on a day-trip to Margate, circa 1951. Back Row L-R: Harry Carter, Jim Neary, Roland Goss (driver), Nev Tuxford (landlord), Sid Radwell. Middle Row: Jack Saunders, -----, Will Radwell, Frank Cripps, Arthur Shillingford, Ken Rolfe, Arthur Cheshire, Horace Holland, T. Brown, "Pigeon" Green -----, Front Row: -----, Jack Cheshire, George Knibb, Bern Holland, Tom Cooper, "Dodger" Brown, Lionel Heritage, Stewart Mulcahy, Joe Pennington, Ben Marlow.

8.56 Another outing, this time mainly females, circa 1953. In the doorway of the coach; Daisy Cherry, Mrs Tom Cooper, Standing L-R: Valerie Haigh, Dave Thomas, Jaqueline Gurney, Gerald Cherry, Barbara Wheeler, ----------, Kathy Charters, Betty Foley, Phyllis Cheshire. Front Row: --------, Elsie Saunders, Averil Cheshire, Glad Bradbury, Evelyn Cheshire, Rose Drydale. The coach is one of Jim Raisey's of Grendon Underwood; in the immediate post-war years Raisey's Coaches were the most likely to be used for the theatre trips, treats and other outings.

8.57 The Waddesdon "Darby and Joan Club," circa 1962, at a function in the village hall. The club enjoyed great popularity as a recreational forum for pensioners during the 1950's and 1960's. the main organiser was Mrs Smith, (the wife of the Church School Headmaster), who was a member of the Women's Volunteer Service. Amongst those in this photograph are: Mrs Mabel Copcutt, Mrs Edith Copcutt (in Invalid chair). Mrs Kibble, Mrs Hattie George, Mrs Parsonage, Mrs Fillingham, Miss Figg, Mr Gilson, Mr and Mrs Alfie Saunders, Mrs E Goss, Miss Moule, Mr Billy Howe, Mr Fred Franks, Mrs Collyer. This photograph provides us with a good view in the village hall, the original entrance lobby and the lamps on the chandelier suspended above. Now both long gone.

8.58 The Darby and Joan Christmas Party circa 1960. In an effort to create a sense of jollity some of the members rather sportingly donned Party Hats but the overall image is rather sombre. This no doubt is partly down to the "dodgy" heating system in the Village Hall which has induced most of the party-goers to continue to wear their outdoor coats. The Darby and Joan Club did a grand job in bringing together the older generation who had lived through a more sociable time in village history, and who derived much pleasure in joining their neighbours at events such as this. Facing the camera at left are Mrs Olive Styles and Mrs Figg whilst in the fez is Mr Billy Howe.

8.59 In 1924 when Waddesdon Woman's Institute was inaugurated, the village fairly buzzed with community activities. With the active support of Mrs James de Rothschild as President, Mrs Woolf wife of the Estates agent, and Mrs Black wife of the village doctor, as Vice Presidents, and with numerous ladies from local farming and professional families in the membership, it could not fail. The first Secretary was Mrs J. Adams and the treasurer was Miss D. Adams. This photograph of circa 1965 brought together members of all ages, some of whom would remember the first meetings of 1924. Amongst those standing are L-R: Daisy Lovell, Betty Beattie, Brenda Davis, Mrs W. Evans, Mrs Franks, Mrs Speed, Margaret Franks, Mrs Burgess, Kath Howe, Faith Fowler, Olive Rhodes, Mrs Parrott, Mrs J. Franklin, Elsie Saunders, Daphne Campbell, Peggy Buckwell, Mrs Creed, Sylvia Southam. Seated: -----, Mrs J. Smith, Mrs Steinhardt, Mrs Littlechild, Mrs Marriott, Mrs Collyer, Mrs H. Read, Mrs Harris, Mrs Marriott.

8.60 One of the most enjoyable functions of the Woman's Institute was to encourage members to participate in light hearted competitions. Here we have a group in Fancy Dress for "Twelfth Night Party" on the 6th of January 1967. L-R: Mrs de Freece, Mrs Speed, Audrey Holland, Daisy Lovell, Daphne Campbell, -----, Sylvia Southam, -----.

8.61 The Golden Jubilee of the Waddesdon Woman's Institute in 1974 was celebrated in the Village Hall. This photograph records the cutting of the celebratory cake by Mrs Dorothy de Rothschild, the original and still serving President. Back L-R: -----, -----, Mrs Jeffery, Peggy Buckwell. Middle: Mrs Hatton, -----, Mrs Steinhardt, Mary Goodgame, -----, Elsie Saunders, -----, Amy Borchard, Gladys Cripps, -----, -----, -----, Dulcie Wilson, Margaret Clifford, Glynis Tucker, Mrs Leybourne, -----, Mrs V. Sharp, -----, Hilda Willis, -----, Mrs Hall, Mrs Washington, Mrs Figg, Mrs Creed. Sitting: Mrs Goss, Daisy Adams, Miss Brassey, Mrs Johnson, Sylvia Southam, -----, Mrs K. Howe, -----.

8.62 The Boy Scout movement has had an intermittent presence in Waddesdon, and photographs have been hard to come by. This photograph from around 1936 admirably records the 1st Waddesdon Scouts in the Rectory garden. Back L-R: Jack May, Jack Evans, Ron Copcutt, Vic Biswell, Ron Snelling, Alec Cripps, Desmond Crook. Middle: Arthur Crook (Assistant Scout Master), Captain John Fluke (Church Army) Scout Master, Rev George Dixon (Rector), Rev Smith (Curate), Vic Burgess (Troop Leader). Front: Eric Goss, Bernard Evans, Rex Cripps, Ken Rolfe, Fred Uff, Tony Figg, Bill Read.

8.63 In 1948 the 1st Waddesdon Scout Troop was re-formed by the Council School Head Teacher, Frank Horner. Most of the boys in the village joined and for a number of years the Scouts provided them with a purposeful use of their spare time and memorable camping experiences. For some years camps were held near The Fox Cover, a small wood at the south-eastern end of Castle Hill off Cat Lane. This photograph from 1950 shows Michael Franks, Norman Carr, Les Carter, and Harry Toy with Harry's grandfather on a bridge in Box, Wiltshire. The boys led by Assistant Scoutmaster Edgar Toy had cycled to Box, with an overnight camp en-route.

8.64 In 1975 the Scouting movement was quite strong in the village with Brownies, Guides, Cubs and Scout groups all flourishing. Here is the squad representing the Waddesdon Cubs in a local football competition. Standing L-R: Robert Wright, Darren Williams, Shaun O'Brian, Andrew Beck, Gary Goodin. Kneeling L-R: -----, Ian Price, Julian Rolfe, Andrew Ryall, Phillip Ball.

8.65 The Waddesdon Singers was formed around 1948 under Mr Joe Smith, the Head Teacher at the Church of England School. It comprised a nucleus of former members of the pre-war Choral Society, and also attracted talented "newcomers" to the village. These were the days when the professional people, school-teachers, doctors, administrators etc, lived in the community, and provided initiative and leadership for cultural activities. The photograph shows Mr and Mrs Smith receiving the tributes of the singers on the occasion of Mr Smith's retirement as leader. Circa 1970. L-R: -----, Mrs Toy, Will Evans, Sybil Jones, Mrs W. Evans, Frank Howe, Dulcie Wilson, Mrs James, Mrs Franks, Margaret Skinner, Mrs Stabler, Eva Rolfe, -----, Will Franks.

8.66 Immediately after the Second World War there was an upsurge in trades union membership including the Agricultural Workers Union. Here we have a meeting of the local branch in Waddesdon Village Hall, where most of those in the photograph are from Upper Winchendon! Circa 1949. Front Row L-R: Charlie Radwell, George Gurney, Mrs A. Gurney, Arthur Gurney, George Read, Gordon Read, -----, Vic Radwell. Second Row: Harold Radwell, Molly Radwell, Margaret Radwell, Mrs G.Gurney, Iris Gurney, George Gilmore, Will Cowley, -----, Pat Radwell, Ernie Dormer. Third Row: Tom Radwell, -----, Len Gurney, Mary Cherry, Mr Cowley (Snr), Sid Walker, Bert Pittam. Back Row: unknown.

8.67 The Waddesdon Allotment Society and its successors had its origins in the lean years of the early nineteenth century, when the Rev. Walton organised a Seed Club to encourage the poor to grow their own food. By the 1860's the annual Church Harvest Festival, (always celebrated on a weekday), included a fruit, flower, and vegetable show and also an athletic sports programme. The average allotment holding at that time amounted to 40 poles (1210 square yards or 1010 square metres), enough in a good year to provide most of the vegetables for a large family. During the 20th century, the annual Allotment Society show and sports, held on August Monday, became the big day of the summer. This event always attracted large crowds, the standards were always high, and in our memories the weather was always baking hot! In fact this photograph proves it did rain sometimes on August Monday, (in those days the first Monday in August). Instead of presenting the show prizes from the front of the Cricket Pavilion, Mrs de Rothschild is shown doing the honours here, a little cramped in one of the marquees. The recipient of the cups is Albert Bradbury, one of a number of gardening experts who succeeded in keeping Waddesdon at the forefront in local show competitions. Circa 1953.

8.68 Len Wood shown here with his wife Joy admiring a collection of rose blooms, was Waddesdon's most successful amateur gardener. Between the 1950's and 1990's he achieved remarkable success at all levels with his rose bloom entries in competitions. In 1978 Len became National Champion of the Royal National Rose Society and in 1987 he was elected President, serving for two years. From start to finish of his rose showing career he never attended a show without winning at least one prize. Not content with showing, he also bred a pink rose "My Joy" dedicated to his wife. Len was a modest village man who was always willing to do his bit, he served as Chairman of the Waddesdon and District Horticultural Society for 25 years, and also for some years as Chairman of the Waddesdon Branch of the Royal British Legion.

8.69 Tom Wheeler the current President of Waddesdon and District Horticultural Society. He is shown at his shed on the Parish Council Allotment field, Sheriffs Closes, down the Quainton Road in 1995. A Waddesdon man through and through, Tom unfortunately is one of a vanishing breed. He has served the village for some years as a Parish Councillor including a stint as Chairman, and has been involved with the Horticultural Society as a member, committee member, Chairman and latterly as President. Tom has had an allotment since completing his service in the Royal Navy in 1954, and still exhibits produce at the annual show.

8.70 Over the years the Society changed its name to represent the interests of the membership. Allotment holding became less popular, so now the name is Waddesdon and District Horticultural Society. However here is Bern Holland amongst the peas on his allotment off Quainton Road (circa 1990); a member of the Society he could therefore purchase his seeds and sundry gardening materials at discount prices. A veteran of the Burma campaign in the Second World War, Bern was a village man through and through, he married a village girl, raised his family, played for the village football team, and worked in the village all his life.

8.71 Bill Fowler has achieved an enviable standard in his gardening for many years and currently is "the man to beat" at the Horticultural Society annual show. In this photograph Bill displays some of the trophies won at the show (circa 1998), whilst on the table rest some of his prize-winning vegetables. In the background of this photograph are Ian Ewers, Secretary of the Society, with his wife Elizabeth, who together with a small team work hard to maintain the regular success of the show.

8.72 In 1960 Cannon Dixon suggested the formation of a Young Wives Club in Waddesdon, and this initiative created the group, which has become the Waddesdon Ladies Club. The monthly meetings are attended by ladies of all ages, including some who were original members. Here we have a group in the Village Hall in 1970. L-R: Coral Soulsby, Vera Marriott, Daisy Lovell, Olive Rhodes, Nina Burnell, Pearl Rolfe, Averil Brown, Doreen Snell, Jean Redding.

8.73 The Ladies Club meets at the Village Hall where members enjoy the interesting talks and activities that are organised, and the friendly informality which the club engenders. Over the years there have been many theatre trips and social evenings, and here we have a photograph of such an evening held at The White Swan in Aylesbury circa 1970. L-R: Rita O'Brien, Betty Beattie, Pearl Rolfe, Mrs Hall, Gladys Cripps, Edna Goss, Rita Richards, Anita Marriott.

8.74 The Wednesday Day Centre in Waddesdon, inaugurated in 1980, was originally held in St Judes Church, but now meets at the Village Hall and is more generally referred to as "The Wednesday Club". Members live in the vicinity, and are mainly elderly; each week they are transported to and from the club, where they enjoy friendly companionship, have their meal together, and participate in various organised activities. This photograph records an outing to a Shire Horse Centre in 1989, and includes, amongst others, the following members and helpers: L-R Con Neary, Ann Payne, Mrs Tom Radwell, Jean Warr, Pat Wright, Mary Norris, Mary Goodgame, Doris Trimm, Lottie Stutchbury, Evelyn O'Shea, Audrey Pegg, Pauline Thompson, and Harold Goodgame.

8.75 The Wednesday Club operates under the auspices of Social Services which provides the Organiser and maintains financial viability, whilst members' charges help to defray costs. In this photograph taken shortly before the Club's transfer to the Village Hall, we have some of the helpers in the kitchen at St Judes, circa 1995. L-R: Audrey Ayris, Pat Wright, Heather Stutchbury, Dorothy Hough and Audrey Pegg. An important element of the Club's success over the years, has been the dedicated work of its faithful band of voluntary helpers, several of whom have given their services continuously, since the beginning.

Section Nine

Shops etc in Waddesdon

Since time immemorial, Waddesdon like other similarly endowed villages, has enjoyed or endured the shopping and service facilities which have been warranted by the custom expended. This basic economic rule lies behind the dire state at which Waddesdon's shopping facilities have arrived at the commencement of the Third Millennium.

Easily within living memory Waddesdon's shops etc could provide all the normal requirements to sustain the community, and the photographs in this section may help readers recall or imagine a less hectic time in our recent history.

Accounts books of Waddesdon's Overseers' for the Poor often mention payments for medicines, food, and clothing for destitute families in the eighteenth century. Obviously there were shops in the village, but little is recorded about them. However the 1798 Buckinghamshire Posse Comitatus informs us the number of male residents were around 230 and of these, two were Shopkeepers, five were Victuallers (Inn-keepers), four were Butchers, two were Tailors, and four were Cordwainers (Shoe-makers). Note; The 1798 Comitatus was a Government return concerned with resources available in the event of a French invasion.

By 1850 the number of Shopkeepers was five and the number of Beer Retailers had risen to eight! There was also a Draper, a Saddler, a Miller, and Levi Crook the Carrier, visited Aylesbury on Wednesdays and Saturdays. Waddesdon was struggling out of a depressed period that had lasted since the enclosures of 1774, but now almost imperceptibly things were showing signs of improvement.

The Kelly's Directory of 1877 informs readers of the recent change of Lord of the Manor, to Baron Ferdinand de Rothschild, and the building of his mansion, now under way. It listed more than fifty trades-persons including seven Grocers, seven landlords of Public Houses, five other shops including two Tailors, three Butchers, one Draper and a Watchmaker. Three Carriers visited Aylesbury on market days, Wednesdays and Saturdays. The population was 1,838 in 1871, (including the hamlets).

Reproduced here is the Kelly's Directory list of Private and Commercial Residents in Waddesdon and Westcott in 1891. This list provides a somewhat distorted perspective, as many

PRIVATE RESIDENTS.

Baverstock Rev. Edward Perry T.A.K.C.L. [curate]
Crook Mrs
Curtis Miss
Davis Rev. John Stratton M.A. [curate]
Dendy Walter Chester
Goss Joseph
Goss Mrs
Hook William John
Kibble John
Payne Mrs. Wescott
Pipkin William, Ada cottage
Rothschild Baron Ferdinand James M.P., D.L., J.P. Waddesdon manor; & 143 Piccadilly, London W
Rothschild Miss Alice de, Eythrope; & 142 Piccadilly, London W
Stretch Mrs
Walker Charles Edward
Williams Rev. Thomas John M.A. [rector], Rectory
Wood Mrs. High street

COMMERCIAL.

Adams Geo. farmer, Wormstone Pk. frm
Adams Wm. dealer, Wormstone Pk. frm
Alcock John, farmer & hay & straw dealer, Lower Blackgrove
Alcock William, corn & coal merchant
Barker Lewis, house steward to Baron F. J. Rothschild M.P
Bell George, shopkeeper, Frederick st
Blake John Walter, mealman & corn dlr
Burnard William, carpenter & builder
Chapman Ephraim, head gamekeeper to Baron Ferdinand Jas. Rothschild M.P
Club & Reading Room (George Alfred Sims, sec. & treasurer)
Cockerill George, White Lion P.H
Collyer Alfred, tailor
Craker Henry, bailiff to Baron Ferdinand James Rothschild M.P. Oving farm
Cripps Sarah (Mrs.), butter vendor
Cripps Thomas, grazier, Wescott
Crook Charles, builder & contractor
Crook Edwin, grocer & baker
Crook Levi, butter dealer & carrier
Dendy Walt. Chester L.R.C.P. Lond. surg
Dodwell Hannah (Mrs.), grocer & baker, Post office
Duntling Obadiah, farmer & landowner, The Grove
Dymock John, Bakers' Arms P.H
Englefield George, shopkeeper
Evans Albert, gas engineer to Baron Ferdinand Jas. Rothschild M.P. Wescott
Figg Henry, beer retailer, Wescott
Figg William, plumber & house decortr
Flowers William, farmer & grazier, Beachenton, Eythrope
Fowler William, Bell P.H
Franklin James, grocer & baker
Garner Edwin, shoe maker
Garner John, shoe maker
Gibbs Edward, land steward to Miss Alice de Rothschild, Eythrope
Gibbs Richard, saddler & harness makr
Gilson Thomas, blacksmith
Goss James, farmer
Goss James, farmer, Wescott Field farm, Wescott
Goss Thomas, farmer, Upper Wescott farm, Wescott
Goss Thomas Griffin, farmer, Wescott
Grace Eli, grocer
Herring Hy. Jas. baker & grcr. Frederick st
Holland Joseph, builder & contractor
Howe Kezia (Mrs.), shopkeeper
Jacques John, head gardener to Baron Ferdinand James Rothschild M.P
MacGregor Alexander, forester to Baron Ferdinand J. Rothschild M.P
McKiernan Michael Peter, foreman to Baron Ferdinand J. Rothschild M.P
Marlow Benjamin, Ship P.H
Marriott Joseph, White Swan P.H. & grocer, Wescott
Monk Charles Henry, farmer, Sheepcote hill, Eythrope
Moscrop William, grocer, draper & bakr
Payne Fred Jn. Matthews, frmr. Wescott
Price Joseph, butcher
Puddefoot Henry, stud-groom to Baron Ferdinand James Rothschild M.P
Roads James, carrier & coal merchant
Rogers Chas. frmr. Lit. Keton, Manor frm
Rolfe Elizabeth (Mrs.), beer retailer
Saunders John Franklin, draper, outfitter & tea dealer
Sharp George, wheelwright
SHERWIN HENRY HAYLES, builder & contractor
Sims Geo. Alfred, land steward to Baron Ferdinand James Rothschild M.P
Sinclair George, herdsman to Baron Ferdinand James Rothschild M.P
Southam Wm. bricklayer, Frederick st
Steele Thomas, joiner, cabinet maker & french polisher; estimates given for all kinds of joinery & builders' work, painting & glazing & general repairs, Frederick street
Strathdee Charles, farm bailiff to Baron Ferdinand James Rothschild M.P
Taylor Jsph. miller (steam) & corn dlr
Thorn Henry, baker
Thorne Geo. & Jn. frmrs. Blackgrove Upper
Treadwell Samuel, farmer, Windmill hl
Turnham Henry, Five Arrows hotel
Uff Thomas, farmer, Wescott
Walker Charles Edward L.R.C.P. Edin. surgeon, & medical officer & public vacc. No. 5 district, Aylesbury union
Walton Richard, watch cleaner
Ward George, blacksmith
Ward William, blacksmith
Watson Horace, farmr. Up. Blackgrove
Webb Frederick, linen draper & tailor
Welch William, builder, Frederick st
West Frederick, hair dresser, High st
Wheelton David, stationer & tobacconist

minor traders did not appear on it.

In 1979 an elderly lady, Mrs Cis Percival provided the writer with a list of businesses she had recalled from her childhood, pre-Great War. Photographs of the period show that some shops were established in purpose-built premises, but many other little businesses were carried on from the front rooms of ordinary houses. Mrs Percival had compiled a list of sixty "shops", and I include a few examples here; John Goss sold cooked meat and sausages from 110 High Street, Edwin Garner was a Shoemaker at 94 High Street, Mrs Betsy Rolfe had the Coffee Tavern at 88 High Street, Mr Collyer was a Tailor and Outfitter at 86, Kitty Allen sold home-made sweets and rock from an old house next to the White Lion Hotel, George Saunders sold milk at his back door where the Indian Restaurant now is, Mr J Gibbs was a Saddler and Harness Maker in the High Street. Mr G Griffin was a Greengrocer at 33 Frederick Street, Mr Jonah Cripps the gravedigger lived at 41, Mr Sandy Cripps, Rat Catcher lived at 74 Quainton Road. Throughout the village were several ladies who had small general shops, and sold all sorts of goods from their front rooms. There were also Thatchers, four Undertakers, two Barbers, six Bakers, two Drapers, a Photographer and two Chimney Sweeps. This was a time when Waddesdon was considered to be very prosperous, although a labourer's wage may have been less than £1 per week; it is likely that all his income would have been expended within the village. The numerous stores and small businesses did not make fortunes for everyone, often they served only to supplement the family income from "proper" work.

The first half of the twentieth century witnessed the best of times for Waddesdon's shops. Despite the two world wars the prosperity of the population steadily improved and reflected in the business success of the shops. Villagers and people in the locality enjoyed the convenience and personal service provided, tastes were unsophisticated and home deliveries were free. Even in 1950 the alternative sources of supply would have entailed a bus journey to Aylesbury, not something to be contemplated on a weekly basis.

Perhaps, for a further ten years the number of shops stayed about the same, some changed ownership, some changed goods, but a downward trend was in motion. Long established names began to disappear, Greengrocer-Tommy Griffin, Baker and Grocer- Emma Grace, Baker and Grocer- Sid Crook (long gone), General Store- Mrs Dodwell, General Store- Mrs Harris, Draper- Mr and Mrs Fillingham, Draper and Hardware Store- Ken Saunders, Butcher- Mr Saunders. The long hours, traditionally a feature of village shop-keeping, and reducing turnover quickened the trend, and shop premises were reverting to living accommodation. The motorcar and the supermarket era had arrived. The population in the parish at the census of 1991 was 1,864.

In this section we include a montage for the record, of the shops etc in the streets of Waddesdon, 2001. For the sake of posterity we include a caption for each photograph containing the names of those persons shown.

9.1 The Coffee Tavern was the next-door business to that of Mr Collyer the village Tailor, (now the premises of the Village Post Office). Mrs Betsy Rolfe shown here at the gate-way had previously owned a Beer shop near Wormstone not far from the present day entrance to Goss Avenue. When the Baron established the plantation strip alongside the Aylesbury Road, Mrs Rolfe was re-housed in Waddesdon's smart new High Street, but this time her business was the more acceptable Coffee Tavern. It is difficult to imagine this was as popular as the Beer house! Photographed circa 1900.

9.2 In this photograph four businesses are on view; the Men's Hairdresser of Mr Frederick West, Humphrey's Bakery, Grocers and Post Office, then the creeper-strewn cottage of Mrs Kitty Allan who sold home-made sweets and rock, finally the White Lion Hotel owned at this time by Halls Brewery of Oxford, circa 1900.

9.3 Will Southam was the third Hairdresser to use these premises previously held by Frederick West and next by a Mr Tombs (who emigrated with his family to Canada). Mr Southam had first set up his Hairdressing business in the house where the Indian Restaurant is now (2001) Photograph circa 1910.

9.4 Saunders' shop at the entrance to Frederick Street circa 1910. This large building titled "Manchester House" provided both business and domestic accommodation for the family of Mr John Saunders. The shop had several departments covering everything from drapery, outfitting, hardware (including paraffin) through to dealing in tea. In this photograph we can see gardening tools and a mattress outside on display, at the hardware entrance. This shop remained in the Saunders family until the 1970's, then was used for a men's Hairdresser's at the old hardware end, whilst an insurance company traded from the old drapery department for a year or two. Eventually the premises were converted to living accommodation and have remained so. (2001).

9.5 Franklins' Shop alongside the Wesleyan Chapel. Since the 1870's this family business provided the village with a first class grocery and bakery shop, first by the founder James Franklin, then through his son Thomas and then his grandson James. This photograph was taken circa 1900. As can be discerned on the notice in the central (false) window, Franklins could supply tea parties and regularly did so until the Great War, each year alternating with Dodwells in supplying the provisions for the Baron's Treat, and later Miss Alice's Tea Party. Franklins bakery had a coke-fired, steam tube, double deck oven, which was modern compared to the other five coal-fired side flue bakeries in the village, and was capable of a higher production rate. In its heyday the bakery produced two hundred 2lb loaves at each baking, and every part of the process was done by hand; mixing the dough, rolling each ball of dough for the cottage loaf, and loading and unloading the oven. House to house deliveries to the village and surrounding farms etc followed and prices in 1912 were, 2d for a large and 1d for a small loaf. Bakers worked exceptionally long hours on six days every week. Franklins continued baking bread until the 1970's, but by 1978 the shop was sold and converted to living accommodation.

9.6 This was the Grocery Shop of Miss Rosanna Adams, later the wife of Michael McKiernan foreman on Baron de Rothschild's estate. Originally this building was erected in 1727, and its purpose was to house destitute families – the Workhouse. Up to 30 people were accommodated here in spartan conditions, males separate from females no matter the marital status! Around 1840 the old Workhouse was abolished and a shop's premises established. In 1905 Miss Alice de Rothschild acquired the roadside strip of land and buildings, from the Ship Inn down the Bicester Hill. From then on the old Workhouse became known as "The Homestead", and became the home of Estate administrators (principally Mr May). In the 1980/90's Phyllis Calvert the famous film star lived here.

9.7 Joseph Price kept a Butcher's Shop in Queen Street in the 1870's, and the premises had the distinction of being the only building considered suitable for retention by Baron Ferdinand, when he acquired the properties in Queen Street. Mr Price seen here circa 1900 transferred his business to the High Street where it continued under his son Robert (Bobby), and later Will Dennis who traded under the Price name.

9.8 Taylor's Mill and Mill House down Quainton Road circa 1910. Mr Joseph Taylor built his first steam powered mill between Silk Street and Back Road, in the mid nineteenth century. In photograph 1.17 the tall chimney can be seen at the original site, and it is thought its prominence inspired the Baron to persuade Mr Taylor to move his business half a mile or so. The new mill shown here was built and the machinery transferred in 1893. Mr Taylor used the mill principally for the production of animal feed from grain imported from Eastern Europe. However he also milled local wheat, including that of allotment holders, often operating a bartering method of payment. He had three sons who locally extended the Taylor milling reputation, Robert at Three Bridge (Water) Mill, Walter at Thornborough Mill and Alfred who took over at Waddesdon. Diesel power replaced steam in the 1930's, and milling at Waddesdon ceased in the 1960's, but feed for farm stock continued to be distributed from the mill premises into the 1980's. After trading ceased the premises were utilised for metal polishing, and to this day D.K.R. Metal Polishers provide this service for customers from near and far.

9.9 Wheelwrights were an essential element in the life of any community until the internal combustion engine totally replaced the horse. Here at the centre of the picture we have Mr George Sharp, at his home and business premises No1 High Street, circa 1910. On the left is George's son Bob, and also within this photograph are numerous examples of the wheelwright's craft. Wheels were manufactured in their totality, as were the wagons, including all the iron work. Standing elm trees were purchased, felled, sawn, seasoned and eventually fashioned into carts, wagons and even wheelbarrows. The rungs of ladders were often made from "retired" wheel spokes. Ted Sharp, son of George, was Waddesdon's last wheelwright. He carried on the business at 1 High Street until the early 1970's, a working link with the past, always a pleasure to visit and always time for a few words.

9.10 Grace's Grocery and Provision Stores circa 1912. One of Waddesdon's six bakeries and a general grocery store which in addition sold pork, bacon and ales and stout (in casks)! The bakehouse was in a cellar under the shop, but where everything was stored is a mystery. At the doorway is Miss Emma Grace who ran the shop and on her left is John Grace, her brother who oversaw things. Graces employed a baker, and bread and provisions roundsman, and here can be seen the smart bread van advertising Hovis. For many years, even after they had ceased baking after the Second World War, the shop exhibited a sign "Daren Bread", (still a puzzle to the writers). Graces ceased trading around 1960. See photograph 9.30.

9.11 Dodwell's Shop was a well established business in Waddesdon since before 1850, and originally the premises were next to the National School at the High Street junction with Silk Street. (see photograph 4.5). Towards the end of the nineteenth century the Baron eventually persuaded Phil Dodwell to part with his coveted property, and re-establish his business about 250 yards away on the site of this photograph. At the time of the move the premises included the Post Office and Telegraph Office, in addition to Baker, Grocer and General Provisions. At some point early in the 20th century there was something of a scandal to do with non-delivering of circulars, and the Post Office was transferred to Humphrey's Shop. For his own reasons Mr Dodwell retained part of the Post Office window sign as can be seen on the left of this picture.

9.12 At the junction of Wood Street with the High Street these two shops have long since closed down and now the complete block and the outhouses at the rear form a complex of apartments. William Figg was a craftsman of renown, being an expert in all aspects of Plumbing and Decorating, and on occasion his standing was confirmed when his technical contributions were published in trade journals. At the time of this photograph circa 1925, the village still enjoyed the benefits of the local gas-works and Mr Figg advertised gas lights and pipe fittings on his shop windows. The business commenced circa 1890 and was passed on to three of Mr Figg's staff in the 1950's. Bob Radwell took on the Plumbing, and Den Ewers and Joe Goss retained the shop and continued with the Painting and Decorating side. Joe and Den retired and closed their business some years ago, but the Radwell family carry on the Plumbing business through Bob's son, John. William Figg's old premises enjoyed a brief respite when Frank Carter ran a Do-it-yourself shop there, before completing the development for private dwellings in the 1980's. George Styles was a foreman on the Estate but was one of the few in the village who found time also to run a business, the village Newsagent. See Photograph 9. 22.

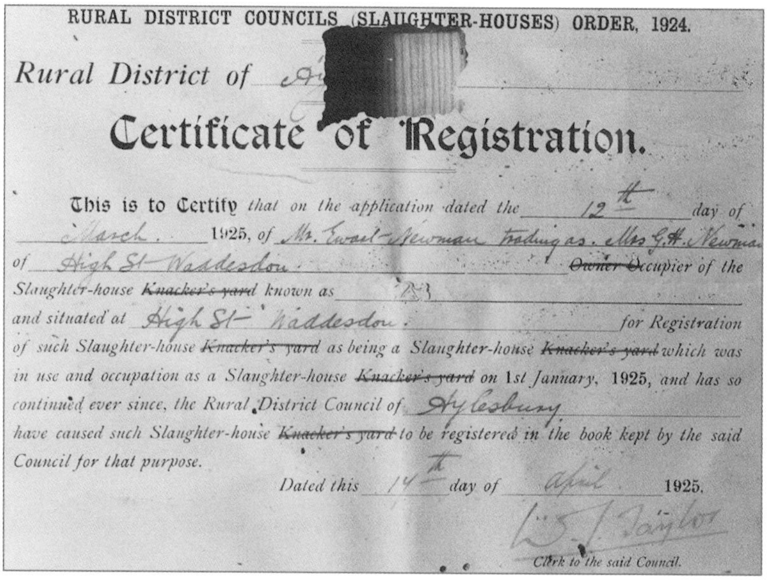

RURAL DISTRICT COUNCILS (SLAUGHTER-HOUSES) ORDER, 1924.

Rural District of Ay

Certificate of Registration.

This is to Certify *that on the application dated the* 12th *day of* March 1925, *of* Mr. Ewart Newman trading as. Mrs G.H. Newman *of* High St Waddesdon ~~Owner~~ *Occupier of the Slaughter-house* ~~Knacker's yard~~ *known as* ... *and situated at* High St Waddesdon *for Registration of such Slaughter-house* ~~Knacker's yard~~ *as being a Slaughter-house* ~~Knacker's yard~~ *which was in use and occupation as a Slaughter-house* ~~Knacker's yard~~ *on 1st January,* 1925, *and has so continued ever since, the Rural District Council of* Aylesbury *have caused such Slaughter-house* ~~Knacker's yard~~ *to be registered in the book kept by the said Council for that purpose.*

Dated this 14th *day of* April 1925.

L. J. Taylor

Clerk to the said Council.

9.13 This Slaughterhouse certificate refers to the premises, which a year later was taken over by Stewart Adams. Ewart Newman had traded there for a number of years whilst also running a small farm from "The Grove" in Baker Street. In the early years of the 20th century a slaughterhouse was a normal and essential feature in any village butchery.

9.14 The cards on the table inform us that Stewart Adams had purchased prize-winning animals from Fat Stock Shows, and the prime cuts are on display. The photograph was taken around 1930 and in the picture, from the left are; Tom Thorp, Eric Russell and Frank Russell. See Photograph 9.25.

9.15 Edward (Ted) Bishop was born in Meerut in India, the son of a regular soldier in the Royal Artillery. Ted joined the Royal Field Artillery in 1913 and was with the B.E.F. in France soon after the outbreak of war. He was wounded and had his leg amputated in 1916, was awarded the Distinguished Conduct Medal and was discharged. In 1918 he set up in business as a Boot and Shoe Repairer in the house on the left of the Britain Lane entrance (opposite Waddesdon Tyres). His workshop was this shed in the garden, and later a lean-to workshop was attached to the house. In the 1940's there were three "snobs" in the village, but as they retired over the next twenty years, no-one took their place.

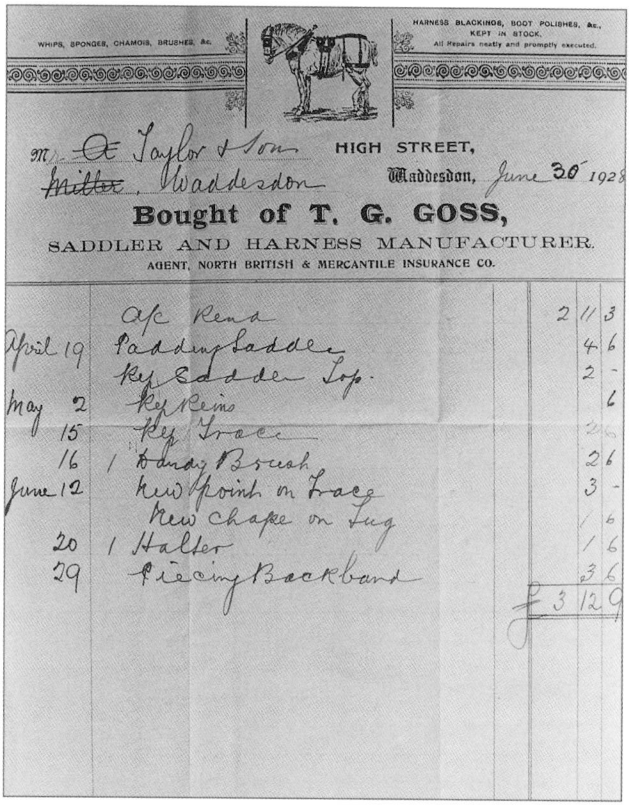

WHIPS, SPONGES, CHAMOIS, BRUSHES, &c.

HARNESS BLACKINGS, BOOT POLISHES, &c., KEPT IN STOCK.
All Repairs neatly and promptly executed.

Mr ~~A~~ Taylor & Son HIGH STREET,
~~Miller~~, Waddesdon Waddesdon, June 30 1928

Bought of T. G. GOSS,

SADDLER AND HARNESS MANUFACTURER.

AGENT, NORTH BRITISH & MERCANTILE INSURANCE CO.

		£	s.	d.
	A/c Rend	2	11	3
April 19	Padding Saddle		4	6
	Rep Saddle Top		2	-
May 2	Rep Reins			6
15	Rep Trace		2	6
16	1 Dandy Brush		2	6
June 12	New point on Trace		3	-
	New Chape on Tug		1	6
20	1 Halter		1	6
29	Piecing Backband		3	6
		£3	12	9

9.16 The Saddler, Thomas Goss had his shop and workshop in the detached house next to Price's Butchers shop in the High Street. Mr Goss sat, visible through the front window, a familiar sight over many years carrying out his craft. In summer the door often stood open, and village boys would venture inside to see at first hand the kind of work done there. The bill reproduced here details work done over three months in 1928 for Mr Taylor of the Mill.

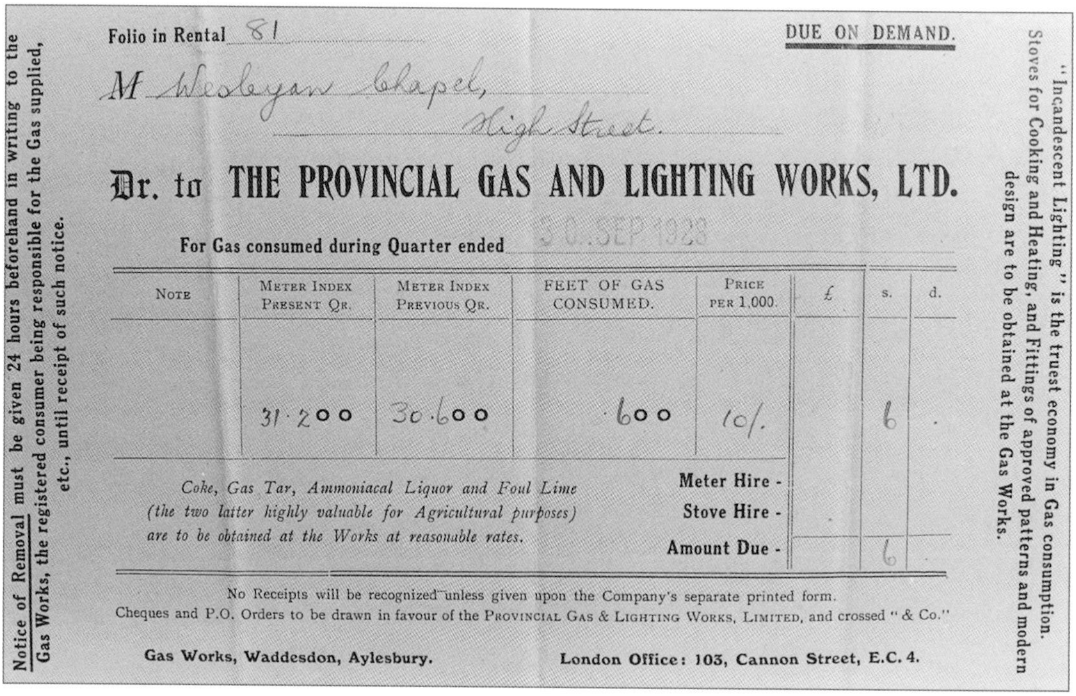

Notice of Removal must be given 24 hours beforehand in writing to the Gas Works, the registered consumer being responsible for the Gas supplied, etc., until receipt of such notice.

Folio in Rental 81 DUE ON DEMAND.

M Wesleyan Chapel,
High Street.

Dr. to THE PROVINCIAL GAS AND LIGHTING WORKS, LTD.

For Gas consumed during Quarter ended 30 SEP 1928

NOTE	METER INDEX PRESENT QR.	METER INDEX PREVIOUS QR.	FEET OF GAS CONSUMED.	PRICE PER 1,000.	£	s.	d.
	31·200	30·600	·600	10/.		6	·
				Meter Hire -			
				Stove Hire -			
				Amount Due -		6	

Coke, Gas Tar, Ammoniacal Liquor and Foul Lime (the two latter highly valuable for Agricultural purposes) are to be obtained at the Works at reasonable rates.

No Receipts will be recognized unless given upon the Company's separate printed form.
Cheques and P.O. Orders to be drawn in favour of the PROVINCIAL GAS & LIGHTING WORKS, LIMITED, and crossed "& Co."

Gas Works, Waddesdon, Aylesbury. London Office: 103, Cannon Street, E.C. 4.

"Incandescent Lighting" is the truest economy in Gas consumption. Stoves for Cooking and Heating, and Fittings of approved patterns and modern design are to be obtained at the Gas Works.

9.17 Another bill of 1928, this one from the village Gasworks for the supply of gas to the Wesleyan Chapel. The Gasworks was sited down Quainton Road, opposite the Mill. (Now Mill Close). It closed down in the 1930's when much of the gas lighting in the village, both in the streets and in the buildings, had been superseded by electric lights. Not many villagers had enjoyed the luxury of gas in the home.

9.18 This photograph shows Les Marriott standing in front of a rick that he has recently thatched, circa 1938. Les was a prize-winning thatcher who worked at this time for Waddesdon Estate, although he took on a small-holding in the 1940's, and thus became self-employed. After hay-making and harvesting, the ricks which stored the crops had to be protected from the elements. This provided a huge amount of work for the thatchers, despite the fact that by winter's end it would all be destroyed.

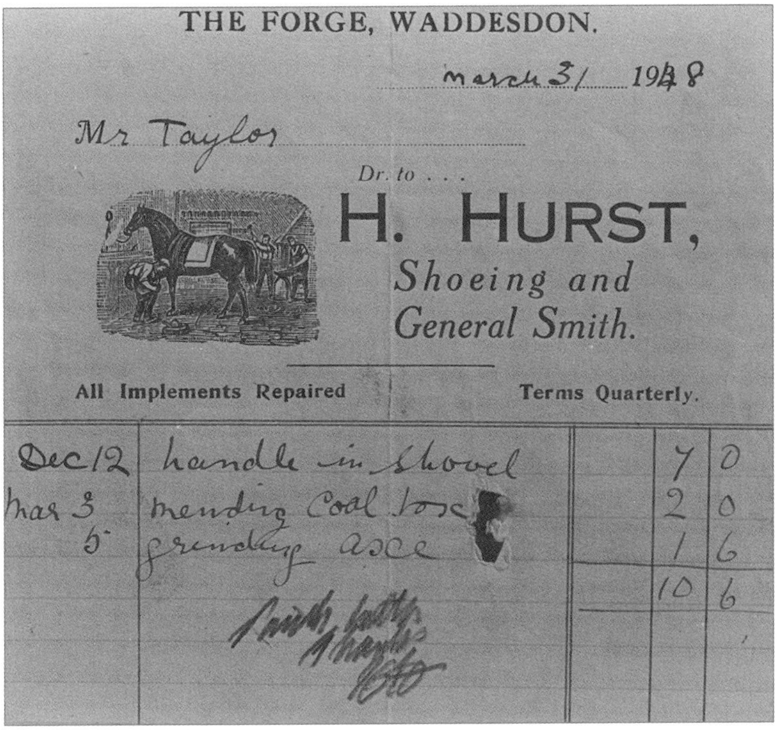

THE FORGE, WADDESDON.

March 31 1948

Mr Taylor

Dr. to . . .

H. HURST,

Shoeing and General Smith.

All Implements Repaired — Terms Quarterly.

Dec 12	handle in shovel	7	0
Mar 3	mending Coal box	2	0
5	grinding axe	1	6
		10	6

9.19 Until the 1960's, Waddesdonians had been familiar with the ring of the blacksmith's hammer, and the instantly recognisable acrid smell of burning hoof, emanating from Harry Hurst's forge, next to the White Lion Hotel. Mr Hurst was the last Blacksmith in business in the village, and like his predecessors he carried out a multitude of tasks, mainly related to agricultural implements as well as the shoeing of horses. The bill reproduced here, from 1948, gives us a reminder of the "make do and mend" era of the past, and the charges made.

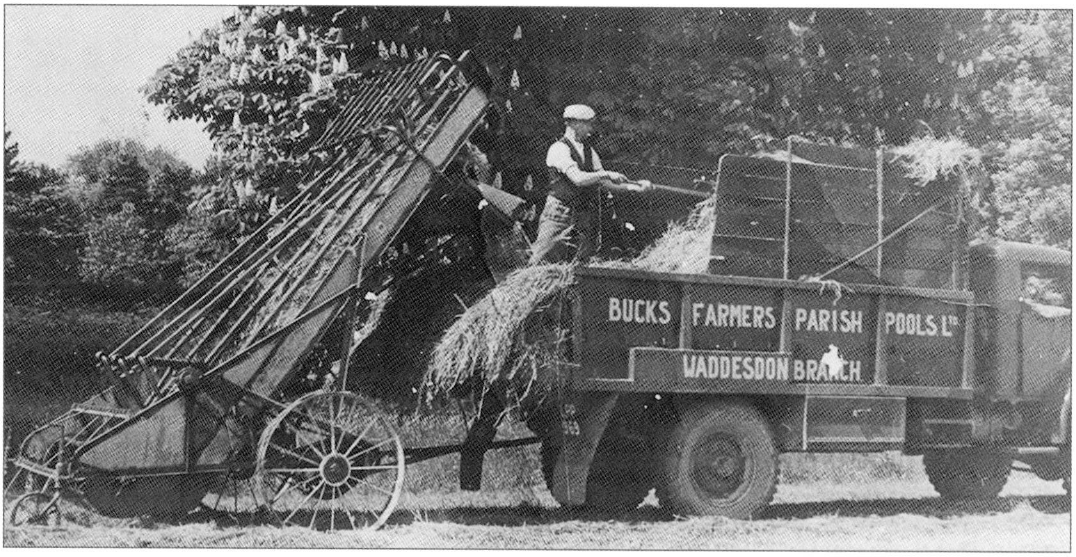

9.20 Vehicles made redundant by the war ending, were sold off to the public, mostly for commercial use. In this photograph of the early 1950's is an ex-army lorry (An ex- "Lease-Lend" Ford or Chevrolet from the U.S.A or Canada), belonging to an organisation set up for local farmers. The Waddesdon Parish Pool operated a large grass dryer and processing plant in huge ex-army Nissen huts at Waddesdon Cross Roads, producing small cubes of animal feed. This plant was operated 24 hours a day for weeks on end. At the wheel is Harold Radwell and Dick Davis is on the back of the lorry. Note: The grass-processing unit was at this time a new concept for the manufacture and storage of animal feed and was perhaps partly responsible for the demise of hay-ricks and thatchers as shown in photograph 9.18. Farmers from other countries were invited to visit the plant, and this photograph was taken for a South African delegate.

SHOPS ETC IN WADDESDON IN 1965

In 1965, members of the Waddesdon Woman's Institute compiled a chronicle of many aspects of village life and included snapshots of many of the shops etc. We have reproduced most of them in the following pages. Numbers 9.21 to 9.33.

9.21 This Garage business was formerly owned by Mr James (Jimmy) Jones, but in 1962 was bought by Mr Clifford Goss and the premises became the hub of Waddesdon Transport. The garage continued to provide a filling station service for passing motorists for a few years, and here we see Mrs Jennifer Goss at the pumps.

9.22 Mr Randall Styles at the entrance to his Newsagents and Tobacconist shop. An old family business which unfortunately was soon to go. The business was transferred to Homeware across the High Street, and the shop converted to living accommodation. See 9.12.

9.23 Peggy Buckwells was a typical village "corner shop" at the time of this photograph. For many years it thrived, and when taken over by Jack Slade and Sons in the 1970's it continued to do well, providing an important and convenient service to those around. It was the last shop of its kind in the village before Roger Slade reluctantly closed its door in 1999. It is now a private house. In the photograph are Olive Holland and Peggy Buckwell.

9.24 Dinah Baron and Susan Parkinson outside Dinah's Ladies' Hairdressers Salon. Previously this shop was the premises used for many years by Gents' Hairdresser, Baden Roads. Mrs Baron gave up this business to lecture on the subject at Aylesbury College. The Ladies' Hairdressers continues to this day. See 9.43.

9.25 Stewart Adams on the right and Sid Kibble at the doorway to Adam's Butcher's shop. The business which had started in the days when deliveries were by horse and trap, (and an essential requirement was a small field and stable, Alcock's Close where Little Britian estate now is), carried on for a few years more, before finally closing down.

9.26 Although the village had a "Co-operative Stores" before the end of the 19th century, we had to wait until 1946 to gain a branch of the Co-operative Society with all the benefits of membership for regular customers. This store was previously one of the premises of Sidney Crook who also traded in the shop originally owned by Phil. Dodwell, (opposite the Five Arrows Hotel). In its heyday around the 1950's. it was possible to purchase just about everything one needed from the "Co-op", and earn a dividend on the expenditure. A boon to the poorer members of society. Waddesdon Co-op was the most successful store in the Aylesbury Society, and it out-lasted the rest, eventually closing down in the 1980's. See 9.42. In the photograph are Christine Simms, Mr Thompson (Manager) and Joy Rhodes.

9.27 Will Dennis shown here with Mrs Dennis took over the butcher's business from Mr R Price in November 1949, and continued until retiring circa 1970. This butchers business then continued for a number of years in the ownership of Joe Jordan, and finally closed in the 1980's. See 9.34.

9.28 Jim Franklin with Mrs Franklin and Doreen Snell, stand at the doorway to the Grocery and Provisions shop, which the Franklin family had owned and ran for the previous century. Mr Franklin retired and closed the business in the 1970's.

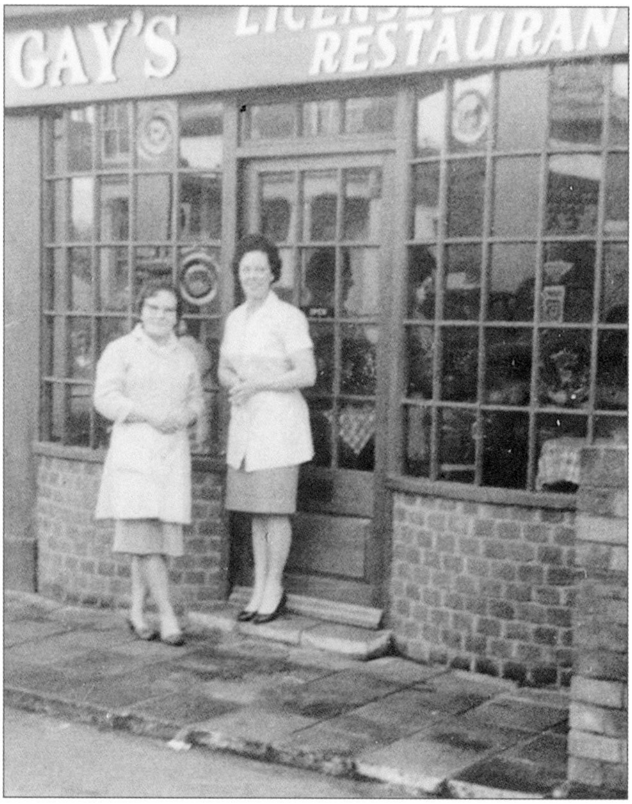

9.29 Gay's Licensed Restaurant was owned by Dulcie Wilson, shown here on the right with Mrs Lee. These premises have a long and diverse business history, starting life as a primitive dairy, a pioneering garage, a toyshop, a traditional English Café, an Italian Restaurant and now an Indian Restaurant. Note: During the period it was an Italian Restaurant the premises were extended to incorporate the house next door (number 45 High Street). See 9.44.

9.30 Grace's shop still in business in 1965, but was then owned and run by Mrs de Freece. Yet another "corner shop" which lasted only a few more years before inevitable closure and modification to living accommodation.

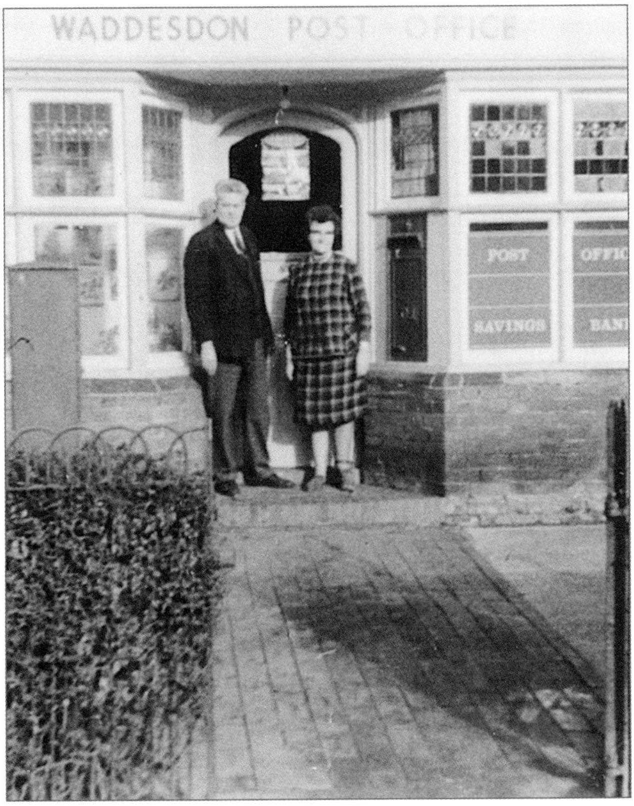

9.31 Waddesdon Post Office has been in these premises since Mr Collyer took it on after closing his Tailoring business in the 1920's. The Postmaster in 1965 was Percy Ashfield shown here with Mrs Ashfield. The postmen then were Fred Casemore and David Blake. Thankfully Waddesdon still has its Post Office, which is currently run by the Patel Family. See 9.40.

9.32 Douglas Toy in the centre of picture with Paul Coyne on his right and son Maurice on his left, bought the premises from Cecil Rhodes in the 1950's and established a good reputation in panel beating, coach work, painting and general engine maintenance. The business progressed to Mr Toy's sons Gordon and Maurice, before they retired in the 1980's. See 9.45. Currently the premises contain the vehicle sales business of George Kamperis.

9.33 A. V. Fillingham's Drapers Shop at the "top" end of the High Street. The premises which included living accommodation was named "London House", whilst Saunders Draper's Shop a few hundred yards farther east, was named "Manchester House". Mrs Fillingham at the doorway in this picture, and her husband provided the village with an extraordinarily comprehensive stock of drapery. Often customers may have already scoured the Aylesbury shops for a requirement, only to find the object in Fillinghham's at a fraction of the cost. The shop closed in the 1970's, but experienced a pleasant revival as an Antique Shop. See 9.35.

9.34 August 1987 and Mr Joe Jordan stands outside his butchers shop at 53 High Street. This was previously the premises of Will Dennis and before that Bobby Price, all butchers, but although Joe was the only full time butcher left in the village, the shop closed when he moved away upon retirement.

9.35 Waddesdon's first antiques shop, "Collectors Corner" had previously been Fillingham's Drapers shop. It was owned and run by Cyril and Kitty Good and their daughter Valerie Grant. In the 1970's and 1980's it was an attractive venue for visitors and locals alike, and on Bank Holidays the sales for charities were highly successful, The shop was closed in the 1990's but the Good family continued to live on the premises and stayed involved in village life.

9.36 The Bell Inn in the High Street 2001 Nigel Bradshaw.

9.37 "Country Seats" in the High Street adjacent to "The Gables"2001 Ian Marden and Dennis Marden.

9.38 The Five Arrows Hotel 2001: L-R Helen Cox, David Panchen, Brian Goss, James Fynn, Gary Moysey, Ralph Symon, Julian Worster, Robert Selbie, Sally Skinner, Becky Harrison.

9.39 "White Gates" bed and breakfast guest-house previously Crooks'Shop 2001. Rosalie and Rex Evans.

9.40 The Post Office 2001 Prashant and Vantia Patel.

9.41 Roger Mead in the doorway of his antiques' shop "Junk and Disorderly", situated next to the Village and Country Property estate agents premises, formerly the Nat West Bank. 2001 Jon Drewe Smythe is on the right with Sally Burnell and Bill Humphries.

9.42 The Chinese Takeaway shop at the old Co-op premises in the High Street 2001 Woon Hei Kwan and Linda Kwan at the doorway.

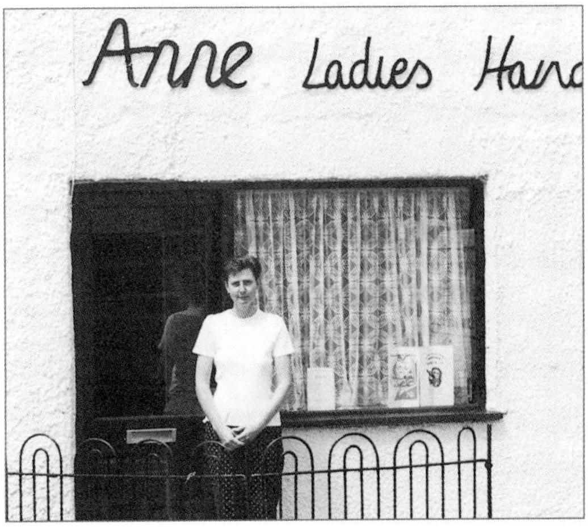

9.43 Anne Ladies Hairdresser's salon with Diane Hunt at the entrance. Waddesdon High Street 2001.

9.44 Chadnis Indian Restaurant 2001. L-R: Amin Uddin, Alam Uddin, Sujon Ahmed, H. Rahman, Nazrul Islam, Ruman Choudhury. Previously "Angelo's Italian Restaurant".

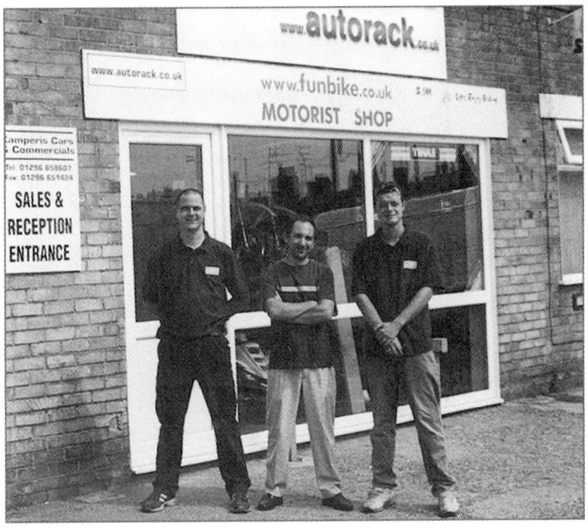

9.45 Kamperis Cars and Commercials premises 2001. Previously Toys' Garage. L-R: Kevin Higgins, George Kamperis, Darren Rolfe.

9.46 Homeware with the new proprietors Kalpesh and Rita Patel, Anne Rampton (previous owner), and Kath Biswell (2001).

9.47 Tom Lovell the proprietor of Waddesdon Tyres 2001. Previously the premises of Thurgers' Garage and before that the Garage of Sam Evans.

9.48 Toulouse Café on the Wormstone lay-by 2001. The proprietor Terry Dersley.

9.49 Chambers Engineering at Wormstone 2001. L-R: Tim Chambers, Martin Smith, Alan Chambers, Nick Chambers, Neil Brindle, Stuart Powell.

9.50 The Bakers Arms with Landlady Christine Tweed 2001.

9.51 E. Johnson Motor Engineers in Frederick Street 2001. L-R: Edward Johnson, Paul Irwin, Paul Davis, Daniel Ridgway.

Section Ten

Miscellany

In our preparations and research for this book we came across a number of fascinating documents and photographs which do not fit easily into the main sections; hence this miscellany.

It includes groups representing essential aspects of community life, and others which record events that would have attracted much attention at the time, or are amusing or "quaint". The Rocket Propulsion Establishment at Westcott is described for a variety of reasons, not least because it was a major employer within the parish, for more than forty-five years.

To represent the many villagers who have left Waddesdon to live in far-off lands during the past two centuries, this section includes six examples of emigration.

10.1 Dr Alexander Thomson Morrison shown here at the wheel of his new Humber around 1910, was appointed Surgeon and Medical Officer for No 5 District (Waddesdon and vicinity) in 1895 and remained until 1924. His first surgery was at his house next door to Crooks the Builders and undertakers, at the entrance to Britain Lane. Next he moved house to the new Rothschild's house facing the Square (where the war memorial now is), and then in 1905 the practice and Dr Morrison transferred to the fine home specially provided by Miss Alice de Rothschild, "The Roses". In the 19th and 20th Centuries the village doctor always lived in the village, and by virtue of his position was expected to be a leader in the community. Dr Morrison and his successors ably fulfilled this requirement for more than 100 years.

10.2 Dr Norman Black and his wife at "The Roses" circa 1935. Dr Black was the village doctor from 1924 to 1945. Medical matters apart, Dr Black was fondly remembered for his ready assimilation into village life, yet he proudly retained his obvious Scottish identity, and his custom of donning his kilt and playing the bagpipes on special occasions.

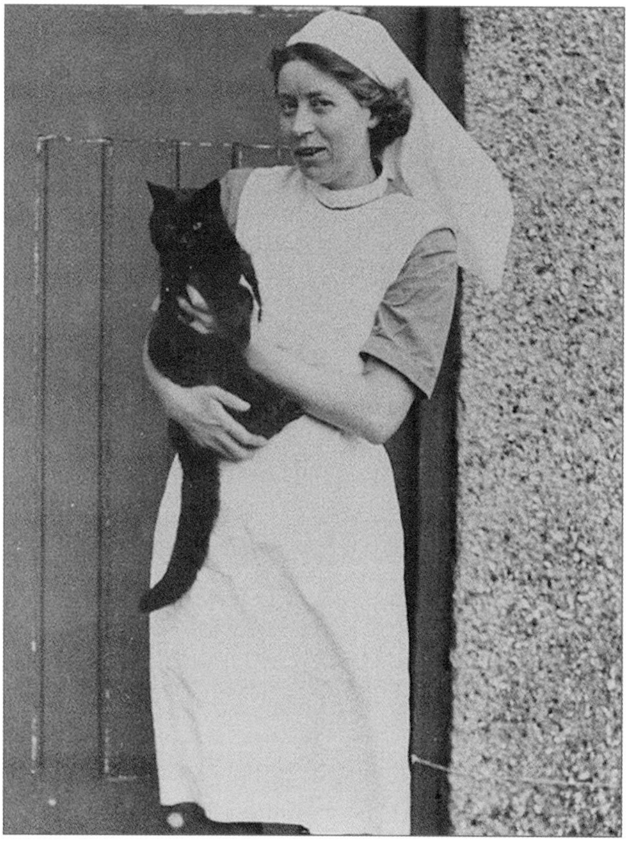

10.3 Nurse Nellie Gunn was the District Nurse from circa 1945 to 1962. She lived at the Rothschild house reserved for the purpose, No 71 Baker Street, and was a dedicated and respected member of the community; remaining here for the rest of her days.

10.4 Dr Colin Campbell came to Waddesdon in 1960, taking over from Dr William Bellamy who had completed 15 years as Waddesdon's G.P. Dr Campbell, shown here in 1965 in Rectory Drive adjacent to his home "The Roses", was the last doctor to live and hold his surgery there. Doctor Colin and Mrs Daphne Campbell raised their family of musically talented daughters and whole-heartedly joined in village life. The Royal British Legion, the Parish Council, the Parish Church and the Women's Institute, are a few of the organisations which enjoyed the benefits of their membership. In 1990 the Waddesdon Surgery in Goss Avenue was inaugurated; one year later Dr Campbell retired from full-time practice, and he and Mrs Campbell left the village to live in Wendover. However, they have still retained a friendly interest in the village and the doctor has acted as a locum at the Surgery from time to time.

10.5 The District Nurse always earned a special place in the affections of the villagers, and none more so than Nurse Honorah George shown here in 1965. She was the District Midwife as well as Nurse, and moved into 71, Baker Street in 1962. The District included Quainton, Over Winchendon and Westcott and the majority of her work was in the care of the very old and the very young.

10.6 The staff of Waddesdon Surgery 2000. Left to right; Dr Alan Watt, Nicky Hole, Jackie Hubbocks, Dr Jennifer Adams, James Adams, Jenny Mansbridge, Kate Wainwright, Lynne Hurry, Ros Hannaford, Cheryl Lewis, Fiona Cavanagh, Teresa Martin, Bernie Halford, Karen Marshall-Falland, Dr Jan Karmali. Dr Watt joined the Waddesdon Practice in 1985, and Doctors Karmali and Adams in 1991. The Waddesdon Surgery was constructed in the late 1980's and opened in 1990. The days of collecting medicines from a wooden cupboard outside the surgery are long gone. The Surgery is constantly busy and provides a valuable service to the local communities, both in-house and through the nursing provided by the dedicated rota of District Nurses.

10.7 P.C George Gale was born in 1882 only 40 years after the formation of the force founded by Sir Robert Peel, but by the time he came to Waddesdon the Buckinghamshire Constabulary had experienced a long-established presence in the village. P.C Gale married and raised his family in Waddesdon, and upon his retirement from the Police he took employment at Waddesdon Manor.

10.8 Police Sergeant Harold Snelling was a big man even by the standards then required by the Police Force, and consequently he needed a large framed bicycle, as is illustrated here outside Crook's shop in the 1930's. Sergeant Snelling stayed on in Waddesdon after his retirement from the force in the late 1930's, for many years operating a village taxi service with his large Austin 16 car.

10.9 Frederick George Lines joined the Buckinghamshire Police Force after serving in the Royal Army Medical Corp in France during the First World War, where he was awarded the Military Medal. He came to Waddesdon as a Police Sergeant from Great Missenden circa 1935, and served as the "Village Bobby" during the Second World War until being posted to Amersham-on-the-Hill during late 1946. He was well respected by young and old alike in the village, but was not averse to giving young lads a "clip around the ears" if he caught them "scrumping" apples from Mr Goss's orchard near the village hall.

10.10 Here we have L-R: P.C. Palmer, P.C. Breecher, P.C.Masterson, and Sergeant Blackman in front of Waddesdon Police Station in 1965. Their area of duty included the surrounding villages where the local "Bobbies" had been withdrawn, and so a motor-car and a motorcycle were provided to support the traditional bicycle and foot patrols. Despite the stretching of resources the officers maintained a "high profile" and were well known by all concerned.

10.11 Constable Ian Newman has been our Community Policeman for the past 11 years. A member of the small team, based at the Waddesdon station, responsible for the day-to- day policing of Waddesdon and the 9 other villages in this vicinity. P.C. Newman has endeavoured to balance everyone's wish for a totally crime-free village with the practicalities of modern policing.

10.12 Waddesdon Fire and Rescue crew in 2000. L-R: Sub Officer John Carter, Leading Fireman Richard Hurrell, Mark Banham, Harry Wells, Leading Fireman Peter Soulsby, Nevile Radwell. Despite occasional changes in official title the village name of "Fire Brigade" has endured for this organisation. For many years call-out alerts were made through the scream of a large siren, but more recently radio "pagers" have informed the crew. The type of incident is now-a-days more likely to be a traffic accident than a chimney fire, and the wide range of materials possibly involved, call for high levels of training in the use of specialist equipment as well as all the traditional disciplines.

10.13 Waddesdon Fire Station in 2000. Ever since the end of the Second World War there has been a steady reduction in the number of Retained (part time) fire stations. Waddesdon is fortunate to have this modern, well-equipped and efficiently manned service at its centre. The tower to be seen at the right rear of the picture is used for rescue practice and hose drying. When the tower was first built it was said the tiled "roof" was added at the request of Mrs de Rothschild, in an effort to make it less conspicuous. Nevertheless it has become something of a landmark in the locality. (Soon to go though in a redevelopment plan!).

10.14 David Blake shown here outside the Post Office in 1965 was probably the last of Waddesdon's village postmen. At this time the other postman was Fred Casemore of Quainton, and the two of them delivered the mail from the Post Office to the surrounding populace. Two deliveries daily. For many years now, mail has been sent out from Aylesbury Post Office for delivery by Aylesbury employees. Progress and more efficient, maybe! One (spasmodic) delivery daily.

10.15 Pettigroves' Fun Fair on "The Green", October 1952. The visit of the fair was the last remaining vestige of Waddesdon's old Feast celebrations, which (naturally) occurred at Michealmas time. September 29th, the Feast of Saint Michael is a Quarter Day, and was traditionally the second hiring day in the year for agricultural labour, (the earlier one was Lady Day, 25th March), when unemployed men stood in a line hoping to be chosen for another six months work. The Waddesdon Feast Day was also known as "Club Day" after the celebrations held by the Sick Club, and this seems to have been held on the first Monday after the 11th October. Pettigroves Fair invariably arrived for that weekend and stayed until the Tuesday, unfortunately this tradition was killed off when "The Green" was sold for the Chestnut Close development.

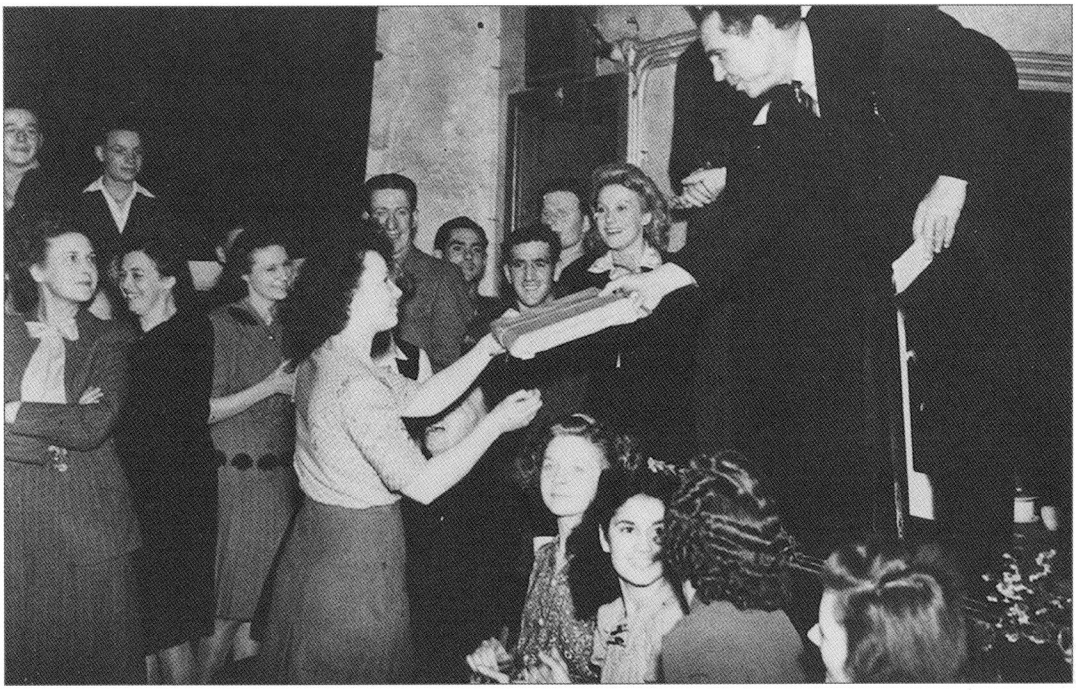

10.16 During the latter part of the Second World War and subsequently, Waddesdon Village Hall was regularly the venue for fund-raising dances organised by numerous organisations within the community. In this photograph Kathleen (Kathy) Scott is being presented with her prize for winning a beauty contest; the presenter is Eugine West the Aylesbury photographer. Also in the picture are from left; Reg Cyster, Mrs Eugine West, Gerald Cyster, Mrs Pennington, Kathleen Scott, Tom Brown, Elsie Sharp. Seated; Brenda Hicks, Daphne Carr, and Olive Callingham. Circa 1948. Although these dances were much enjoyed by the locals it was a rare occasion indeed if there was not at least one "punch up", and when the itinerant construction workers from the Westcott establishment attended, pitched battles sometimes resulted. This was many years before licensed bars were allowed at events in the Village Hall.

10.17 It was often said that one should be careful in passing on village gossip, for many of the villagers were related! To illustrate that point most of the persons in this wedding photograph of 1930 lived in Waddesdon. Back Row L-R: Will Speed, Doll Cripps, -----, ------, Jack Tompkins, Iris George, George Gurney, Dolly Fowler. Standing: Will Harding, Annie Wood, Mr and Mrs Alf Saunders, Edith Harding, ------, Mrs W. Speed, ------, Dick Wood, Harold Harding (Bridegroom), Kitty Speed (Bride), ------, --------, --------, -------, Edna Howe, Kathy Creed, Mrs Creed. Front: ---------, ---------, Mrs Martha Harding, Joan Harding, M. Wood, Betty Harding, Ruby Jones, Len Wood, Mrs Speed, Andy Speed, Mr Speed.

10.18 The reception after the wedding of Jimmy Jones was held in Waddesdon Village Hall. Here we see the very smartly attired wedding party photographed at the side of the Hall circa 1925. Note the bridegroom is wearing spatterdashes (spats).

10.19 In December 1931 George Gurney married Dolly Fowler, and here is the family group photographed outside the house, 40 Quainton Road, where they were to live for many years. Back Row: Horace Shirley, "Diddy" Dormer, Peggy Russell, Ellen Gurney, Middle Row: Florence Gurney, George Gurney Snr, Arthur Gurney, Bridegroom and Bride, Tom Fowler, Zilpha Fowler, Emily Fowler, Front Row: Cyril Gurney, Len Gurney, Winnie Loader, --------.

10.20 Members of the Waddesdon Estate Fire Brigade formed a Guard of Honour when Willy Wheeler married Lilian Wheeler in 1927. The bridesmaids were Amy Wheeler and Gladys Wheeler sisters of bridegroom and bride respectively. Weddings were something of a village occasion, and neighbours and friends would line the entrance road in a gesture of goodwill as can be seen here.

10.21 Once again a large gathering for the family photograph at the wedding of Ron Southam and Dorothy Cook in 1928. Back Row: -------, Mrs Parsonage,---------, Charlie Scott, George Franks, Ernie Brown, Will Heritage, Norah Southam, Bernard Cripps, Amy Ewers, Florence Cherry, Philip Ford, ------,-------,------,------, Mollie Franks. Middle Row: Ern Cripps, Vi Cripps, Alice Cripps, Frank Cripps, Emily Brown, Ernie Southam, Bridegroom, Mrs Harry Crook, Bride, ------,------,------,------, Liz Jessup, Ethel Scott, Jinnie Birch, -----. Front Row; -------,------, Ernie Brown, Alec Cripps, Gladys Southam, Arthur Southam with Rex Cripps, Nellie Southam with Gladys Brown, Bertha Cripps, Joan Cripps, Evelyn Scott, Alice Birch, Drue Cook, Jim Cook, Nance Cook, Kathy Scott, Doris Scott.

The plan for facilitating the emigration of agricultural labourers seems to be viewed in a favourable light by the rate-payers of parishes in the neighbourhood of Aylesbury. On Thursday last nearly eighty persons were put on board two boats to be conveyed by canal to Liverpool, from whence they will take their passage to New York. A few of the number will pay their own expenses, but the greater part are to have their expenses defrayed by the parish officers. There did not appear to be any indications of regret among these poor people at leaving their native land. The following list will show the names of the parties, and the parishes whence they have emigrated.

Aylesbury.—Mrs. Warr and 6 children, to join her husband, already settled; John Boddington and 3 children; — Spencer, his wife, and 2 children.

Cublington.—Robert Row, Thomas Cutlow, and Jesse Hall, all single men.

Stone.—Francis Carter, Elijah Carter, Sarah Carter, and John Miller, all single, and John Miller, widower.

Waddesdon.—James Showler, wife, and 2 children; Moses Cowell, wife, and 4 children; John Showler, wife, son, and 4 orphan children; William Crook, wife, and 3 children; John Embro, wife, and 3 children; Samuel Allcock, wife, and 3 children; Jonathan Taylor, Rose Holland, William Bailey, John Speed, James Speed, Henry Crook, and Elijah Showler.

Winchendon.—John Keys, wife, and 4 children; John Spencer, wife, and 1 child; James Spencer and wife; Richard Spencer, wife, and 1 child; James Spencer, Richard Venemore, William Capel, and Eliza Burbridge.

10.22 The March 1832 editions of The Bucks Herald carried advertisements offering passage from Liverpool to New York, with provisions provided by the captain, at £6 – 0s – 0d for adults and from £2 – 0s – 0 d for children. Labourers it was said could earn £30 –0s – 0d per year whilst blacksmiths etc could command 7s – 6d per day. America was already renowned as a land of freedom and opportunity. This cutting is from an April 1832 Bucks Herald. It is not surprising the Overseer for the Poor in Waddesdon saw emigration of some of his destitute charges as a partial resolution of his problem. Whether the 39 persons were volunteers is not known. The Overseer sold some parish properties to pay the passage and because at the last moment the fund was found to be inadequate, the Beck and Fetto Charities granted £50 to bridge the gap. On 12th April Benjamin Crook conveyed the emigrants to the Aylesbury canal where they boarded Mrs England's two barges (horse drawn narrow boats) for their journey to Liverpool, (at 2 miles per hour!). An eye-witness, Mr Robert Gibbs "witnessed the sad scenes at the canal wharf when the paupers were packed into coal barges". A letter from Henry Crook described poverty and hardship in America in the years which followed their arrival, but the writer knows of no other communication from the 1832 emigrants or their descendants.

10.23 The family name of Craker has a long association with the parish and this locality. Zechariah Craker was born in Waddesdon at Walkers' Green (near to the present Bowls Green) in 1811. He was a member of the Waddesdon Baptist Chapel and when he married Rebecca Rhoda Barrett in 1831 he was living at Hogshaw. Exactly why, just two years' later Zechariah, Rebecca, and their infant daughter emigrated to the United States of America is not known. However we can list a few factors which would influence any of us today: nonconformists were held in suspicion by the majority; living standards for workers were lower than in living memory; prospects for improvement were poor; Waddesdon was amongst the most deprived of the Vale villages. On the other hand, advertisements and newsletters advised that America offered complete freedom, opportunity and good pay. The Craker family travelled on the ship Ajax to New York and settled initially in Erie County, New York, then later in Wisconsin. Rebecca bore nine children, but died prematurely and Zechariah remarried, fathering a further nine children. Note: the mortality rate for very young children was high in those days. This photograph shows Zechariah, presumably in his sixties, after a hard but successful life. He died in 1881, and today has around 200 known descendants in America. They have arranged family gatherings, and some have visited Waddesdon in the past few decades.

William Davis, Wm. Cripps, and James Davis, were indicted for stealing two south down sheep, belonging to Woodfield Blake Eagles, Esq., of Aylesbury, on the 24th Dec. last.

Mr. Rose conducted the prosecution, and Mr. Taylor appeared for the prisoners.

George Cannon.—I am shepherd to Mr. Eagles. On Wednesday, December 24th, had some south down sheep under my care, and the following day missed two of them. I examined the field and found a gap in the hedge, through which I think the sheep had been drawn, leads into the turnpike-road from Aylesbury to Bicester, and I traced them to the ground of Mr. Ledbrook of Fleet Marston. I traced them along the bridle way to a break belonging to Mr. Monk. I saw a mark on a tree as if two sheep had been hung up there; the reason I thought so was by the quantity of blood there; it appeared as if they had been hung up to two different trees. I traced the footmarks to a pond where I found a skin and the inside of the sheep, and a large stone was in the skin. I recognized the head directly, as well as the skin; the head was cut away from the skin. Went with Mr. Cross and Lennard the next day to Davis's where we found two bits of the breast, and three pieces of a neck of mutton. I saw the prisoner James Davis the day before, he was coming towards his house, but when he saw me he turned back and ran away. I saw him again in the neighbourhood, and he ran away again, leaving the footpath and taking to the fields, but did not see him again till in custody. I was with Cross when the shoes were fitted to the marks; they appeared to correspond with the shoes worn by the prisoner. I saw stones on the road, and we proceeded to the prisoner's home, where I found two ends of two breasts, three pieces of neck, a small bone, and a large suet-pudding (the parts were produced in court). I went back and took W. Davis into custody. The meat was discovered under one of the beds. I told him what I wanted, and he asked what was the matter, and I told him on what charge I took him into custody, and he said that he knew nothing of the affair, but that some one brought it to his house on Christmas-day, and he had part of it for his dinner, and the same party who brought it to him was with him again at 7 o'clock next morning, and he asked him where he got it, who replied that was no affair of his, prisoner bought it, and in consequence of what passed I went to Cripp's house, leaving Lennard at Davis's. I went with Barton and Adams, both officers of Waddesdon, where we found the basket I produce, with suit in it. I enquired of the prisoner's wife, in the presence of the prisoner, where he bought it, and she said she could not tell me, but they bought it of some butcher in Aylesbury market; and Cripps said that if she had bought it of him (witness) he would know it. I took him into custody and examined his shoes and compared them with the marks on the road, where I saw Mr. Ridgeway and the constable, who gave James Davis to me and I took him to the place and tried his shoes, which corresponded with the impressions on the road, as did those of Cripps. I have not the slightest doubt that the impressions were from the prisoners' shoes. I lost the impression of the shoes until I came to a ditch where the marks were perfect with the shoes of Cripps; there were three rows of nails and a small portion of wool was on the shoes; it was a bridle road, leading to a bridge, but the marks were not quite so strong as those of the other prisoner.

10.24 Reproduced here are cuttings from the Bucks Herald report of the trial of three Waddesdon men, at the Epiphany Quarter Sessions on 31st December 1833, on a charge of sheep stealing. Only a few years earlier the trial would have been conducted at the Assize Court, but in the "enlightened" age of the 1830's sheep stealing was no longer a capital (public hanging) offence. The British colonies needed labour! Along with James Davis, William Cripps was found guilty and sentenced to be transported for life, just seven days after the offence, and at the season of goodwill too! In 1834 William Cripps sailed for Tasmania in the convict transport ship Augusta Jessie, whilst his wife Eliza and baby son Adam remained in Waddesdon. Eliza was to all intents and purposes, widowed, and in fact was described as such when she remarried in 1852. William Cripps obtained his "ticket of leave" and became an apple grower near Hobart in Tasmania. He married Elizabeth (nee Pace), fathered thirteen children and their descendants are now scattered around Australasia and across the world.

10.25 When poor people emigrated to the colonies in the nineteenth century they were aware that it was "goodbye" for ever. However some of them prospered and occasionally Waddesdon received a visit from one of its exiles; even from the other side of the world. This photograph records just such a visit, circa 1910. L-R: Mrs Clara Fowler (nee Cripps) of Frederick Street, Alice Walker of Brisbane, Queensland, Australia, Mr Walker, Mrs Kate Cripps of Frederick Street, Mrs Margaret Walker (nee Cripps). Mrs Walker was the daughter of parents who had emigrated to Queensland in 1873. (They were related to William Cripps. See 10.24). In the early 1870's the rural economy was in a parlous state and for agricultural workers the prospects were grim. The government was anxious to colonise Queensland and depending upon circumstances, free and assisted passages and cheap land were offered to emigrants. The sailing ship "Ramsey" embarked around 300 emigrants from Oxfordshire and Buckinghamshire in March 1873, including sixteen adults and eighteen children from Waddesdon. (The largest contingent from a single parish). Amongst these Waddesdon emigrants were five adults and three children by the name of Cripps. The voyage took over 100 days, and the conditions on board probably served as a strong disincentive to those who may have wanted to return.

10.26 Grace Griffin shown here in her uniform as a nanny in Adelaide, South Australia in the 1950's, was a daughter of Tommy Griffin, the village Greengrocers. She emigrated to Australia at the age of 21 in 1949. (See 10.27).

10.27 In May 1959 Grace married Eddie Edema in Perth, Western Australia and they have lived there ever since. She does however; keep in touch with Waddesdon news through correspondence etc with old friends.

10.28 Clive Burnell was born in 1957 and until he was 24 years of age lived in Waddesdon. Educated at the village school then apprenticed as a toolmaker in Aylesbury, Clive could have been destined to spend the rest of his life in local engineering workshops, but for his hobby as a Brass Bandsman. Following in the footsteps of his paternal grandfather, and with the keen support of his parents, Clive received professional tuition in cornet playing from an early age. Over the years he won numerous solo awards and progressed in the Brass Band world, playing with the Morris Concert Band (Oxford) at all the major venues in England, and performing for television, radio and recordings. Meanwhile he retained his ties with local village bands, often helping out at engagements, and was a stalwart member of Marsh Gibbon Silver Band for a number of years. He is shown here receiving one of the many trophies he won in cornet solo competitions while still a schoolboy.

10.29 In 1981 the Gisbourne, New Zealand, Civic Brass Band advertised in "The British Bandsman" for cornet players. Clive responded, was selected and was thus sponsored to emigrate to Gisbourne. In the following years Clive has played with a number of bands in New Zealand travelling extensively with them to contests and engagements and with a large measure of success. As so often happens with emigration, this is a tale of personal success, Clive's hobby has become his profession. Opportunities arose, were grasped, study led to qualifications and Clive now teaches Brass and Woodwind at schools in the Waikato area. In 1983 he married Raewyn and now has a daughter and two sons, all playing in Brass Bands.

No. CLVII.—WADDESDON.

The Stocks.—The punishment of the stocks seems to have been within the province of the parish constable, without the aid of any superior authority, judge or jury; this often led to public squabbles. In 1825 a man who had paid a visit to Waddesdon from a neighbouring village was pounced upon by the constable on a charge of drunkenness and forthwith consigned to the stocks. In this case the constable found his match, for the man floored not only him but his helpmate also, and both constables were sprawling on the ground at the same time; further help was obtained, and eventually the constables succeeded and the man was much punished by the orifice of the stocks being too small for his limbs; this unseemly squabble took place on a Sunday and was brought about by the needless officiousness of the parish constable, as the man would have gone home quietly if left to himself. The stocks were again brought into use in 1839, on the occasion of a garden robbery. The culprit had not been long confined when he feigned a swoon and faintness, and by the advice of the doctor he was released; no sooner did he find himself at liberty than he took to his heels and far outstripped his pursuers, taking good care afterwards to keep a respectful distance not only from the stocks but from other people's gardens. The Waddesdon stocks disappeared altogether several years ago.

10.30 A cutting from a Bucks Advertiser and Aylesbury News edition of the 1880's, recalling the use of the Stocks in Waddesdon in the nineteenth century. The first sentence of the account provides an interesting view of how petty crime was dealt with in those days.

THE CORMORANT.

A Cormorant, a sea bird, very rarely seen so far inland, was, on Saturday, September 17th, shot by A. E. Deane, Esq., while resting upon the Church Tower. "The Cormorant, or Corvorant,—as it is sometimes called," says Cassell's Natural History, "inhabits the New as well as the Old Continent. In the latter it is very widely diffused, being spread over a considerable portion of Europe, especially in the North; and is common in England. This bird swims very low in the water; even in the sea the body is deeply immersed, little more than the neck and head being visible above the surface. It dives most expertly, pursuing the fish, that forms its food, with great activity under water. It flies with the neck outstretched, and may often be seen drying its drenched plumage on the shore or on insulated rocks."

10.31 Another revealing comment upon the values of the nineteenth century, this time from the Waddesdon Parish Magazine for November 1870. Why the weary bird was shot dead whilst on the Church Tower is not clear. No sign of mercy or sanctuary in this story!

SALE OF MR. JOHN TREADWELL'S SHEEP.

A RECORD.

ONE SHEEP MAKES 85 GUINEAS.

The annual sale of the Oxfordshire Downs took place at the Model Farm, Winchendon, on Wednesday last, the auctioneers being Messrs. Mumford and Bond, of Brill and Thame. The company began to assemble at about 12 o'clock, parties arriving by brakes, etc., from Aylesbury, Thame and other places. A first-rate luncheon was served by Mr. G. Cockerell, of Waddesdon, in the large barn near the dwelling house recently occupied by Mr. Treadwell, and which was recently destroyed by fire. The ruins were inspected by most of those who attended the sale, and Mr. Treadwell's many friends expressed their sympathy with him. When the time, 1.30, arrived for the sale a good company surrounded the ring. Mr. Bond, in a few introductory remarks, said he was sorry to say the Model Farmhouse was not the same it had been, and he was sure everyone present expressed great sympathy with Mr. Treadwell in the trouble which had overtaken him (hear, hear). Fortunately Mr. Treadwell had a temporary abode near his old house, and he hoped next year they would see him in his new house, which he trusted would be as comfortable as the old one (hear, hear). With reference to the sheep for sale, he might say that Mr. Treadwell had returned to the show-yard, and had taken prizes at the Royal, Glasgow, Harrogate, and other shows. He thought the company would agree with him that the sheep for sale that day was the very best lot Mr. Treadwell had offered. That, he believed, was the opinion of one of the best breeders of Oxford Downs. They had dark faces, were fleshy, with plenty of bone, and possessed all the characteristics of good Oxford Downs. Mr. Bond then offered lot 1. for sale, and this made 20 guineas; lot 4, a twin ram by Warwick, made 33 guineas, and lot 7, a sheep by Oxford, 46 guineas. There was keen competition for No. 8, a twin sheep got by Hobbs' Choice. The biddings quickly rose until the price became somewhat sensational, and it was not until 85 guineas had been reached that the hammer fell, the purchaser being Mr. Hobbs, of Maisey Hampton. Good prices continued to be made, and when the end came it was found that the record had been broken, not a single sheep having been sold for less than two figures. Although the average has been better, this has never before been achieved, at other sales the tail end generally making 7, 8, and 9 guineas. Mr. Poel purchased no less than 18 sheep for South America, and Mr. Olde bought six for the same destination. Another was purchased for Ireland, whilst sheep go to the distant counties of Norfolk, Yorkshire, and

10.32 Mr John Treadwell, a renowned sheep breeder of Model Farm, Upper Winchendon, was also prominent in the local heirarchy, being an important employer of agricultural workers and a Poor Law Guardian for the Parish. The importance of his annual sales reflected his success in the show ring and as this cutting from 1897 informs us, his breeding stock was highly valued across the world.

10.33 Four generations of the Fowler family who had farmed and lived at 75 Frederick Street in 1902. L to R: -----, George Fowler, Thomas Fowler, Zilpha Fowler, Zilpha Fowler (aged 85), Emma Fowler, Richard Fowler. In 1874, the elder Zilpha Fowler was living in a "Dirt House" which was purchased by Baron de Rothschild. A young chestnut tree growing in Zilpha's garden was bought for 10 shillings by the Baron and transplanted at the South Front of the Manor.

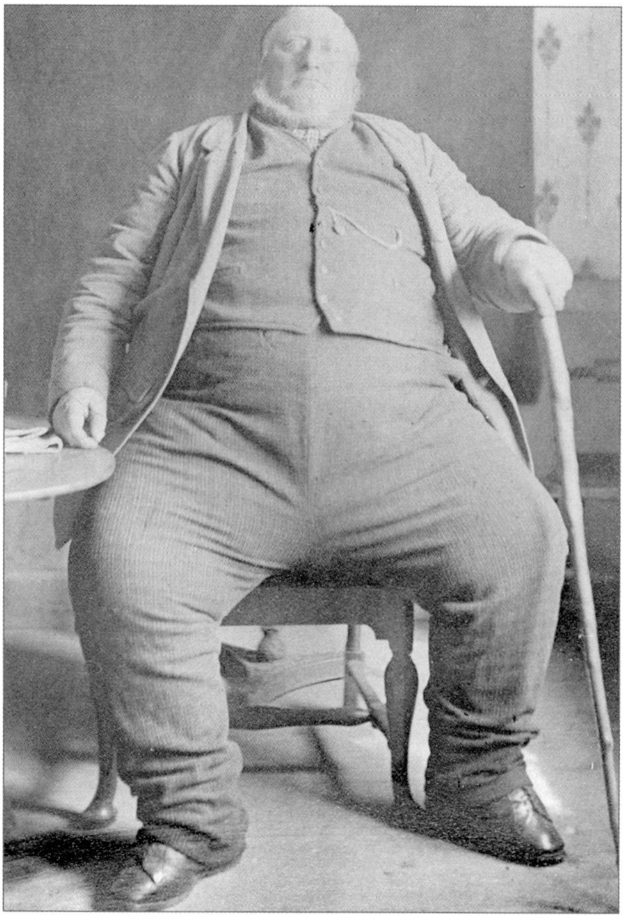

10.34 The story of William Stevens is a curious tale for it describes the destruction of a man who appeared to relish the notoriety, which his gluttony attracted. This photograph was taken in the old Five Arrows Inn two days before his death on Good Friday 1877. In earlier years at Lodge Hill Farm, Mr Stevens had been the last tenant to keep the "Bunter Cow" whose milk was to be supplied to poor families in Waddesdon. This charity was a condition of the tenancy of Lodge Hill Farm, and somehow was allowed to fail when the cow died in the 1860's.

WADDESDON.

SACRED HARMONIC SOCIETY.—The members of this society, with the aid of a few friends, gave their annual concert in the British schoolroom on Good Friday. The subject selected was an oratorio by Fawcett—"Paradise." The bâton was wielded by Mr. Bridle. The room was crowded, many being unable to obtain a seat. The concert was a success both from a musical and financial point of view. The proceeds are in aid of the funds of the British School.

DEATH OF A GREAT MAN.—Waddesdon has lost, physically at least, its greatest man, in the decease on Good Friday of William Stevens, once known in the hunting field as "The Shah," and more recently in the neighbourhood generally as the Buckinghamshire Giant. William Stevens was formerly a farmer, and lived for some years at Lodge-hill, but about four years ago he took up his abode at the Five Arrows, Waddesdon, where he has ever since resided. At that time he did not weigh more than 18 stone, but having, it is stated, seen a fat woman in a show at one of the neighbouring fairs, he made up his mind to achieve the same exaggerated dimensions, and set about doing so with great success. His appetite was good, and his flesh-forming properties still more so, and as he devoted himself mainly to the consumption of enormous quantities both of meat and drink he gradually became enormously fat, weighing the last time he "scaled" no less than 35 stone. His reputation as a local curiosity becoming known, drew many persons to the Five Arrows, thereby facilitating Stevens' fattening process by frequent treats, which he was rarely known to refuse. It is said that he has taken 40 glasses of grog in one day, without being much the worse as regarded intoxication, and without any diminution of his appetite for solids. Towards the close of his life he became so fat that he could hardly sit upon a chair. On Good Friday Mr. Cockerell, the landlord of the Five Arrows, on entering his gigantic guest's bedroom, thought he did not look well, an opinion which was also shared by Mrs. Cockerell, though Stevens himself did not think there was much wrong with him. However, medical help was obtained, and on the doctor seeing the patient he immediately adjudged him past help, and suffering from internal mortification. Deceased died about ten o'clock in the evening of the same day, and was interred on the following Monday in the parish churchyard. The measurements of the coffin were as follows:—6 feet 10 inches long; 3 feet 6 inches in extreme width; 3 feet 4 inches wide at the head; 1 foot 11 inches at the foot; and 2 feet 4 inches in depth. The breast-plate bore the inscription: "William Stevens, who died March 30, 1877, aged 46 years." The coffin was brought by twelve men from the bedroom, through a hole which it was necessary to cut in the side of the house, and the remains of the deceased, placed on a truck, were drawn to the grave by his favourite old mare, which had been in his possession for upwards of twenty years. About thirty relatives and friends attended the funeral, which was witnessed by no less than 500 persons. The rector of the parish, the Rev. T. J. Williams, officiated. The height of the deceased when living was not more than the comparatively common one of 5 feet 11 inches. Two days before his death his photograph was taken, and the host of the Five Arrows has, we understand, copies for sale. It is not calculated to make other persons enviable of a bulk which, even in the portrait, is obviously such as to be a source of suffering to any human being of ordinary instincts and inclinations. However, poor Stevens is gone to the bourne whence no traveller, fat or lean, returns; and the Waddesdon people, especially the worthy host of the Five Arrows, may echo the Shakesperean lamentation of—"Take him for all in all, we ne'er shall look upon his like again." We are requested to add that the deceased was a retired farmer, with a good income, and was not maintained for exhibition, as incorrectly stated in some of the London papers.

10.35 Underneath a report of a concert by the Sacred Harmonic Society the Bucks Advertiser of April 1877 gives us some details of the life, death and funeral of William Stevens, the "Waddesdon Giant".

10.36 This photograph commemorates the Diamond Wedding Anniversary of Mr and Mrs William Fowler in July 1934. They received a telegram of congratulations from the King and memorably a visit by H.R.H. Princess Mary together with Mr and Mrs James de Rothschild. Mr and Mrs de Rothschild presented the couple with an inscribed cut-glass bowl containing almost 100 carnations, and Mrs Fowler recalled the old village of 1874 before Baron Ferdinand de Rothschild set to work on the Manor and Estate. Mr Fowler who had started work at the age of seven, (earning one shilling per week for six days' work), was one of the first recruits to join the Baron's work-force. He continued in Rothschild employment until injury forced him to retire at the age of 71.Mrs Fowler (nee Clara Ann Cripps) was born and raised in a cottage at "the Green", (where the Bowling Club now is), and she found work as a weaver at the Silk Factory for many years.

10.37 When this photograph of Pillow Lace makers was taken, early in the 20th century, this type of cottage industry was already a thing of the past. L to R : Mrs Kitty Cripps, Mrs Phillips, ------, Mrs P Atkins, Mrs Fields. The lace was produced on a tightly packed straw "pillow" as illustrated on the photograph. Early in the 19th century when it was estimated that a third of all girls in Bucks were employed in Lace making, a "Lace school" existed in Waddesdon. Pupils entered at three years' of age into working conditions that were recognised as bad even by the standards of the day. Space, light, ventilation, heating and sanitation levels were deficient, and there was official concern at the loose morals of some within this type of employment. Cleanliness for practical reasons was paramount however, the lace must not be soiled; therefore the girls were not allowed outside for exercise or rest, but in order to relieve their eyes and fingers they learned elementary reading, writing, and arithmetic largely by rote. Hence it was not unusual for women to sign their names whilst men often made their mark, "X". In 1862 many women in Waddesdon still made Pillow Lace to supplement family incomes; in 1800 it had been possible to earn up to 1shilling and six pence per day but by 1850 daily earnings were just a few pence.

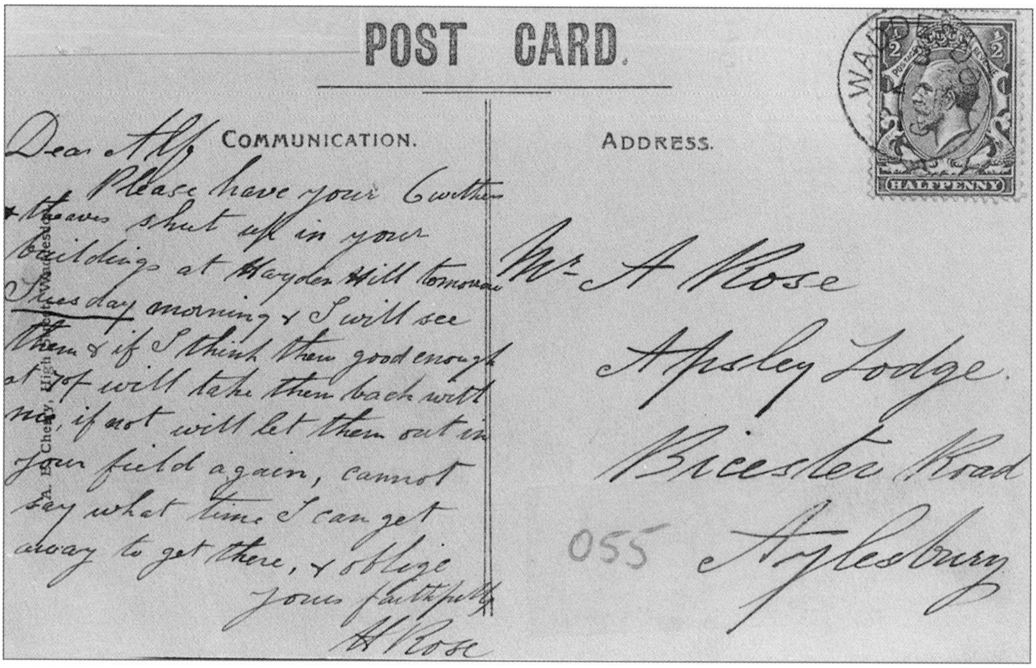
POST CARD.

COMMUNICATION.

Dear Alf

Please have your 6 wethers + theaves shut up in your buildings at Haydon Hill tomorrow Tuesday morning & I will see them & if I think them good enough at 70/- will take them back with me, if not will let them out in your field again, cannot say what time I can get away to get there, & oblige

Yours faithfully

H Rose

ADDRESS.

Mr A Rose

Apsley Lodge

Bicester Road

055 Aylesbury

10.38 One hundred years' ago although there were some telephones in use, most people had to depend upon the Royal Mail, and they could rely on it, implicitly. This card of 1903 was expected to arrive at Apsley Lodge in time for Mr Alf Rose to pen six of his sheep at Haydon Hill Farm the next day, for Mr Herbert Rose to evaluate against their 70 shillings price-tag. With all our modern means of transport etc, not many of us today would wish to travel six miles by horse and cart on such an arrangement. Note: Up until the introduction of commercial motor vehicles for moving farm animals it was common place to "drive" animals to and from farms and markets. Mr Cyril Gurney recalled that as a boy in the early 1930's he and his father George "drove" over 150 sheep "by road" from Aylesbury Station, where they had arrived from Kent, to Upper Winchendon. There again, not something one would contemplate with today's traffic.

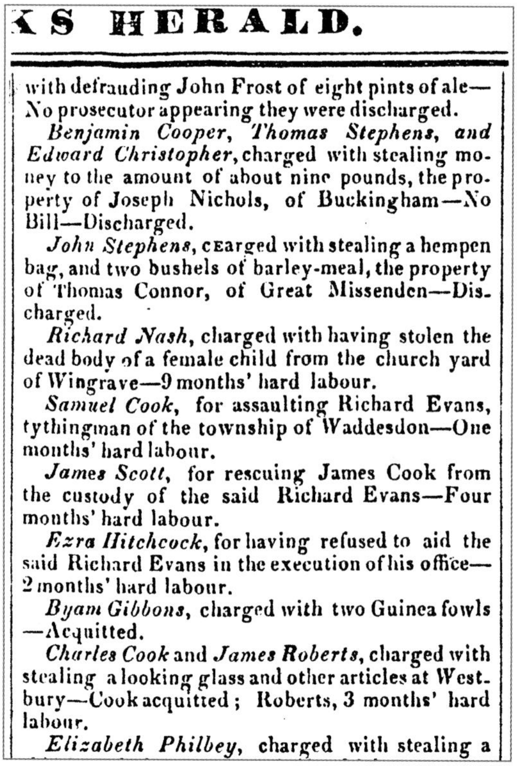
KS HERALD.

with defrauding John Frost of eight pints of ale—No prosecutor appearing they were discharged.

Benjamin Cooper, *Thomas Stephens*, *and Edward Christopher*, charged with stealing money to the amount of about nine pounds, the property of Joseph Nichols, of Buckingham—No Bill—Discharged.

John Stephens, cEarged with stealing a hempen bag, and two bushels of barley-meal, the property of Thomas Connor, of Great Missenden—Discharged.

Richard Nash, charged with having stolen the dead body of a female child from the church yard of Wingrave—9 months' hard labour.

Samuel Cook, for assaulting Richard Evans, tythingman of the township of Waddesdon—One months' hard labour.

James Scott, for rescuing James Cook from the custody of the said Richard Evans—Four months' hard labour.

Ezra Hitchcock, for having refused to aid the said Richard Evans in the execution of his office—2 months' hard labour.

Byam Gibbons, charged with two Guinea fowls—Acquitted.

Charles Cook and *James Roberts*, charged with stealing a looking glass and other articles at Westbury—Cook acquitted; Roberts, 3 months' hard labour.

Elizabeth Philbey, charged with stealing a

10.39 A cutting from the Bucks Herald of 1846 shows us how misdemeanours were dealt with by the local courts. The actual offence by Samuel Cook and the ensuing struggle involving James Scott, Ezra Hitchcock and the tythingman Richard Evans, would seem almost comical were it not for the terms of "hard labour" handed down as a result. Tythingmen were of course unpopular officials and no doubt the magistrates, usually including clergymen, would have wished to show maximum support to these gatherers of church dues.

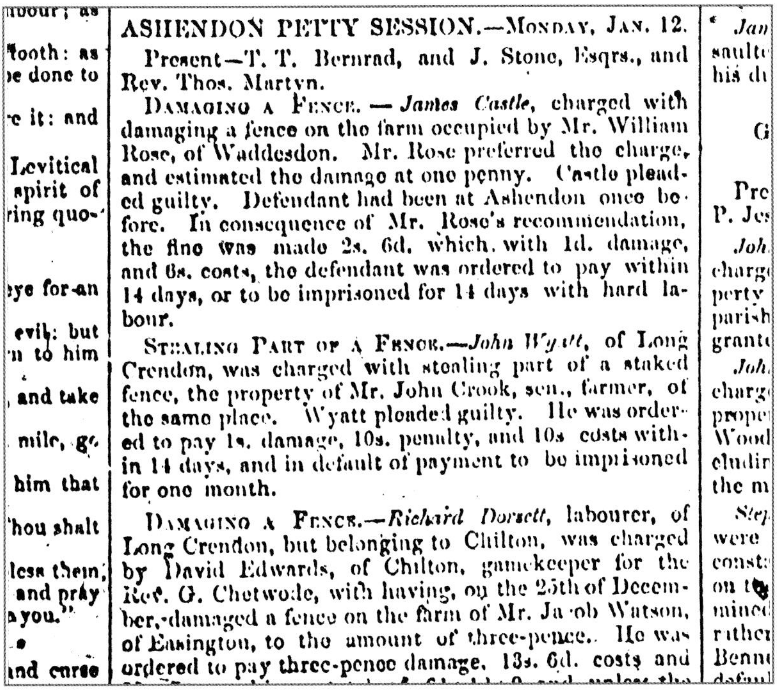

ASHENDON PETTY SESSION.—MONDAY, JAN. 12.

Present—T. T. Bernard, and J. Stone, Esqrs., and Rev. Thos. Martyn.

DAMAGING A FENCE.—*James Castle*, charged with damaging a fence on the farm occupied by Mr. William Rose, of Waddesdon. Mr. Rose preferred the charge, and estimated the damage at one penny. Castle pleaded guilty. Defendant had been at Ashendon once before. In consequence of Mr. Rose's recommendation, the fine was made 2s. 6d. which, with 1d. damage, and 6s. costs, the defendant was ordered to pay within 14 days, or to be imprisoned for 14 days with hard labour.

STEALING PART OF A FENCE.—*John Wyatt*, of Long Crendon, was charged with stealing part of a staked fence, the property of Mr. John Crook, sen., farmer, of the same place. Wyatt pleaded guilty. He was ordered to pay 1s. damage, 10s. penalty, and 10s costs within 14 days, and in default of payment to be imprisoned for one month.

DAMAGING A FENCE.—*Richard Dorsett*, labourer, of Long Crendon, but belonging to Chilton, was charged by David Edwards, of Chilton, gamekeeper for the Rev. G. Chetwode, with having, on the 25th of December, damaged a fence on the farm of Mr. Jacob Watson, of Easington, to the amount of three-pence. He was ordered to pay three-pence damage, 13s. 6d. costs and

10.40 Another cutting from 1846 again illustrating the harsh sentences handed down for acts, which today hardly warrant an admonishment. At Ashendon Petty Sessions, James Castle found guilty of damaging a fence to the value of one penny, had now to find 8 shillings and 7 pence within 14 days, or would be given 14 days hard labour.

10.41 For those of us more than 40 years of age it is difficult to believe that so many old barns that had served local farms for perhaps 200 years have been demolished within living memory. This group of farm buildings stood in Severidge Field on Glebe Farm, but as with numerous other examples were redundant, as the rapid transposition from horse to mechanised power took place in the second half of the twentieth century. As these isolated barns became redundant they were neglected and eventually demolished.

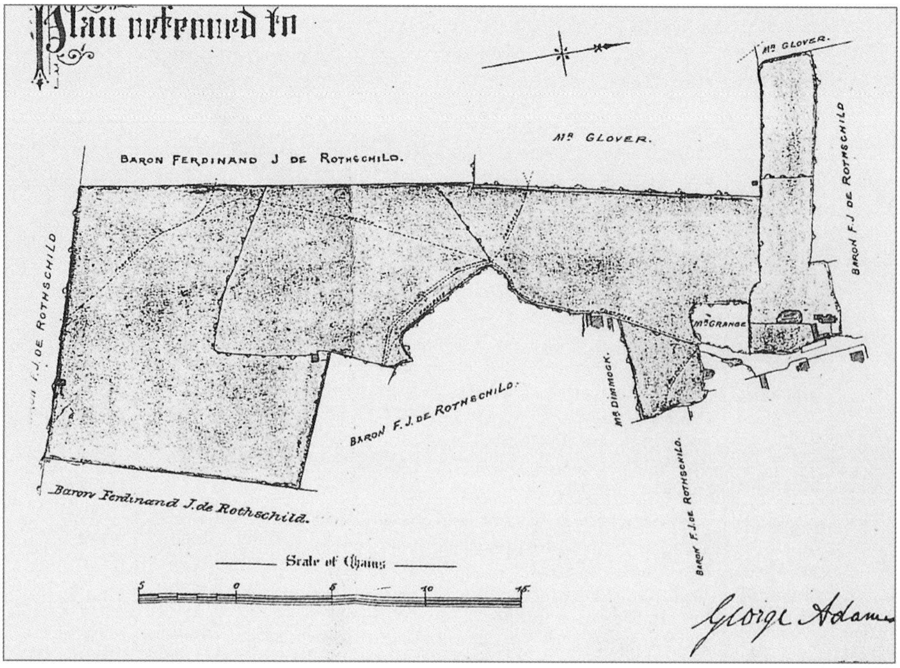

10.42 In 1877, farmer George Adams of Warmstone sold the land and farm buildings shown in this plan, to Baron Ferdinand de Rothschild. As can be seen, the Baron had thus almost completed his purchase of all the land at Warmstone. At the lower right hand side of the plan can be seen the southern end of Warmstone Lane. The farmstead outlined on the west side of the lane was later replaced by a new "Rothschild style" farm opposite, and woods were planted on the site. George Adams continued as tenant of the large Warmstone farm, and remained the owner and resident of Warmstone House, which he had built some years earlier. His son John carried on the tenancy until 1935. However on the sale of the house in 1965, the six hundred year period of land holding at Warmstone, by the Adams family, came to an end.

10.43 Peter Adams is our last remaining farmer of that name within the old parish. He has carried on the role, which innumerable ancestors have fashioned before him in the Waddesdon locality, and happily he is joined in this tradition by his son Matthew, who farms in nearby Wotton parish. Over the centuries the Adams family have provided continuity and service to worthy community activities, including during the mid-nineteenth century, prominently supporting the parish church, and also the struggling British School. This set an example for tolerance and the public good, well in advance of the times. In Section Eleven in this book the reader will see that the old tradition of Beating the Bounds, has long enjoyed their support. In 1928, the Rev. Moreton wrote of three family names, Adams, Crook, and Franklin, whose ancestry in the village, could be traced back to the thirteenth century. Easily within living memory, all three family names were involved in village businesses, and were leading members on community activities. In recent years the latter two families have disappeared from the parish. Village life is changing apace!

WADDESDON COMMUNITY SPIRIT.

I am greatly disturbed by the paragraphs in the December issue of the Newsletter which seriously maligned the village people by stating they show little interest in elderly residents. I am an elderly person (over 80 years) and have been unwell for much of the year, with a short stay in hospital. During this hospital period and throughout the year I have been amazed and delighted with the wonderful help given to me by the villagers, and I cannot speak too highly of the great happiness they have brought to my life.

I must register a strong protest about the wording of these paragraphs, especially coming from a resident of another village. I suggest it would have been advisable to review village activities as a whole - doing so would have shown that there is indeed community spirit in the various activities and a great interest in what is going on in our own village.

(EDGAR TOY).

WADDESDON COMMUNITY SPIRIT.

With reference to your article about the community spirit in Waddesdon, I find it very hurtful to tar the whole village with the same brush. I took over the village playgroup about 18 months ago, and then found I was pregnant and thought I would have to give up a job I very much enjoyed. Not so. The ladies I worked with all rallied round and took over from me while I had my baby. They did their own jobs and mine. The support and care they showed has continued now my baby has arrived. The extra work they have incurred receives my thanks and those of the parents. I think there are many people in Waddesdon who are willing to help; community spirit is not just helping at the local clubs, it is being there when your neighbour needs you. Waddesdon is not a village of "passers-by" as you will find out if you live in the village as I have and ever need help. (ROSEMARY BISWELL).

12

CARE OF THE ELDERLY.

Mrs. Lear may be entitled to stress the need for more helpers at the Wednesday Day Centre. What she is not entitled to do is to assume from this that the residents of Waddesdon do not look after their old people. An enormous amount of quiet, kindly, unpublicised care is given by neighbours and relatives every day - not just once a week. Mrs. Lear will have done her cause no good at all by adopting such a hectoring tone and may well have offended many kind and good-hearted people.

(BRIDGET HOPPS).

ANOTHER REPLY.

Lack of community spirit in Waddesdon? Thank God for the work of our volunteer firemen who, apart from their obvious contribution to this and other villages, have found time to raise a noteworthy sum of money for "Children in Need". A "thank you" also for the work of the Play and Toddler Groups and for those good ladies who care for our senior citizens at the Wednesday Club. The White Lion Social Club also expresses concern for the elderly in the special social activities arranged for them, and so do the dedicated men and women who take Meals on Wheels round the village twice a week. We now have a cub pack in Waddesdon, but led by an experienced scouter from outside the village.

Having listed the good aspects of community concern, it is sad to learn that volunteers are not coming forward to help with local shopping and to provide the guidance our youth badly needs through a village youth club and Brownie and Guide packs. The old and the young are the least able to organise help for themselves. Does the village still have a conscience in such matters? The Christian community just about manages to maintain three churches in Waddesdon, but it is debateable how long the Anglicans can act as custodians of an ancient monument for the rest of us and keep churches open in Westcott and Winchendon in addition to their more important moral and charitable commitments.

13

10.44 Since 1978 the Newsletter has informed the villagers of Waddesdon, Over Winchendon, Fleet Marston and Westcott of the activities, events, organisations and services in the locality. This cutting of January 1989 contains some response to an article of the previous month, demonstrating that some people at least, did not agree that the community spirit had died. The newsletter began publication in 1978 after Jim Christopher, the Head teacher of the Secondary School brought together a small group of volunteers for that purpose. Financed by advertising and donations this otherwise free newsletter is printed by the school, and then delivered to every household by a band of volunteers. There have been only two editors from the start; first Jim Christopher who at that time lived in the village, and since then for many years Mrs Pat Wright, ably assisted by Mrs Bridget Hopps. They have been involved from the beginning, and with their team of helpers provide a valuable continuity to this community project.

The Rocket Propulsion Establishment

Westcott 1946 to 2000

The ex-Royal Air Force air-field and some of the accommodation areas at Westcott, totalling around 700 acres was taken over by the Ministry of Supply in April 1946. Initially entitled the Guided Projectile Establishment, the site was to become the British research and development centre for rocket propulsion.

Soon a group of German scientists, who had worked on enemy war-time rocket projects, arrived to join the founding groups on site; in due course their families followed and the children attended local schools. The scientists, engineers, administrators and support staff who were drawn to Westcott, were just returning to "normal life" after the Second World War. Together they amassed a core of knowledge and experience, (unparalleled in peace-time), derived from their war-time service, whether in the forces or in civilian work of a secret nature.

Early work concentrated upon liquid bi-propellant engines similar to those produced for the German war effort, but in 1949 solid propellant motors were included in the programme. Generally solid propellants were preferred for military applications, and liquid propellants for space, however there were some notable exceptions. More than five hundred motors were developed at Westcott, forming the foundation for post-war British military and civil rocket propulsion.

In 1947 a serious accident, involving a wartime German bi-propellant aircraft boost motor on a Westcott test site, caused three fatalities. This accentuated the dangers associated with testing innovative rocket propulsion units. The nature of the work demanded unique facilities for testing the engines, and for storing, handling and processing the propellants. By 1951 some 24 test beds for the static firing of solid and liquid propellant rocket motors of various sizes and thrusts had been constructed. The liquid propellant test beds usually incorporated a complex pressure vessel system for containing the oxidants and fuels, and these test sites were connected to an effluent treatment plant, which culminated with a reed-bed and finally a goldfish tank which proved the integrity of the outflow.

Research laboratories and workshops were located around the establishment, and maintenance and support staff recruited such that in the early 1960's more than 1200 persons were employed on the site. The engineering and instrumentation apprenticeship scheme was second to none, and up to twenty young men were recruited each year. On completion of their training some stayed, and the remainder were readily absorbed into private industry. The site infrastructure was constructed and maintained by staff of the Ministry of Works (or later titles). Workers commuted from all the local towns and villages, for many years transported in fleets of buses operated by the establishment; Waddesdon had a full bus-load, and of course a large number walked or cycled in from Westcott village where around forty "Prefabs" and two housing sites were provided.

A Social Club known originally as the V 100 Club, was centred at the ex-Sergeants' Mess.

It catered for most popular activities including drama, snooker, squash, tennis, cricket, football, archery, indoor bowling and dances. For a time there was a Brass Band, a Radio Club and a Gliding Club. Although many of the groups activities are now extinct, the Westcott Social Club still exists after more than fifty years of success.

There was a period when the establishment had a local reputation as a "holiday camp", particularly perhaps in the view of ex-farm labourers etc for whom the working conditions and light tasks were a revelation. Undoubtedly Westcott, deep in rural Buckinghamshire, was a happy establishment. The quality of the research and development work was renowned and morale was invariably high. In 1958 work on the British ballistic missile Blue Streak galvanised the site, and in 1971 the British Black Arrow launch vehicle, whose first and second stages were powered by engines of Westcott pedigree, and whose third stage was produced entirely at the establishment, was launched from Woomera, and placed the satellite Prospero into orbit.

The adoption of the American Polaris nuclear deterrent for use from British submarines led to Westcott's most successful military contribution in the design, development and production of the warhead propulsion unit. This was a highly complex project incorporating the use of packaged liquid propellants. It was successfully concluded in the 1990's with the decommissioning of the Polaris deterrent, after many years of satisfactory service.

No doubt a number of reasons caused successive British governments to move to the margins of the European civil space programmes, whilst costs precluded going it alone. In the 1970's the numbers employed at Westcott gradually diminished although there was still a very wide range of research being undertaken.

Recognition of the market potential in small liquid propellant rocket engines for satellite positioning, resulted in Westcott producing the highly successful Leros "family" of thrusters. These have been fitted to many of the satellites now in earth orbit, enabling constant positioning and attitude control.

Over the years the site was given different titles as it was passed from one ministry department to another, and finally it was absorbed into the Royal Ordnance Factory organisation, which in 1985 was privatised. Subsequently, Royal Ordnance plc was procured by British Aerospace. The Westcott establishment was stripped of most of its solid propellant and associated capabilities and staff were either transferred or made redundant. A large test-firing site and other specialised structures in a secure enclave, have been retained by British Aerospace and are in continuous use.

The highly specialised liquid engine part of the business was sold to A.R.C. (an American company) in 1998, and is still in existence on the Westcott site.

The remainder of the old airfield has been sold off, and is now let for a wide variety of private business ventures.

10.45 Launch of the very first Skylark test vehicle August 1957. Between 1957 and 1996 the Westcott establishment produced and developed the Skylark family of test vehicles. These were based upon the Raven solid propellant motor, and the Skylark Upper Atmosphere Research Vehicle could attain an altitude of more than 100 miles in its early days. Ultimately when boosted by the Goldfinch and Cuckoo motors, it was possible to attain altitudes of 500 miles. The Skylark was an extremely reliable test vehicle that was used for more than 400 launchings including a number for Germany, Sweden, Norway, Argentine and the European Space Research Organisation. The Raven motor measured 17 feet in length, 18 inches in diameter and contained one ton of plastic propellant; this produced a thrust of 11,500 pounds for 30 seconds. They were in production until a few months before the Westcott Solid Propellant Factory was closed down in 1996.

10.46 This photograph shows a test firing under way of the R.Z.1 Kerosene / Liquid Oxygen engine which was to be used in the Blue Streak, the British ballistic missile, circa 1958. The P2 test site was by far the largest liquid engine test bed in the country, and in the two years before the Blue Streak project was cancelled, more than 500 engine tests had been successfully undertaken on this facility. In this picture the R.Z.1 engine can be seen mounted vertically at the right of centre. The exhaust is directed down over a steel chute, which is cooled by water jets, hence the steam and spray emerging with the flame at the lower area of the photograph. After 1960 work continued for some years, developing the R.Z engines for Europa 1, the vehicle to be used by the European Launcher Development Organisation (ELDO). With the demise of the RZ engines there was no further requirement for the P.2 firing site, and eventually it was converted to a drop testing facility.

Section Eleven

Beating the Bounds

In the dim and distant past, man followed the basic instinct present in many species of animals to claim, mark and defend his territory. As civilisation evolved so the importance of this practice grew, often with disputes over conflicting claims, sometimes bloodshed, and when the territory bordered national boundaries the claimants would often resort to all-out war. However at local level the demarcation of territory was generally a mutually accepted fact, which became an essential feature of community organisation. For example, responsibility of the parish for the welfare of its poor was the basis of the Poor Law which originated in Elizabethan times, and continued into the twentieth century. For the Poor Law to succeed it was crucial that parish officials knew precisely where their territorial responsibilities ended.

Parish boundaries were established long before records and maps were produced, and we can be sure that by the reign of Elizabeth I the parish limits were already recognisable, beyond dispute and re-established with sufficient frequency to imprint upon the memory of those concerned. The boundary lines followed natural features where-ever practical, waterways being the most obvious and best, but ancient hedges, and trees were utilised, according to the terrain in question. At suitable intervals of time the boundaries were patrolled and at notable points, where the line changed direction for instance, marks were made and a ceremony enacted. This formal patrolling of the boundary is known as "Beating the Bounds". In 1652 George Herbert wrote in "The Country Parson" of four reasons why clergy should beat the bounds:

"A blessing of God for the fruits of the fields. Justice in the preservation of bounds. Charitie in living, walking and neighbourly accompanying one another, with reconciling of differences, at that time, if they be any. Mercie in relieving the poor by a liberal distribution of largesse which at that time is or ought to be made."

The ecclesiastical parish of St Michael and All Angels consists of the area later designated as the civil parishes of Wormstone, Waddesdon, Westcott and Woodham, and its boundary is thought to exceed 40 miles in length. (See Field Map 1.21). It is perhaps no coincidence that this area formed a considerable portion of the Waddesdon Hundred originating more than 1000 years' ago. Mr Long, a curate at Waddesdon in1921, mentions in an historical note, "the parish priests with churchwardens and other parish officials, with a number of youths and boys, beat the border-stones of the parish with green boughs. The boys themselves were frequently whipped and bumped on the boundary stones, (or the ground), in order to impress the matter on their memory. (Occasionally boys were stood on their head at certain points). I advocate the use of all these methods in order to leave no doubt on the matter!" He also remarked that the Roman festivals of Ambarualia and Terminalia involved processions of priests, farmers and others, walking the boundaries, marking them and carrying out religious ceremonies for the protection of crops, and that the laws of King Athelstone required the marking of boundaries.

When in 1460 the papal tax known as "Peter's Pence" was levied on parishes according to their size, Waddesdon had the distinction of paying 10 shillings $3^1/_2$d. This was slightly less than Ivinghoe, the largest rural parish in Buckinghamshire. Waddesdon was a larger parish than High Wycombe, Chesham, or Slough.

Churchwardens' and other accounts record "Beating the Bounds" at Waddesdon on more than 30 occasions since 1693, and given the inferences drawn from the foregoing paragraphs we may assume this tradition was already an ancient custom in the 17th century. The perambulations of this long parish boundary take two whole days and are carried out at Rogationtide normally, at seven year intervals. Although the custom is by no means unique in England, it is fairly unusual for a parish to have such a long unbroken record to the present day.

During the twentieth century, the bounds have been beaten regularly except when the contingencies of the two world wars interrupted the sequence. Each event is recorded in a small (black) book where changes due to fallen trees, stream diversions or hedge removals are noted. Preparations for each occasion, keeping the records intact, and actually walking the boundary, has always fallen upon a dedicated group of stalwart parish families, and the incumbent clergy of the parish church. Permission from farmers and other landowners has to be obtained, as the boundary rarely follows public footpaths, and needless to say the control of those taking part demands attention, for these days many more people have the time and inclination to participate.

Seven years after each perambulation of the boundaries, at Rogationtide, the "Beating the Bounds" ceremony commences once again. On the morning of the Monday preceding Ascension Day, a short religious service is held at the Osier Beds on the Quainton Road at the boundary with the parish of Quainton. The Rector leads those present in a prayer asking for God's blessing on the land and the harvest to come, then the first of nearly 150 crosses is re-cut in the turf. A young boy or girl is spanked whilst held upside down over the cross and the procession prepares to move off.

Walking just outside the Waddesdon boundary, which at that point is a stream, the organisers lead off in an easterly direction. At long established points, crosses (mostly cruciform, but some diagonal) are re-cut, bottoms are spanked, the book checked and occasionally maps studied. By lunchtime the boundaries of Quainton, Pitchcott, Quarrendon and Fleet Marston have formed the route where they meet with the parish boundary of Waddesdon, and lunch is taken where the boundary crosses the Akeman Street (A41). Then comes the hardest part; almost a straight line to the River Thame near Eythrope, over the river onto the Stone, Dinton and Cublington parishes, back across the river (wet feet at least!), and up onto Upper Winchendon land. A long hard meandering climb up to the Winchendon road, and thankfully a stop for tea, before the short stumble down to Moor Close which brings the first day to an end. There is just the small question of the mile or so trudge home to the village!

Moor Close is a field at the northernmost point of the parish of Upper Winchendon and it brings the procession to the point where the Wottesbroke, a stream that rises in Waddesdon, forms the boundary.

The second day commences much, as did the first, except for one traditional and inexplicable difference. The cross re-cut in the turf at Moor Close comprises the removal of four separate square spits of soil, so leaving in effect a raised cross. Thrice more on the second day this peculiar style of cross is utilised, once at Bansells Meadow, the junction of the Wotton boundary, the others at junctions with Ludgershall parish and Doddershall in the parish of Quainton. It is thought the raised cross may have signified the meeting with perambulators from adjoining parishes, but time has long erased the certainty of that.

The first part of the route for the second day follows the Wottesbroke for about one mile before the procession turns where the Ashendon boundary meets that of Westcott. After crossing the old Second World War airfield the walkers take lunch at New House Farm. The afternoon is a long slog along the boundaries of Wotton Underwood, Ludgershall, Grendon Underwood and Quainton where they meet with the parishes of Woodham, Westcott and Waddesdon. Streams, hedgerows and woods are negotiated, visibly ancient crosses are re-cut into trees which are even more ancient. Tea is taken and finally at around 6.00pm the weary perambulators complete the course back at the Osier Beds. The book is brought up to date, and the names of those who have "Beaten the Bounds" are added to the record.

Since the end of the nineteenth century the practical reasons for Beating the Bounds have disappeared, but this ancient custom is more popular now than ever, if we judge by the numbers who take part. However the record of beating Waddesdon's boundaries continues thanks to the dedication, conscientiousness and meticulousness of generations of particular parish families. They continued the tradition when it would have been far easier to let it slip away. Prominent amongst those family names are; Rose, Goss of Waddesdon, Goss of Westcott, Adams of Westcott, Taylor, Crook and Biswell. Although some of these family names have now disappeared from the locality, the remainder are still committed to Beating the Bounds and all that goes with it. Long may it continue!

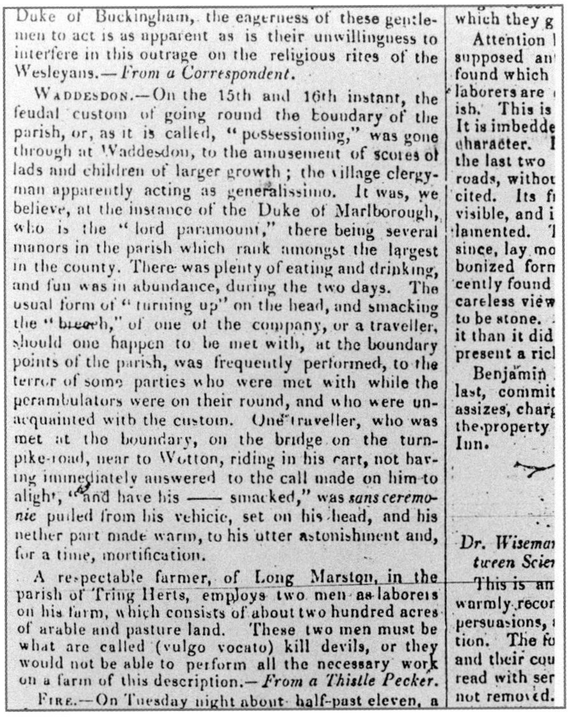

Duke of Buckingham, the eagerness of these gentlemen to act is as apparent as is their unwillingness to interfere in this outrage on the religious rites of the Wesleyans.—*From a Correspondent.*

WADDESDON.—On the 15th and 16th instant, the feudal custom of going round the boundary of the parish, or, as it is called, "possessioning," was gone through at Waddesdon, to the amusement of scores of lads and children of larger growth; the village clergyman apparently acting as generalissimo. It was, we believe, at the instance of the Duke of Marlborough, who is the "lord paramount," there being several manors in the parish which rank amongst the largest in the county. There was plenty of eating and drinking, and fun was in abundance, during the two days. The usual form of "turning up" on the head, and smacking the "breech," of one of the company, or a traveller, should one happen to be met with, at the boundary points of the parish, was frequently performed, to the terror of some parties who were met with while the perambulators were on their round, and who were unacquainted with the custom. One traveller, who was met at the boundary, on the bridge on the turnpike-road, near to Wotton, riding in his cart, not having immediately answered to the call made on him to alight, "and have his —— smacked," was *sans ceremonie* pulled from his vehicle, set on his head, and his nether part made warm, to his utter astonishment and, for a time, mortification.

A respectable farmer, of Long Marston, in the parish of Tring Herts, employs two men as laborers on his farm, which consists of about two hundred acres of arable and pasture land. These two men must be what are called (vulgo vocato) kill devils, or they would not be able to perform all the necessary work on a farm of this description.—*From a Thistle Pecker.*

FIRE.—On Tuesday night about half-past eleven, a

which they g
Attention l
supposed an
found which
laborers are
ish. This is
It is imbedde
character. I
the last two
roads, withou
cited. Its fi
visible, and i
lamented.
since, lay mo
bonized forn
cently found
careless view
to be stone.
it than it did
present a ricl
Benjamin
last, commit
assizes, charg
the property
Inn.

Dr. Wisema
tween Scie
This is an
warmly recor
persuasions,
tion. The fo
and their cou
read with ser
not removed.

11.1 A cutting from the Bucks Advertiser of Saturday May 27th 1843, describing something of the ancient traditions of possessioning, "Beating the Bounds". It seems the perambulators assumed the licence to give strangers a little reminder that they were at the boundary of Waddesdon Parish! In his "History of Aylesbury" Robert Gibbs quotes from a 1667 publication:

"That ev'ry man might keep his own possessions, Our fathers us'd, in reverent Prossession.
With zealous prayers, and with praiseful cheere, To walk their parish-limits once a yeare;
And well-known marks (which sacriligeous hands. Now cut or break) so bord'red out their lands,
That ev'ry one distinctly knew his owne; And many brawles, now rife, were then unknown.

11.2 Monday May 2nd 1921, 9.30 am. The perambulators at the start of the Beating of the Bounds at the Osier Beds' corner on the road to Quainton. The Rev. Long officiated at the short religious ceremony. To his left is Albert Cherry the photographer who took this picture by "remote control"! A long rubber tube buried in the road-dust connects a rubber bulb in his hand to the shutter mechanism on the camera. Also in the photograph are F. Webb, A. Goss, E. Sims, J.W. Goss and son, Hubert St John Wildridge, A. Collyer, G. Finch, Arthur Collyer, F. Turnham, H. Rose.

11.3 1928. The party about to move off on the first day. L-R ; Bernard Crook, Herbert Rose, ------, ------, Arthur Goss, ------, ------, Rev George Dixon, S. Dexter, -------, Mr Herbert, -------, Alf Taylor, Bobbie Price, Ralph Adams.

11.4 May 27th 1935. The finish of the second day. At the Osier Beds the party recorded here are; Vic Burgess, Bobbie Price, Alf Taylor, Rev George Dixon, Arthur Goss, Mrs Long (nee Copcutt) from America, the first lady known to have completed the two-day course.

11.5 Monday May 19th 1952. Seven years after the end of the war saw many of the village stalwarts joined by a new generation of school-children at the Rogation-tide ceremony at the Osier Beds. Some of those in the picture are L-R ; Norman Butler, Bernard Linnell, David Harris, Tony Cherry, Les Carter, John Saunders, John Dormer, Alan Golby, Les Mills, then adults ; Herbert Rose, Canon Dixon, Charlie Cherry, Alf Taylor, Will Dennis, Raymond Griffin, Mrs Biswell, Joe Biswell, Sid Kibble, Peter Adams, Peter Cannon (Church School teacher), Miss Rose.

11.6 Crossing the brook at Eythrope on the first day 1952. Alf Taylor assisted by Will George uses a fallen tree to avoid wet feet on this occasion.

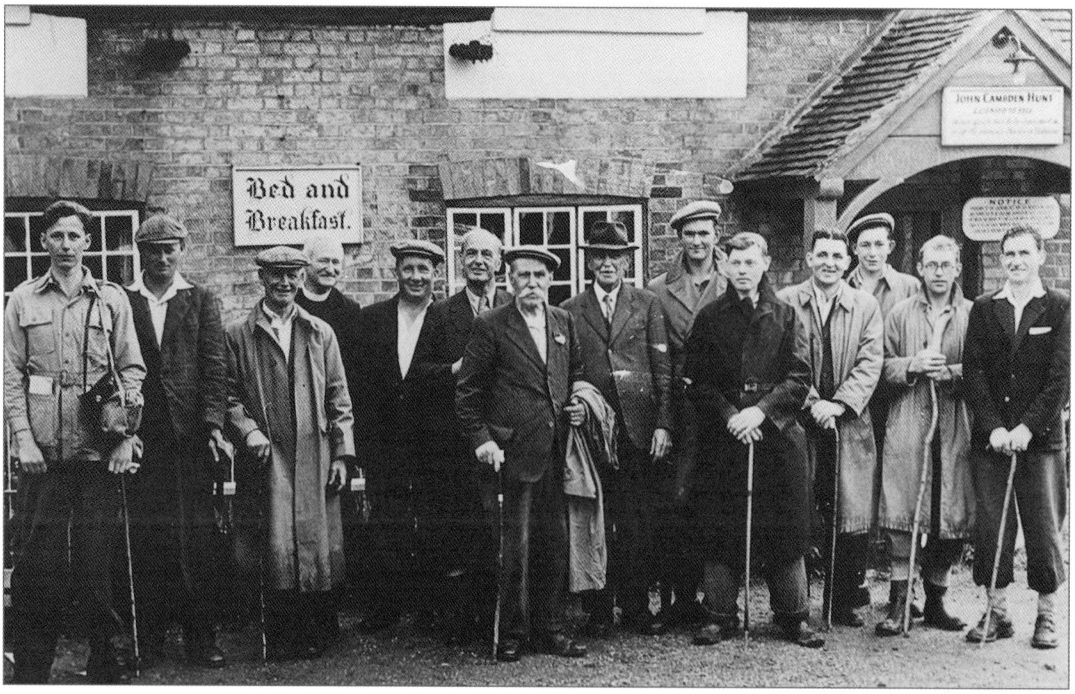

11.7 May 20th 1952. Mid afternoon on the second day at the Crooked Billet, Ham Green. L-R ; Ron Copcutt, Peter Adams, Charlie Cherry, Canon Dixon, Joe Biswell, Alf Taylor, Arthur Goss, Herbert Rose, Roger Goss, Will Dennis, Hywel Evans (head teacher County School), Stan Goss, Raymond Griffin, Peter Cannon.

11.8 This Picture of Tuesday 5th May 1959 shows the walkers resting at lunchtime at Newhouse Farm near Westcott with buildings of the Rocket Propulsion Establishment (R.P.E.) in the background. At the left of picture is Mr Ralph Adams the host of this picnic, a member of probably the oldest local family and a stalwart supporter of traditional community life. Standing L-R: Mr Adams, Ian Slade, Mr Peebles (R.P.E.), Mrs R. Adams, Roger Goss, Colin Marriott, John Goss, Una Taylor, Joe Biswell, Mrs Dennis, Cyril Copcutt, Alec Harding, -----, John Franks, Basil Wheeler, Arthur (Pete) Goss, Ron Copcutt, Sid Kibble, -----, Graham Smith, -----, -----, Cannon Dixon, -----, -----, David Slade, -----, Roy Cheshire (at the back), -----, -----, -----, -----, Mr Webster (R.P.E.), Mr Warne (R.P.E.). Among the boys on the grass: Colin Willis, Bill Biswell, Robert Willis, Timmy Collins.

11.9 Tuesday 5th May 1959. Here we see the perambulators about to leave the secure site at Westcott by climbing a specially arranged ladder platform. On the ladder L-R ; Inspector Harvey, Mr Dixon (Canon Dixon's brother), Joe Biswell, Roger Goss, Colin Marriott, Bernard Cherry, then nine school-boys including Colin Willis, John Adams, Cyril Copcutt.

11.10 Lunchtime at Newhouse Farm, Westcott on the second day, 1967. L-R ; Bill Biswell, Roger Goss, Joe Biswell, Rev H.Parker, Mrs Doll Biswell, Janet Biswell, Jim Collier, -----Mr Golby, Sylvia Southam, --------, Brian Finch, ------,-------, -------, --------, Ron Wright, --------, Des Sharp,--------,Will George, --------, Mrs Dennis, Mrs Johnson, Mrs Stormont Mowatt, Alec Harding, Ernie Hill, Robert Fowler, Fred Marriott, Mrs D. Campbell, Cyril Copcutt, Bill Read, Mr Whalley, John Goss, Oliver Franklin, Ron Copcutt, Eric Goss. The seven-year interval between perambulations was upset in 1966 when preparations were delayed, and the ceremony was postponed to 1967, and incidentally featured in the nationwide B.B.C television programme "Tonight".

11.11 1974 and here we have a lad being given the ritual spanking, "to impress the matter upon his memory", administered and witnessed by stalwarts of the tradition: Jack Slade with spade, Roger Goss and Bill Biswell holding the boy, and behind is John Goss in trilby and Pete Atkins. The boy looking on is Paul Lawrence.

11.12 Roger Goss is shown here re-cutting a cross in a poplar tree in the Westcott establishment 1981. L-R: Jack Slade, Les Beaman, Pete Atkins, Norman Carr.

11.13 The second day 1981, the perambulators pass through the Rocket Propulsion Establishment at Westcott. In the background is the old R.A.F. Control Tower. L-R; (Adults); Jack Slade, Norman Carr, Rev. Pearson-Miles, Bill Biswell, Pete Atkins, Roger Goss, Sid Biswell, Dave Sanderson, Bill George, Les Beaman, Mrs Dennis, Des Sharp. Amongst the younger element are; Mark Saunders, Andrew Ball, Paul Green, Sean O'Brien, Stephen Arnaud, Louise Biswell, Stephen Kemp, Charles Beaman.

11.14 1988 at the Osier Beds, the walkers are just moving off after the short sevice and are obviously in a cheerful mood. Amongst those nearer the camera are; Adrian Lesurf, June Masters, Bill Read and Ian Ewers whilst further to the rear are Bern Holland, Eric Goss, Billy Masters, Ivor Burnell, George Blake, Sally and Charles Beaman.

11.15 Inside the Westcott establishment in 1988. Roger Goss displays the re-cut cross on this young ash tree whilst onlookers enjoy the sunshine and admire his handiwork. L-R ; (Adults) Gary Savin (Site Maintenance Foreman), Rev Colin Hutchings, Barbara Hood (Site Admin Officer), Pete Atkins, Antony Saunders, Roger Goss, Bill Biswell.

11.16 1988 and one of the easiest obstacles for the walkers to negotiate as they cross the Westcott site, a single strand safety fence around one of the rocket installations. Amongst those in this photograph are L-R ; -----, Mathew Eason-Bassett, Janet Eason-Bassett (nee Biswell), -------, Adrian Eason-Bassett, Sally Beaman, ------, Geoff Dixon, Antony Saunders, Des Sharp, Ian Ewers, -----, -----.

11.17 1995, first day and the Rev Hutchings conducts the opening service alongside a thoughtful Bill Biswell who since 1974 has organised the Beating the Bounds ceremony. Also in this picture at the Osier Beds are Anne Richards and Richard Jeffery.

11.18 A pause at the bridge on the road to Stone from Eythrope, mid-afternoon on the first day. 1995. Sid and Kath Biswell stand by the bridge and at the centre of the picture is Mrs Delphie Evans who is the oldest person on the walk, next is Elizabeth Khalvat and right of picture is Brian Warr. Sitting on the parapet of the bridge is Colin Wright.

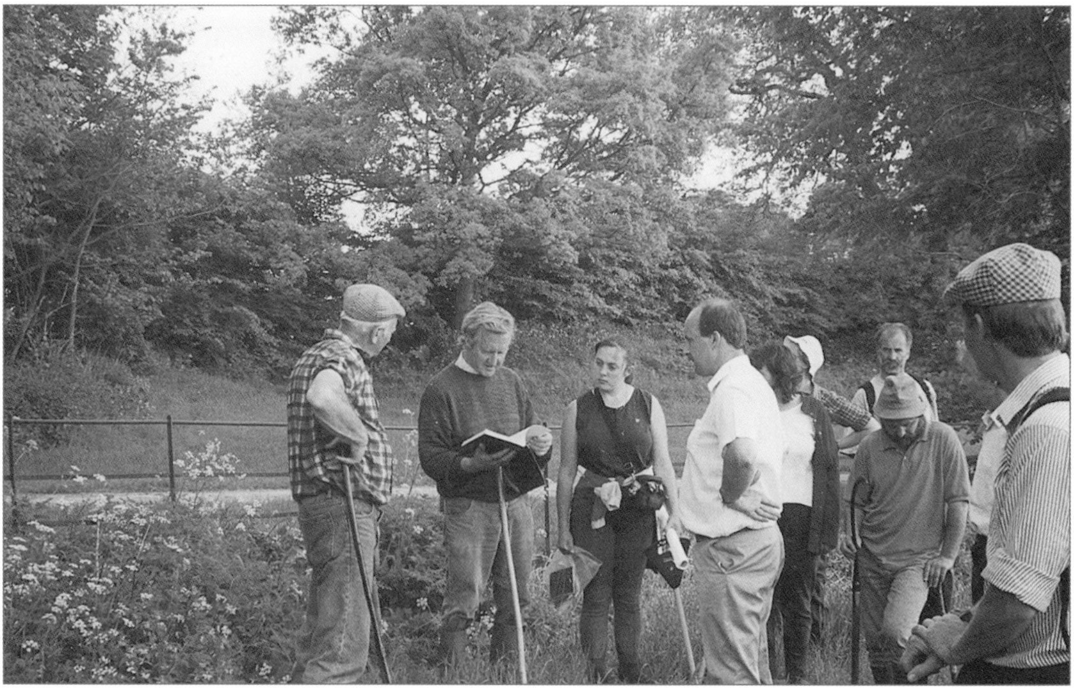

11.19 1995 and nearing the end of the first day. Bill Biswell consults "the book" at the point where the boundary crosses the private road leading to the "Wilderness". At numerous locations around the parish the old markers have been lost as trees and hedges have disappeared in the last few decades, and now it is not unusual for the walkers to change direction in the middle of a ploughing as they faithfully retrace the boundary of old. L-R; Antony Saunders, Bill Biswell, Louise Biswell, Mike Busby, Simon Millard, Pete Atkins, Matthew Adams.

Section Twelve

Schools

In "Waddesdon and Over Winchendon" the Revd C.Oscar Morton mentions references in Overseers accounts, a christening register and other records, which prove that for periods of time schooling was provided in the village during the 17th and 18th centuries. In 1809 rectors sponsored the schooling of two boys, and in 1829 the Trustees of the Charity School required "all boys receiving parish relief from 6 to 12 to be sent to the School Room. John Hitchcock to teach them for 5 to 6 shillings per week". This school was partly funded by grants from the Lewis Fetto Charity, the Trustees of which were instructed to expend the income in schooling and apprenticing poor children of the Towne of Waddesdon. One or more of the three rectors of the living regularly donated other schooling grants. There is no record of where the School Room was, nor whether satisfactory results were achieved; however the neat and concise accounts and records kept by the Churchwardens and Overseers, (which still exist today), indicate some success from these ancient schooling initiatives.

Early in 1845 the clergy and officials of the Church of St Michael decided to provide a National School for 150 pupils, (National Society for Promoting the Education of the Poor in the Principles of the Established Church). The planned capacity was far short of the total requirements of the village.

In July 1845 an open-air public meeting was held at The Bell Inn, when it was resolved, "to provide a cheap and popular school for the education of the poor and labouring classes of Waddesdon". Notable amongst the supporters of the resolution were John Gibbs and Robert Gibbs of Aylesbury, the former was the proprietor of The Aylesbury News, and both of them champions for the establishment of non-sectarian schools.

Before the year was out the National School was in operation, the first purpose-built school in the village, funded by public subscription and administered by the Church of England. The number of scholars to be accommodated was 150, later increased to 200 (mixed). It was situated on the south side of the High Street on land previously part of "Motons", the Manor of the Second Portion. This building was destined to serve as a school for 65 years, then as The Institute for a similar period. It was a sick bay during the Second World War, and now provides homes for Waddesdon Manor employees of the National Trust.

The British School in 1845 on the other hand, was struggling. Land off Silk Street, given for the new building was temporarily withheld due to the influence of "a non-resident clergyman". Meanwhile around 120 boys were crammed into a room adjoining the Wesleyan Chapel, to "be taught by a competent master procured from the Borough Road Institution". Despite all their difficulties, the supporters of the British School raised the necessary £313, built the school and opened for business in 1846. The capacity was initially for 150 scholars, but this was soon extended to 220, (mixed).

Attendance at school was not compulsory, and a subscription was levied upon those who could afford it. The funding, operation and maintenance of the schools was a local responsibility, the National School under the auspices of the Rector of the First Portion, the British School under a Chairman of Managers.

On the 18th of October 1850 the Government Inspector of Schools, in his report on the British School, stated "it is situated in what was once one of the darkest villages in Buckinghamshire". However the thirst for enlightenment was not generally maintained over the ensuing decades, for in 1869 an Inspector reported that, "most young persons are growing up without any useful education as they mostly attend school between the ages of three and eight only". Boys in the parish, aged 10-13 years, could earn three shillings for six days' work! Fortunately the Elementary Education Act of 1870 established free schooling for children up to 12 years of age, and further legislation placed controls on child employment. Consequently, school became a more attractive choice.

The first British School survived for less than 50 years; it was condemned in 1894 and incredibly, the managers were required to provide a new school building "in the course of 1895". They set-to immediately.

Public meetings were held to test and rally support. Baron de Rothschild attended, pledged generous financial help and by taking the chair, provided crucial leadership and assurance. A committee to serve under the chairmanship of Mr Obadiah Duntling was elected: Messrs Rose, Monk, Treadwell, Flowers, Crook, and Lane, with extra help from Messrs Cockerill, Franklin, Webb, and Holland. Most of the important farmers and businessmen in the village.

The new site, almost adjacent to the old school, faced onto Baker Street and was presumably taken in exchange for the original land. The estimated cost of the building with enlarged playing area was £1500. Baron de Rothschild promised £600, practically all the ratepayers promised "to do their share", numerous donations from "good connections" were pledged, and consequently Mr Rose the Treasurer announced, the objective could be achieved.

On April 16th 1895, approved plans for the new school to accommodate 242 pupils were inspected at a public meeting held in the old British School. A Building Committee comprising Baron de Rothschild, Messrs G. Sims, Levi Crook, W.Figg, and all the original committee etc was appointed. Subsequently the architect W.J. Taylor and builder C.Crook were engaged. The building contract was for £1495-2s-0d including all furniture and fittings, and the certificate of completion was presented to the committee in December 1896. Gas lighting was installed at a later date and also a schoolhouse in due course.

20th Century Developments

Miss Alice de Rothschild had long been unhappy at the presence of the National School by the Manor entrance gates on Waddesdon High Street. It was said she was becoming worried about the risk of accidents due to the increased use of motor vehicles. In 1910 she made a rather generous deal with the Church, a new school for 180 pupils, in exchange for the old school and schoolhouse plus the triangle of land (known as "The Square" or "The Green") formerly at the junction of Silk Street and High Street. How the villagers allowed the old Square (common land) to be appropriated and sold from under their noses is beyond the author. Barely a decade later, and after some argument, the village War Memorial was sited on the Square and ownership no longer mattered.

The new National School along with Elmdene and Ivydene the schoolhouses, were models of modern design. The school was situated in Baker Street not far from the British School, it had large windows for maximum use of natural light, gas lighting for winter etc, and coke fired central heating. For the pupils it was probably more comfortable than many homes.

As the years passed the two schools happily existed, co-operated even! At some point after the Great War the old titles were exchanged for "Church School" and "Council School," and 17 years after the Second World War the pupils were amalgamated from the age of 11, in to the new Church of England Secondary School. This of course depleted the numbers on role for the two schools, and inevitably a new County Combined Infant and Junior School was built adjacent to the new Secondary School. The redundant National and British School sites were sold circa 1982, the former demolished and the School Lane houses built there, the latter retained but transformed into a private accommodation complex.

Into the 21st Century

Today Waddesdon's schools are situated on an enviable site, (the gift of Mrs Dorothy de Rothschild), adjoining the parkland of Waddesdon Manor Estate.

The infant and junior school, now renamed Waddesdon Village Primary School, provide the young children of the immediate neighbourhood with their early groundings in education. Examinations for selection to the Aylesbury grammar schools at the age of eleven is still a feature of local education, but at the age of twelve all pupils transfer to secondary education, whether to grammar school or to Waddesdon Church of England Secondary School. There are around 200 pupils at the school with eight teachers and eleven part and full-time support staff. The school is owned by Buckinghamshire County Council and operates under the auspices of a Board of Managers assigned by village organisations.

The establishment of Waddesdon's Church of England Secondary School was the result of a long-term ambition of the rector, Cannon George Dixon, who as chairman of the Governors laid the Foundation Stone in 1962. The Church of England subscribed a quarter of the £125,000 cost, and the school became the only Anglican voluntary aided secondary school in Buckinghamshire. The school is owned by the Anglican Church, which is represented by church appointed Trustees, but the school operates under the auspices of a Board of Governors.

Opened in 1963, the school was designed for 240 pupils and had ten teachers aided by four non-teaching staff. The school catchment area included the ten villages and hamlets surrounding Waddesdon, and this remains the case today. The school soon began to establish a good reputation in the locality. Scholars achieved well in their academic and sporting activities, and school-leavers have always been eminently employable.

Science laboratories were constructed in 1980 and a programme of additions to the buildings during the 1990's included new art and music rooms, a gymnasium, and extra classrooms at a cost of £1.1m. Student numbers had climbed to 560.

The special relationship Waddesdon schools have enjoyed with the Rothschild family was accentuated recently when the Dorothy de Rothschild building was opened by Jacob Lord Rothschild. It comprises two modern computer rooms, general teaching and technology facilities, offices and a meeting room. In addition a range of school enhancements including more drama, physical education and music facilities were provided at a project cost of £1.6m.

The school has received approval for an extensive programme of improvement works including a coach parking area, planned for completion by 2004. Of the £3.6m projected cost, 10% is to be raised by the church and the school.

Waddesdon C/E Secondary School was awarded Beacon Status in 1998, one of only 75 schools in England to receive this accolade. The school now has 945 students, including 200 Sixth Formers, with 58 teachers and 30 support staff. Pupils travel from near and far to attend the school, which has so many applicants from outside the catchment area that a selection procedure has evolved. Those from outside the village are in the majority, and their transportation brings traffic problems to Baker Street, each school morning and afternoon. The school is a priceless asset to the young scholars of the community, and an object of pride to all in the locality.

TO THE FRIENDS of POPULAR EDUCATION.

A DESERVING CASE.

THE Village of WADDESDON, one of the largest parishes in the County of Bucks, which, with its hamlets and immediate neighbourhood, contains a population of 5,000 souls, is purely agricultural, and in a deplorable state of ignorance, with but one small endowed Church School in the district, and has for some time drawn the attention of a few friends of Education, who with several resident farmers, determined to attempt the establishment of a public school upon the Royal British System. A Chapel was borrowed for this experiment, which succeeded beyond expectation; 120 Boys soon attended; the place was too small; a new convenient and substantial room was built, 57 feet by 27 feet, to accommodate 150 scholars, (140 are now on the books,) the costs of which is £313; in aid of this the Government Board of Education have promised £121 when the remainder is forthcoming. Every effort in the power of the projectors of the School has been used, and £117 have been raised (as below), leaving them deficient £75, for which this appeal to the public is respectfully made to enable them to give the blessings of a good Education to this poor and populous neighbourhood. The following non-resident Gentlemen have lent their assistance as stated:—

Mr. Richard Herons, of Horley, near Banbury	The Site of Building.		
John Hull, Esq., Ramsgate	10	10	0
J. D. Bassett, Esq., Leighton Buzzard	3	0	0
The Baron M Rothschild, London	5	0	0
John Lee, Esq., Hartwell House	3	0	0
Mr. John Gibbs, Aylesbury	5	5	0
John Houghton, Esq., Sunning-hill	2	2	0
Two Farmers of Waddesdon	10	0	0
Subscriptions under £5 each	44	0	0
Tea Party Collection	15	0	0
Various other means, and Three Lectures	19	3	0
Promised aid from Government when all the other Cash is forthcoming	121	0	0
	£238	0	0
Required to obtain the above Grant	75	0	0
	£313	0	0

Donations toward the above will be thankfully received by Mr. John Gibbs, of Aylesbury; or Mr. Charles King, of Waddesdon, near Aylesbury.

N.B. A Lay Member of the Committee will with pleasure give a plain, practical, and amusing Public Lecture on the necessity and advantages of Education, particularly on the British System, at any place within fifty miles of Aylesbury, upon being allowed to make a Collection for this Case.

12.1 The Aylesbury News of 2nd January 1847 carried this article giving the background, progress and financial position of the British School. In fact the school was in use by the end of 1846, but the debt required the stalwart efforts of a dedicated group for a further four years, before it was paid in full. John and Robert Gibbs of Aylesbury were the prime movers in this group, which achieved so much for the village.

GOVERNMENT REPORT OF THE NATIONAL SCHOOL.

"The School has made good progress during the past year. The infants are remarkably well taught. The children are generally presented in standards suitable to their ages. There are very few girls as compared with the number of boys; this is accounted for by the prevalence of lace-making and straw-plaiting, and the disregard of the Workshops' Act. Hence also the needlework is unsatisfactory."

IMPORTANT TO PARENTS AND EMPLOYERS OF CHILDREN.

Act to Regulate the Employment of Children in Agriculture (*5th August* 1873).

This Act comes into full operation on the 1st January, 1875.

Its provisions should be complied with during the year 1874.

After January 1st, 1875, no employer, or his agent, may employ any child under 8 in agricultural labour, unless he be its parent or guardian, and then only on land in his own occupation.

After January 1st, 1875, no employer, or his agent, may employ any child over 8 and under 12, unless the parent or guardian can produce a certificate to the following effect:—

If the child be over 8 and under 10, he must have completed 250 school attendances (that is, 25 weeks at least,) within the 12 months immediately preceding the issue of the certificate.

If he be over 10 and under 12, he must have completed 150 school attendances (that is, 15 weeks at least,) within the same period. (N.B.—No children, whether boys or girls, can be excepted from these rules but those who have passed the 4th Standard.)

No child under the age of ten years shall be employed in any agricultural gang.

Morning school and afternoon school each count as one attendance.

The school must be a school recognised by Government as efficient, if there be one within 2 miles of the parents' home.

Every employer, or agent of an employer, guilty of an offence against the Act shall be liable to a penalty of £5.

Any other person committing an offence against the Act shall be liable to a penalty of £1.

But no penalty shall be inflicted for employing children above 8 years of age during School Holidays, or temporary Closing of the School—

Or in Hay Harvest, Corn Harvest, or gathering of Hops; and the Magistrates have the power to entirely suspend the Act during a few weeks in the busy seasons of the year.

N.B.—Parents are earnestly advised to send their children at once to school, that they may complete the proper number of attendances, otherwise while they are under 12 they cannot be employed in agriculture after January 1st, 1875.

12.2 Even though the two schools in the village had existed for two decades and more, family finances were often stretched to breaking point, and children were put to work at lace making and straw plaiting. It was possible for a girl to earn as much as two shillings and six pence by the age of 16, in return for a 50 to 60 hour week. Her labourer father would earn about 17 shillings for a similar period; if he had a job! Various Acts of Parliament were enacted to raise literacy and educational standards, and here we have two cuttings from the Parish Magazines of February (top) and January 1874 illustrating the point.

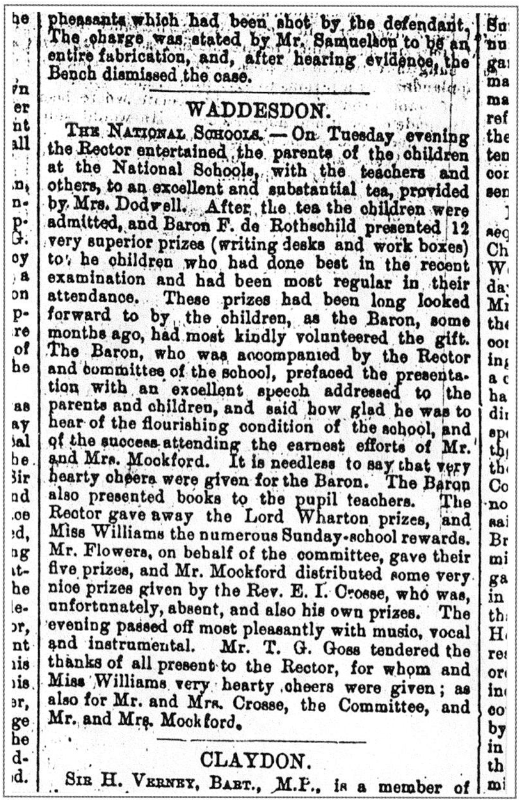
pheasants which had been shot by the defendant. The charge was stated by Mr. Samuelson to be an entire fabrication, and, after hearing evidence, the Bench dismissed the case.

WADDESDON.

THE NATIONAL SCHOOLS.—On Tuesday evening the Rector entertained the parents of the children at the National Schools, with the teachers and others, to an excellent and substantial tea, provided by Mrs. Dodwell. After the tea the children were admitted, and Baron F. de Rothschild presented 12 very superior prizes (writing desks and work boxes) to the children who had done best in the recent examination and had been most regular in their attendance. These prizes had been long looked forward to by the children, as the Baron, some months ago, had most kindly volunteered the gift. The Baron, who was accompanied by the Rector and committee of the school, prefaced the presentation with an excellent speech addressed to the parents and children, and said how glad he was to hear of the flourishing condition of the school, and of the success attending the earnest efforts of Mr. and Mrs. Mockford. It is needless to say that very hearty cheers were given for the Baron. The Baron also presented books to the pupil teachers. The Rector gave away the Lord Wharton prizes, and Miss Williams the numerous Sunday-school rewards. Mr. Flowers, on behalf of the committee, gave their five prizes, and Mr. Mockford distributed some very nice prizes given by the Rev. E. I. Crosse, who was, unfortunately, absent, and also his own prizes. The evening passed off most pleasantly with music, vocal and instrumental. Mr. T. G. Goss tendered the thanks of all present to the Rector, for whom and Miss Williams very hearty cheers were given; as also for Mr. and Mrs. Crosse, the Committee, and Mr. and Mrs. Mockford.

CLAYDON.

SIR H. VERNEY, BART., M.P., is a member of

12.3 Prizes for attendance and examination successes were an established feature of school life. In the New Year of 1884 the Baron de Rothschild prizes were introduced. For many years they were the most keenly anticipated of all the school prizes, and sooner or later most families in the village had at least one such treasure. The Baron's School Prizes were awarded in Westcott and Upper Winchendon as well as Waddesdon, and after the death of the Baron in 1898, the tradition was continued for some years by his sister, Miss Alice de Rothschild.

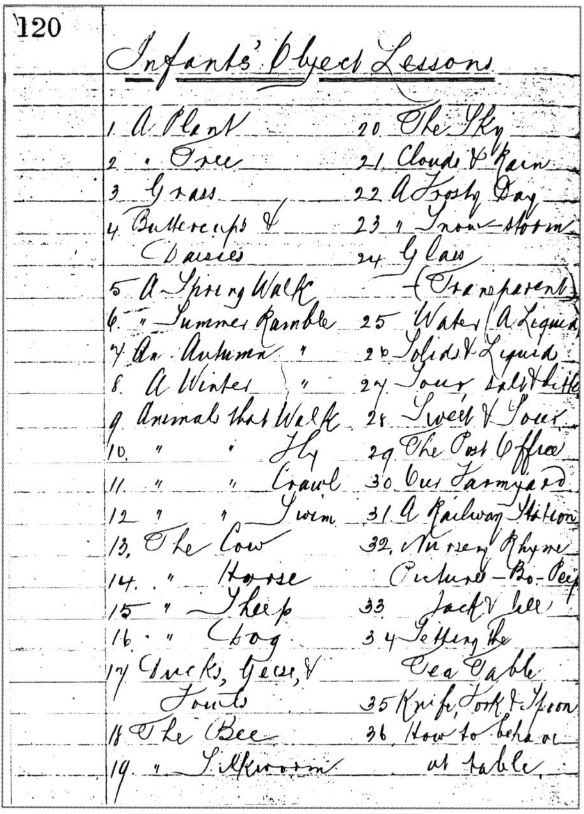
120

Infants' Object Lessons

1. A Plant — 20. The Sky
2. " Tree — 21. Clouds & Rain
3. Grass — 22. A Frosty Day
4. Buttercups & Daisies — 23. " Snow-storm
5. A Spring Walk — 24. Glass (Transparent)
6. " Summer Ramble — 25. Water (A Liquid)
7. An Autumn " — 26. Solids & Liquids
8. A Winter " — 27. Sour, Salt & Bitter
9. Animals that Walk — 28. Sweet & Sour
10. " " Fly — 29. The Post Office
11. " " Crawl — 30. Our Farmyard
12. " " Swim — 31. A Railway Station
13. The Cow — 32. Nursery Rhyme Picture—Bo-Peep
14. " Horse — 33. Jack & Jill
15. " Sheep — 34. Setting the Tea Table
16. " Dog — 35. Knife, Fork & Spoon
17. Ducks, Geese, & Fowls — 36. How to behave at table
18. The Bee
19. " Silkworm

12.4 Although the schools were expected to concentrate upon the three "Rs", there was still time to educate in the broader sense. This Infants Object Lessons' list covers practically all aspects of everyday village life. The list was subject to the approval of the School Inspector when he visited the British School in 1903. Item 36, "How to behave at table", might prove a little novel these days!

12.5 The National School (Church School) photographed from the air in 1931. This school built in 1910 by Miss Alice de Rothschild, in exchange for the original* school buildings (The Institute), comprised all the traditional amenities, and included additional facilities such as central heating with an underground boiler room, and folding partitions between classrooms. *See 4.5 In this view the double doorways on the south side lead to the cloakrooms. The large playground was divided by a fence separating the girls and infants on the right, from the hurly-burly activities of the older boys. The buildings left and right at the edge of the playground were the lavatories, the boys' urinal being totally uncovered. In winter quite a trek for mid-lesson visits!

12.6 The British School (County School) photographed around 1965. It was built in 1895 at a cost of less than £2000, all raised by voluntary subscriptions and donations. The project took around 18 months, from condemnation of the original school to completion of this substantial structure and its outbuildings. At the right of the picture can be seen part of the single storey lavatories and storage sheds. The ornate cast iron railings immediately in front of the school were considered for removal for scrap during the Second World War* but were reprieved; there were no sentiments allowed when the school was sold for development in the 1970's, suddenly the railings were gone, what a shame! (* Metal objects such as railings, gates, old pots and pans etc were collected for the construction of ships, guns, aircraft, etc).

12.7 This photograph is unique amongst our collection of pre-Great War school groups, we can name everyone in the picture. The setting is the playground of the British School, the date circa 1905 and the group seems to comprise a combination of family members and relatives. Back Row L-R: George Copcutt, Harry Cripps, Jack Wheeler, Fred Stanton, George Ewers, Alf Fowler, Ron Crook, Ralph Rolfe, Ralph Saunders, Stan Biswell, Fred Cripps, Mr Rushden, (Headmaster). Fourth Row L-R: Lionel Cannon, Jack Rolfe, Alf Fowler, Bert Saunders, G. Stanton, Rufus Fowler, Ted Sharp, Hubert Biswell, Stan Southam, Henry Thorpe, Horace Saunders, Maurice Saunders. Third Row: Annie Pollard, Ethel Atkins, Florie Price, Jess Figg, Lilly Blake, May Atkins, Alice Allen. Second Row: Min Copcutt, Em Southam, Nell Church, Ethel Sharp, Bessie Evans, Annie Biswell, Winnie Ford, Daisy George. Front Row: John Thorpe, May Allen, Win Sharp, Charlie George, Madge Thorpe, Elsie George, Alice George.

12.8 Council School pupils circa 1928. Back Row L-R: Stan Ewers, Charlie Cripps, Percy Saunders, Muriel Cannon, Chrissie Hicks, Ivy or Mabel Cripps, Kitty Read, Reg Harding, Jack Scott, Will Sharp. Middle Row: Alf Carter, Joe Fowler, "Ginger" Bailey, Harry Biswell, Alf Taylor, Oliver Franklin, Arthur Copcutt. Front Row: Ena Pacey, May Biswell, Winnie Read, Dolly Harding, Kathy Rolfe, Eva Copcutt.

12.9 A class at the Church School circa 1931. Back Row L-R: Cyril Rolfe, Peter Adams, Jim Meager, Ron Loader, Betty Carter, Mararet Hicks, Margaret Faulkner, Ken Jeeves. Middle Row: Margaret Neary, Vera Brown, Iris Atkins, Peggy Rhodes, Gladys Evans, Maireni Wood, Peggy Cyster, Kathy Scott, Florrie Field, Grace Cannon. Front: Keith Bishop, Harold Allen, Jim Neary, Bill Mulcahy, Tony Biswell, Gerald Sullivan, Billy Dewhurst.

12.10 The Senior Class at the Church School circa 1932. Back Row L-R: Tom Brown, Ray Carter, Len Harms, Vic Syrett, Jim Slade, -----, Vic Burgess, Frank Brackley. Third Row: Edwin Harris (Headmaster), Diana Adams, Gwen Smith, Mabel Faulkner, Mary Slade, Joan Massey, Joan Bishop, Daphne Horwood, Dorothy Hinton, Mary Adams, R. Oakley. Second Row: Sylvia Atkins, Madge Walker, Molly Varney, Ruby Webb, Joan Cripps, Minnie Eldridge, Margaret Cannon, Dorothy Syrett, Jean Bateman. Front Row: Jim Wicks, Don Saunders, Laurie Goss, Bob Fountain, Vic Biswell, Bill Jones, Harry Franks, Will Dennis, Jack May.

12.11 A class of juniors at the Church School circa 1933. Back Row L-R: Len Cannon, Geoffrey Harms, Andy Speed, -----, Jack Slade, Arthur Barratt, -----, Len Wood, Desmond Crook. Third Row: Evelyn Scott, Rita Crook, Gladys Biswell, Queenie Cyster, Joan Jeffs, Iris Oakley, Audrey Hedges, Elsie Walker, Sybil Jones, Joan May, Vic Biswell. Sitting: Amy Evans, Hilda Brackley, Joan Eldridge, Win Loader, Doris Scott. Front Row: Ruby Webb, John Boughton, Percy George, Rose Evans. Teacher: Mrs Shaddock.

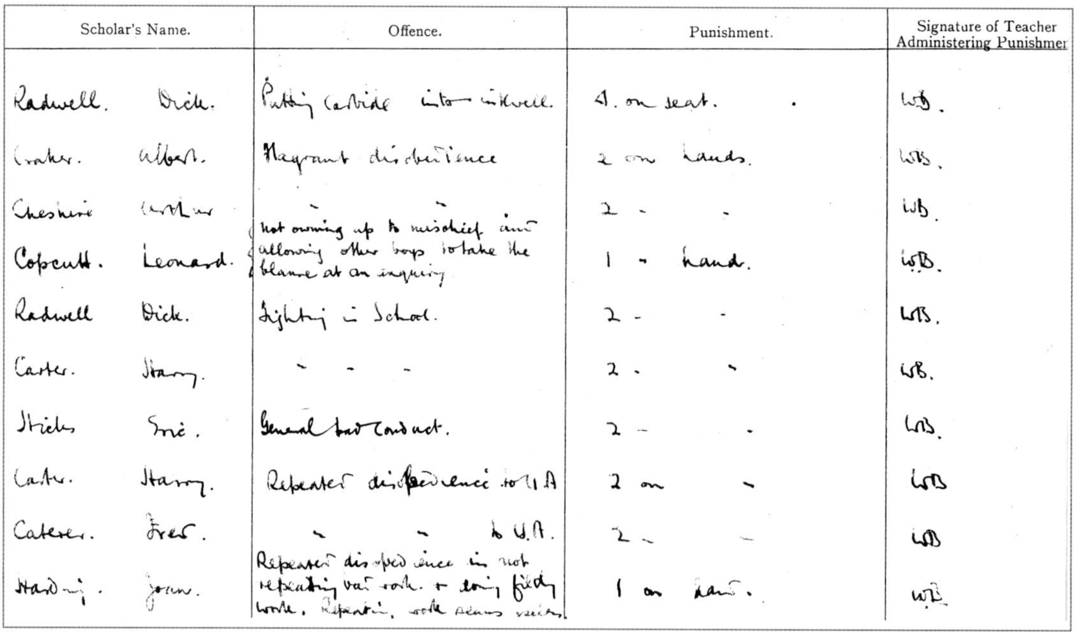

Scholar's Name.	Offence.	Punishment.	Signature of Teacher Administering Punishmer
Radwell. Dick.	Putting carbide into inkwell.	4. on seat.	WB.
Croker. Albert.	Flagrant disobedience	2 on hands.	WB.
Cheshire Arthur	" "	2 " "	WB.
Copcutt. Leonard.	Not owning up to mischief and allowing other boys to take the blame at an inquiry	1 " hand.	WB.
Radwell Dick.	Fighting in School.	2 " "	WB.
Carter. Harry.	" " "	2 " "	WB.
Hicks Eric.	General bad conduct.	2 " "	WB.
Carter. Harry.	Repeated disobedience to U.A	2 on "	WB
Caterer. Fred.	" " to U.A.	2 " "	WB
Harding. Joan.	Repeated disobedience in not repeating [illegible] work & doing filthy work. Repeating work [illegible]	1 on hand.	WB

12.12 This cutting was taken from the Punishment Book of the British School, and records a few of the instances when Mr Bullock the Head Teacher made use of the cane. We read that on the 4th December 1931, Dick Radwell was caned on the seat for "putting carbide into inkwell". No doubt Dick was carrying out a scientific experiment, but Mr Bullock did not appreciate the disturbance and mess that resulted when the ink erupted in a fizzing stream! The chemical reaction of carbide and water produces acetylene gas. Carbide lamps were used on early motor vehicles and cycles, and carbide was readily available from garages. Restricting the drip of water onto the particles of carbide controlled the reaction in the lamp. See 7.17.

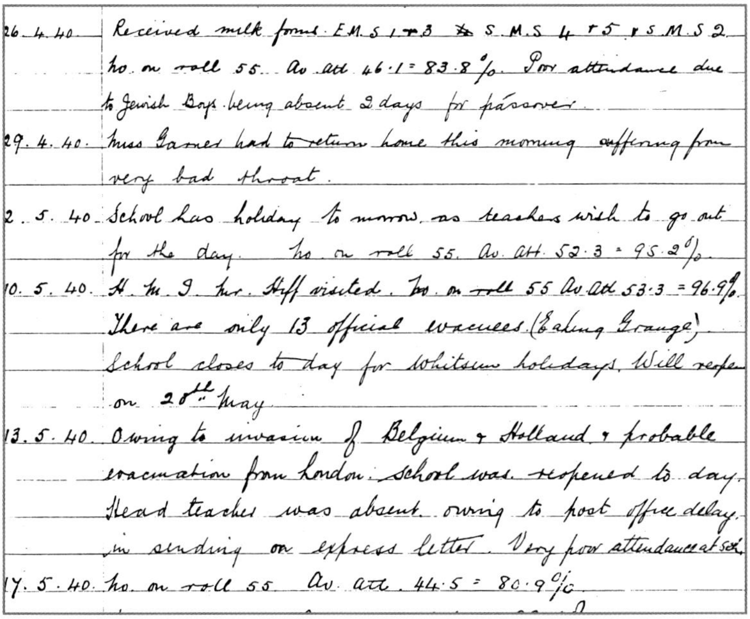

26.4.40. Received milk forms E.M.S 1+3 & S.M.S 4+5 & S.M.S 2.
No. on roll 55. Av. att. 46·1 = 83·8%. Poor attendance due
to Jewish Boys being absent 2 days for passover.
29.4.40. Miss Games had to return home this morning suffering from
very bad throat.
2.5.40. School has holiday to morrow, as teachers wish to go out
for the day. No. on roll 55. Av. Att. 52·3 = 95·2%.
10.5.40. H.M.I. Mr. Stiff visited. No. on roll 55 Av. Att. 53·3 = 96·9%.
There are only 13 official evacuees (Ealing Grange).
School closes to day for Whitsun holidays. Will reopen
on 20th May.
13.5.40. Owing to invasion of Belgium & Holland & probable
evacuation from London school was reopened to day.
Head teacher was absent owing to post office delay
in sending an express letter. Very poor attendance at sch.
17.5.40. No. on roll 55. Av. att. 44·5 = 80·9%.

12.13 An interesting page from the Chairman of Managers' records for The Council School in 1940. On the 26th April the attendance was down, due to the Cedars Boys' absence to celebrate the Feast of the Passover, on the 3rd May the teachers "wish to go out for the day!" Was this a case of mutiny? On the 10th May only 13 evacuees from Ealing Grange remained, in December 1939 there were 25, but as the expected bombing of London had not materialised some children had returned to the comforts of their own homes. However, the report for 13th May heralds the end of the "Phoney War," and evacuees would soon be on the move again.

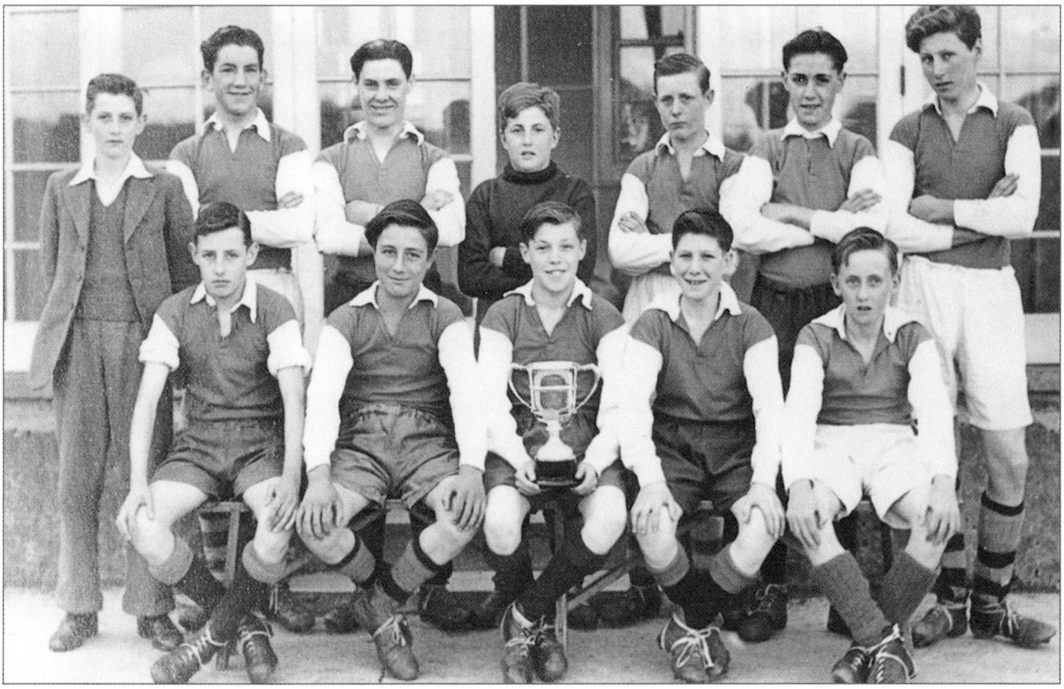

12.14 The Council and Church Schools joined forces on the sports field in the late 1940's and immediately tasted success. Thanks to the influx of senior scholars from the surrounding villages there was an abundance of talent for selection. Here we have the Senior Boys Under 14 team of 1948, the winners of the Aylesbury District Cup photographed on front of the Waddesdon Football Pavilion. Standing L-R: Brian Cross, Brian Bates, Dave Thomas, John Cripps, Tom Wilson, Brian Carr, Ray Spooner. Sitting: Ralph Evans, Fred Saunders, Terry Fowler, Robert Drydale, Sid Biswell.

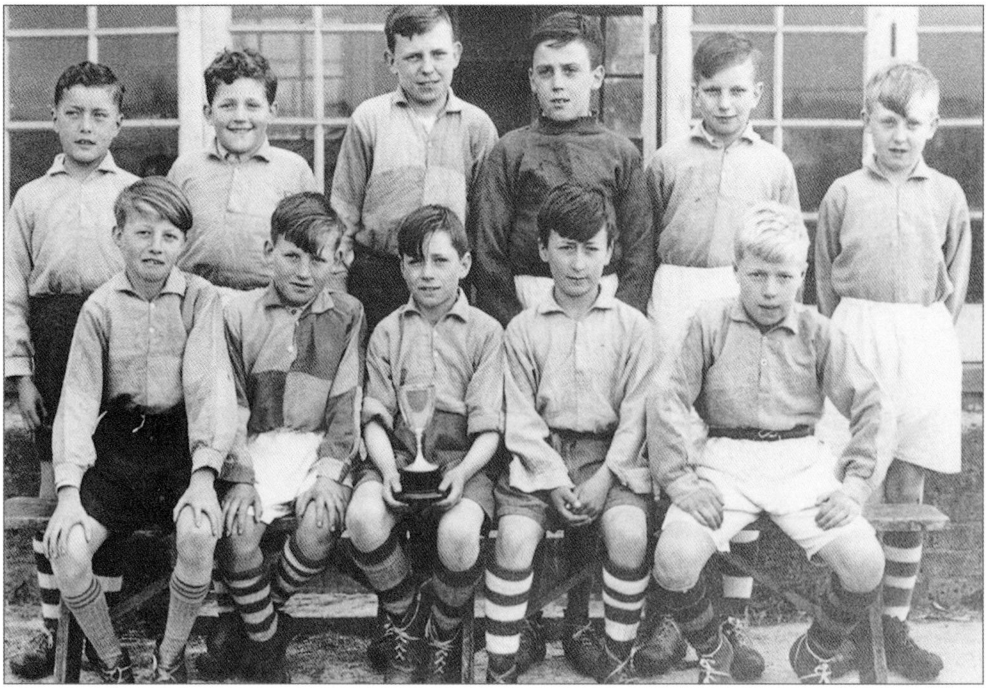

12.15 In 1950 the combined Waddesdon Schools' Junior Team won the Aylesbury District Cup. Standing L-R: Arthur Richards, Bryan Goss, Peter Williams, Ray Sharp, Antony Saunders, Malcolm Wheeler. Sitting: Basil Wheeler, Les Mills, Doug Rolfe, Les Sharp, Terry Marriott.

12.16 School Sports' Day for the Council School 1950. Back Row L-R : Eileen Bonson, -----, Ann Bignell, June Baylis, -----, Phyllis Cooper, Ann Churchill, John Fowler, Ivor Gurney, Pat Smith, Barbara Speck, Mavis Sharp, Lorna Fowler, Violet Wallace, -----, Peter Williams. Fourth Row: -----, -----, Marie Fowler, Vera Cripps, Peter Atkins, -----, -----, Margaret Rand, Doreen Saunders, Norman Carr, Bern Johnson, Miss Hallet (Teacher), -----, -----, Mr Horner (Head Teacher), Alan Evans. Third Row: Barry Atkins, Bill Fowler, -----, -----, -----, -----, -----, -----, -----, -----, Jill Speck, Anna Fowler, Mavis Carr, Gwenda Carr, Phyllis Saunders, Beryl Baylis, -----, Roy Bradbury. Second Row: Ann Cheshire, Roseanne McKenna, Linda Cheshire, Roy Cheshire, -----, Edward Fowler, Desmond Sharp, Keith Vaughan, -----, Pete Johnson, Buster Williams, Ruby Biswell, Veronica Sharp, Jennifer Cripps, -----, Rita Cannon, -----, -----, Rosemary Ewers, -----, Ian Ewers, -----. Front Row: Geraldine Ashfield, Barbara Sharp, Douglas Rolfe, Ivor Smith, Les Sharp, -----, Roger Hillier, Beth Sharp, -----, Alan Bignell, -----, Ruth Vaughan, -----, Malcolm Wheeler, -----, Janice Hicks, -----.

12.17 School leaving age had progressed from 14 to 15 years. This was the Waddesdon Senior Team, all Church School boys but only four from the village. Circa 1951. Standing L-R: Richard Charters, David Harris, Mick Sharp, Alan Small, Graham Golby. Sitting: Peter Bradbury, Don Marlow, Tony Carter, John Dormer, Tony Cherry, Les Carter.

12.18 School Sports' Day for the Church School circa 1952, and some of the participants pose for the camera. Boys at the rear of the photograph L-R : -----, Alan Bonson, David Harris, Bernard Wheeler Cherry, John Morris, -----, -----, Richard Davis, Meldwyn Price, John Dormer, Colin Bates, Lennie Richards, Terry Marriott. Girls Standing: Georgina Collins, -----, Pam Coles, Janet Jones, -----, June Goss, Rosemary Howes, Pat Green (Helper), Margaret Buckingham, Jean Carter, Mary Davis, Violet Shirley, Joy Gurney, Jessie Emerton, Murial Copcutt, Patricia Hayes, -----. Two Boys Standing at centre: -----, Maurice Fowler. Sitting on bench : -----, Harold Pennington, Keith Fennimore, Ken Cherry, David Slade, John Howe, Sandra Lee. On the grass: Barbara Saunders, Rowena Evans, -----, Rosemary Cherry, Brenda Saunders, Sally Walters, John Mathews, Josie Biswell, Roy Cyster, Susan Cherry, Alan Carter, -----, Rear: Jill Alliband, Front Dorothy Brown, Rear: Bryan Goss, Front: Angela Gurney.

NETBALL

The netball season began in September and during the season we have played twelve matches several of which we won.

The season was rounded off with a tournament at Queen's Park school on February 28 th. Fourteen teams took part.

Last year we were in the bottom division but this year we were promoted to the top division, and finished fourth. We were all very pleased that one of our team was chosen as a reserve for the Aylesbury and District team.

At the Tournament held in Aylesbury on April 25 th. the Intermediate Team gained 2 nd. place winning 5 out of the 6 matches played.

SCHOOL SUCCESSES

Scholarships to Grammar School

Joyce Franks Freda Fowler

LEAVERS

John Harvey is serving an apprenticeship at Westcott.
Alan Small works for Mr. Rickett, the coal merchant.
Colin Marriott works on his father's farm.
Graham Golby works on his father's farm.
Peter Crawford works on his father's farm.
Michael Sharp works on Mr. Ridgeway's farm.

(20)

David Harris works on Mr. King's farm.
Peter Tombs works on a farm at Hogshaw.
Delwyn Mills works on Mr. Jones' farm.
Colin Bates works for his father.
William Taplin works at Mr Busby's farm.
Leslie Carter works at Woodham Brick Co
John Dormer works at Mr Brooker's the electrician at Aylesbury.
Anthony Cherry works at Woodham Brick Co.
Richard Charter works at Mr. Shippley's farm.
Norman Butler works at Mr. Gostelow's farm.
Pauline Sharp works at Dominion Dairy.
Judith Uff works at Hazell's Printing Works.
Brenda Robinson helps at home
Betty Radwell works at Woolworth's.
Doris Drydale also works at Woolworth's.
Jill Alliband works at Hazell's.
Mary Wilson went to live in Aylesbury.
Patricia Hayes works at Waddesdon Gardens.
Dorothy Goss works at her father's cafe.
Rosemary Howes works at Woolworth's.
Judith Parker left to go to another school.

CORRECTION. Junior Football Team Page 19
Alan Carter omitted.

Printed by - D. Mills K. Marriott R. Davis B. Linnell.
Silk-Screening by - L. Carter J. Dormer M. Riley C. Howell.

(21)

12.19 During the Headmastership of Mr J.Smith, the Church School senior boys produced a school magazine each term using a small printing press and silk screening techniques for the illustrations. We reproduce here pages 20 & 21from a 1952 magazine that provide us with a fascinating list of school-leavers' employment choices. Of 16 boys who left school, ten found employment on farms.

12.20 Sports Day for Church of England School-children 1952. This group of mixed ages includes a significant number of pupils from surrounding villages, who were amongst the first local generations to be bussed-in to Waddesdon. Girls at the back L-R: -----, Shirley Ball, Winnie Wood, Gwen Rolfe, Dorothy Goss, Betty Radwell, Margaret Collins, Rosemary Howse, Joy Gurney, Jennifer Preston, Jill Roads, Lily Biswell. Small girls standing L-R: Josie Biswell, Ruth Brown, Brenda Saunders. Boys standing L-R: Andrew Tomlinson, Meldwyn Price, Chris Cyster, Harold Pennington, Dave Harris, Les Kibble, Danny Price, Michael Charters, Terry Marriott, -----, Alec Ewers, Don Marlow. Boys kneeling L-R: -----, Norman Emerton. Girls sitting L-R: Margaret Evans, Jean Carter, Doris Drydale, Rosemary Cherry, Freda Fowler, Joan Fowler, Daisy Cherry, Edna Parker, Violet Shirley, Glynis Foley.

12.21 A junior class from the Church School 1954. Rear L-R: Brian Battershill, John Wood, John Howe, Alistair McLaren, Judith Matthews, Sheila Ellis, Anita Knibb, Rita Saunders, David Slade, Irwin Green, Percy Richards, John Matthews. Sitting: John Franks, Roger Hiscock, -----, Susan Cherry, Paula Rhodes, Carol Shillingford, Sally Walters, Angela Gurney, Yvonne Lee, Diane George, Valerie Cherry, Rita Saunders, Vincent Miller, Keith Lee. Front Row: Robert Smith, Bill Biswell, Timmy Collins, David Bonson.

12.22 The Waddesdon schools' netball team, victorious in the 1956 District Cup competition. Standing L-R: Rita Cannon, Linda Cheshire, Doreen Saunders, Vera Cripps. Sitting: Angela Harrison, Gwenda Carr, -----.

12.23 A junior class from the Church School 1957. Back Row L-R: John Wood, Sandra Millar, Alan Marriott, Coral Styles, Chris Price, Marie McLaren, Ray Butt, Rosemary George, John Green. Third Row: Pam Saunders, Dennis Foley, Rosemary Goss, David Blake, Pauline Scott, Richard Norris, Ann Smith, Frank Carter, -----. Second Row: -----, Eileen Stone, Stephen Andrews, Gillian Carter, Derek Price, Janet Biswell, Derek Beattie, Catherine Harms. Front Row: Stewart Shillingford, Sue Knibb, John Walters, Gillian Mills, Brian Saunders, Pauline Franks, Austen Price.

12.24 A photograph of the newly established Waddesdon Church of England Secondary School 1963. The Rector of Waddesdon, Cannon G. Dixon, had worked long and hard to ensure the Church of England maintained its control of the planned new secondary school for this area, despite the protests of a strong minority who preferred a non-sectarian school. The succeeding decades have witnessed a success in every possible field, and there are very few pupils and parents who would wish to alter any aspects of the school.

12.25 The junior football squad 1966/7. Back Row L-R: -----, Roy Wheeler, Clive Carter, Patrick Fennessy, Stephen Rhodes, Phillip Carter, -----, Stephen Garrard. Front Row: Eddie Ridgway, -----, Andrea Needham, Alan Hughes, Anthony McKenna, Graeme Fowler.

12.26 A group of Waddesdon Church Junior School pupils photographed in the playground circa 1970. Standing L-R: Dawn Marriott, Kevin Rolfe, Peter Wood, Stewart Williams, Brian Read, -----, -----, Hilary Brown, Trudy Lovell, -----. Kneeling: Tina Marriott, Linda Wheeler, Ian Lewis, Nicholas Garrad, Diane Alburg, Jane Powell, Heather Rhodes, Lynne Evans, Geraldine Cherry.

12.27 The Infants at Waddesdon County School circa 1972. Back Row L-R: Shaun Maitland, Braddan Evans, Stewart Powell, Malaky McGirr, -----, -----, Mrs Hough. Middle Row: Susan Warrington, -----, -----, -----, -----, Tracy Saunders, -----, Sharon Maitland. Front Row: Susan Foley, Nicholas Gilson, Gary Oselton, Richard Ellery, Jane Pilcher, David Bonson, Stephen Arnaud, Kevin Furber, David Tucker.

12.28 A junior class at Waddesdon County School circa 1972. Back Row L-R : Moira Thompson, Sheila O'Brien, -----, -----, Peter Tearle, Peter Coyne, Stewart Taylor, Mark Pilcher, Andrew Brown, Mrs Fuller. Middle Row : Beverly Sharp, Linda Spagarni, Keith Rimmer, Terry Warrington, Lorrainne Brown, Stephen Linnell, Wendy Coles, Linda Clarke. Front Row : Paula Mathews, Wendy Ridgway, Janet Saunders, Patrick Onn, Paul Lingard, Mark Hughes, Deborah McKenna, Colin Carpenter.

12.29 The juniors at Waddesdon County School circa 1972. Back Row L-R: Clifford Oselton, -----, -----, Mary McGirr, Caroline Redding, Sheila Coker, Simon Watts, Andrew O'Brien, Paul Clements. Middle Row: Richard Jeffery, Zsa Zsa Czap, Moira Thompson, Karen Bonson, Vivienne Lynch, Kerry Lingard, Beverly Kelly, Janet Carpenter, Janice Wooller, Julie Ayris, Kay Arnaud, Paul Lawence. Front Row: John McGirr, Russell Hughes, Glyn Ridgway, Jeremy Ayris, Colin Walters, Robert Mathews, Mark Chambers, Stephen Zealey, Mark Edwards.

12.30 An historical pageant performed by the school children attracted crowds of relations and friends to the County School. Here we see a group of pupils enacting the tale of Sleeping Beauty (?) closely watched by the attentive audience. Amongst the performers can be recognised, Suzan Alburg, and Sarah Furber, whilst the audience includes from the left ; Leslie Carter, Thelma Carter, Doreen Snell, George Blake, Mrs Blake, Anita Marriott, Andrew Carter, Mrs and David Kemp, Ian Price, Arthur Evans, Elsie Cheshire, Mary Praeger, Christine Cheshire, Sandy Young, Beth Young, Arthur O'Brien.

12.31 Another photograph of the audience at the Pageant performed at the County School circa 1978. Amongst those shown here are, from the left; Dave Powell, Arthur O'Brien, Doris Jenkins, Kathy Cannon, June Powell, Rita O'Brien, Joy Rhodes, Jennifer Tearle, ? Tearle, Mrs Cripps, Sybil Jones, Antony Saunders, Mrs Jones, Mrs Gold, Margaret Wallis, Violet Atkins, Mrs Atkins, Albert Atkins, Doreen Furber, Geoff Furber, Phylis Carter. The building behind the spectators is the school's canteen. It was built in the late 1940's, and for the following 30 years served as a canteen providing meals at subsidised prices, to all the school-children requiring them. The canteen was demolished to make way for the housing development associated with the old Council School.

12.32 The football squad at the new County Combined School circa 1981. Back Row L-R: -----, Matthew Woodhouse, Paul Green, Tim Cheshire, Darren Willis, Neil Holdsworth, Peter Clark, Mark Pretty. Front Row: Chris Raynor, Richard Blaydon, David James, Marcus Powell, -----, Colin Cracknell, Gary Carter, -----.

12.33 This aerial view of 1995 shows Waddesdon schools' complex in its magnificent setting nestled between the village and the Waddesdon Estate parkland. At the near centre of the photograph is the Church of England Secondary School, which has more than doubled in size over its lifetime. It then accommodated around 400 scholars drawn from the original catchment area, and these numbers were bolstered by additional pupils bussed in from local towns and villages. At the far centre is Waddesdon Village Primary School, sited where the garden plots for the earlier schools were located. Around 200 pupils from the village are given their elementary education here.

12.34 Some of the "Little Oaks" Play-group photographed in the Village Hall in November 2000. The children standing are L-R; Megan Richards, Jordan Brooker, Molly Lynch, Hattie Bradshaw, Georgia Herman, Chloe Hill, Georgia Barr. Middle Row: Niamh Thompson, Keone Wilson, Henry Connor, Ryan Saunders, Jamie-Lee Grady. Front : Katie Thurkettle, Megan Higgins, Jamie Ward. Ladies : Julia, Denise, Dawn, Sally. Waddesdon has had a pre-school group accommodated at the Village Hall since the 1960's. For many years the leader was Mrs Dilys Todd who gave a valuable continuity to the organisation. Latterly the group has survived thanks to the sterling work of a succession of leaders and helpers, who have had to contend with constrained finances and modern operating bureaucracy. A valuable element of community life in the 21st century.

12.35 Photographs 12.35 to 12.39 are of pupils attending Waddesdon County Combined School in the year 2000. In 1997 a scheme was introduced whereby children could gain school experience in the year before they were due to commence full-time education. Initially half-day attendance, and progressing to whole day, the children are taught in the "Reception Class". Here we have the County Combined Reception Class of November 2000. Back Row L-R: Leah Johnson, Charlie Vere-White, Katie Armstead, Jack Richards, Alice Armstrong, Jordan Skinner, Zoe Thurkettle, Liam Johnson. Middle Row: George Nixon, Danielle Price, Shaun Busby, Joseph Walls, Dean Ridgway, Jenny Crane, Christian Powell, Ben George. Front Row: Lizzie Allars, Liam Arnold, Alex Bishop, Lewis Irwin, Micheala Hiscock, Charlie Carr, Rosie McGuckin, Joshua Grady.

12. 36 Back Row L-R: Keelan Higgings, Joshua Dunn, Lewis Brigginshaw, James Busby, Catherine Chau, Lewis Hubbard, Fraser Prendergast, Ben Lynch, Francessca Matoso, Joshua Bedford, Damon Bull, Rebekah Clements, Daniel Parry-Jones, Ben Higgins. Third Row: Emily Crane, Karl Tearle, Elizabeth Lucas, Hannah Neal, Steven Ardley, Samuel Blore, Jennifer Wilson, Helena Lloyd-Miller, Amy Poulton, Luke Jackson. Second Row: Kenneth Cliffe, Jake Webb, Harriet Bell, Louise Liddiard, Lucy Johnston, Amber Chalmers, Natalie Ward, Freddie Banham, Bethany Arnaud, Michael Butler, Josephine Davies, Poppy Furber. Front Row: Liam Ross, Henry Gayler, Robin Newport, Hollie Barr, Samantha Saunders, Katherine Dersley, Thomas Thurkettle, Liam Hustwick, Jack George, Abigail Randall, Daniel Caterer, Naomi Ryder-Green.

12.37 Back Row L-R: Jade Lucas, Joseph Cox, Hannah Clements, Daniel McCutchion, Ruby Escott, Charlotte Johnson, Ros Brown, Oliver Prendergast, Connor Hursey, Hamish McCutchion, Lewis Ashton, Peter Stiefel, Daniel Barr, James Smart. Third Row: Tom Williams, Jonathan Tattam, Hannah Lear-Cairnie, Kirsty Dean, Patrick Blore, Marcus Zakrzewski, James Garey, Nicholas Grady, Sophie Liddiard, Sarah May. Second Row: Jamie Butler, Amelia Rabone, Jasmin Davies, Joshua Little, Jack Williams, Joshua Poulton, Jenna Hodges, Rosie Short, Emily-Rose Nixon, Jodie Lewis, Sophie Bridger, Luke Lancaster, Darren Sewell. Front Row: Bethany Goss, Ben-Marcus Lake, Ryan Shepherd, Thomas Williams, Rachel Vere-White, Charlotte Price, Oliver Slaughter, Daniel Skinner, Kathryn Williams, Emily Stoiljkovic, Rachel Wilkins.

12.38 Back Row L-R: Darcy Lloyd-Miller, Jonathan Barnes, Ruth Mackay, Michelle Acum, Cammille Ahmid, Jack Bevan, Robert Bruce, Alex Allars, Melanie Mackie, Andrew Norman, Robert Middleton, William Jackson. Third Row: Laura Bradford, Steven Peters, Tim Allars, Martin Lester, Lucy Bradford, Hayley Price, Jake Hillier, Lauren Hales. Second Row: Helen Randell, Zoe Little, Craig Ross, Megan Thorne, Harriet Olliffe, Laura Bull, Lana Jay, Bianca Brandon, Lizzy Shaw, Christian Hubbard, Karl Neal, Lewis Agostinelli. Front Row: Sophie Ayris, Rocky Escott, Kimberley Saunders, Jessica Rabone, Abbie Garrad, Jenny Harsey, Alec McCutchion, Amber Ewers, Lucy Coates, Jucy Inwood, Lynn Marlow, Abby Meek, Daniel Chapman, Stephen Sewell, Charlie Conner.

12.39 Back Row L-R: Jacqui Stiefel, Ella Zakrzewski, Richard Williams, Michaela Hillier, James Caterer, Marie Biswell, Michael Graby, Alicia Kilty, Christine Ardley, Elaine Chambers. Third Row L-R: Florence Chau, Laura Ashton, Adam Dalwood, Dean Hodges, Carla Hyde, Rebecca Booroff, Jade Butler, Sam Short, Helen Simms. Second Row L-R: Callum Wilkins, Charlotte Sewell, Kimberley Saunders, Katie Higgins, Lewis Thomson, Lesley Bridger, Rebecca Swatton, Christopher Garey, Graham Iddon. Front Row: Hester Ort, Fiona Johnson, Livvy Meek, Samantha Ayris, Charlie Dersley, Nicholas Wilson, Angela Wetherall, Craig Smithies, Michael Kelly, Ben Curtis, Luke Holland, Rebecca Inwood, Roxanne Kingsman.

12.40 Photographs 12.40 to 12.44 are of scholars from Waddesdon, Westcott, and Upper Winchendon attending the Church of England Secondary School 2000. Year 7: - Back Row- L-R: Sarah Coats, Rachel Cox, Tom Short, Paul Watson, Sarah Norman, Vanessa Francis, Ben Howlett. Third Row: Blair Slaughter, Dominic Kilty, Chris Cox, Barry Saunders, Rachel Adams, Cali Whitley, Antony Weatherall, Harriet Rosling, Adam Jeffrey. Second Row: Lucy Garrard, Tim Blore, Stephanie Fisher, Rory Francis, Jamie Saunders, Jade Markham, Freja Markham, Nichola Johnson, Ross Gehnich, Front Row: Pascale Descrettes, Hannah Barfoot, Nick Brooker, Ashley Hollings, Aron Ridgway, Kirsty Brown, Richard Campion, Nick Howlett, Darren Wells, Nathan Kirk.

12.41 Year 8: - Back Row L-R: Gemma Ferguson, Victoria Allars, Rachel Cole, Rebecca Shute, Gemma Lambourne, Emma Warner. Third Row: James Broome, David Francis, Katherine Cox, Gareth Dench, Mathew Barnes, Peter Tompkins, Sarah Robson. Second Row: Emily Cross, Aimee Holland, David Baker, Giles Foster, Lynette Bridger, Daniel Spinks, Faye Chadbone. Front Row: Charlie May, David Mansfield, Catherine Davies, Lee Garrard, Robert Bellis, Thomas Wayland, Rebekah Tyler.

12.42 Year 9: - Back Row L-R: Suzane Stuchbury, Jade Campion, Jenny Lacey, James Olliffe, James Shaw, Carl Perrin, David Barnes, Bobby De'ath. Middle Row: Carl Chambers, Daniel Brown, Stephanie Fox, Jason Fisher, Peter Kingsman, George Ort, Nathan Hollings. Front Row: Simon Lewis, Daniel Wright, James Rosling, Stevie Ryder, Rebecca Pumphrey, Laura Coyne, Jamelia Chaudry.

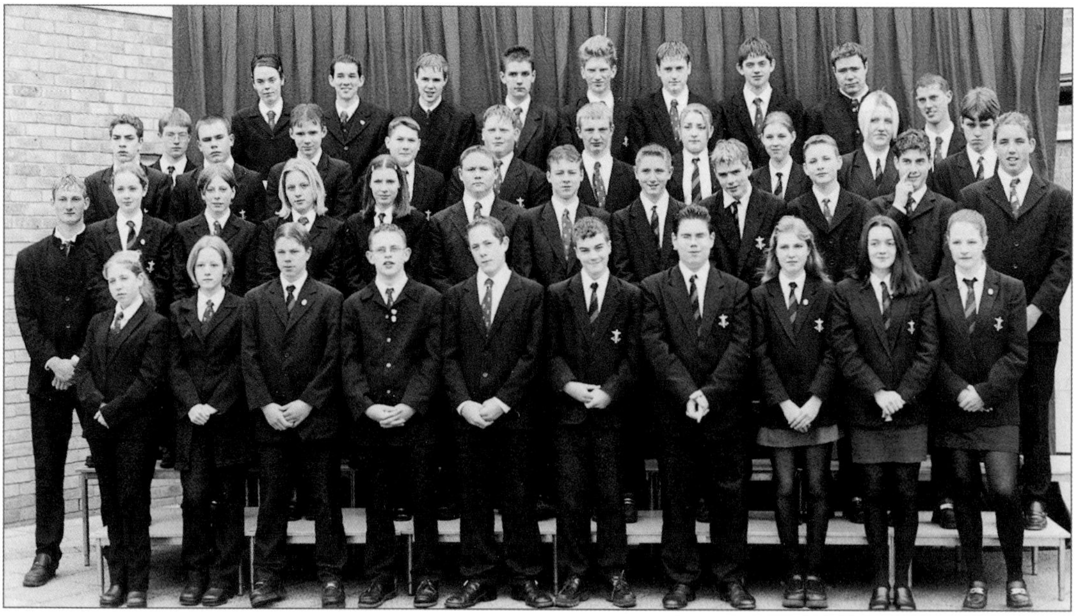

12.43 Year 10 and 11: - Back Row L-R: Sarah Shute, Jeremy Rose, Aaran Green, Allan Iddan, Gary White, Simon Mathews, Marcus Hollings, Kevin Baker. Third Row: Liam Biswell, Simon Cox, Oliver Farnell, Simon Garey, Nick Barfoot, Mark Lewis, Craig Chambers, Holly Markham, Nicola Mansfield, Hayley Golder, Mathew Cole, David Tompkins. Second Row: Jamie McCulloch, Fiona Makay, Melanie Coyne, Sally Thornton, Katie Zverko, Mathew Webster, James Davison, Lee Coyne, Aubrey Green, Mark Leadbeater, Richard Chaudry, Michael Doyle. Front Row: Rachael Bellis, Amy Coyne, Shane Brooker, Jack Wooller, Jonathan Pumphrey, Phillip Deamer, Ross Slaughter, Lisa Swatton, Zoe Curtis, Elizabeth Wayland.

12.44 Sixth Form: - Back Row L-R: Adam Davies, Sarah Lacey, Claire Holland, Elliott Green, Lewis Bleasedale, Dennis Stray. Middle Row: Chris Sturch, Martin Deamer, Emma Newell, David Gardener, Katie Jones. Front Row: Lucy Bonson, Gemma Pointon, Kerry Biswell, Louise Benley.

12.45 Of the 88 adult staff employed at the Secondary School, the eight shown here all live in Waddesdon. Back Row L-R: Tom Holdsworth, Gill Carter, Val Homewood, Jeremy Davies. Front: Jenny Carr, Hilary Lambourne, Annie Norman, Coral Soulsby.

12.46 The Chairman of Governors and the Head Teacher of Waddesdon Church of England Secondary School 2000, the Rev. Tom Thorp and Mr Alan Armstrong. Under their direction and thanks to excellent staff, the school has progressed to Beacon status in the English schools' system.

Section Thirteen

Treats, Fetes and Jubilees

Mention Treats, Fetes and Jubilees to older Waddesdonians and prepare to be engulfed under a tidal wave of nostalgic reminiscences. The summertime events of Waddesdon's past have become legendary, and when one discovers the facts, it is no wonder.

By far the biggest and most popular annual event in the locality was the Waddesdon Schools' Treat of the late 19th century. Known then and ever since as "The Baron's Treat", it developed from separate school treats held each year for National and British Schools' scholars, in the 1870's to hugely popular combined events in the 1880's and 1890's. The general public were welcomed and by 1898 as many as 20,000 visitors descended upon the grounds of Waddesdon Manor, whilst the scholars and families from Waddesdon, Upper Winchendon and Westcott enjoyed their teas, races and entertainment; all provided by Baron Ferdinand de Rothschild.

The baron died in 1898 and there was just one more Treat (1899) on the previous scale. Miss Alice de Rothschild, the Baron's sister and heir, continued the School's Treat but reduced the event to entertain just the villagers. This in no way reduced the anticipation and pleasure for the locals, and although it was officially entitled "Miss Alice's Tea Party" no expense was spared to provide a "treat" worthy of comparison with the early events.

Apart from the Treats, Waddesdon discovered a vitality for summer-time entertainment and fund-raising. All the organisations held their annual celebrations and Fetes whilst practically every year the Baron and later Miss Alice, were hosts to events such as The Bucks Show, Athletic Sports and district and county fetes, all drawing large numbers of visitors. Then there were the exceptional events such as Queen Victoria's Diamond Jubilee in 1897, and spectacles such as the annual summer manoeuvres of the militiamen.

Inevitably the above events were affected by the First World War, most were suspended for the duration, some including Miss Alice's Tea Party were never resumed, (due to Miss Alice de Rothschild's ill health). During the inter-war years the community organisations maintained Waddesdon's renown for the excellence of its summertime events, and this reputation enjoyed an additional fillip after the Second World War, thanks to the great spirit of comradeship and commitment, which the recent conflict had imparted.

In the pages that follow we have assembled representative illustrations covering the past 130 years and from these we hope to convey to the reader something of the flavour and atmosphere of events from Waddesdon's past.

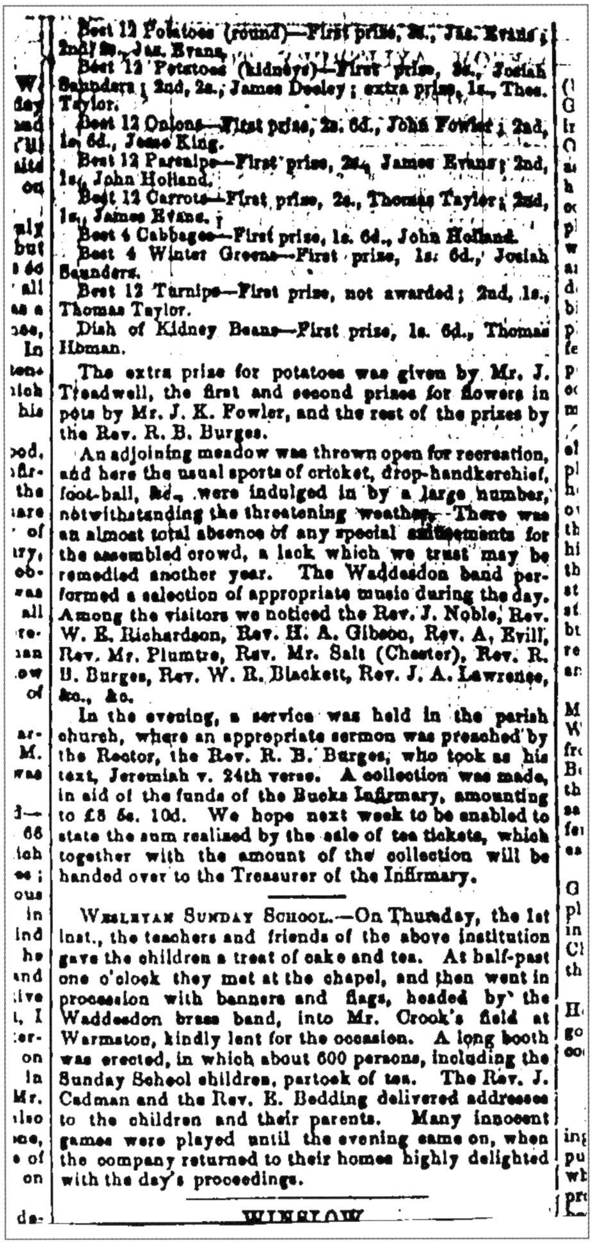

Best 12 Potatoes (round)—First prize, 3s., Jas. Evans; 2nd, 2s., Jas. Evans.

Best 12 Potatoes (kidneys)—First prize, 3s., Josiah Saunders; 2nd, 2s., James Deeley; extra prize, 1s., Thos. Taylor.

Best 12 Onions—First prize, 2s. 6d., John Fowler; 2nd, 1s. 6d., Jesse King.

Best 12 Parsnips—First prize, 2s., James Evans; 2nd, 1s., John Holland.

Best 12 Carrots—First prize, 2s., Thomas Taylor; 2nd, 1s., James Evans.

Best 4 Cabbages—First prize, 1s. 6d., John Holland.

Best 4 Winter Greens—First prize, 1s. 6d., Josiah Saunders.

Best 12 Turnips—First prize, not awarded; 2nd, 1s., Thomas Taylor.

Dish of Kidney Beans—First prize, 1s. 6d., Thomas Hbman.

The extra prize for potatoes was given by Mr. J. Treadwell, the first and second prizes for flowers in pots by Mr. J. K. Fowler, and the rest of the prizes by the Rev. R. B. Burges.

An adjoining meadow was thrown open for recreation, and here the usual sports of cricket, drop-handkerchief, foot-ball, &c., were indulged in by a large number, notwithstanding the threatening weather. There was an almost total absence of any special amusements for the assembled crowd, a lack which we trust may be remedied another year. The Waddesdon band performed a selection of appropriate music during the day. Among the visitors we noticed the Rev. J. Noble, Rev. W. E. Richardson, Rev. H. A. Gibson, Rev. A. Evill, Rev. Mr. Plumtre, Rev. Mr. Salt (Chester), Rev. R. B. Burges, Rev. W. R. Blackett, Rev. J. A. Lawrence, &c., &c.

In the evening, a service was held in the parish church, where an appropriate sermon was preached by the Rector, the Rev. R. B. Burges, who took as his text, Jeremiah v. 24th verse. A collection was made, in aid of the funds of the Bucks Infirmary, amounting to £8 6s. 10d. We hope next week to be enabled to state the sum realised by the sale of tea tickets, which together with the amount of the collection will be handed over to the Treasurer of the Infirmary.

WESLEYAN SUNDAY SCHOOL.—On Thursday, the 1st inst., the teachers and friends of the above institution gave the children a treat of cake and tea. At half-past one o'clock they met at the chapel, and then went in procession with banners and flags, headed by the Waddesdon brass band, into Mr. Crook's field at Warmston, kindly lent for the occasion. A long booth was erected, in which about 600 persons, including the Sunday School children, partook of tea. The Rev. J. Cadman and the Rev. E. Bedding delivered addresses to the children and their parents. Many innocent games were played until the evening came on, when the company returned to their homes highly delighted with the day's proceedings.

WINSLOW

13.1 The Bucks Advertiser and Aylesbury News of 10th September 1864 carried accounts of two recent events at Waddesdon. The first account was the "Harvest Tea" held on Wednesday 7th September in "Benthems" Rectory grounds and adjoining paddock. Part of the article is reproduced in the upper part of this copy; it informs us that a horticultural show, sports and the Waddesdon Band constituted the entertainment for the "assembled crowd", (which was 1,075!). The sport of "drop handkerchief" is unknown to the writer. Of particular interest to us in the 21st century, is the apparent normality of holding events on weekdays and the relatively high value of the show prizes, (12 onions, first prize 2s 6d) roughly one day's pay, if in work! The account of the Wesleyan Sunday School Treat held on Thursday 1st September, splendidly conjures up the utopian ideals of that era, when "innocent games" were played and pleasures were so much simpler. The popularity of the event is indicated by the attendance figure of 600!

SCHOOL TREAT.

The School Treat took place at Mr. T. G. Goss's farm on August 2nd. The day was very fine, and all was most enjoyable. The children, in number over 80 (who shall say that our population is not increasing ?), behaved so well, and were so thoroughly happy ; their behaviour and pleasant manners reflect no little credit upon their good and painstaking governess, Miss Custerson. An abundant tea was provided, and Mrs. Goss and her family deserve our warm thanks for the pains they took, as did many other friends, to make the day a success. The event of the day was the distribution of the rewards. Those given by the Rector were properly appreciated, but when Miss Williams began to give away the rewards sent all the way from India by the children's kind friend, the Lady Caroline Grenville, their happiness was unbounded. The presents themselves were valued, but far beyond their value was the kind remembrance which they proved the Wootton family to have in Madras of the little children of Wescott. Many hearty cheers for the Duke and his daughters, for the Rector and Miss Williams, Mr. Iremonger, Mr. Baldwin (whose letter to the children was read by the Rector) the Governess, Mr. and Mrs. Goss, &c., ended a very happy day.

T. J. W.

Over-Winchendon.

HOLY COMMUNION.

Thirteenth Sunday after Trinity—Communicants, 23 : Alms, 10s. 6½d.

HOLY MATRIMONY.

August 6—Francis Andrews (Wescott), to Drusilla Reynolds.

SCHOOL TREAT.

The Annual School Treat for Waddesdon and Winchendon Schools took place at the Manor House, on August 9th, on which occasion Baron F. de Rothschild most liberally entertained all the children of these parishes. Between 400 and 500 were present, besides very many visitors ; his wish being that the children should long remember the day on which he laid the corner stone of the mansion which he is building on Lodge Hill. The Winchendon children were on the ground first. It was a grand sight to see the Waddesdon party on the road in eight waggons, preceded by the Rifle Corps band, banners and flags flying. The heavy rain did not damp their spirits, and and a most happy day was spent. The tea was provided by Mrs. Dodwell, and was excellent : it was spread in the large tent. Games were played, races run for valuable prizes given by the Baron, and these were not confined to the children, as one of our most respected farmers was the fortunate winner of half-a-dozen of Champagne. Some of the company enjoyed a dance or two. It was a day to be long remembered as one of great enjoyment. The Church Sunday School children of Waddesdon and Winchendon were, as usual, presented by their several teachers with little presents, the gifts of the Rector.

Printed by Lewis Poulton, Market Square, Aylesbury.

13.2 This cutting from the September 1877 edition of the Parish Magazine gives us another view of the typical Treats provided for the school children. The upper report is of the "Westcott School Treat" held on Mr Goss's farm, and significantly describing the benevolence of the Duke of Buckingham's daughter. The Duke, the principal local landowner, had provided both the school and church for the village. The lower account, of the Treat for the Waddesdon and Winchendon school-children, informs us that the corner-stone of Waddesdon Manor was laid by the Baron on that day, 9th August 1877. This Treat was held at the "Manor House", that is the Manor house of Over Winchendon, now known as "The Wilderness". This was the first of the combined schools' Baron's Treats. Thereafter they were held in Spring Hill Field on Lodge Hill, (formerly Glebe Land).

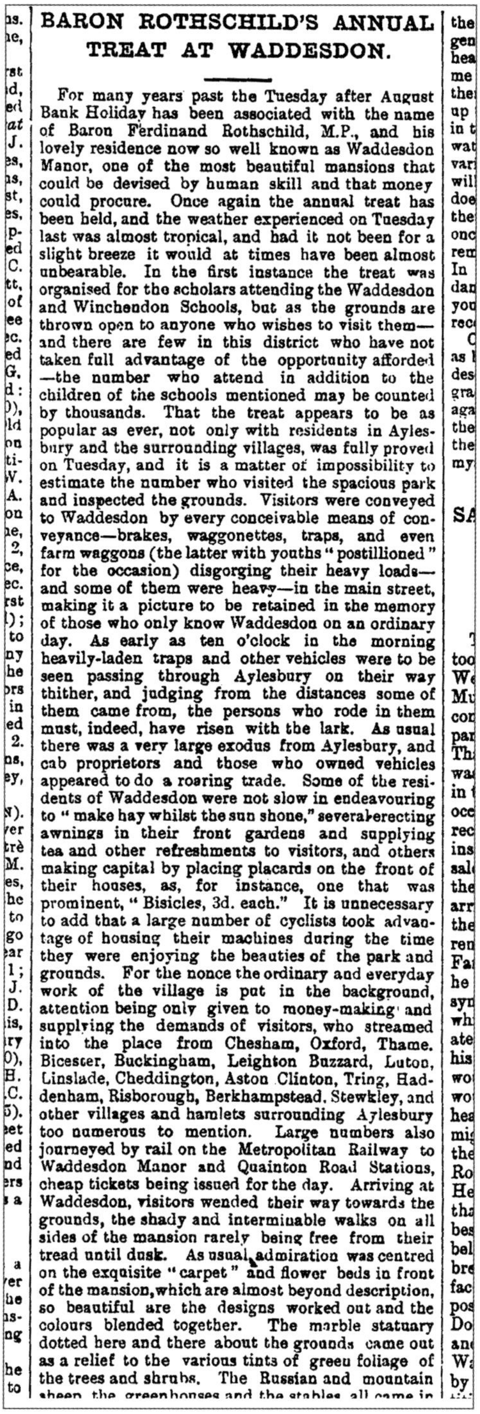

BARON ROTHSCHILD'S ANNUAL TREAT AT WADDESDON.

For many years past the Tuesday after August Bank Holiday has been associated with the name of Baron Ferdinand Rothschild, M.P., and his lovely residence now so well known as Waddesdon Manor, one of the most beautiful mansions that could be devised by human skill and that money could procure. Once again the annual treat has been held, and the weather experienced on Tuesday last was almost tropical, and had it not been for a slight breeze it would at times have been almost unbearable. In the first instance the treat was organised for the scholars attending the Waddesdon and Winchendon Schools, but as the grounds are thrown open to anyone who wishes to visit them—and there are few in this district who have not taken full advantage of the opportunity afforded—the number who attend in addition to the children of the schools mentioned may be counted by thousands. That the treat appears to be as popular as ever, not only with residents in Aylesbury and the surrounding villages, was fully proved on Tuesday, and it is a matter of impossibility to estimate the number who visited the spacious park and inspected the grounds. Visitors were conveyed to Waddesdon by every conceivable means of conveyance—brakes, waggonettes, traps, and even farm waggons (the latter with youths "postillioned" for the occasion) disgorging their heavy loads—and some of them were heavy—in the main street, making it a picture to be retained in the memory of those who only know Waddesdon on an ordinary day. As early as ten o'clock in the morning heavily-laden traps and other vehicles were to be seen passing through Aylesbury on their way thither, and judging from the distances some of them came from, the persons who rode in them must, indeed, have risen with the lark. As usual there was a very large exodus from Aylesbury, and cab proprietors and those who owned vehicles appeared to do a roaring trade. Some of the residents of Waddesdon were not slow in endeavouring to "make hay whilst the sun shone," several erecting awnings in their front gardens and supplying tea and other refreshments to visitors, and others making capital by placing placards on the front of their houses, as, for instance, one that was prominent, "Bisicles, 3d. each." It is unnecessary to add that a large number of cyclists took advantage of housing their machines during the time they were enjoying the beauties of the park and grounds. For the nonce the ordinary and everyday work of the village is put in the background, attention being only given to money-making and supplying the demands of visitors, who streamed into the place from Chesham, Oxford, Thame. Bicester, Buckingham, Leighton Buzzard, Luton, Linslade, Cheddington, Aston Clinton, Tring, Haddenham, Risborough, Berkhampstead, Stewkley, and other villages and hamlets surrounding Aylesbury too numerous to mention. Large numbers also journeyed by rail on the Metropolitan Railway to Waddesdon Manor and Quainton Road Stations, cheap tickets being issued for the day. Arriving at Waddesdon, visitors wended their way towards the grounds, the shady and interminable walks on all sides of the mansion rarely being free from their tread until dusk. As usual, admiration was centred on the exquisite "carpet" and flower beds in front of the mansion, which are almost beyond description, so beautiful are the designs worked out and the colours blended together. The marble statuary dotted here and there about the grounds came out as a relief to the various tints of green foliage of the trees and shrubs. The Russian and mountain sheep, the greenhouses and the stables all came in

13.3 This cutting of an account of the 1897 Baron's Treat requires no caption. Just read the fascinating article for a lesson in descriptive writing.

13.4 The Baron's Treat in 1897 and all the fun of the fair especially for the local school children who each had tickets for free rides. On this bright and hot summers' day the crowd around the steam powered round-a-bout (Gallopers) remain quite formally dressed and every head wears a hat!

13.5 Baron Ferdinand de Rothschild hosted the Royal and Central Buckinghamshire Agricultural Show on several occasions, and Miss Alice de Rothschild continued this tradition after her inheritance. This photograph taken from the slopes of Lodge Hill in Springhill Field, gives a view of the entrance pavilion adjacent to the Manor drive (now the exit road) at the 1909 Show. A large crowd is enjoying the spectacle in the Main Ring, and nearer the camera several cars have privileged parking position. The village church of St Michael seems remarkably near in this shot, proving how deceiving the camera can be.

13.6 Another view of part of the Main Ring of the 1909 Bucks Show. Once again the motor vehicles catch the eye, as do the ladies' clothes and the formal attire of the men. Waddesdon Manor Park continued as the venue periodically until 1939, when Mr James de Rothschild was to have hosted the show, but the outbreak of war caused its cancellation.

13.7 The Waddesdon Athletic Sports circa 1910. The extremely difficult obstacle for the competitors of this event must have provided much amusement for the spectators as well as those taking part. The entry fee for adult events was 3d, but the first prize was a sovereign, and second prize a half sovereign, therefore competition was very fierce, when a week's wages for most was less than £1.

13.8 The Athletic Sports included bicycle races as well as the normal running and jumping events, and they attracted athletes from the surrounding area. However, there was a snag for youngsters wishing to progress in amateur athletics, for once they had accepted money prizes in adult events they were considered to be professionals, and therefore barred from A.A.A. competitions. One young man, Ernie Atkins, was re-instated after much difficulty, and competed at County level. The packed crowd in this photograph exemplifies the popularity of the sports, despite the apparent poor weather. Two of the entries are wearing sports clothes, but the man in the centre appears to have just taken off his jacket in the hope no doubt of snatching a prize. Note: At this time Waddesdon had a Cycle Club of more than 25 members, which regularly mounted competitive runs to local places of interest.

13.9 The crowd at the "Prize-giving" after completion of the Waddesdon Athletic Sports circa 1912, as viewed from the balcony of the Cricket Pavilion. The Athletic Sports were inaugurated at the Harvest tea events in the mid 19th century, and were continued in the 1890's under the benevolence of Baron de Rothschild. After the death of the Baron, Miss Alice de Rothschild sponsored the sports until the outbreak of the Great War. Subsequently sports featured in the programmes of events at the annual Allotment Society Shows, up to and after the Second World War.

13.10 An almost identical view as 13.9, but separated by about 30 years. On this occasion it is the prize giving at the Allotment Society Show and Sports circa 1938. As with most functions in the village, the presenting of prizes usually fell to Mrs James de Rothschild, deputising for her husband, who was the President of the Society.

13.11 To celebrate the Coronation of King George V on Thursday 22nd June 1911, the combined population of Waddesdon, Upper Winchendon and Eythrope were invited to a day of events at various venues. First was a church service at 10.30,followed by a "Ladies verses Gentlemen" cricket match, and then sports. This photograph shows some of the crowd in Britain Field, where 20 events were contested in the early afternoon. Typical of the period, everyone seems to be in Sunday best dress including hats; hardly suitable for competitive sports! Two Temperance Band members can be discerned here, the Old Prize Band was engaged in the Westcott celebrations.

13.12 Some of the younger element enjoying light refreshments, each holding a Coronation mug, in this picture taken in Britain Field on June 22nd 1911. At 2.30 all the children were gathered in the British School for tea, whilst at 3.30 the adults were entertained to an "excellent meat tea" in Waddesdon Hall. Each person who partook of tea was presented with a commemorative Coronation medal, which together with all the teas, was the gift of Miss Alice de Rothschild. The caterer was Mr J Franklin on this occasion.

13.13 The Ladies' egg and spoon race on 22nd June 1911. The day's events were organised by The Sports Committee, and apart from those mentioned in the two preceding captions there followed singing and dancing by school children in the Hall, and between 8-12pm dancing to the Waddesdon String Band, assisted by Miss Edith Garner on the piano, in the Rectory gardens. Tasteful illuminations were provided by Mr Figg.

13.14 Morris Dancers in the Square at Waddesdon circa 1908. Unfortunately we have no evidence of exactly why the High Street was so packed with people on this occasion. It is obvious that a large number of visitors are present from the wagonettes parked opposite the Five Arrows Hotel, and it is safe to surmise that many more would have come on foot and bicycles. Behind the nearest wagonette can be seen the cart shed and workshop of Mr Joseph Holland a builder, who had prospered lately, as evidenced by his stylish residence at this end of the village, (now known as The Gables).

13.15 The Waddesdon Schools' children marching behind the Temperance Silver Band on their way to Miss Alice's Tea Party circa 1914. Although not such an occasion as the Baron's Treat, which it had succeeded, the Tea Party was the biggest summer-time event for the children of Waddesdon, Upper Winchendon and Westcott. For them, all the attractions were the same, but the total numbers attending were limited by invitation, to people of the villages. "The Gables", the large house behind the procession, had by now been purchased by Miss Alice, given the Rothschild treatment, and gained a street gas-lamp, as can be seen.

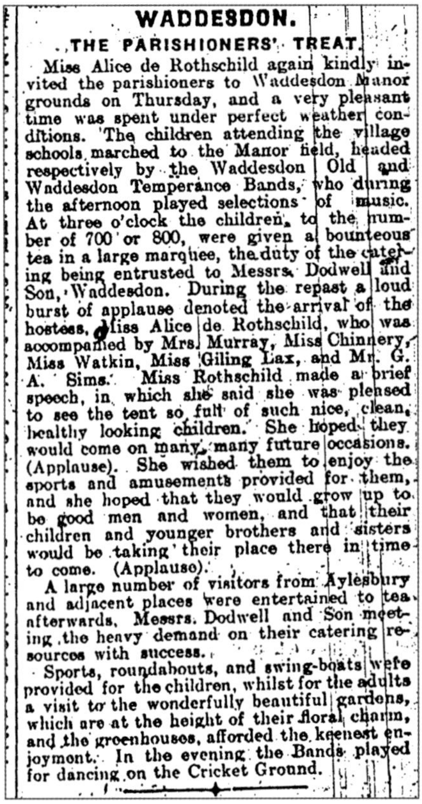

WADDESDON.

THE PARISHIONERS' TREAT.

Miss Alice de Rothschild again kindly invited the parishioners to Waddesdon Manor grounds on Thursday, and a very pleasant time was spent under perfect weather conditions. The children attending the village schools marched to the Manor field, headed respectively by the Waddesdon Old and Waddesdon Temperance Bands, who during the afternoon played selections of music. At three o'clock the children, to the number of 700 or 800, were given a bounteous tea in a large marquee, the duty of the catering being entrusted to Messrs. Dodwell and Son, Waddesdon. During the repast a loud burst of applause denoted the arrival of the hostess, Miss Alice de Rothschild, who was accompanied by Mrs. Murray, Miss Chinnery, Miss Watkin, Miss Giling Lax, and Mr. G. A. Sims. Miss Rothschild made a brief speech, in which she said she was pleased to see the tent so full of such nice, clean, healthy looking children. She hoped they would come on many, many future occasions. (Applause). She wished them to enjoy the sports and amusements provided for them, and she hoped that they would grow up to be good men and women, and that their children and younger brothers and sisters would be taking their place there in time to come. (Applause).

A large number of visitors from Aylesbury and adjacent places were entertained to tea afterwards, Messrs. Dodwell and Son meeting the heavy demand on their catering resources with success.

Sports, roundabouts, and swing-boats were provided for the children, whilst for the adults a visit to the wonderfully beautiful gardens, which are at the height of their floral charm, and the greenhouses, afforded the keenest enjoyment. In the evening the Bands played for dancing on the Cricket Ground.

13.16 On Saturday 1st August 1914, the Bucks Advertiser carried this report on what was to be the very last "Treat" of its kind, in Waddesdon. Troop and naval fleet movements were under way across Europe and within three days Great Britain would be at war with Germany. This typical account from "the good old days" would never be repeated in quite the same style. Thankfully the future is still unknown to us all.

13.17 The fountains and parterre at the south front of the Manor 1927. Baron Ferdinand had often invited those attending Shows, Treats and Fetes, to enjoy the Manor grounds on the day of the event; indeed this aspect became a favourite attraction. James de Rothschild hosted several British Legion and Liberal Party fetes, held in Spring Hill and in the Cricket Field, when the Manor grounds and gardens were open to the visitors. This photograph is thought to record how the many visitors to the British Legion Fete of July 23rd 1927, enjoyed the opportunity to relax in such grand surroundings.

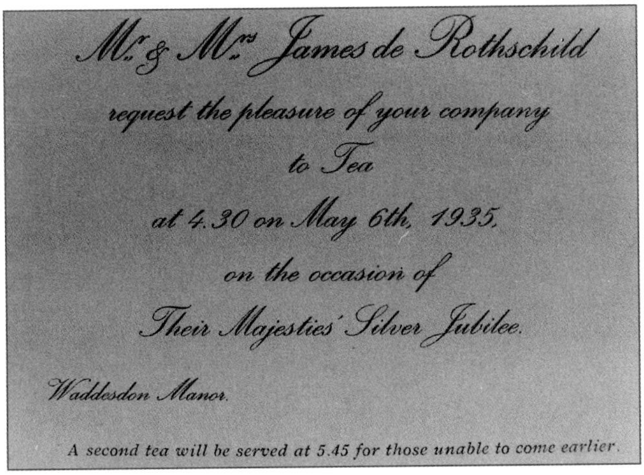

Mr & Mrs James de Rothschild
request the pleasure of your company
to Tea
at 4.30 on May 6th, 1935,
on the occasion of
Their Majesties' Silver Jubilee.
Waddesdon Manor.
A second tea will be served at 5.45 for those unable to come earlier.

13.18 & 13.19 To celebrate the Silver Jubilee of King George V's accession to the throne, a national holiday was proclaimed for Monday 6th May 1935. In Waddesdon a day of appropriate activities was arranged. "A merry peal of bells" awakened the village at 7 a.m followed by a service of thanksgiving, led by the Rev G. Dixon in a packed parish church at 10 a.m. This began one of the happiest days the village has ever known. Every house in Waddesdon, Fleet Marston, Over Winchendon and Eythrope had previously received invitations (reproduced here 13.18) to tea, from Mr and Mrs James de Rothschild. The tea was taken in an enormous marquee and the guests were greeted at the entrance by Mr and Mrs de Rothschild. At the end of the "generous meal" there were speeches, and Mr and Mrs de Rothschild were introduced to five generations of the Cheshire family. Around 1200 people were able to accept the invitation. The small silver embossed effigies of King George V and Queen Mary (13.19) were used as table decorations.

13.20 At 12.30 p.m. the Silver Jubilee Carnival Parade commenced its tour of every street in the village. This photograph shows the parade at the War Memorial, nearing the end of its tour before entering the Manor grounds, to start the afternoon celebrations in Spring Hill Field. On the left of the photograph are Mr and Mrs Arthur Gurney with Pat Radwell and Cyril Gurney.

13.21 The Bucks Herald reported that almost every house in Waddesdon was decorated in bunting, streamers and coloured paper. Here we have No 2 Baker Street, the home of Mr F Sibley, "Boot and Shoe Repairer," a prizewinner. Silver Jubilee 1935.

13.22 The row of Rothschild houses in Baker Street with bunting stretched across the road. Silver Jubilee 1935. The houses looking very new and the robust wooden fence at the right of picture informing us that Grove Way is still to be started. At the near gate is Mrs Jones and further down are Willy Wheeler and Mrs Wheeler.

13.23 The winning entry in the Carnival Parade was "A Gypsy Caravan" with Mr Woolf, Mrs Woolf and their daughters suitably attired. Photographed here in Springhill Field after the circuit of the village. Silver Jubilee 1935. There were races for the children, folk dancing and later in the afternoon Mr de Rothschild formerly opened the new Bowling Green, by bowling the first wood. The new Green had been entirely laid out by the members.

13.24 Another entry in the 1935 Silver Jubilee Carnival Parade was the Estate Fire Engine patriotically decorated as shown here, after the judging. Included in the Parade were a large number of individuals in fancy dress who walked around the route; they were grouped in categories for the judging and the results were; Children:- 1st Miss Pauline Atkins (Jubilee Girl), Ladies:- 1st Miss Snelling (Britannia), Men:- 1st Mr E. Slade (Farmer Giles) and the prize for most original was to Mr W. Franks (Traffic Signals). The day was completed with a crowded dance in the Village Hall for adults, and a party for youngsters held in the Council School, organised by Mr Bullock and Miss Garner.

13.25 The Waddesdon and District Branch of the British Legion was extremely active in the inter-war years. Only a few weeks after the Jubilee celebrations in 1935 the Branch organised a very large fete and gymkhana known as "The Glorious First Of June", to raise funds for the relief of unemployed ex-servicemen in Durham and Northumberland. The teas sold during the afternoon were organised by Mrs Woolf, and she was aided by "about 60 ladies", some of whom are photographed here along with some young boys. Back Row L-R: - Miss Emily Murphy, Mrs R.Allen, Miss Peggy Russell, Standing: - Wally Mason, Mrs Evelyn Hicks, Miss Allen, -----, Mrs G.Sharp, Mrs H.Saunders, Mrs Walton, Mrs M.Carter, Miss Ethel Richards, Mrs Harding, Arthur Hill, Mrs Dennis, -----, -----, -----, Mrs Loader. On Chairs: - Mrs W.Evans, Miss Audrey Holland, Mrs P.Woolf, Mrs G.Neary, Mrs H.George, Mrs M.Harding, Miss Dorothy Harding, Miss Annie Edwards, -----, Mrs L.Walton. Sitting on grass: - Mrs C.Atkins, Mrs H.Olliffe, Mrs Whitlock, Les Mason, Norman Wheeler, Ron Saunders, Harold Allen.

13.26 Fun for everyone was the order of the day, at the "Glorious First of June" fete and gymkhana. Throughout the afternoon there were bands, cabaret, fire brigade contests, a pony and dog circus, comic dog show, old English Morris Dancing, costume cricket match and much much more, not least the children's costume parade. Here we have the Scott sisters, L-R: - Evelyn (Vegetable Stall), Dinah (Baby), Kathy (Golliwog), Doris (Work Basket). There were six classes and a total of 50 entries; Dinah was the winner of class 3. This fete, probably the largest and most successful of all the fetes held in Waddesdon, illustrated the standard that could be attained with the aid of enthusiasm, good leadership and support throughout the community.

13.27 A snap-shot of Mr and Mrs James de Rothschild at the British Legion Fete and Gymkhana on the Glorious First of June 1935. Mr and Mrs de Rothschild opened the Manor grounds and gardens, (an opportunity eagerly seized by hundreds of visitors), and entered into the spirit of the day by visiting numerous side-shows and displays. Mrs de Rothschild entered her dog "Shaggy" in the Comic Dog Show, where it was awarded two runner-up prizes; the shortest nose and most obedient.

13.28 Another group of entrants for a fancy dress competition circa 1935, and photographed here in Golden Knob allotment ground. L-R: - Vic Sharp (?), Gladys Holland (Work Bag), Ena Sharp (Odds and ends), Harold Sharp (Carpenter). Behind the group, and in the garden of Mr and Mrs R. Sharp's bungalow, can be seen the wooden caravan which was the home of Willy Creed, a well known, gentle little man who unfortunately died when the caravan caught fire in the 1950's.

13.29 The Allotment Society August Monday Show and Fete was Waddesdon's largest annual open-air event. Always held on the first Monday in August, the proceedings for the public commenced with the start of the Eight Mile Walking Race, at about one hour before the opening of the fete. This photograph shows "the off " in front of The White Lion circa 1937. The many bicycles to be seen will be used to carry the judges and supporters around the circuit; Waddesdon Cross Roads, Quainton via Pitchcott Road, Rag Hall, Hall Farm, up the A41 to Waddesdon Cricket Field, and twice around the running track in front of the expectant crowd at the fete.

13.30 The finish of the Eight Mile Walking Race circa 1936, a grim dual between Fred George on the left and Jack Scott. The knowledgeable crowd watching intently to check whether the very fast walk has developed into a run, in which case disqualification was the penalty. The walking race resumed as a feature of the Fete after the Second World War, and the Winner's Cup was won outright by Fred Cripps, who came first on three consecutive occasions.

13.31 Fancy dress parades were invariably included in the village fetes, and adults entered into the spirit as well. This photograph circa 1935 shows Baden Roads very topically attired as Adolf Hitler. He had paraded on his horse, but is shown here with admiring spectators Jack Atkins (left) and Teddy Sharp, in front of the cottages at the War Memorial. Baden was the village Barber and a talented pianist who often performed at local concerts. For some years he was engaged to play the organ for services at Fleet Marston church.

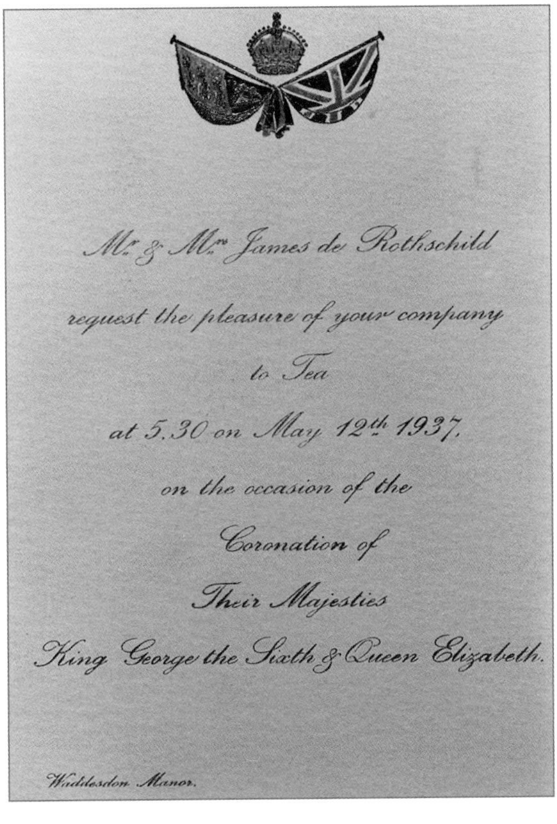

Mr. & Mrs. James de Rothschild

request the pleasure of your company

to Tea

at 5.30 on May 12th 1937.

on the occasion of the

Coronation of

Their Majesties

King George the Sixth & Queen Elizabeth.

Waddesdon Manor.

13.32 The village celebrations for Coronation Day, 12th May 1937, included a peal of bells, church service, Carnival Parade, Fun Fair, races for the children, tea, and a Pageant of Empire in the evening, followed by a dance in the Village Hall. We reproduce an invitation card from Mr and Mrs James de Rothschild, who once again provided a tea for all the villagers. The caterer was Mr Gargini of The Bulls Head, Aylesbury, and the number of teas provided was 1,400 at one sitting.

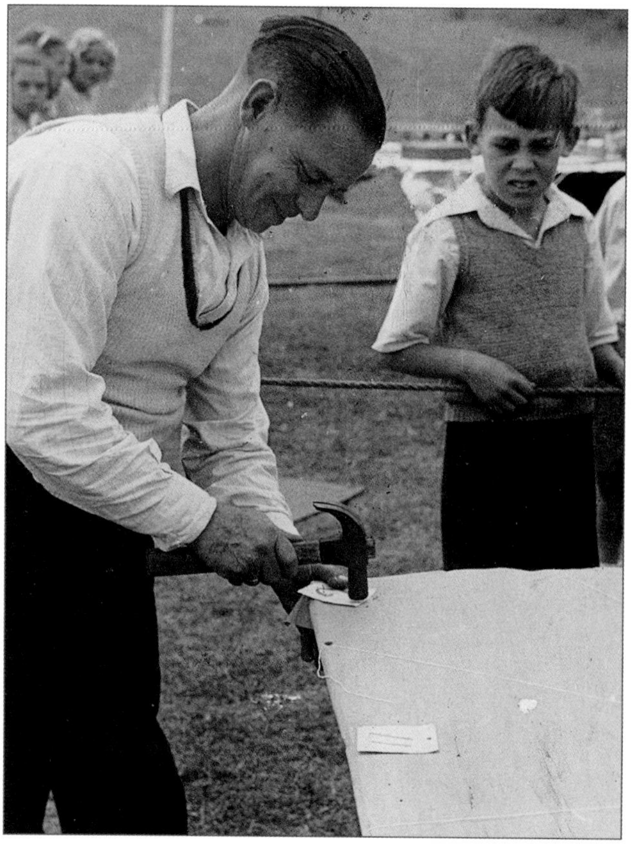

13.33 August Bank Holiday Monday circa 1947. The Allotment Society Show and Fete is as popular as before the war, and preparations are in full swing. John Hayes secures numbers to the "Spinning Jenny" table, while Ivor Gurney looks on.

13.34 Again circa 1947, some of the spectators at the main ring containing the running track, at the August Monday Show. L-R: - -----, Margaret Atkins holding son Peter, Brenda Hicks, Tim Hicks, Gracie Sharp, -----, -----, Betty Beattie, Fred Beattie.

13.35 Circa 1947. One of the events was the "Slow Bicycle Race," a competition where the first over the line was not necessarily the winner. In this case Brian Carr was first past the winning post, but came second! At the back L-R: - Will Franks, Michael Franks, Joe Biswell, Vivian Hayes, Maurice Johnson, Ivor Gurney, Kneal Marriott. Near the camera Terry Marriott and John Murphy.

13.36 A bevy of local beauties at the Show circa 1947. L-R Dinah Scott, Pat Rhodes, Gracie Sharp.

13.37 Family spectators at the August Monday Show circa 1948. Adults L-R: - Ambrose Biswell, Sybil Jones, Mrs Jones, Bert Jones, Kathy Eldridge, Mr Harms, Mrs Roads, Baden Roads, -----, Doris Rolfe. Boy at right is Norman Roads.

13.38 A happy Kathy Scott with fiancé Ron Snelling applauds competitors at the August Monday Show, circa 1950. Next to Kathy is Mrs P. Evans with her daughter Margaret, behind the two younger girls.

13.39 In 1947 the Waddesdon British Legion and Allotment Society combined their efforts to stage a grand fete, along the lines of the legendary pre-war events. This is a poster for the fete, showing the ambitious attractions that bolstered the traditional sports etc of yesteryear. This initiative was a resounding success, as will be seen from the large crowd in the following photographs.

13.40 "Standing room only" remaining for latecomers to watch the conjurer perform on the makeshift stage.

13.41 A closer view of a section of the crowd enjoying the entertainment at the 1947 Show and Fete. Amongst those sitting are L-R; Tom Evans, Vera Brown and friend, Sylvia Atkins, Harry Read, Mrs Read, Mr and Mrs Sharp, Joyce Thompson, Myrtle Atkins. Amongst those standing L-R; Mr W. Figg, Mrs McKenna, Mr (Jock) McKenna, Tom Cooper, Mrs Cooper, Mr Golby, Jim Wicks.

13.42 The eight mile walking race that for years had heralded the commencement of the Allotment Society Show and Fete was succeeded by a road race of around four and a half miles. Here we see Roy Southam sprinting off at the start in 1952, followed by Gorden Linnell and the rest of the competitors (out of picture). Roy went on to win the event, which required the runners to race down Quainton Road to the cross roads near the station, turn left along Rag Hall, left again at Hall Farm and back to Waddesdon Cricket Field, finishing with a lap of the running track.

13.43 Just returned from National Service in the Royal Air Force, a very fit Roy Southam wins the One Mile track event in 1952, after earlier winning the Road Race. Also in the picture are L-R: - Lionel Heritage in black shorts, Mr Winstanley, Dick Schneider with tape, Will Franks and a very young John Franks.

13.44 The Coronation of Queen Elizabeth II on 2nd June 1953 gave everyone the opportunity to join in the fund-raising and preparations necessary before the big day. In this photograph a group of ladies are busy sewing bunting for the street decorations. The sewing circle met in the Village Hall Committee Room. Sitting L-R: - Mrs K.Howe, Mrs Cripps, Mrs M.Read, Mrs Read, Mrs Dymock, Mrs Reynolds, Mrs Brown. Standing: - Dorothy and Ruth Brown.

THE WADDESDON SINGERS

present

A CONCERT

in aid of Coronation Funds

IN THE VILLAGE HALL
ON SAT. MAY 9th. 1953
AT 7. 30. p m.

Conductor

MR. J. H. SMITH

Accompanists

MRS. A. TAYLOR
MR. C. H. F. EARL

Price 2d

13.45 Fund-raising was very much a community activity supported and aided by the Manor Estate and numerous businesses in the village. The Waddesdon Singers did their bit as shown here, raising money towards the target figure of £500, which was achieved in a variety of ways. At one stage it was planned to roast an ox on Coronation day, and one was donated by Mr James de Rothschild, but in the event it was thought better to sell the ox, and put the proceeds towards the fund. The concert by the Singers featured solos by Mr W.Evans, Mr J. H. Smith and Mr W. Franks,a duet by Mr and Mrs W. H. Evans, and songs by the choir, all melodious compositions and mostly from an earlier era. Very well received!

13.46 The Waddesdon Coronation Day Parade led by the Hazel Watson and Viney Printing Works Band on June 2nd 1953. The weather was miserable but everyone was determined to make the day memorable and enjoyable, so the turnout was not greatly diminished. All along the High Street poles, had been erected to support pennants and bunting, as is just discernable in this photograph. The man with hands in his pockets is Jock Millar.

13.47 The Fancy Dress entrants formed part of the Coronation Day Parade. Here they are passing "The White House Café". Adults recognisable in this photograph include L-R: - Percy Ashfield, Mrs Claridge, Mrs Adamson, Mrs Steve Goss, Mrs Joe Goss, Mrs Lily Rhodes, Harold Sharp.

13.48 The Coronation Day Parade included "Ye Ancients" musical vehicle, shown here in Frederick Street. Rather reminiscent of a Cairo bazaar it was mounted on a trolley and contained Vic Radwell playing popular songs on his accordion, and was propelled by Bill Walters, "Dodger" Brown, Henry Haigh, Will Radwell and a dubious unknown Arab! Visible in this picture are L-R: - Mrs Rose Drydale, Mrs Phylis Cheshire, John Walters, Mrs Walters, Bill Walters, Arab, Will Radwell, Henry Haigh, Jacqueline Gurney, Wendy Saunders.

13.49 The Coronation Day Parade terminated in the village Playing Field but the fun for some continued despite the drizzle. In the carriage Vic Radwell continued to play whilst the children gaze in wonderment as the Arab conducts. The children include, L-R:- Malcolm Wheeler, John Speck, Glenda Owen.

13.50 Coronation day entertainment continued with a Married versus Singles football match, won by the Married men shown in this photograph. The score was 1-0 and the goal was scored by George Rolfe who had played for Aylesbury many years before. The teams are Standing L-R: - Ivor Burnell, George Rolfe, Harold Price, Eric Rhodes, George Knibb (captain), behind George is the goalkeeper Eric Hicks, Bern Holland, Ivor Hicks. Sitting: - Jim Ryder, Jack Cheshire, "Nobby" Brion. Others in the picture are L-R: - Henry Haigh, "Skib"Carter, Vic Radwell, Will Radwell. The prize for the winning team was a barrel of beer. The Married v Singles Coronation Cup was still being contested into the 1990's.

13.51 The losing Singles side in the Coronation Cup football match. Standing L-R: - Laurie Powell, Jim Fowler, Danny -, Jim Neary, Ken Jeeves, Norman Carr. Front Row: - Derek Lovell, Stuart Malcahy, Ken Rolfe, Roy Southam, Don Marlow.

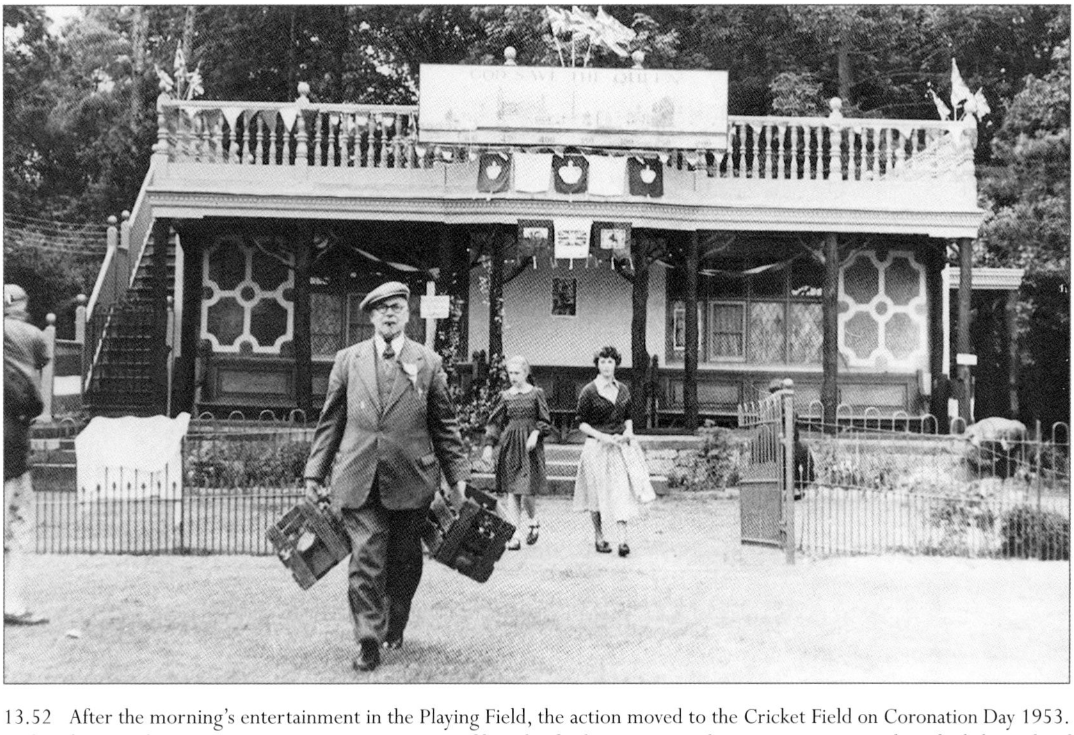

13.52 After the morning's entertainment in the Playing Field, the action moved to the Cricket Field on Coronation Day 1953. In this photograph Jim Carter is conveying two crates of liquid refreshment out to the marquees. Mounted on the balustrade of the Cricket Pavilion roof is the fund-raising progress board that had previously been displayed from the balcony of The Five Arrows Hotel. The two girls at the gateway are Susan Newman (left) and Doris Cripps.

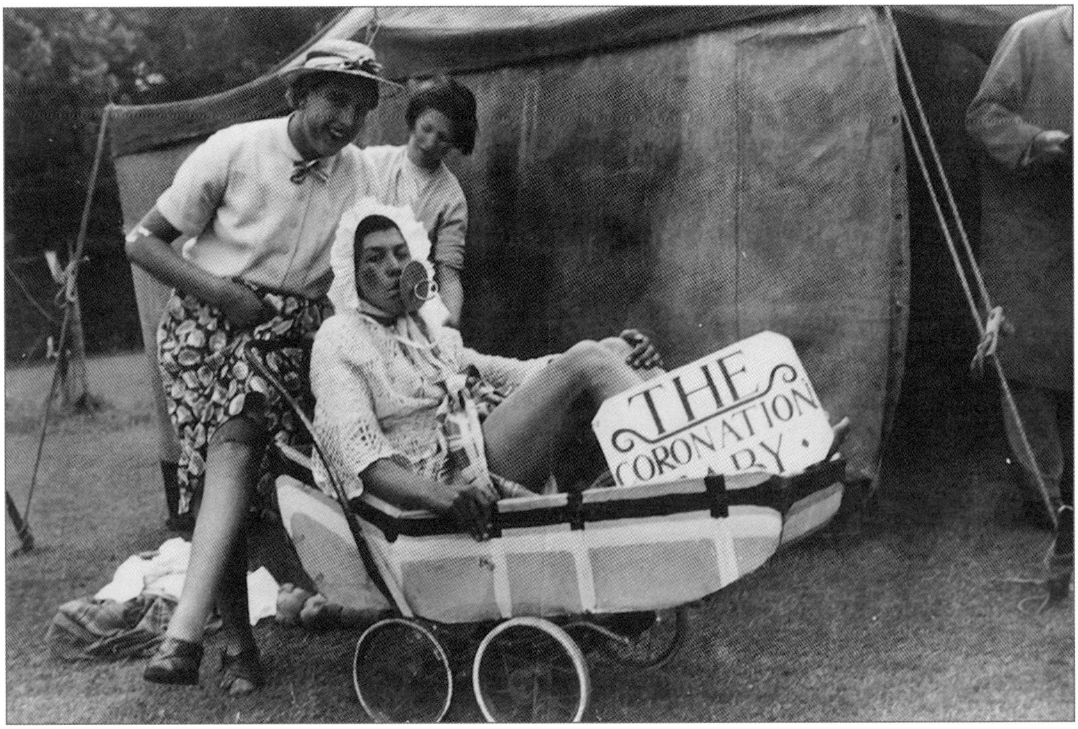

13.53 One of the winning entries in the Fancy Dress Parade, John George (Mum) and Michael Franks (Baby). Molly Franks makes final adjustments at the rear.

13.54 Some of the participants in the Comic Cricket Match held in the afternoon of Coronation day 1953. L-R: - George Fowler, Jack Uff, -----, Jim Ewers, Hywel Evans, Jock Millar, George Slaymaker, Tom Reed, Tom Mortimer, Joe Biswell. The afternoon events included races and "sweet scrambles" for different ages of children.

13.55 The weather on Coronation Day 1953 was damp to say the least; just look at the clothes people were wearing, but that did not stop them from enjoying themselves! The three-legged race for adults had from left Eric (Roddy) Rhodes and Joy Carr, Arab and Phyl Cheshire, Bill Walters and Doreen Church, Mrs H.Sharp and Michael Franks, -----, and Tom Fury, -----, -----.

13.56 The ladies of Waddesdon were well used to catering at big events, but the task of providing a tea for the whole village in the marquees at the Cricket Field must have been rather daunting. At long last the teas in the two sittings were over and the helpers are shown taking a well-earned break and refreshments. At the back table L-R: - Mrs Hilda Sharp, -----, -----, Mrs Pat Davies, Mrs Margaret Atkins, Mrs Mabel Copcutt, Mrs Cotterill, Mrs Eva Rolfe. At the near table: - Mrs Glad Bradbury, Mrs J.Carter, Mrs Wheeler, Mrs Wheeler. Standing: - Mrs Faith Fowler and Mrs Josie Dormer.

13.57 No record of fetes etc in Waddesdon would be complete without mention of the stalwart men and women who continuously gave their time and talents to the various causes. In particular we have Mr Herbert Owen, (nick-named Roo-key), who invariably provided the coconut stall and manned it, sometimes a risky task! (" How much for hitting the nut with the cap Herbie? ") In earlier years a veteran member of the Old Prize Band and throughout his life an active member of the Allotment Society, Mr Owen earned his living by selling small items from a barrow, which he pushed around the local villages. His wares included paraffin oil, through to custard powder, and his longest day each week was his Westcott- Ashendon- Upper Winchendon round. He continued well into the 1950's.

13.58 1954 and another wet August Monday! For those organising fetes etc a succession of wet events can be devastating. For many lesser functions it became normal for advertising posters to bear the annotation " If wet in Village hall", and people continued to support them for many years. However, the Allotment Society Show and Fete was too big to move undercover, so here we have a typical group defying the miserable weather. L-R: - Ernie Southam, -----, Mrs Ron Southam, Mrs Rush, Sylvia Rush, -----, Mrs Reynolds, Mrs Jones.

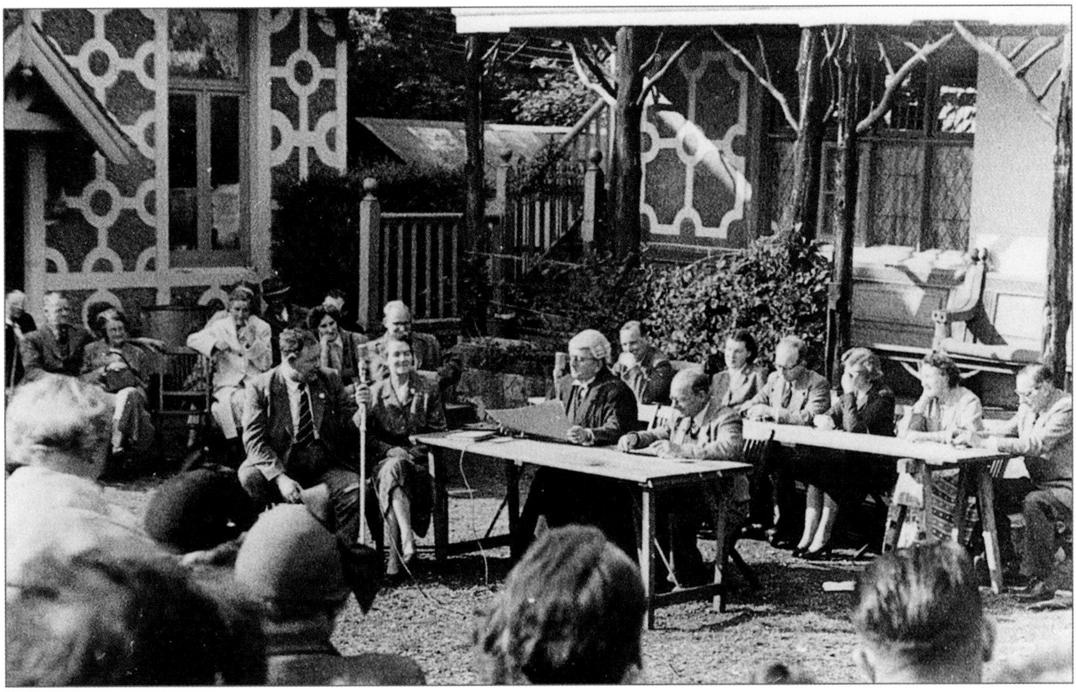

13.59 At the August Monday Show in 1957 one item of entertainment was "The Dunmow Flitch" trial. This consisted of couples competing to win the title of "Happiest Married Couple," after being cross-questioned in public. At the table are Frank and Kathie Howe, the eventual winners, who received the prize – a flitch of bacon. Behind them are Ivy and Bill Read, and at the left are Bill and Mrs Reynolds, all awaiting interrogation. Also recognisable in the picture are Mr and Mrs Willie Evans and Mr Stormont-Mowatt. The judge's clerk is Frank Gowlett.

13.60 A "Men versus Ladies" football match was an attraction at the event held circa 1960 in the village Playing field. This photograph taken at the front of the Football Pavilion shows the ladies dressed as bona-fide footballers, whilst the men dressed up as anything but! Back Row L-R: - Linda Marriott, Betty Wallis, Glad Bradbury, Joyce Franks, Gwen Powell, Gillian Price, Rita Saunders, -----, Fred Beattie, -----, Tommy Mole, Josie Dormer, Frank Gowlett, -----, Laurie Powell, Will Radwell, Tom Fury, -----. Front Row: - Ruby Oselton, Rosemary Bradbury, Gill Speck, Joan Shillingford, Phyl Cheshire, Betty Cherry, Tim Carter, -----, -----.

13.61 Over a very long period the Whit Monday Fete, held in the Rectory, was a popular first open-air event of the year. Although the weather was sometimes inclement, the fete was invariably a financial success, and as can be seen from this happy crowd of youngsters (circa 1965), the entertainment was riveting. Amongst the children in the picture are: Michael Holland, Charles Jenkins, Roger Slade, Margaret Norris, Francis Norris, Robert Barker, Ivor Southam, John Sturch.

13.62 The Parish Council instigated the formation of a committee to organise celebrations to commemorate the Queen's Silver Jubilee. Fund-raising for the celebrations included a musical concert held in the Village hall in May 1977. The performers are shown here. L-R Back Row: - -----, -----, Ralph Hopps, Colin Campbell, David Kemp, -----, Vincent Benyon, Simon Dickinson, Colin Wright. Middle Row:- Gladys Cripps, Mary Goodgame, Heather Campbell, Jenny Campbell, Barbara Robinson, Margaret Woodstock, Susie Campbell, Daphne Campbell, Una Taylor, Margaret Campbell. Front Row:- Glenys Tucker, -----, Janet Jones, -----, Evelyn Lee, Pauline Bevans, Dorothy Hough, Mary Stabler, Pat Wright. The children include the two sons of Janet Jones.

THE QUEEN'S SILVER JUBILEE
7th June 1977

Residents of Waddesdon, Upper Winchendon, Eythrope
and Fleet Marston are warmly invited to attend the
Waddesdon Jubilee Celebrations

PROGRAMME

----

*10.30a..m	Cricket quarter finals
1.00 p. m	Carnival Procession led by the Waddesdon Jubilee Queen, Miss Sheila Coker
	Route: Sharps Close, Goss Avenue, High Street, Quainton Road, Frederick Street, High Street to the Village Hall, Baker Street, recreation ground
*2.15	Fancy Dress Competition
*2.30	Children's sports and Cricket semi-finals and final
*3.30	Baby Show
*4.00	Commencement of tea (to ticket holders only)
*5.30	Tug-of-war
6.30	Comic Football
8.30	Bonfire and singsong
9.00	Dance on recreation ground (Village Hall if wet). Licensed bar. Music provided by the Rob K Trio.

• indicates that events will be held in grounds of secondary school.
All other events will take place on recreation ground.
All the above activities are free.

****

Special Church Services

Sunday, 5th June	11.00 a.m.	Jubilee Thanksgiving Service at Waddesdon Parish Church
Tuesday, 7th June	8.00 a.m	Holy Communion at Waddesdon Parish Church
	9.30 a.m.	Jubilee Thanksgiving Service Westcott Church

****

Local Jubilee Beacon

At about 10.00 p.m. on Monday, 6th June a beacon will be lit At Mr. J. Tapping's Farm at Upper Winchendon. Celebrations will start at 9.30 p.m. It is hoped that a licensed bar and food will be available.

****

This programme is issued by Miss P.J. Fender, 17 Grove Way, Waddesdon, on behalf of the Waddesdon Jubilee Committee

13.63 The programme of events held in Waddesdon to celebrate the Queen's Silver Jubilee on the 7th June 1977 is reproduced below. The cricket competition was a 6-a-side, 5 overs tournament, won by Quainton Road neighbours Goodin, George and Carr ("Three in a Row"). Three fathers and three sons. The Beacon at Upper Winchendon, lit as part of a nation-wide chain, was a great success, starting the local celebrations in fine style.

13.64 A snap-shot of the Carnival Queen, Sheila Coker, with attendants on their decorated float, leading the carnival procession down Quainton Road. Silver Jubilee 1977.

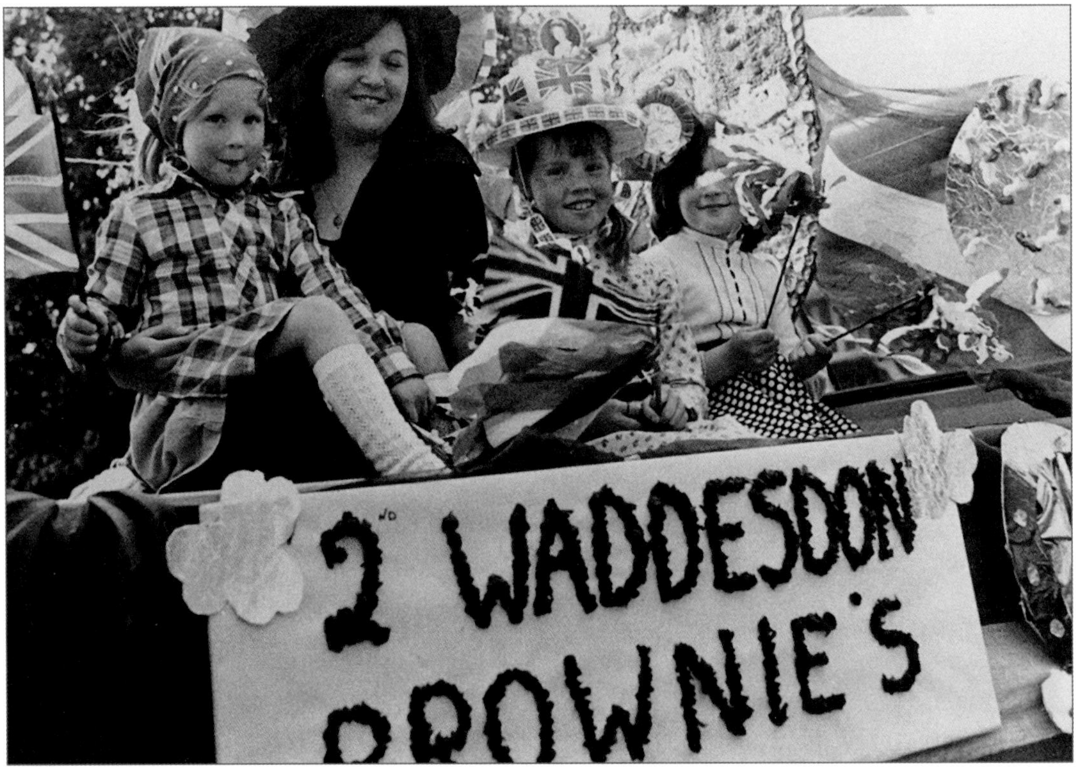

13.65 The Waddesdon Brownies' float in the carnival with L-R: - -----, Valerie Homewood, Fiona Campbell, -----. Silver Jubilee 1977.

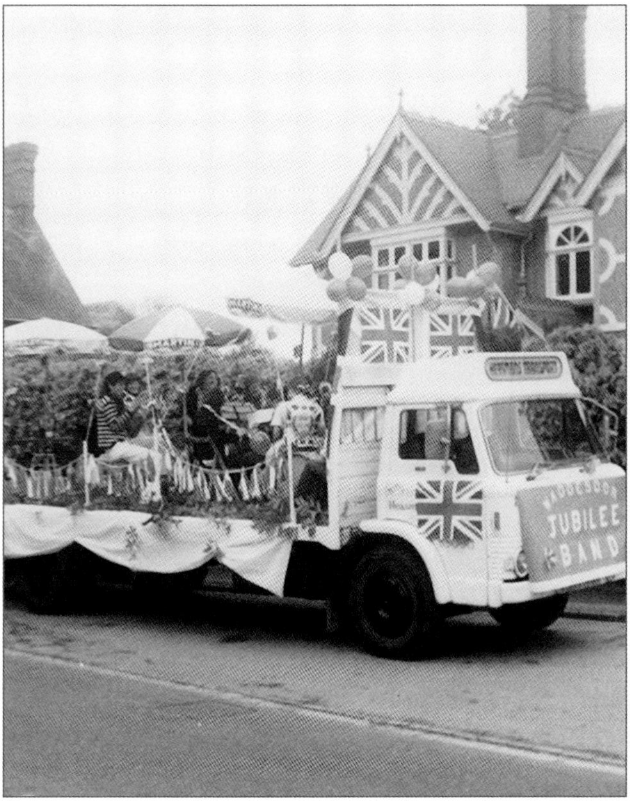

13.66 The Jubilee Band float halted outside "The Roses," before setting off in the procession. A motley collection of instrumentalists, who somehow blended to play the same Souza's "Liberty Bell" over and over again for the whole route; they found only one musical score was available! Silver Jubilee 1977.

13.67 Anita Marriott in a regal pose on the Young Wives Club float which depicted "25 years of Fashion", in the Silver Jubilee procession. 1977.

ADMIT ONE №0812 £2.75

KENNY BALL
AND HIS JAZZMEN
plus SOUNDS FAMILIAR
DANCE

Friday, 1st June 8 p.m. - 1 a.m.

The Great Barn, Glebe Farm,
Quainton Road, Waddesdon

LICENSED BAR Pig Roast FREE PAR

in aid of WADDESDON VILLAGE HALL IMPROVEMF'

13.68 Since 1968 the Village hall has operated as a Charitable Trust under a management committee. To raise funds towards Hall improvements, a group of representatives from all village organisations held highly successful "Dances" featuring Kenny Ball and his Jazzmen in 1976 and 1979. Colin Wright, who at that time farmed the Glebe land down Quainton Road, was the main force behind these initiatives, but all the various groups including some notable individuals who were "roped in", did their bit. On each occasion crowds of around 1500 duly paid up, and enjoyed a remarkable evening of Traditional Jazz in the great barn. The normal farmyard scents were conveniently masked by the smoky aroma arising from the large hearth at the pig-roast.

13.69 Despite an apparent waning of public support for fetes by the mid 1970's, the Waddesdon Fire Brigade hosted two grand events on consecutive years in Britain Field. circa 1980. They were fetes of the vintage variety with plenty of exciting entertainment in the arena, but were not well supported. Principal organiser was Frank Carter who was enthusiastically aided by the members of the Fire Brigade and their families. This photograph shows a Tug-o-War competition under way at the western edge of Britain Field.

13.70 The 50-year anniversary of the end of the Second World War was celebrated in Waddesdon on Saturday, September 2nd 1995. A committee representing various organisations and none gathered on 12th June and commenced work to organise a special fete for the entire village. On the day, the celebrations were preceded by a unique Service of Remembrance (in a rain storm) during which 76 young children each placed a labelled flower posy at the base of the War Memorial, one for each of the Waddesdon men killed in the two world wars, and whose names are inscribed in the memorial. This photograph records the scene afterwards. The Rev. Hutchings, who officiated at the service, is to be seen at the back, and on the right is Gillian Carter with John Carter and Peter Soulsby, two members of Waddesdon Search and Rescue Crew, which paraded with the other village organisations.

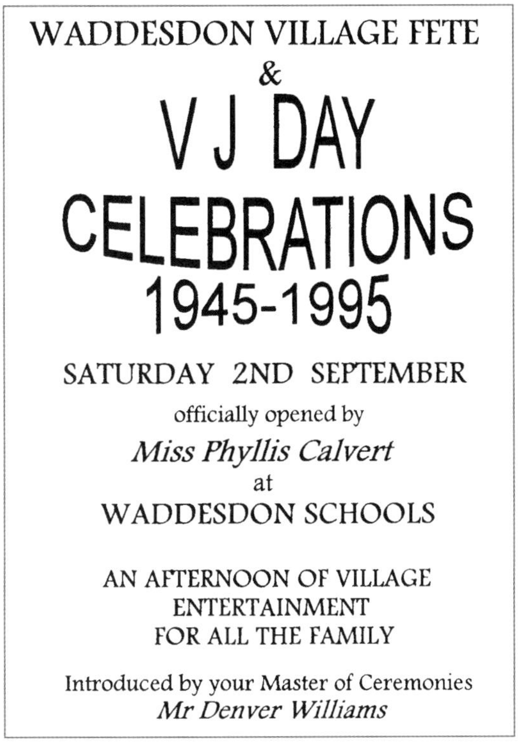
WADDESDON VILLAGE FETE
&
V J DAY
CELEBRATIONS
1945-1995
SATURDAY 2ND SEPTEMBER
officially opened by
Miss Phyllis Calvert
at
WADDESDON SCHOOLS

AN AFTERNOON OF VILLAGE
ENTERTAINMENT
FOR ALL THE FAMILY

Introduced by your Master of Ceremonies
Mr Denver Williams

13.71 V.J. Day 50 Year Anniversary. Following a few weeks of intense activity by the organising committee the Celebrations officially commenced when the Film Star, Phyllis Calvert (a village resident for some years) declared the fete open. There was a Fancy Dress competition, an inter-pub "It's a Knockout" tournament, Wolverton Town Brass Band, numerous Sideshows, an exhibition of stationary engines and old vehicles, Races for the children, Refreshments and Ice-cream, a late afternoon Disco and an evening Dance (with a live band!). The afternoon's event was well attended and judged a success by all, however the dance was not well supported, and the committee members who loyally attended were too exhausted to enjoy themselves. A lesson there!

13.72 In 1995 the Parish Council requested ideas from villagers as to how they wished to celebrate the 50th Anniversary of the end of the Second World War. There were no suggestions, and V.E day (May 8th) came and went without note. Mrs Margaret Hills, the Warden at Anstey Court, with the support of a dedicated band of helpers, was determined the anniversary of the end of the war should be celebrated by those who had lived through it. At very short notice they organised a highly successful party for the senior citizens of Waddesdon, Ashendon, Upper Winchendon and Westcott, held in August at Westcott Leisure Centre. L to R: Ken Slade, Tim Carter, Edie Washington, Harold Cripps, Doris Blake, Audrey Ayris, Jack Slade, Sid Carter, Edie Rolfe, Gwen Spencer, Harold Allen, Margaret Hills sitting in chair.

13.73 The success of the V.J. Day Anniversary Celebrations prompted those involved to form the Waddesdon Special Events Committee. The object was to organise events and raise money so the proceeds could be accumulated in the Millennium Celebration Fund for the year 2000. This photograph records a typical scene at the June fete held each year in the Playing Field; in this case it was 1998. The emphasis was always upon entertainment and value for money, and the inter-pub fun-competition ensured the younger villagers were involved. The usual fete sideshows and tea provisions were often staffed by village organisations whilst bands, dancing groups, animal displays and novelties were engaged to give continuous entertainment. At the right of this picture a young Irish Dancing Troup is taking a bow. Behind them is the large marquee purchased by the Committee, and used to accommodate Tea and Bar facilities at most events.

Waddesdon Special Events Committee
proudly present

GRAND FIREWORK DISPLAY
& BONFIRE

at
The Football Ground, Frederick St

on
Saturday 2nd November
Gates open at 6.00 pm for 7.00 pm start

Entertainment includes:
Disco, Barbeque, Licensed Bar, Hot Soup

'Best Guy' Competition for the children
Entries must be delivered by 6.15 pm

FREE ENTRANCE
(Raffle proceeds to subsidise "Christmas Cheer")

Safety Notes!!
Children under 12 to be accompanied by adult
No fireworks to be brought into field
SORRY ... no on-road or field car parking available

13.74 In 1995 and each year thereafter until 1999 the Special Events Committee staged a Bonfire and Fireworks Display around November 5th, and a Christmas Cheer tour of the village in December. This firework poster of 1996 lists an exciting programme, which in the event was to be completed in little more than two hours, and saw off fireworks to a value of more than £1000. Annually a crowd of about 800 attended the event.

13.75 During 1999 innumerable parties and Balls planned for Millennium New Years Eve, were either cancelled or reduced as the general public became disenchanted with the exceptional demands of many people in the service industries. The Waddesdon Ball, organised under the auspices of the Special Events Committee, suffered from this unexpected turn, and ran at a loss to the value of fourteen tickets. In this picture we show some of the party-goers and the spread, in the marquee, which had been specially hired for the ball.

13.76 After years of fund-raising by the Special Events Committee, Waddesdon's Millennium Festival was held on Saturday June 24th 2000. The festivities commenced at midday with a Carnival Parade down the High Street, along Baker Street and into the Playing Field. This photograph shows the mustering of the groups in Silk Street with the Police Land Rover at the front. The decorated lorry of F.T.Evans carries the Steel band, which provided an appropriate musical accompaniment to the proceedings, and set a carnival atmosphere for all the participants. Unfortunately the weather, cool and overcast, did not help.

13.77 The Waddesdon Fire and Rescue Tender bought up the rear of the parade, behind this immaculate float entered by the Bowls Club, which was also celebrating its 75th Anniversary. Amongst the members present on the float are: Phyllis Carter, Doreen Spooner, Stuart Shillingford, Les Carter and Maureen Shipperley.

13.78 As always the Scouts did their bit as shown in this picture. Their float in the Carnival Parade was a tractor and trailer with a campsite scene, and the troop members marched behind. The Scout Leader is Steve Hewitt, with scouts Kamil Ahmid, Charlie May, Sebastian Decrettes, Janice Simmons and David Francis (Standard bearer). Cub Leader Sue Francis, with cubs Amellia Gunn, Zouie Little, Oliver Wright, Callum Wilkins, Nicholas Wilson, Josuah Little, Sam Short and Joseph Cox.

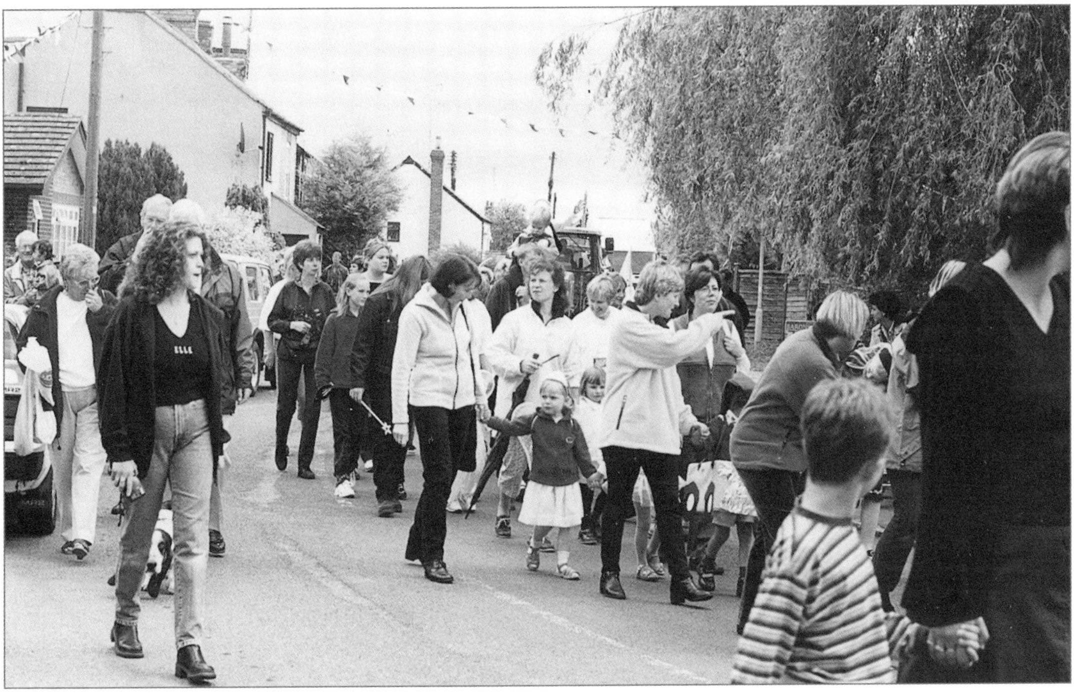

13.79 House-holders allowed bunting to be strung along the Carnival Parade route, adding a special something to the day. Here we see the crowd and some of the Little Oaks Playgroup entry walking with the Parade in Baker Street, while the bunting flutters overhead.

13.80 The Millennium Carnival Parade entering School Lane, with Mrs Hawkins in her electrically powered chair leading the Mothers Union contingent including: Valerie Grant, Ted Hawkins, Pat Wright, Anne Payne and Mildred Jones. Leading the Junior Football Club members is Simon Blore.

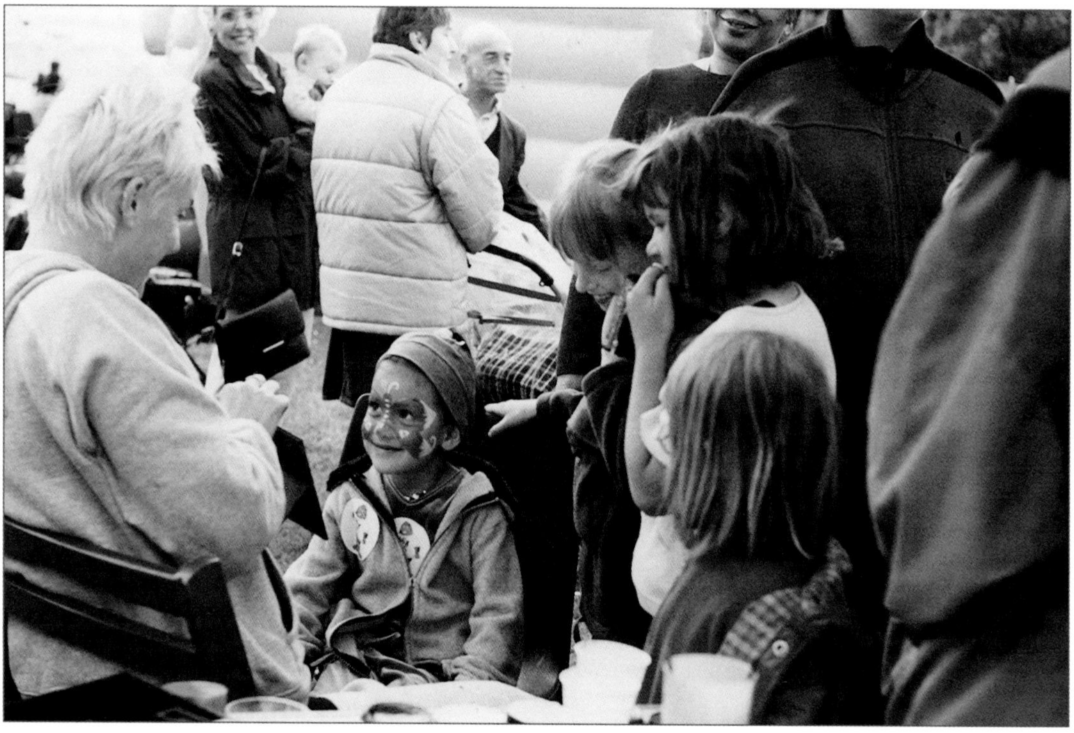

13.81 The Waddesdon Millennium Festival of 24th June 2000 was opened with a short ceremony conducted by the Revd Simon Dickenson (C of E) and the Revd Peter Dudeney (Methodist). There followed a full programme of events and entertainment, in addition to a range of free sideshows and attractions. As this picture shows, the face-painting was both popular and amusing.

13.82 Monster-Mix-96, (advertising the local radio station), holds no fears for these youngsters at the Millennium Festival. The boy in Cubs uniform is Mathew Powell. The entertainment in and around the arena included: a Balloon Artist, a Caricaturist, Singers and Instrumentalists, Irish Dancers, two Children's dancing Schools, the Oxford Morris Men, and of course the Steel Band.

13.83 For the younger children there were two fairground round-a-bouts and a bouncy castle, whilst the bigger children competed on a "bungy run", gladiator joust and a bouncy boxing game. Senior citizens enjoyed tea in and around a large marquee, and listened to popular songs by "Claire". Everything was funded from the Millennium Festival account. In this photograph we have young children enjoying the novelty round-a-bout, watched by the Sweetland family amongst others. Surplus funds were subsequently disposed of, in grants to children's organisations in the village.

Section Fourteen

Waddesdon In 2000

Preceding sections in this book illustrate how different aspects of life in Waddesdon have changed over the years. Photographs and articles enable the reader to contemplate the rapid rise in prosperity and all that went with it, over one hundred years' ago; and to witness the loss of many shops, and the lessening of community activities during the past few decades. This trend is common everywhere, but Waddesdon in 2000, appears to have lost more than some of its contemporaries. It may be said; this in part at least, reflects the perceived needs of the villagers, whose work, habits and interests now range far beyond the confines of the parish.

Despite no longer "having everything," Waddesdon remains an extremely popular village and retains many of its special attributes gained from the past. The people are friendly, welcoming newcomers who wish to become involved in village life, and tolerating those who seek a quieter existence. Most householders are owner-occupiers. Since the Second World War there has been very little development at the western end of the village. At the eastern end, larger building projects have been limited to the local authority estates of Anstey Close, Goss Avenue, Sharps Close, and Warmstone Close, and the private estate of Little Britain. Infilling however, by building on any available closes, ex-orchards, gardens and yards has increased the density of the housing. The south-eastern edge of the village is marked by the spacious building and recreation facilities of the Primary and Secondary schools.

Property prices are above average for the area, this in part reflects the excellent reputation of the secondary school, but makes it more difficult for young villagers to set up home here. Many do stay, and others return when opportunities arise, giving an indication of the attraction the village still holds. However modern life-styles demand more than ever, that people be prepared to move for their work, and this inevitably results in a growing proportion of residents who have no previous connection with the parish. Thankfully, those who settle here, sometimes bring fresh energy to community endeavours, helping to mark the difference between urban and village life.

This final section contains colour photographs, which we believe illustrate some of the physical factors that make Waddesdon unique. They include panoramic views from vantage points not normally available to the general public, and not surprisingly we have given due prominence to Waddesdon Manor, the estate and the Rothschild end of the village. These elements give the village its memorable style, and through their accessibility, enrich all our lives.

14.1 This was the view when Ivor Gurney took the opportunity afforded by workers' scaffolding at the Village Hall in 1996. Waddesdon High Street looking towards the Church Tower, just visible at left centre. The new traffic calming measures visible at the roadside.

14.2 Another view of Waddesdon's fine wide High Street and a new "traffic calming bottleneck", again taken from the weathervane on the Village Hall, 1996.

14.3 The practice tower at the Fire Station provided the platform for this view of Grove Way and the Secondary School in 2000. The large plots for the houses inform us they date from more than 30 years' ago. The levelling effect of photography from this height disguises the stiff climb one has to take, to reach the woods on Waddesdon Hill at left rear.

14.4 This view looking north from the practice tower 2000. The soon-to-be-modified Fire Station, with Frederick Street climbing away in the centre. In the distance the flat Vale of Aylesbury leading to the Claydons.

14.5 At the rear is the Hoddy Houses Wood which backs the village Playing Field. The five chalet type houses are in School Lane and the near right properties lie in the former farmyard at the Grove. Photographed from the Fire Station practice tower.(2000).

14.6 Again from the practice tower Baker Street looking eastwards. A mixture of young and older properties with Little Britain just visible at the far centre.

14.7 The Old Rectory as seen from the church tower 1996. In the distance is Frederick Street and farther off the fields of Glebe Farm.

14.8 Silk Street with its mantle of Horse Chestnut blossom as viewed from the church tower in May 1996.

14.9 This view of Queen Street in 1996 may be compared with 3.28 that was also taken from the church tower about 90 years earlier. Miss Alice de Rothschild would doubtless be satisfied with the mature and robust cedar tree that now obscures our view of Home Farm.

14.10 When the army arrived in 1941 to construct the fuel dump on Waddesdon Estate, the ornate wrought iron gates at Princes Lodge were removed. The brick pillars with their sculpted dogs atop remained for fifty-five years, before the gates shown in this photograph were re-erected to complete the picture. The gates are the original and had been used as the front gates to the Pavilion at Eythrope since 1957. We show them shortly after completion of the gilding work, with a backdrop of autumnal shades in the surrounding woods. 1997.

The Five Arrows

14.11 This splendid example of decorative wrought ironwork is mounted on the north gable-end of the Buttery at the Dairy. Significantly, within the laurel wreath suspended on the left, is a miniature milk pail and a cream setting pan, but the five arrows on the right is the main reason for including this photograph in this book.

Five arrows are used to represent the five sons of Mayer Amschel Rothschild, the founder of the banking dynasty. In the early nineteenth century four of the sons went out from the family base in Frankfurt, to establish branches of the Rothschild bank in Austria, France, England and Naples, (at that time Naples was part of the Kingdom of Sicily). The eldest brother remained at the original bank in Frankfurt.

The family coat of arms, which was commissioned in 1822, includes two depictions of five arrows clenched in a right hand with the arrows pointing downwards. The Five Arrows crest of the Rothschild family in this country is normally shown like that, but not at Waddesdon! The Waddesdon version of the crest always has the arrows pointing upwards.

Suffice to say that very soon after the Baron purchased the estate the Five Arrows crest began to appear on buildings, probably earliest of all on the sign of the erstwhile Marlborough Arms, renamed the Five Arrows Inn. The Baron's policy was to prominently display the crest circumscribed by the Rothschild motto "Concordia, Integritas, Industria," within a plaque on all his buildings as they were constructed, or having undergone "the Rothschild treatment". The only exception known to the writer is "The Limes" in Queen Street, which has a rather splendid terracotta F de R emblem, to mark its reprieve and renovation back in the 1880's.

As a general rule, the building plaques installed during the lifetime of Baron Ferdinand, depict the arrows restrained at their centre by a ribbon; during Miss Alice's time by a coronet; and during James de Rothschild's time by a simple strap.

Today, the mention of "Five Arrows" mainly conjures images of Waddesdon's prominent and memorable hotel, but elsewhere the crest is everywhere before one's eyes, it is even incorporated in the Church of England Secondary School badge, and the Parish Council letterhead.

14.12 In a project worthy of comparison with the original construction by Baron Ferdinand over a hundred years earlier, the redundant dairy and lakes in Queen Street were partially rebuilt and revitalised, in the early 1990's. This photograph of 1995 provides us with an extraordinarily good example of how precise and new so many developments in and around Waddesdon would have looked in the 1890's. The Waddesdon Dairy is now a Conference and Administration Centre, in demand for commercial seminars, and often at weekends for wedding ceremonies and receptions.

14.13 This was the picture in 1995 after completion of extensive renovations to Waddesdon Manor. Only the maturity of the surrounding woods betray the fact that one hundred years have elapsed since the photographer set up his camera for 3.10 and 3.11.

14.14 The staff at Waddesdon Manor have earned a high reputation for imaginative innovation, to maintain the Manor's standing as one of the outstanding visitors attractions in the country. In the late 1990's an award-winning presentation of floodlighting was inaugurated for autumnal display. Here we show the fountain at the North Front, illuminated and contrasted against the last of the daylight in the early evening.

14.15 Later the same evening (as 14.14), the South Front provided our camera with this first public view of the floodlit Manor.

Colour photographs 14.12 and 14.13 by kind permission of Mr Alan Lesurf, the remainder by Ivor Gurney.

BIBLIOGRAPHY

Buckinghamshire Miscellany. Robert Gibbs.
History and Antiquities of the County of Buckingham. George Lipscomb.
Victoria History of Buckinghamshire.
Records of Buckinghamshire.
Waddesdon and Over Winchendon. C.Oscar Moreton.
The Buckinghamshire Commitatus. Bucks Record Society.
The Rothschilds at Waddesdon Manor. Mrs James de Rothschild.
The Country Parson. George Herbert.
The Aylesbury Agitator. John R Millburn and Keith Jarrott.
St Michael and all Angels & the Parish of Waddesdon. A.E.Hawkins.
The Bucks Advertiser.
The Bucks Herald
The Buckinghamshire Records Office (Parish records etc)
Kelly's Directory.
Waddesdon Parish Magazine.
Waddesdon Deanery Magazine.
The Brill Tramway. Bill Simpson.
The Wotton Tramway. Ken Jones.

POUNDS, SHILLINGS AND PENCE

Prior to 1971 the British currency was as follows:
Pounds (£), Shillings (s), Pence (d).

1 Pound	=	20 Shillings or 240 Pence,
1 Shilling	=	12 Pence ,

Other denominations of coins used, included:

Farthing	=	1 quarter of 1 penny (d), Ceased to be legal tender 1961.
Halfpenny	=	1 Half of 1 penny (d),
Threepenny Bit	=	3 pence (d),
Sixpenny Piece	=	6 pence (d),
Half a Crown,	=	2 Shillings and 6 pence,
Florin,	=	2 Shillings.

After 1971 (Decimalisation) the value of the £ was the same but divided into 100 pence (p).

ACKNOWLEDGEMENTS

We are truly grateful for the co-operation we have received from every quarter, during the compilation of this book. Our task in researching the details for "Waddesdon Through the Ages," over the past few years, has rewarded us with innumerable pleasant acquaintanceships and renewed friendships. Sadly, inevitably, some of these contributors have now passed away; however their names remain on the record.

We wish to thank all the persons and organisations listed, for providing photographs, documents and information. Unfortunately, despite our best efforts, there may be some omissions and mistakes, for these we beg the indulgence of the reader.

Particular gratitude is due to Ivor Burnell who allowed the authors free access and use of the unrivalled Burnell Collection of postcards and documents. Also our thanks go to the curators of the "Rothschild" archive at Waddesdon Manor, who gave us access to their unique collection of photographs, and permission to allow them to be published in our book.

Additionally we wish to record our special thanks to Andrew and Ann Langton who read and corrected the draft "Waddesdon's Golden Years" in 1995, and so willingly undertook the same, more lengthy task, for "Waddesdon Through the Ages."

Last but not least, thank you to our families. We wish to mention the invaluable help of Ivor's son Antony in word processing, and the essential support of our wives respectively Sylvia and Freda, who have tolerated, encouraged and assisted us to the conclusion of this project.

The Alice Trust

The authors wish to express their sincere appreciation, for the encouragement and backing they have received over the years, from The Alice Trust and staff of the National Trust at Waddesdon Manor. Particular thanks are due to Fabia Bromovsky, Pippa Shirley, Jane Cliffe and Christopher Campbell, who through their good offices, assured the successful completion of this book.

Waddesdon, The Rothschild Collection (The National Trust)

Photographs: 1.9, 1.11, 2.7, 3.3, 3.5, 3.12, 3.13, 3.14, 3.22, 3.33, 3.35, 3.37, 3.63, 4.9, 6.54, 6.55.

The Burnell Collection

Photographs: 3.21, 4.34, 6.7, 6.9, 6.13, 6.23, 6.45, 6.46, 6.52, 7.14, 7.27, 8.31, 8.34, 8.35, 8.57, 9.2, 9.8, 9.12, 9.13, 9.16, 9.17, 9.19, 10.28, 10.29, 12.4, 12.13, 13.14, 13.15, 13.22.

Alan Armstrong, Secondary School.
Harold Allen, Westcott.
Peter Adams, Westcott
Barry Atkins, Aylesbury.
Myrtle Atkins, Waddesdon.
Yvonne Barham, Waddesdon.
Dinah Baron, Aylesbury.
Betty Becket, Aylesbury.
Michael Bevington, Stowe.
Bill Biswell, Waddesdon.
Amy Borchard, Waddesdon.
Averil Brown, Waddesdon.
Helga Brown, Abingdon.
The Bucks Advertiser, Aylesbury.
The Bucks Herald, Aylesbury.
Clive Burnell, Hamilton, New Zealand.
Ivor Burnell Collection, Waddesdon
David Butt, Dinton.
Doris Butt, Waddesdon.
Sandra Butt, Dinton

Christopher Campbell, Waddesdon Manor
Dr and Mrs Campbell, Wendover
Freda Carr, Waddesdon.
Harry Carr, Haddenham.
Les Carter, Waddesdon
George Collins, Upper Winchendon.
Ron Copcutt, Waddesdon.
Malcolm Craker, Aylesbury.
Mr and Mrs Will Dennis, Aylesbury.
Delphie Evans, Waddesdon.
Grace & Eddie Edema, Perth, Australia.
Oliver Franklin, Waddesdon.
"Tucker" and "Chalkie" George, Waddesdon.
David George, Waddesdon.
Violet Gilbert, Aylesbury.
Angela Gilmore, Aylesbury.
Anne Golder, Waddesdon.
Eric Goss, Waddesdon.
Myrna Green, Linslade.
Jacqueline Green, Haddenham.
Rita Greenlaw, Dunstable.
Rosamund Griffin, Waddesdon Manor.
Antony Gurney, Turweston, Brackley.
Cyril Gurney, Stone.
Len Gurney, Upper Winchendon.
Sylvia Gurney, Leighton Buzzard.
Jean Hammond, Crafton, Bucks.
Tim Hicks, Waddesdon.
Rita Holland, Aylesbury.
Valerie Homewood, Waddesdon.
Brian Hughes, Dunstable.
Matthew Hirst, Waddesdon Manor.
The Rev Colin Hutchings, Waddesdon.
Ken Jones, Aylesbury.
Sybil Jones, Waddesdon
Joe Jordan, New Milton.
Elizabeth Khalvat, Waddesdon
George Knibb, Waddesdon.
Dinah Law, Waddesdon.
London Transport Museum.
Derek Lovell, Waddesdon.
Ken Machin, Westcott
Freda Maltby, Northhampton
Anita Marriott, Waddesdon.
Colin and Vera Marriott, Waddesdon
June Masters, Cranwell
Alistair McLaren, Quainton.
Joe and Janet Novak, Traverse City, U.S.A.
Rita O'Brien, Waddesdon.
Oxford Publishing Co, Yeovil.
Rosemary Parnell, Waddesdon.
Ken Pearson, New South Wales, Australia
Les Pittam, Aylesbury.
Max Prestwood, Waddesdon C.C. School.
B Quinlan, Hunting Aerofilms Ltd -
Borehamwood Herts.
"Railway Magazine", London.
Harold Radwell, Winchendon.
Paul Record, Leighton Buzzard.
J. Rogers, Aylesbury
Ken Rolfe, Waddesdon.
Pearl Rolfe, Waddesdon.
Royal British Legion, - Waddesdon Branch.
Barbara Sanderson, Aylesbury.
Don Saunders, Waddesdon.
Ria Scott, Winslow.
Uri Sellor, Tel Aviv, Israel.
Lora Sharples, Taylor and Francis Ltd,
London.
Mick Shaw, Bradwell, Milton Keynes.
Bill Simpson, "The Brill Tramway".
Ken Skinner, Westcott.
Margaret Skinner, Aylesbury.
Edie Slade, Waddesdon.
Jack Slade, Waddesdon.
Philip Slynn, Peterborough.
Grace and Bill Smith, Bierton.
Charles Smith, Waddesdon.
Gerry Smith, Dunstable.
Kathy Snelling, Aylesbury.
Ron Snelling, Aylesbury.
Roy Southam, Waddesdon.
Peggy Stevens, Quainton.
Margaret Stone, Waddesdon
Una Taylor, Waddesdon.
A Turner, Fleet Marston.
Len Thorne, Stratford upon Avon.
Joyce Wicks, Wing.
Len Wood, Waddesdon.
Wilf and Winnie Washington, Waddesdon.
Waddesdon Girl Guides.
Betty Wheeler-Cherry, Waddesdon.
Waddesdon Bowls Club.
Marilyn Whittam, Aylesbury.

Preparation of Postscript Files

Prior to final negotiations for the printing contract, we were advised to enter all relevant data, text, pictures, page layout and printing parameters onto Postscript digital files. This specialised transposition process was carried out by Mark Brandon, an expert who happens to live in the village. What a stroke of luck!

This professional and local service provided by Mark, was of great importance in the completion of the book, and his patient explanation of our numerous technical queries was extremely helpful.

INDEX OF ILLUSTRATIONS

Numbers refer to section and illustration numbers